Vampire Capitalism

Paul Kennedy

Vampire Capitalism

Fractured Societies and Alternative Futures

Paul Kennedy
Department of Sociology
Manchester Metropolitan University, UK
Manchester, United Kingdom

ISBN 978-1-137-55265-5 (hardcover)   ISBN 978-1-137-55266-2 (eBook)
ISBN 978-1-349-71607-4 (softcover)
DOI 10.1057/978-1-137-55266-2

Library of Congress Control Number: 2016961824

© The Editor(s) (if applicable) and The Author(s) 2017, First softcover printing 2019
The author(s) has/have asserted their right(s) to be identified as the author(s) of this work in accordance with the Copyright, Designs and Patents Act 1988.
This work is subject to copyright. All rights are solely and exclusively licensed by the Publisher, whether the whole or part of the material is concerned, specifically the rights of translation, reprinting, reuse of illustrations, recitation, broadcasting, reproduction on microfilms or in any other physical way, and transmission or information storage and retrieval, electronic adaptation, computer software, or by similar or dissimilar methodology now known or hereafter developed.
The use of general descriptive names, registered names, trademarks, service marks, etc. in this publication does not imply, even in the absence of a specific statement, that such names are exempt from the relevant protective laws and regulations and therefore free for general use.
The publisher, the authors and the editors are safe to assume that the advice and information in this book are believed to be true and accurate at the date of publication. Neither the publisher nor the authors or the editors give a warranty, express or implied, with respect to the material contained herein or for any errors or omissions that may have been made.

Cover Image: © miss_Tea / iStock / Getty Images Plus
Cover Design: Fatima Jamadar

Printed on acid-free paper

This Palgrave Macmillan imprint is published by Springer Nature
The registered company is Macmillan Publishers Ltd.
The registered company address is: The Campus, 4 Crinan Street, London, N1 9XW, United Kingdom

To Jasmine and Camille

Acknowledgements

In this book, I have stood on the shoulders of so many giants that it is difficult not to feel dizzy as well as extremely privileged to have enjoyed a career that allowed me to draw so freely and often on the knowledge, wisdom, inspiration and practical skills of such a vast number of scholars and thinkers. They have not all been mentioned in this writing but their influence over me during decades of study, teaching and writing is nevertheless embedded firmly in this work.

Then there are all those work colleagues in addition to associates and friends through my affiliations to professional organizations, particularly the UK and North American Global Studies Association, who have shaped my ideas and offered support in countless additional ways over many years. Among valued colleagues and friends at Manchester Metropolitan University (MMU), I would particularly like to thank Shoba Arun, Colin Barker, Susie Jacobs, John Jordon, Steven Miles, Phil Mole, Gary Pollock, Chris Porter, Scott Poynting, Berthold Schoene and formally, Derek Wynne. Beyond the walls of MMU, the following have been more influential and helpful than they probably realize: Barrie Axford, Marco Caselli, Robin Cohen, John Eade, Stephen Edgell, Jerry Harris, Ray Kiely, Roy May, Darren O'Byrne and Leslie Sklair among many others.

Special thanks are due to those who have bravely endured, read, critically reviewed and handsomely advised on this manuscript during the past year as it evolved. They are Robin Cohen, Stephen Edgell, Jerry Harris, John Jordan, Ray Kiely, Tony Nixon, Phil Mole and Scott Poynting. I tried to follow their suggestions as much as possible but clearly I remain fully responsible for any flaws, omissions or mistakes that may lurk within this writing.

Beyond academia, the team at Palgrave has been patient and supportive at all times and I thank them sincerely. Finally, many thanks are due to my family who have always provided enthusiastic support and emotional solace during the long period of preparation and writing, especially my long-suffering wife and partner, Sue.

Contents

1 Introduction: Capitalist Modernity in Question   1

2 The Rise of Vampire Capitalism (and not a slayer in sight)   29

3 The Roots of Vampire Capitalism   61

4 Living with Twenty-First-Century Capitalism   99

5 The Juggernaut of Science and Technology: Friend or Foe?   131

6 Individualization and the Cultures of Capitalism   169

7 Global Capitalism and the Biosphere: Our Future in Jeopardy   203

8 Does Capitalism Have a Future?   239

9 Alternatives: Exploring Possibilities   273

Bibliography   315

Index   339

List of Acronyms

AI	Artificial Intelligence
AOSIS	Alliance of Small Island States
CCS	Carbon Capture and Storage (systems/technologies)
CDOs	Collateral Debt Obligations
CEO	Chief Executive Officer
CEPGs	Corporate-funded Climate and Environmental Policy Groups
CO_2	Carbon Dioxide
COP	Conference of Paris
EA	East Asia
EU	European Union
EU ETS	European Emissions Trading System
EPOS	Electronic Point of Sale (systems)
EPZ	Export Processing Zone
FAO	Food and Agricultural Organization
GATT	General Agreement on Trade and Tariffs
G20	World's Largest Economies
GDP	Gross Domestic Product
GHGs	Greenhouse Gasses
GPT	General Purpose Technology
HNWI	High Net Worth Individual

IAASTD	International Assessment of Agricultural Knowledge, Science and Technology for	
ICT	Information and Communication Technology	
IGO	Intergovernmental Organization	
IF	Intergenerational Foundation	
ILO	International Labour Organization	
IMF	International Monetary Fund	
IPCC	Intergovernmental Panel on Climate Change	
IWGIA	International Work Group for Indigenous Affairs	
LIBOR	London Interbank Offer Rate	
MENA	Middle East and North Africa	
MIT	Massachusetts Institute of Technology	
NASA	National Aeronautics Space Administration	
NAFTA	North American Free Trade Association	
NATO	North Atlantic Treaty Organisation	
NHS	National Health Service (UK)	
NGO	Non-governmental Organization	
NIC	Newly Industrializing Country	
NLT	Neoliberal Thought Collective	
OECD	Organisation for Economic Cooperation and Development	
OPEC	Organization of Petroleum Exporting Countries	
PEC	Private Equity Company	
PES	Payment for Ecosystem Services	
PPM	Parts Per Million	
SA	South Asia	
SAPS	Structural Adjustment Programmes	
SSA	Sub-Saharan Africa	
TJN	Tax Justice Network	
TNC	Trans-national corporation	
TTIP	Transatlantic Trade and Investment Partnership	
UKIP	UK Independence Party	
UN	United Nations	
UNDP	United Nations Development Programme	
UNEP	United Nations Environment Programme	
WB	World Bank	
WHO	World Health Organization	

WSF	World Social Forum
WMO	World Meteorological Office
WTO	World Trade Organization
WW1	World War One
WW2	World War Two

1

Introduction: Capitalist Modernity in Question

It is 16 years since celebrations and exuberant optimism greeted the new millennium. Much of the euphoria then on display has largely dissipated, and the world now looks alarmingly different. A number of events and crises account for this radical and depressing transformation: chiefly the financial crash of 2008–2009 and the colossal scale of government, domestic, business and bank indebtedness that it revealed. This was followed by high unemployment, austerity and, eventually, timid moves by governments to re-impose some degree of regulation on the financial sector. A long, slow and piecemeal return to something like normality has followed. Yet even this belated 'recovery' is looking increasingly fragile.

Now, in addition to economic crises, there are widening fears of environmental catastrophe as we are battered by storms of unrivalled ferocity and forced to face the reality of melting polar icecaps. Anxious voices now seriously question whether an apparently unaccountable corporate capitalism allied to a scientific and technological juggernaut must be reined in. Many ask why governments and politicians seem so determined to defend corporate and financial interests rather than those of ordinary people or smaller, local businesses. Moreover, they ask why these same governments offer only vague promises in respect to actions that might rectify this destructive imbalance.

If anything, the world of *geo-politics* since 2000 has been even *more* frightening than the economic world. The 2001 destruction of New York's World Trade Organization (WTO) twin towers is perhaps the most iconic moment in this new era of fear. A US-led 'war on terrorism'—including aggressive conflicts in Afghanistan and Iraq—not only reactivated long-standing sectarian, tribal, national and regional rivalries in the Islamic world, but also heralded a terrifying era of international war, neoliberal 'interventionism' and expanded terrorist atrocity. Partly by destabilizing local governments, neoliberal interventionism has provided the opportunity and excuse for the spread of ruthless new terrorist movements across the Middle East and Africa, led particularly by Al-Qaeda, and more recently 'Islamic State' and its offshoots. Car and suicide bombings are still regular occurrences in Baghdad and other Iraqi cities, not only causing a loss of civilian life sometimes running into hundreds for single attacks but also amounting to appalling tallies of over a thousand deaths during certain bloody months. In Europe and elsewhere, 'lone-wolf' copycat killers have murdered innocent civilians, journalists and cartoonists, with guns, trucks and machetes. Russia, in part responding to North Atlantic Treaty Organization (NATO) attempts to absorb more former Soviet states into its membership, has revived its imperial ambitions by annexing Crimea and invading mainland Ukraine.

High expectations created across the Middle East and the world more widely, raised by the Arab Spring of 2011, were quickly dashed as democratic experiments collapsed under military dictatorships and/or civil wars. An exodus of desperate refugees numbering in their millions followed, with many—particularly from Syria—attempting to reach Europe. Yet the European Union (EU) itself is now dogged by the rise of populist, Far-right movements.

China's legal—and questionably legal—moves to safeguard its future access to resources have seen it engage in a muscular assertion of naval power across South Asia's seas, raising regional tensions. China's wider ambitions are also evident through their involvement in deals with corrupt African and Central Asian governments to acquire vast tracts of tribal land and mineral resources as one route for securing its own economic development.

Meanwhile, the EU patently failed to show unity when it dealt unfairly with Greece's vast debts. Yet it did show a somewhat blinkered humanity in the summer of 2015 when it offloaded much of the Syrian refugee crisis to Turkey. EU timidity in the face of such problems is partly explicable in relation to the continuing decline in citizen support for its institutions and elites and the rise of Far-right populist parties across many countries including France, the Netherlands, Hungary Denmark, Italy, Austria, Sweden, Germany and others. The spate of violent Isis-sponsored terrorist attacks, particularly in France during 2015 and 2016 but also Germany, almost certainly further contributed to citizen suspicion of refugees and the presence of Muslim migrants in particular.

Indeed, 2016 seems to have been a year in which a defiant retreat into—even an angry reassertion of—nationalist identities and concerns, accompanied by the demand on the part of many citizens that governments prioritize local needs, were thrust unashamedly into the global limelight. This, in turn, is partly a response to decades of rapid globalization. Here, many—especially the relative losers, and perhaps those who are less well educated—are reacting not to one, but two sources of discontent. One concerns the wider loss of national economic autonomy and job/income security from offshoring, de-industrialization and outward flows of capital. But equally some share a perception that continued waves of migrants represent a more immediate threat to local and regional cultures and shared identities, as well as jobs, and even more so at a time of economic recession.[1] One event in the summer of 2016 which highlighted this turn towards nationalism was the UK's June 2016 majority vote to leave the EU, which was particularly strongly supported among those living in small towns and regions suffering from under-investment who perhaps felt excluded from years of economic growth and ignored by London politicians. Brexit may also have placed the very existence of the EU in jeopardy since there are fears it may trigger similar responses among the disillusioned and possibly neglected citizens

---

[1] Case study 2 in Chap. 4 explores some of the reasons for growing support for EU populist parties in more detail.

of several other countries. Another such event was signalled by Trump's presidential nominee acceptance speech to numerous working-class as well as traditional Republican voters in July 2016. Here, he declared unequivocally that future US policies would prioritize American rather than global interests.

This résumé of recent economic as well as geo-political events suggests that there is a strong underlying and direct connection between the current worldwide economic crisis and the kinds of global as well as local, national and regional conflicts and discontents briefly outlined above. This sets the stage for the main theme of this book: namely, the current crisis of capitalism and its likely trajectory in respect to the future prospects for humanity and the planet's biosphere. In *The Enigma of Capital and the Crises of Capitalism* (2011), David Harvey dissects not just the causes and trajectory of the 2008 crisis and its aftermath but also the underlying contradictions that have always beset capitalism. In doing so, he argues that it is the built-in drive to accumulate capital and pursue economic growth that constitutes the fundamental problems confronting humanity, rather than the dilemmas associated with any particular crisis. So long as capitalism is dominant, every individual—jostling with four to five billion others for an economic perch in what has basically become a world labour market after decades of globalization—but also every company, small, medium or large, profession, service, town, city, region and nation, has no alternative but to compete against each other for their very economic survival and for a share of global growth. Drawing on Marx, Kliman (2012: 183) throws further light on Harvey's argument that the vast treadmill that is capitalism, pressing relentlessly onwards through periods of booms and crises, permits few to escape. He observes that the 'goal is the continued self-expansion of capital … the accumulation of value for the sake of the accumulation of value—not for the sake of the consumption of the rich'. The latter, and the companies some own or serve, are as much ensnared by capitalism's unquenchable thirst for value, growth and competition as we more ordinary humans. Thus, when the 2008 financial crisis hit, it hit banks, investors, share values and jobs hard and threatened total collapse of the economy. The US government intervened by pushing up Federal debt 40 per cent over two years in order to bail out—effectively nationalize—leading private banks. But Kliman argues that the priority here was not to save individual capitalist firms, even though they were supposedly too big to be allowed to fail, but rather to 'serve the interests of capitalism itself' (p.183). It could not be allowed to collapse.

Continuing for the moment to think in these generalized and abstract terms we add the following arguments. First, unless constrained by counter-forces, the inner mechanisms of profit, competition and accumulation, which constitute capitalism's DNA and which drive it forward, endow socio-economic life with a one-dimensional character where material development dominates all other considerations. This closely resembles what Weber (1968) said about the economic rationality which he believed had swept through not just economic but all spheres of human action by the early twentieth century. Here, calculability and the prioritization of least-cost efficiency over all other considerations in the pursuit of goals thrust alternative, substantive—that is, moral and social—concerns into the background. In later chapters (particularly Chaps. 2, 3 and 4) we argue that certain historical constraints, such as the primarily national basis of economic life, the power of organized labour and the impact of two world wars on political priorities, were sufficiently strong to constrain capitalism and keep it within certain bounds. But these have been severely weakened since the early 1980s. In part, this is due to deliberate government policies, usually referred to via the umbrella term, neo-liberalism. These were designed to remove most obstacles to the mobility of capital, to champion the market and private ownership and to deregulate corporate and financial power. For example, despite its declared commitment to the social market and the protection of workers' rights, the EU commission operates with a gamut of pro-market, pro-profit and pro-competition policies. These include tough restraints on trade union action; strong discouragement of government aid for declining businesses, nationalization or re-nationalization; the imposition of rigorous austerity measures across Europe in response to the 2008 financial crisis, even though those who did least to cause the latter are being hurt most by them; and prioritizing the need to attract foreign investment even to the point of exposing local public or private enterprises to the risk of being out-competed and taken over by business interests controlled from overseas.[2] All this means that market capitalism has become 'unfettered' (Sandel 2016: 29) and is now free to roam across all social, cultural and natural domains, colonizing and commoditizing virtually all commonly owned resources, or attempting to do so. Everyone, it seems, now bears an inescapable duty to passively accept the rigours and insecurities of the market while resting content with whatever material benefits and individual freedoms it may or may not bring. As Hayek—one of the key figures in developing neoliberal thought—himself insisted, any gains the market economy might bring to particular individuals have little to do with virtue, merit or justice but rather are shaped by chance (cited in Turner 2008: 124).

Thus, the second argument of this book is that during the last 40 years or more, the world's economies and citizens have been engulfed by fundamental transformations working their way through social and economic life—one of them being this same overwhelming and scarcely questioned support by governments for neoliberal capitalism. These structural transformations have created new uncertainties for many although they have brought some economic improvement in their wake as well. We say more about this later. Of course, ever since the factory system, based on hired labour working with machinery and concentrated in one place, first became established in the British textile industry from the 1760s, capitalism has never stood still. As Marx and Engels famously observed in their 1848 *Communist Manifesto*, under capitalist production:

> All fixed, fast frozen relations ... are swept away, all new-formed ones become antiquated before they can ossify. All that is solid melts into air, all that is holy is profaned, and man is at last compelled to face with sober senses his real condition of life.

Arguably, however, the cumulative impact of the intersecting structural economic transformations associated with capitalism during recent

---

[2] This refers to the much contested Transatlantic Trade and Investment Partnership deal (TTIP) which the EU Commission has been negotiating with America for some time. It is opposed by trade unions, NGOs, environmentalists and others who fear that the emphasis on freer access to EU markets will override existing safety, work and other protective legislation and ultimately expose those who resist such changes—including sovereign governments—to the risk of being sued through international law.

decades, and which have engulfed most of the world, have unleashed challenges and dilemmas on a scale, of an intensity and at such a speed that they call into question the very capacity of capitalism to adapt and even survive these changes. We explore these transformations and their likely causes and consequences in much more detail throughout the chapters that follow. In outline, however, they include the recent addition in the Global South to the world's stock of industrializing economies, all competing for investment and market share; simultaneously, we confront the massive financial linkages which connect all these economies together around a core of rapidly intensifying globalizing processes; and a swathe of technological advances, with their accompanying occupational and job changes, which have permeated industrial, service, financial and socio-cultural life, including robotization and artificial intelligence (AI) while giving rise to the knowledge economy.

Set against this background two questions are paramount. One concerns the present but also the future prognosis for capitalism as a worldwide economic system. How probable is it that whatever form it eventually takes, capitalism will prove capable not just of adapting to the changes and problems just outlined but will also survive their impact in its own right? But there is a second and far more important question, the obverse of the first. If we are compelled to continue relying on capitalism as the dominant engine of economic life, and given recent, current and impending transformations, and the risks they bring, what are humanity's prospects of surviving over the next century without being overwhelmed by vast and perhaps scarcely controllable employment, environmental, food, water, geo-political and perhaps other crises and conflicts? Although probing for answers to these two questions underlies the entire discussion throughout this book, Chap. 8 focuses specifically on interrogating possible answers.

Clearly, these are very big questions and it is crucial to establish a framework within which to assess and test their remit in a convincing way. To do this we now discuss three topics. The first concerns the reasons for discussing modernity and the characteristics of 'the modern' as a co-agent in helping to forge our world today, alongside capitalism, and even though the latter has become the dominant partner. Then, second, we consider a number of compelling counter-arguments which challenge the book's central theme of an overweening but simultaneously inept and dangerously unequal capitalism, the potential benefits of which are being progressively outweighed by cumulative risks and contradictions. Hopefully this will focus the reader's attention more acutely on what is at stake in the discussions to come. The final section returns to the original theme and briefly indicates the main dilemmas and problems that lie ahead if we continue to give free rein to the relentless, explosive logic and power that capitalism and—to a lesser extent—modernity have displayed till now.

1.1 The Partnership of Capitalism and Modernity

As the study of societies evolved and the different disciplines mapped out their various spheres of interest, a bifurcation became established between the focus on modernity, its origins, character and consequences, and the study of capitalism. To an extent this separation cuts across various disciplines. But in general, sociologists, anthropologists and social geographers tended to incorporate modernity into their repertoire, while economists and political economists staked out capitalism as their primary field of investigation, though in very different ways. This separation of interest has been unfortunate in a number of respects. For one thing, both capitalism and modernity share and depend upon almost identical and largely secular rationalities and orientations focused around the simultaneous re-making of personal life and society in pursuit of control over nature, material improvement and the belief in a more inclusive society and polity. They also emerged out of the same historical circumstances. Moreover, the vast majority of social scientists from all disciplines, along with political leaders, share the presumption that capitalism and modernity have always provided, and still do, the only realistic path to achieving 'progress' in relation to enhancing humanity's well-being and access to social justice and freedom. Both are argued to be universal and timeless and capable of taking us into the indefinite future, ultimately encompassing every society.

Although, as will be evident in later chapters, capitalism in the twentieth century became the controlling force, steering most of what happens, the ambitions, dreams and discourses associated with modernity have always been, and remain, important. Depending on who wields them at any one time, they underpin and weave in and out of the turbo-dynamo that is capitalism. In short, our world today has not been made by capitalism alone. Nor does the one-dimensional or instrumental rationality that dominates capitalism spring solely from the relentless drive to accumulation. Indeed, despite capitalism's overwhelming resources and urge to dominate technology and science, the relationship was never completely one-sided.

First, European science was already in the process of establishing its own dynamic and momentum through such figures as Bacon, Copernicus, Galileo, Kepler and Newton, inheritors of an intellectual and social movement that had its origins in the thirteenth century, culminating in the scientific revolution of the seventeenth century. Clearly, this was long before the birth of industrial capitalism. Scientific thought also drew on the legacy of Greek and Islamic thinking going back centuries. Moreover, as Mouzelis (1999: 149) argues, advances in scientific thought gradually led to a new and superior kind of knowledge based on criteria of validation that crossed all political boundaries and cultures and superseded thinking tied to religious or moral precepts. This, in turn, laid the basis for the development of technologies that made possible the evolution of more complex societies consisting of increasingly specialized institutions and roles. These same technologies also exposed local communities to influences diffusing from the centre on a previously unknown scale and at the same time permitted the increased mobility of citizens.

Second, additional kinds of knowledge that preceded industrial capitalism were also simultaneously exercising their own independent influence on the evolution of European society and thought while helping to underpin scientific thinking (Seidman 1998). The Renaissance and Reformation were certainly two of these. However, the eighteenth-century European Enlightenment, with its insistence on the capacity and right of autonomous individuals to exercise reason in the face of superstition, bigotry, religious fundamentalism and feudal/absolutist tyranny, was particularly powerful. As Seidman suggests: '[t]he power of science was thought to lie in its capacity to liberate human kind from material want, from illusions that mired us in fear and ignorance, and from a world that felt beyond human control. The Enlighteners imagined science as a vehicle of human progress'.

Together, scientific and Enlightenment thought fused to form a tide of expectations, orientations and demands that sociologists and other social scientists have called the drive to modernity. According to Wagner (2001: 61–63), for example, at the core of modernity lay the conviction that the world is shaped by human action rather than by nature and natural events or supernatural agencies. This, in turn, leads to the belief that individuals have both the obligation and the right to make choices (Wagner 1994: xii) and to forge their own identities. Closely tied to these views there is also an emphasis on scepticism and critical reflection and so the need to question knowledge and test it against independent truth criteria. Further, in his book *All That Is Solid Melts Into Air* (1982), Berman shows how much of the energy propelling modernization processes forward emanated from the marriage between individuals striving to assert their autonomy and their attempt to express this through seizing hold of the material world all around them and transforming it to meet their own needs and desires. This creative energy and egocentric determination took many forms: scientific and technological achievement, business practice, political action, institution-building or the sphere or art and ideas. Clearly, the search for valid knowledge, scientific discovery and technological experimentation were always central to the impulse to modernization before capitalism, and its one-dimensionality, was released and allowed to capture huge swathes of social, intellectual and scientific life.

Third, there was another way in which modernity along with science and technological development exercised a role in shaping our world, partly independently of capitalism. On one hand, as Mann (1986) and Giddens (1985) have argued, the fragile balance of power between competing European nation-states, which erupted frequently into violent conflicts, prevented any single state from consolidating its hold permanently over the continent as a whole and establishing an empire. But this same competition and fear of foreign war also gave rulers an incentive to strengthen and centralize their state institutions. This state-building took many forms, such as suppressing regional identities perceived as likely to undermine central power, encouraging technological—and therefore, military preparedness—and craft development, improving communications and national transport systems and nurturing local trading classes who could then be used as a source of tax revenue and state loans. Much of this also required some attempt to break with the status rigidities of the existing quasi-feudal system by fostering a limited meritocracy. The absolutist rulers who pursued state-building did not realize that the modernization processes for which they were unwittingly laying the foundations—alongside science and Enlightenment Thought—would culminate eventually in economic and political revolutions destined to either eliminate or reduce the powers wielded by their descendants while preparing the ground for industrial capitalism.

Last, the emergence of industrial capitalism in one country after another was only possible because of the deliberate policies pursued by modernizing state elites. These were anxious not to allow their own indigenous markets to be out-competed by rival economies or to risk military domination by countries whose own industrial revolutions were equipping them with superior war technologies. To this end, a number of European governments took steps to remove customary restrictions on free markets and to unify the national economy, to abolish serfdom and encourage agricultural experimentation. But they also opened government offices to able non-aristocratic contenders, transferred advanced technology to local businesses while subsidizing and protecting the latter from foreign competition, and assumed much of the financial burden of funding essential transport and other infrastructure where the market was still too weak to do so (Gershenkron 1966). The governments of the USA from the early 1800s onwards, and in Japan following the Meiji Restoration in 1868, undertook similar measures, and for the same reasons—crucial steps that neither India nor China were able to take until they had shaken off European domination.

Thus, everywhere the birth and later trajectories of capitalism depended on the visions of a 'modern' future pushed by different elites and driven by national motivations and interests within the wider context of the actual or perceived threat of competition from rival or former colonizing nations in an international system of sovereign states. By the same token, albeit to varying degrees, each country's transition was led by the state since only organized, centralized and focused power could remove or neutralize the obstacles to modernization (see Skocpol 1979). Much of this has been forgotten, especially by neoliberal thinkers. These three background contingencies to early and later phases of modernization—the reality of an international order, nationalist motivations and the centrality of state-led industrialization—continue to shape not just the institutions and politics of each country but also the expectations and perceptions of citizens and political elites. However, there is a sting in the tale of this story. The national identities and interests forged or consolidated in competition with rival states and coupled to the attempts to unleash a viable national capitalism have left a legacy of states zealously guarding their sovereignty and citizens who believe they are united around the sense of an 'imagined national community' (Anderson 1983) that they wish to protect. This, in turn, inhibits the transition to a more collaborative world of cooperating nation-states at the very time when economic production, finance, commercial culture and science, and their consequences, have outgrown a national frame and desperately require and depend upon such inter-state collaboration.

1.2 Counter-arguments: The Miracle of Capitalist Modernity

Even to pose the question of whether capitalism and modernity can continue to dominate and shape the world's future as they have done for more than two centuries while providing the only viable vehicle for taking humanity to a fairer and safer world, seems a risky and perhaps foolhardy endeavour. At the very least it invites incredulity and probably complete indifference from both Left and Right political interests in addition to many working in the humanities and social sciences, particularly orthodox economists. It is not difficult to understand why this is so, since there are at least three very obvious and powerful reasons for doubting the necessity to respond to this question: the proven capacity of capitalism to adapt as it confronted various economic crises; its long-term survival in the face of serious challenges to its existence; and the trail of successes that have followed in the wake of capitalist modernity.

Continuous Adaptation and Creativity

Experts differ concerning how many major technological leaps, phases or waves industrial capitalism has passed through, along with corresponding changes to work practices, modes of business organization and arrangements for financing investment and international trade. Nevertheless, the reality of almost continuous, relentless transformation is obvious and irrefutable. By the later decades of the nineteenth century, strenuous efforts were being made by political-economic elites in Germany, France, the USA and later Italy, Tsarist Russia and Japan, to catch up with Britain's industrial lead. This soon gave rise to fierce competition for shares of growing national and international markets. The reality of trade rivalry in an ever more complex world economy has continued unabated ever since. Thus, from the 1960s a host of Asian and other countries in the Global South have joined the race for industrial modernization—most notably China and India. The following gives an approximate outline concerning these various phases.

The early era of factory production based on coal, steam power, canals and textiles was followed from approximately the 1830s by the age of the railway, steam ships, the telegraph and the diffusion of factory production—with an ever-increasing scale of production—to a range of manufacturing processes (especially steel) and including the manufacture of machines for making other machines. Then, from the 1890s, and led by Germany and the USA, industries more dependent on scientific research rose to the fore. These included not only electrical engineering and chemical industries but also the telephone and later the radio. The motor car based on the internal combustion engine was a notable product of these technologies, along with the beginnings of suburbanization. The era of mass production, or Fordism, also began at this time (from the 1910s)—though as a general model for business organization it continued through to the 1970s, and sometimes beyond. Fordism involved huge integrated factories with a highly specialized and efficient workforce whose productivity made it possible to pay employees relatively high wages. The latter could be spent on buying the products of their own labour as well as enjoying the new leisure industries such as cinema.

The middle decades of the twentieth century saw the spread and continuation of the Fordist model but accompanied by the development of a further wide range of new technologies and products: synthetic materials, nuclear power, aerodynamic systems, automation in manufacturing and the growing sophistication of communication, data storage and analysis. Finally, we reach the current era dominated by the revolution in communication and information technology and digitalization. But a range of other scientific advances, including the mapping of the human genome and the advance of AI are also crucial. We scrutinize these changes in Chaps. 5 and 8.

The point about these vast scientific, technological and accompanying social, cultural and economic transformations—with all the conflicts and upheavals to everyday life they imposed on the generations living through them—is that they demonstrate the capacity of capitalist modernity to endlessly adapt and to move along a trajectory which has often brought material benefits to many.

Survival in the Face of Multiple Crises

Unsurprisingly, such colossal technological, business and international transformations have not passed without generating crises. Indeed, capitalism has always been riven with political, financial, economic and ecological crises. They are part and parcel of the inherently volatile and largely unregulated character of a market system based on the search for profit, the vagaries of changing tastes, competitive pressures and the apparently unstoppable thirst for new knowledge and innovation. These, in turn, are linked to the highly uneven manner—by region, sector, social class and gender—through which the transformations capitalism wrought worked their way through each nation. In parallel with this there were numerous mini booms and slumps as business, bank and investor confidence rose and fell in response to bouts of over- and under-production, speculative surges and rising or falling prices. Concrete historical examples of these major crises will now be considered.

The Europe-wide revolutionary fervour of the 1840s was closely tied to the exposure of citizens to the full pressure of market forces. In Britain's case the chief culprit was the 1834 New Poor Law which removed previous local and statutory systems of protection against unemployment and economic distress. Then there was a long period of relative economic stagnation and falling prices during the last decades of the nineteenth century, sometimes referred to as the 'Long Depression'. This was linked not only to over-production, as the USA and Germany became major exporting nations of manufactured goods, but also to the rise of vast corporations whose proprietors sought monopolistic prices and low wages through suppressing worker organizations. A fierce eruption of worker discontent preceded and followed—and to some extent continued during—the First World War (WW1) which alarmed governments and business elites across Europe and North America. In Russia this contributed to a revolution in 1917 which culminated in the Bolshevik takeover of political power, thereby providing an ideological and potential economic rival to Western capitalism for the next 70 years. The financial crash and subsequent unemployment and contraction of the world economy from 1929 onwards helped trigger the rise of fascism in Germany and Japan—and consolidated fascism in Italy—culminating in World War Two (WW2). But it also opened the path to greater government intervention in the post-war management of market economies and 30-plus years of unprecedented worldwide economic growth, in addition to full employment and a regime of social-democratic consensus between labour and capital in the advanced economies.

Then, in the 1970s, severe inflation accompanied by falling profits and widespread industrial unrest in many countries brought strong pressures to end the post-war consensus. Inflation had several causes, including the end of world currency stability following the devaluation of the dollar in 1971, and the fourfold oil price hike of 1973. Trade union pressure on governments and businesses, however, received most of the blame—especially from politicians and thinkers on the Right who argued that the preceding era of regulated markets and capitalism since the 1940s threatened to supress both freedom and enterprise. Indeed, the crises of the

1970s provided a pretext for the major turn towards neoliberal economic policy, beginning with Thatcher in Britain in 1979, and Reagan in the USA from 1981. Neoliberalism subsequently became one of the crucial, though not the only, force which accelerated and deepened processes of globalization, particularly through the greater openness to world markets and capital flows which it demanded. In addition, neoliberal policies and globalization were also backed by US policies operating through the 'Washington Consensus'. All this is examined at some length in Chap. 3.

There is wide agreement that deregulation of the finance industry, supported by neoliberal policies and coupled to globalization, created the conditions for the implosion that led to the most recent capitalist crisis, one that has affected the Western economies with particular intensity (see e.g. Elliott and Atkinson 2008; Dardot and Laval 2013; Gamble 2014; Stiglitz 2013; Quiggin 2010; and Mirowski 2013, to name but a few). This began in 2008 with the collapse of Lehman Brothers in New York and was soon followed by the huge financial losses suffered by a series of investment banks and other financial businesses. Dealing with this required massive government borrowing across the EU and the USA in the attempt to prevent the crisis bringing down a far wider range of businesses and causing citizen distress from unemployment and, ultimately, even the inability to draw money from their banks. Estimates vary, but one observer placed this amount at $5 trillion (Gowan 2009). The financial crisis gave rise to a period of austerity, unemployment and insecurity in the Western countries which continues till the present time. This might have been much worse had it not been for the resort to quantitative easing on a massive scale by some Western governments, and also the ability of the Chinese economy, with its astonishingly high rates of economic growth until just recently, to keep demand expanding in the world economy as a whole. We return to a deeper examination of this most recent crisis in Chaps. 3 and 4.

For the moment, and with the partial exception of the 2008 crash, it is crucial to note how again and again capitalist modernity has recovered and risen, phoenix-like, from the ashes of crisis: bank failures; the rise and fall of markets and different technologies; extreme international competition; the destruction of huge swathes of employment and wealth during major recessions; periods of political instability; bouts of prolonged and organized worker resistance and demands; and major cataclysmic events, particularly the two world wars. One key explanation for this survivability in the face of almost constant upheavals is the role that interventionist governments have played at different times. In addition, capitalist enterprises frequently developed and demonstrated strategies of their own that enabled them to respond to local and international competition and economic change. Schumpeter, another influential thinker on the nature of capitalism in the first half of the twentieth century, talked about the process of 'creative destruction' as critical to business and economic change. Here, new innovation destroys the old but the overall gain outweighs the harm and losses brought by change. Similarly, investment in more efficient machinery and labour processes, perhaps driven by conflict between workers and owners, raised the productivity and output of workers. In principle, therefore, businesses could afford to pay such workers higher wages and/or improve their working conditions without hurting profits. But such investments also increase the demand for the products of other businesses, probably in the form of heavy industrial goods. In this way change or expansion in one sector drove through increased demand and perhaps investment in other sectors. Marx called this process expanded reproduction.

In any case, capital has continuously invaded ever more fields of social, economic cultural and domestic life that were previously outside the market and organized through family, household or communal modes of work. This process of commoditization involves turning goods and services that had no previous market value into products made for sale. Obvious examples are food and beverage production, leisure activities and entertainment, the disposition of holiday or vacation time, health and medical remedies and education. Even natural biological processes and resources in the plant, animal, insect, bacterial and genetic spheres have, in recent years, been progressively colonized by capital and the scientists it employs. Once legalized through the award of internationally recognized patent rights, businesses then sell any resulting products back to the world at high prices.

Changing ideas have also played a large role in this process, in that intellectual and academic theory, shaped by the varying historical circumstances associated with each country's particular route through modernity, have constantly adjusted to the changing circumstances and epochs of capitalist economic life. This began in the mid-nineteenth century when the destructive social impact of Britain's virtually free and unregulated market policies were causing concern. The ideas developed by various thinkers then helped to alter the way governments, politicians, the public and businesses altered their own expectations and demands concerning the changes and crises they were experiencing. At the same time these same ideas reflected the underlying structural realities which thinkers themselves were struggling to understand.

Keynes's work from the 1920 to 1940s was a landmark example. Keynes 'envisaged a transition from the individualism and anarchy of *laissez faire* capitalism to the order and social stability of a system of managed capitalism' (Turner 2008: 50). Among other things this required a greater involvement by governments in steering capitalism in the attempt to reduce the economic dislocation, and therefore the distress from mass unemployment and recession, that occurred when the market failed to align the productive output and investment of private businesses with the consuming or market power of workers and citizens. In different ways, Keynesian demand-management policies later became central to the conventional economic wisdom and practice of many Western governments more or less right through until the 1970s when a new and different crisis, of inflation or stagflation and falling profits, came to the fore. This convinced many that comprehensive government intervention in economic life had become one of the main causes of crisis rather than its solution. It was at this point that the pro-market and anti-collectivist ideas that Hayek (e.g. 1944) and other neoliberals had been developing since the 1930s began to influence certain politicians and others. We examine these ideas and their considerable impact on capitalism since the 1970s and today in Chaps. 3 and 4.

The Development of the Productive Forces and Material Advance

Capitalist modernity also demonstrates a trail of successes in improving the material well-being of humanity and to some degree the increased access, for many, to greater social justice, democratic politics and personal freedom—albeit in a highly uneven, unequal fashion. Just a few pieces of evidence illustrate this point.

First, according to Maddison (2001: 264)—a historian who has amassed an impressive data base of world statistics on population and economic growth—between 1820 and 1870 Europeans from 12 nations enjoyed an average per capita increase in their incomes of 60 per cent. This had risen by another 77 per cent by 1913 and a further 36 per cent by 1950—the latter period probably held back by the Great Depression and two world wars. For the same group of countries, particularly in Europe but also including Japan, the really astonishing improvement in per capita incomes came between 1950 and 1973 with a rise of 151 per cent. These were the 'golden' years of American leadership of the Western world, post-war recovery, huge investments in depleted capital stocks and government willingness to prioritize the goals of full employment and the need to establish or upgrade welfare systems. Such rapid, huge and almost continuous improvements in material prosperity had been virtually unknown across Europe and the world prior to the arrival of industrial capitalism.

Second, and turning to the rest of world—much of it under imperial control in 1900—apart from Japan the West's capitalist leap forward in the nineteenth century was scarcely replicated elsewhere. If anything, living standards and national gross domestic product (GDP) remained stagnant or declined even in China and India which, until the early nineteenth century, had enjoyed wealthier economies than those in the West, though with much larger populations. However, this global inequality began to flatten out from roughly the middle of the twentieth century onwards as China and the newly independent countries such as India, South Korea and Indonesia began to pursue a path of independent economic growth (Therborn 2013: 145–7). In doing so their governments adopted a capitalist growth path, but one which frequently involved a mix of state and private investment with governments playing a much more pro-active, even direct role, in managing growth than anything ever practised in the Western countries.

There have been three highly significant consequences of the industrialization achieved by the Global South since the 1970s. Largely due to a combination of very high rates of economic growth and high populations—especially in China and India—there is general agreement that the relative world balance of economic power is shifting away from the West and back to Asia and countries such as Brazil and Russia (Gamble 2014). Further, during the last 20 years or so, a new highly educated, technically proficient and/or entrepreneurial middle class has emerged in many countries. To an extent they are capable of out-competing their Western equivalents across a range of advanced industries and services. Moreover, as relatively affluent citizens within their own countries, they are fuelling a consumer economy and demanding lifestyles little different from those in the West. According to Milanovic (2012) there are now perhaps 200 million of such individuals in China, 90 million in India and a further 30 million or so across countries such as Brazil, Indonesia and Egypt. It is *their* incomes which are rising fastest in the global economy, apart from those of the world's top wealthiest 1 per cent, to whom we return in Chaps. 2 and 4.

Last, Milanovic argues that between 1988 and 2008, albeit with the exception of the poorest 5 per cent, the bottom one-third of the world's people living on slightly more than $1.25 per day as measured by the World Bank's (WB) indices enjoyed a 40–70 per cent increase in their living standards. Not all of this is due to national and global capitalist growth. Fluctuations in the prices of food, water and raw materials also played a key role along with government policies. WB and other statistics on changing income levels are notoriously difficult to collect and analyse (see Cohen and Kennedy 2013: 108–10). Thus, the claims by various global institutions and scholars to the effect that there have been huge falls in world poverty primarily because of globalization and the adoption (or imposition) since the 1980s of more open market economies, need to be assessed cautiously. In particular, Chen and Ravallion (2008) showed that it has been China's success in reducing national poverty that accounts for the greater part of the world poverty reduction. By 2005, there were 600 million fewer Chinese citizens living on less than $1.25 per day than in 1981. If these figures are subtracted from world totals, the global picture of poverty reduction at the bottom looks less rosy. Nevertheless, it is undeniable that as in the West, different varieties of capitalism are now working their 'magic' in many countries across the world that until recently were economically stagnant.

1.3 Thinking the Unthinkable: The End Game for Capitalist Modernity?

Given this remarkable capacity for capitalism to adapt, survive and generate fairly continuous material gains during 200 years of perpetual change and frequent crises, why should the situation facing capitalist modernity be any different today? Certainly, most of the writers whose work is discussed in detail in later chapters are deeply concerned about the current state of world capitalism. But although they see a capitalist machine which is taking us temporarily into an era of slow or no growth, they do not believe the entire world system of capitalist modernity is running down entirely, like a gigantic clockwork machine whose key has been permanently lost. Rather, it seems, they presume that provided key reforms are set in place, capitalism can and will return to its previous capacity to steadily improve the lives of most people.[3] Nor is the critical restraint evident in these and other mainstream assessments new or unexpected. For more than 200 years it has been the scarcely questioned view of political and other leaders and scholars of all disciplines that capitalist modernity provides the only realistic path to achieving something we may loosely call 'progress'. From the 1980s postmodern thinking seriously challenged the ontology of modernity as an irresistible historical force bringing a universal moral justification for the inevitability and rightness of progress. Yet, postmodernism did not seriously dislodge the idea or the promise of material improvement from the popular mind. Rather, the pursuit of modernity and market capitalism will proceed, like technology and scientific advance, almost of its own accord and as if driven by a mysterious and unstoppable global force (Bauman 2002: 143–4).

However, the recent changes we alluded to above may prove more difficult to overcome, or weave into the existing dynamics and repertoires of capitalist modernity, than the crises and conflicts of the last 250 years. Here, we merely outline these but the central themes to which they refer are explored separately in later chapters.

---

[3] Of course, this is very different from the boundless optimism and hype concerning the role of innovation, enterprise and growth in bearing humanity towards a future universal economic nirvana frequently on display on our TV screens from politicians, media spokespersons, business tycoons and others.

1.4 In Recent Decades a Vampire form has Largely Disengaged Capitalism from Society[4]

As we see in Chap. 2, vampire capitalism refers both to particular kinds of capitalist enterprises and also to a general tendency now intrinsic to vast swathes of investment practice—but not usually to most small and medium enterprises. It points to the reality that today a considerable proportion of the wealth generated from economic growth is not reinvested back into long-term production. Instead, much wealth is diverted into the largely deregulated financial industry, selling a variety of risky products, or moves in search of rising asset values and unearned rent. This reflects the reality that government policies have tended to play to the 'needs' of capital rather than those of citizens, believing this to be essential for attaining economic growth. The result is a capitalism whose elites exist in a separate socio-economic dimension from that of workers and citizens and who act as if this scarcely mattered either to the latter or to capital's own future.[5] Taibbi's reference in 2010 to Goldman Sachs in *Rolling Stones* magazine as 'a great vampire squid wrapped round the face of humanity' brilliantly and daringly captures the meaning intended except that the term 'vampire' is being applied here to a much wider range of contemporary capitalist actions and actors.

The Current 'Model' of Economic Practice Stifles Economic Growth

Neoliberal assumptions concerning what constitutes 'sound' economic policy by governments and intergovernmental organizations (IGOs) severely inhibit future economic prospects. Globalization and the rise

---

[4] Marx described capital as 'vampire-like' in *Capital* Volume 1. He was referring to the reality that all capital originated in labour and the continuous process of extracting surplus value. Though today knowledge and technology play a far greater role in wealth creation, Marx's fundamental insight regarding labour as the source of value remains key. The term 'vampire capitalism', used here, means something much broader than exploitation at the point of production.

[5] See Chap. 8 for a full discussion of this last point.

of a much more diverse world of competing industrial economies further constrain the range of policy alternatives available. Chief among these policies are: tolerating growing inequality and a low tax regime for the super-rich to avoid 'restraining' innovation and wealth generation; avoiding public investment or borrowing in pursuit of infrastructural and employment-creating projects for fear that these might push wages up too high and divert investment from the (largely unproven) super-efficiency of private businesses; allowing and even encouraging debt—whether as a substitute for wage rises or as a central plank of business expansion; and avoiding any moves to re-regulate the global financial system. But the resulting race to the bottom in terms of wage levels undermines effective demand and further limits the prospects of absorbing surplus investment funds in new investment. Similarly, dwindling tax revenues and massively skewed income distribution prevent governments from spending more on ageing populations and improving education levels without the need to charge students, and so on.

Relentless Technological—Scientific 'Advance' Threaten a Jobless Future

Technological advance—increasingly dependent on science—has been the other leading driver of material progress. Even though they have been largely brought under the domination of capital (and the state) some sectors of technology and science struggle to retain some autonomy. As we will see in Chap. 5, this capacity to replace human labour with increasingly sophisticated machines which replicate ever more aspects of AI is spreading rapidly to a range of activities in transport, farming, surveillance systems, medical and business assessment, distribution, education and much else besides. Some observers see a future governed by the near certainty that an ever greater number of occupations will be engulfed by unemployment as capital replaces human labour. Nor is it certain that their poverty and low wages will save those still waiting to be absorbed by capitalism in the Global South from the same fate, given the constant fall in the costs of investing in machines.

We are faced then, with a capitalism which permits 1 per cent to secrete nearly half of the wealth from economic growth into tiny protected havens while all but 10 to perhaps 15 per cent of the remainder—who work in the remaining high-tech jobs—are left chronically insecure and struggling on declining incomes, or simply excluded as structurally irrelevant to economic life.

Individualization and Lifestyle Cultures Dissolve Social Coherence and Collective Action

The Enlightenment and modernity held the promise that the free individual would be empowered to exercise reason in making choices concerning what s/he wanted to be. This would equip social actors with the capacity to determine the directions that modernity could or should take within the constraints set by living in a society governed by humanistic principles and scientific knowledge. In Chap. 6, we suggest that there is a danger that the material affluence brought by capitalism has driven the ideal of individual self-autonomy off-course by fostering a version of self-realization concerned almost exclusively with the personal quest for self-promotion and narcissistic enjoyment, which divides rather than unites us. Instead of steering modernity and capitalism by exercising reason, we have allowed a particularly narrow kind of rationality to dominate based on egoism and a relative indifference to community. This prevents us from challenging the system through collective action even though the insecurities tied into the cultures of capitalism undermine rather than promote genuine individualization processes.

Our Plunder of the Earth's Bio-Sphere Leaves a Legacy of Dangerous Environmental Risk

In Chap. 7 we show how the cumulative impact of capitalist modernity is nowhere more clearly visible than in respect to the damage inflicted on the earth's biosphere, particularly in relation to climate change and global warming. What stands out is the unquestioned belief in humanity's right to exploit all nature's resources from mineral deposits and the oceans to virtually all animal and plant life. For millennia, human actions have always been partly responsible for environmental change, and the very idea of 'nature' is in some ways a conceptual construct. Also the environment itself is an entity that constantly adapts both to human Also geophysical changes. It is undeniable that Western industrialization is responsible for most environmental damage. Yet the rapid industrialization of the Global South, especially China and India, is already contributing massively to greenhouse gas emissions and the despoliation of seas, forests and so on and can only intensify. One of the huge imponderables concerning how to reverse environmental risk, before it lurches towards climate changes we can no longer contain or survive, concerns the burden of who will be required to pay the cost.

1.5 Thinking About Alternative Futures

The impact of all of these transformations will surely intensify in the coming years because they are all direct consequences of the trajectory of capitalist modernity. None have emerged out of nowhere, sui generis and without a history or cause. Living in an interconnected global economy with a single shared climatic system means that these transformations and processes form an interlocking and mutually reinforcing syndrome. As each or any of the above plays out so it will trigger, aggravate or worsen one or more of the others through a dangerous trail of synergies. At the very least, and given the narrow logic defining market capitalism's DNA, it is difficult to see how left to its own devices it will manage all these dangers without huge interventions from governments, the scientific community and above all the exercise of citizen power. But such external interventions are likely to alter capitalism irrevocably and may reinforce the changes that are already altering it from the inside, for example, through the rise of cognitive capitalism or the knowledge economy. These changes are examined in Chaps. 8 and 9.

None of this means that capitalist modernity is likely to disintegrate any time soon into a world recession even deeper and more prolonged than that of the 1930s. Nor does it follow that civil and national wars will ignite at any moment culminating in a series of socialist or Right-wing, quasi fascist revolutions—though neither are these prospects impossible. Yet, it will be no easy task to redirect capitalist modernity into safer avenues through serious reforms even on the scale of a single nation. It is also possible to imagine severe crises pushing the world into a situation where the usual levers of successful management associated with capitalist modernity and the institutions of international governance prove incapable of preventing some regions fragmenting into anarchy and violence.

There is another possibility. Capitalism may struggle and splutter into the future in various forms but in the meantime there may be serious attempts to replace it in whole or part with a multiplicity of mostly small-scale, primarily locally based alternative social formations. Indeed, this is the theme we explore in Chap. 9. Two sections of humanity are perhaps particularly likely to seek refuge in these alternative social formations. First are those who are already disenchanted by the life now under offer from capitalist modernity. A second group consists of a growing number who are currently being excluded from, and/or pushed to the margins of, the current world system by the transformations outlined above and which render it unlikely their precarious situation will or can be changed in the coming decades.

Overall, then, this book not only explores the present impact of neoliberal capitalism on societies today and their various lines of fracture and division, but also considers the alternatives, both potentially dystopic and positive, that seem to loom ahead.

Bibliography

Anderson, B. (1983). *Imagined communities: Reflections on the origins and spread of nationalism.* London: Verso.
Bauman, Z. (2002). *Society under siege.* Cambridge: Polity.
Berman, M. (1982). *All that is solid melts into air.* New York: Simon and Schuster.

Chen, S. and Ravallion, M. (2008). *The developing world is poorer than we thought, but no less successful in the fight against poverty*. World Bank. Retrieved August 9, 2016, from http://elibrary.worldbank.org/doi/abs/10.1596/1813-9450-4703

Cohen, R., & Kennedy, P. (2007). *Global sociology* (2nd ed.). New York: New York University Press.

Cohen, R., & Kennedy, P. (2013). *Global sociology* (3rd ed.). New York: New York University Press.

Dardot, P. and Laval, C. (2013). *The new way of the World: On neo-liberal society* (trans: Elliot, G.). London: Verso.

Elliott, L., & Atkiknson, D. (2008). *The gods that failed: How blind faith in markets has cost us our futures*. London: Bodley Head.

Gamble, A. (2014). *Crisis without end? The unravelling of western prosperity*. Basingstoke: Palgrave.

Gershenkron, A. (1966). *Economic backwardness in historical perspective*. Cambridge, MA: Harvard University Press.

Giddens, A. (1985). *The nation state and violence*. Cambridge: Polity.

Gowan, P. (2009). Crisis in the heartlands: Consequences of the new Wall Street system. *New Left Review, 55*, 5–28.

Harvey, D. (2011). *The enigma of capital*. London: Profile Books.

Hayek, F. A. (1944). *The road to Serfdom*. London: Routledge.

Kliman, A. (2012). *The failure of capitalist production; Underlying causes of the great recession*. London: Pluto Press.

Maddison, A. (2001). *The world economy: A millennial perspective*. OECD. Retrieved August 10, 2016, from http://theunbrokenwindow.com/Development/MADDISON%20The%20World%20Economy--A%20Millennial.pdf

Mann, M. (1986). *The sources of social power: A history of power from the beginning to AD 1760*. Cambridge: Cambridge University Press.

Milanovic, B. (2012). *The real winners and losers of globalization*. The Globalist. Retrieved August 11, 2016, from http://www.theglobalist.com/the-real-winners-and-losers-of-globalization/

Mirowski, P. (2013). *Never let a serious issue go to waste: How neoliberalism survived the financial crisis*. London: Verso.

Mouzelis, N. (1999). Modernity: A non-European conceptualization. *British Journal of Sociology, 50*(1), 141–159.

Quiggin, J. (2010). *Zombie economics: How dead ideas still walk among us*. Princeton, NJ: Princeton University Press.

Sandel, M. (2016, June 10–16). The energy of the Brexiteers and Trump is born of the failure of elites. *New Statesman*. Retrieved August 11, 2016, from http://www.newstatesman.com/politics/uk/2016/06/michael-sandel-energy-brexiteers-and-trump-born-failure-elites

Seidman, S. (1998). *Contested knowledge: Social theory in the postmodern era*. Oxford: Blackwell.

Skocpol, T. (1979). *States and revolutions: A comparative analysis of France, Russia and China*. Cambridge: Cambridge University Press.

Stiglitz, J. (2013). *The price of inequality*. London: Penguin.

Therborn, G. (2013). *The killing fields of inequality*. Cambridge: Polity.

Turner, R. S. (2008). *Neo-liberal ideology: History, concepts and policies*. Edinburgh: Edinburgh University Press.

Wagner, P. (1994). *A sociology of modernity: Liberty and discipline*. New York: Routledge.

Wagner, P. (2001). *Theorizing modernity: Inescapability and attainability in social theory*. London: Sage.

Weber, M. (1968). *Economy and society, Volume 1*. New York: Bedminster Press.

2

The Rise of Vampire Capitalism (and not a slayer in sight)

A glance at any dictionary provides a definition of a 'vampire' that runs pretty much along the following lines: a person or entity which sustains its own existence by preying on the blood of living beings. Its actions as an extortioner leaves its victims weakened and perhaps likely to die. In traditional European folklore the remedies against vampires included destroying it by thrusting a stake through its heart or exposing it to the cleansing wholesomeness of holy water or a crucifix. This chapter argues that during the last 40 years or so a disruptive and largely predatory model of capitalism has become established, especially, but not solely, in the Western economies. We use the term 'vampire' as a metaphor for this recent form because of its tendency to create the conditions whereby a minority of low- or non-tax paying capitalists, their actions facilitated by political allies, have been able to commandeer a large proportion of the wealth generated from economic growth while failing to either re-invest this in ways that create jobs and raise the incomes of everyone else or to remunerate their employees in proportion to the latter's contribution to creating new value. Of course, there is a vast spectrum of private companies and other entrepreneurial organizations and it is unfair and misleading to attach this label to all or even most. These provide measurable benefits to society through employment and the production, and perhaps export, of marketable goods and services. Also, their profits partly return to the national system through taxation, new investment, the demand they create for the inputs of other businesses, the wider diffusion of innovations and/or research, contributions to charities, endowments and so on.

Nevertheless, there are strengthening trends running in the opposite direction whether demonstrated by particular companies, certain types of businesses or economic sectors. Arguably, we are witnessing the rise of a capitalism which is no longer willing or capable of contributing to the development of the world's productive forces in ways that can continue to benefit the majority of people over time. That sector of capitalism which falls within the designation 'vampire' has reached the end of its useful life because it now disproportionately serves a tiny minority rather than humanity as a whole. This theme is also taken up in Chap. 8. Moreover, under present conditions—examined below and in greater detail in Chap. 3—we have little prospect of fundamentally changing this situation. Before examining the dimensions of this claim in detail we briefly consider the general nature and logic of capitalist enterprises.

2.1 Generic Capitalism

The primary duty of capitalists is to seek and exploit market opportunities in the pursuit of maximum profits and as a central plank in the accumulation of capital. Caring first and foremost about the interests of those who have invested in a company is a legal responsibility. It follows that it cannot be the duty of, nor is it possible for, capital in general or of particular businesses to develop national economies or overcome poverty, *per se*. These are projects of an altogether different order. Nevertheless, capitalism has played a leading role in advancing, albeit unevenly, the productive forces over time. In a sense some of the crises capitalist societies now face are due to its unplanned successes. The key examples here are an ageing society and the continuous technical advances which reduce the demand for labour and create unemployment (Beck 2009: 22–23). Such changes are largely the cumulative result of unintended and uncoordinated actions on the part of innumerable competing economic actors. Private businesses contribute to such processes but through the operation of Adam Smith's invisible hand—or the serendipity of accident rather than design.

2 The Rise of Vampire Capitalism (and not a slayer in sight)

As we saw in Chap. 1, the pressure to return a profit, outwit competitors and ceaselessly expand market reach give capitalism, as a wider entity, a one-dimensional character. Its sole rationale is capital accumulation and it will constantly push against the constraints on its field of operation if allowed to do so. In Weberian terms, the formal rationality and calculability associated with modernity and the growing dominance of scientific thought spills out in all directions but becomes especially central, indeed essential, to capitalism. The capitalist market possesses 'no inherent moral character' (Stiglitz 2013: xii) nor is it engaged in any wider project other than facilitating the process of making profit.

Yet, capitalism does not operate alone. Nor, given its one-dimensionality and the unpredictable nature of its achievements, can it be allowed to do so by other key actors. We refer here not just to the state but also society: that dense network of overlapping and interacting relationships enacted by millions of social actors through micro- and macro-levels, including those who organize in order to challenge and shape capitalism at various times. In the case of the state, every country's struggle to establish a national capitalist base required state-led actions to remove the remaining traditions and elite interests which obstructed free markets, the mobility of labour and the emergence of a bourgeoisie. If anything the central role of governments in nurturing the rise of an indigenous capitalism has intensified since the 1960s, especially in the case of the Asian Tiger economies of South Korea, Taiwan, Vietnam, Malaysia, Thailand and of course China with its combination of communist central control and private business opportunity. This mutual dependence of market and state continues today. Certainly, Western governments responded to the financial crash of 2008 by socializing the losses of corporations that had always been totally opposed to such state interventions, in addition to propping up businesses such as the car industry in the USA.[1]

This last point highlights the contemporary dilemma. For perhaps a 100 or so years up to the late 1970s, a number of forces and processes, including nationalism and national economic rivalry, imperial

---

[1] Falling demand for gas-guzzling cars at a time of rising fuel prices and the impact of the 2008/9 recession brought the US auto industry to a state of financial collapse. Between them, Presidents Bush and Obama spent around $80 billion on rescuing Chrysler, General Motors and their suppliers in 2009.

opportunities and ideologies, middle-class reformist pressures on governments, and especially the growing power of labour organization, kept capitalism's narrow instrumentality under a certain degree of constraint.[2] Since the 1970s, however, a number of transformations have largely freed many of the larger and global companies from these earlier limitations—in the context of a vast world labour market replete with nations competing for investment. At the same time, technological change and the growing significance of knowledge have altered the terms of exchange between capital and most forms of labour—though, not always to the benefit of capital as we see in Chap. 8—while the expansion of the financial industries have provided new opportunities for profit-making.

This is the context for arguing that many large enterprises now demonstrate vampire-like features. We now identify and explore four criteria for establishing the dimensions of vampire capitalism. These are as follows: the relative shift to shareholder value as the most significant avenue to profit maximization strategies by many companies and investors, often at the cost of long-term investment; the growing gap between wages and the new wealth resulting from economic growth, as capitalists, including financiers and others, extract the greater share from their own businesses and the wider economy; the enhanced role and impact of tax-avoidance strategies by the wealthy; and the growing dependence of some businesses on rent-seeking activities, helped by political allies. It is important to understand and see each of these as part of the whole.

2.2 The Shareholder Economy

Changing Shareholder Demands Since the 1980s

For most of capitalism's history the majority of businesses, large and small, operated primarily within a national framework. The leading investors in their business, their employees, the bulk of their customers—whether other companies or household consumers—and rival businesses were all fellow nationals. Of course, some companies always pursued

---

[2] This discussion is taken up in detail in Chap. 3.

2 The Rise of Vampire Capitalism (and not a slayer in sight) 33

export markets and had to contend with imports from foreign companies. Nevertheless, in Britain's case, for example, even during the late 1960s firms owned by nationals and based in the UK still supplied nearly 90 percent of the British market for manufactured goods (Webster 2002: 67). This was the era of Fordism and the same pattern was repeated in the USA, Germany, France and many other major industrial countries.

When finance, competition and leading markets were all primarily nationally based, businesses faced a political and economic climate where some accountability to the expectations and scrutiny of other players was difficult to avoid. The dividends paid to shareholder/investors out of profits probably varied over time. But in general a sense of obligation to the national economy, awareness of how the media might interpret company decisions and the desire to grow and out-compete business rivals ensured that a considerable proportion of annual profits was ploughed back into business expansion. Depending on the particular business, schemes for training and re-training employees were also necessary to survival. In addition, businesses operated within an immediate economic and cultural environment where their awareness of, and responsiveness to, various stakeholders—upon whose resources and/or approval they depended—were highly significant. Such stakeholders included: existing and potential shareholders, banks from whom they had secured loans and who might provide future funds, their workers and trade unions, the local community who looked to their firm to supply secure employment opportunities and charitable services, a network of business and technical advisors/consultants, and local universities whose science laboratories were engaged in research or relevance to their further product development and so on. Faced with these pressures, businesses strove to achieve a balance between the dividends earned by shareholders and the proportion of profits they re-invested for long-term growth. Share prices as measured in stock markets were always important because they provided an indication of the overall asset value of a company, but they were not normally the only consideration.

This sketch probably offers an idealized and over-optimistic picture of the typical company prior to, say, the 1970s. Nevertheless, many observers have argued that a radical re-shaping of the decision-making processes and priorities of many businesses has taken place during the last 40 years or so. In particular, managers have altered the key relationships and the balance sought between business profit, dividends, long-term investment and share value. In what specific ways and why has this happened?

The needs of shareholders and their primary concern that the value of the shares they hold should keep rising, wherever possible, has become the central concern. Increasing share values, in turn, depends on profitability and dividend payments. If potential buyers—the investment banks, investment and pension fund managers, and brokers who buy shares on behalf of their clients, wealthy individuals such as Oil Sheiks or Russian Oligarchs—see that the dividends paid out by a company are healthy and perhaps increasing, they are likely to pitch into the market and add some or more of this company's stock to their existing portfolio of income-earning securities. Three key changes increasingly evident from the 1980s strengthened these processes.

One was the increased role of the financial industry in economic life, especially in the UK and USA, along with the abolition of most controls on the flows of capital between countries. The huge growth of saving and investment schemes on behalf of pensioners and others also contributed to a rapid surge in the volumes of money searching for profitable havens. But, second, both individual buyers and the investment and pension fund managers looking for higher yields for their clients—and for themselves in respect to the transfer fees they could charge for turning over their clients' money—were increasingly interested in scouring stock markets for company shares that seemed likely to increase in value. Often, the potential for share prices to rise was more important than the dividend payments their clients might receive on these same shares. This shift towards 'empowered investors' (Sennett 2006: 41) endlessly buying and selling shares in the pursuit of higher value has been compounded by a third change taking place within the management structures of many companies. Here, increasingly, the CEO and other company executives have demanded or won the right to have part of their salary and bonuses linked directly to share prices. Obviously this provided incentives for managers to drive up profits in such a way as to further increase share prices thereby adding to the forces pushing in the same direction from outside the firm.

On the general question of who actually owns private shares and therefore who benefits concretely from rising asset values it is important to note that some governments have tried to encourage policies designed to widen the distribution of share ownership. During the 1980s, in the case of the UK, this mainly took the form of tying the privatization of public utilities such as gas, water and electricity to widely publicized share offers at below likely and future market prices to all citizens. Many responded to these opportunities and then later sold their stock when prices duly rose. Despite such market-oriented policies, however, the actual ownership of private stock remains highly unequal in most countries. In the USA, for example, the top 1 percent wealthiest people in 2010 owned 35 percent of all private stock, trust funds, mutual funds, bonds and business equity. In stark contrast the bottom 90 percent owned only 12 percent of all such stock while the least wealthy 50 percent possessed less than 1 percent (Domhoff 2016). Since the 2008 crisis the proportion of US citizens owning shares has also diminished.

Short-Termism and the Losers

In Chap. 3 we discuss the deeper macro-transformations that have underpinned these processes but for now we consider the main consequences of this relative shift towards prioritizing share values. One change emphasized by numerous observers (e.g. Sennett (2006); Elliott and Atkinson (2008); Gowan (2009); and Lansley (2011)) is that CEOs and their managerial staff have tended to assign a lower priority to profit re-investment and company growth, preferring to pay out higher dividends in order make their company shares more attractive to investors. Over time this relative change in the ratio of investment to dividends is likely to push up share value and enable investors and managers to earn good returns while moving their assets elsewhere if company prospects begin to look less favourable. Secondly, this essentially short-term perspective on business performance is likely to shrink the long-term prospects for company expansion. According to Andy Haldane, chief economist at the Bank of England, the practice of putting immediate shareholder interests before those of employees and customers poses a threat to the growth prospects of the economy as a whole. Referring to Britain during a TV interview in July 2015, Haldane observed that whereas during the 1970s around 10 percent of company profits went to shareholders this figure was now between 60 and 70 percent (Giugliano 2015). If such practices are widely employed across an entire economy the result is likely to be not only slower overall economic growth but also reduced or declining employment prospects.

A third adverse result of short-termism concerns the tendency for various kinds of financial crises and speculative bubbles to become more commonplace. A notable case involved the dot-com bubble of 2000 where brokers and investors hugely over-estimated the likely short-term returns on businesses and products caught up in the communications revolution. Their actions pushed up share prices in these companies to unrealistic levels, drawing in unwary investors in the process until the inevitable collapse. More generally, most investors possess little expert knowledge of particular companies or of the workings of financial markets so they sometimes hire the services of 'experts' to act on their behalf. Driven by the need to maximize their own financial return the latter are likely to keep switching their clients' resources between different assets so they can charge various commissions and fees. This not only leads to a misallocation of resources but also pumps up market instability. One observer (Gowan 2009: 7) argues that this kind of 'speculative arbitrage'—the constant dealing in and transferring of financial products between different markets—constitutes a kind of gambling. Indeed, some traders actively create price differences by deliberately entering a particular market in order to drive up prices, thereby tempting other investors to follow suit. Once asset prices reach a particular level the trader then sells their share of the assets, in the process retrieving a handsome profit for themselves or their clients, while their actions burst the bubble and lead to tumbling prices for everyone else. The doubling of oil prices in 2007/08 was very likely caused, in part, by this kind of behaviour and there have been many other cases.

Fourth, the short-term orientation and strong leaning towards quick returns demonstrated by company managers and investors accentuates economic instability. Here, the drive to higher and quicker returns may encourage takeover bids for the ownership of other companies perceived, perhaps, as rich in resources but whose share prices do not currently reflect their overall asset values. Private Equity Companies (PECs) and venture capitalists have increased rapidly in numbers and weight in recent decades and they tend to specialize in this specific kind of business. Often the aim is not to increase profitability by expanding a firm's productive capacity or the productivity of its employees and plant by pouring in new investment—though this is possible—but rather to strip out its more lucrative and valuable assets and/or maximize earnings within a few years before selling it on. Normally, such takeovers are based on leveraged buyouts. These are financed in large part by external borrowing either from onshore or offshore banks or from other companies rather than from the PEC's own resources. Such loans enable PECs, and other firms, to set the interest payments on these loans against tax relief while it is likely that profits will be moved to tax havens. All this pushes more debt into the financial system and enables the PEC's investors to make tax-free quick profits without necessarily adding much value to the productive economy.

The overall result is economic fragmentation and the running down or even demise of the companies caught up in these bids, not to mention the likely loss of employment. According to Hutton (2007: 26), between 1995 and 2005, the total value of these and other kinds of takeovers deals in the USA amounted to $9 trillion. As in the case of other takeover booms the motives driving such activities are mostly short-term rapaciousness rather than any serious attempt to generate further economic growth, create employment, improve productivity or stimulate technological and other kinds of innovation.

A fifth case of short-term profiteering centres around the wider strategies increasingly pursued by many large corporations with global reach. Together, the revolution in communications and the economic strategies pursued successfully by a growing number of countries in the Global South since the 1960s, in training workers and establishing local infrastructure, has also enabled companies to diversify and spread their business networks across vast distances. In response, many corporations have either downsized some of their home operations to these cheaper locations or increasingly outsourced part of their production to local businesses in these countries, often on a huge scale. Such offshoring actions are not harmful in themselves. Indeed, they usually benefit those seeking work in the Global South and help to swell these countries' export earnings. In theory, the cheap imports of such goods into Western countries also helps keep inflation low and to some extent compensate consumers for falling real incomes. However, when combined with the wider impact of the other forms of short-termism and reduced investment discussed above, they worsen the prospects for economic growth as well as the income and employment security available to many Western workers by allowing companies to play one workforce against another. Frequently, this results in a continuous squeeze on wages, the deterioration of work conditions and moves to reduce the numbers of permanent workers through the progressive casualization of the labour force.

2.3 The Gap Between Wages and Productivity

Siphoning New Wealth into Few Pockets

A number of scholars, Inter-governmental Organization (IGOs) and informed observers have become concerned about the extent to which inequality has been increasing and indeed accelerating across many countries during recent decades (Piketty 2014; Quiggin 2010; Streek 2014; Freeland 2012; Stiglitz 2013; and Lansley 2011, to name but a few). In its 2008 report, *World of Work,* the International Labour Organization (ILO) observed that in the case of 51 out of 73 countries for which it had data, the share of total income accruing to wage earners during the previous 20 years had fallen. In contrast the income share taken by the top 10 percent of income earners rose considerably, while the gap between the top and bottom 10 percent widened by around 70 percent in the countries they surveyed. Indeed, by 2007 average executive pay in the 15 largest US private corporations was 500 times higher than that earned by average employees compared to a ratio of 300 to one only four years earlier in 2003. However, the ILO argues that growing income gaps of similar proportions are also occurring in countries such as Germany, Hong Kong, Australia, the Netherlands and South Africa.

The US case is especially significant because of its continuing central role in global capitalism. Among the researchers who have examined inequality in the USA are Dew-Becker and Gordon (2005). They tracked the growth in productivity from 1966 onwards against rates of inflation. They argue that when spurts of productivity growth occur this tends to hold down inflation while the reverse occurs when the former falters or stagnates. Interestingly, their data suggests that in the years between 1995 and 2005, when average productivity rose across the private economy quite substantially (reaching nearly 4 percent each year, 2001–2005), the average hourly earnings for the non-farm population scarcely increased at all. Had it not been for lower-than-average rates of inflation during that same period workers' incomes would have fallen in real terms despite productivity gains. In fact, over the entire period from 1966 to 2001, the top 10 percent of income earners enjoyed a growth rate of real income equal to or higher than that of the average rate of economic growth in productivity. In stark contrast the earnings of the bottom 90 percent either fell behind economic growth or gained no benefit at all.

Moreover, much of the national growth in productivity achieved between 1995 and 2005 came from laying off workers and various cost-cutting activities so that the growth in jobs overall was limited. Drawing on the work of other observers, Dew-Becker and Gordon identify two groups benefiting from extreme inequality at the very top levels of the US economy: the superstars in sport, media celebrities and CEOs and their leading executive managers in private corporations. The super earnings among the former, they suggest, can be largely attributed to the technological change of recent decades (including the Internet, cable and satellite TV) which has hugely broadened the audiences for these superstars and sharpened public appetites for, and therefore improved the earnings of, the performers judged to be top-ranking. Dew-Becker and Gordon argue that the huge rise in payments accruing to top corporate and financial executives, on the other hand, is more difficult to explain and certainly seems to bear little relationship to any realistic measure of rising performance or competency. Rather, what seems to operate, they claim, is a 'scratch my back model' whereby top executives draw on each other's networks of mutual support and interaction in order to persuade compensation committees of their eligibility for further rewards. In addition, the latter do not wish their executives to appear any less deserving or super-competent than in similar companies. US society's tolerance of this procedure, in turn, is almost certainly linked to the ability of economic elites to capture the support of leading politicians and both main parties.[3]

More is at stake here than rising inequality, however—even the excessive degree to which this is happening among the very richest citizens across many societies. Thus, Lansley (2011: 57) argues that what we are seeing is 'a dangerous productivity-wage gap' whereby most of the gains from economic growth accrue to the richest people in society. This is dangerous because its consequences may feed growing citizen discontent with the democratic process and conventional politics. In addition, this decoupling of wage earnings from productivity also undermines the ability of ordinary people to afford to buy goods and services in the capitalist economy without falling back on credit cards and dependence on rising debt. This, in turn, places the entire edifice of market capitalism at risk given that it is predicated on almost continuous economic growth along with a more or less equitable distribution of the gains from such growth, over time, so that demand will mostly keep pace with rising output. Without these, capitalism loses not just lose its legitimacy but its very momentum and inner dynamism. We return to this theme in Chap. 4.

Feeding the Wages–Productivity Gap Through Finance

As we will see in Chaps. 3 and 4, increasing inequality is being caused by a number of changes. One of these has a particularly strong bearing on the wage–productivity gap, namely the rise of the financial industries, especially since the 1980s, and the associated growing significance and influence of financial processes and products, including bonds, stocks shares and derivatives, in the wider economy. For example, Lapavitsas (2013: 203) shows how the ratio of financial assets to GDP in the USA increased from 500 to 800 percent between 1984 and 2009—a trend repeated in several other countries such as Germany and Japan.

---

[3] Piketty (2014) is also dubious concerning the usual reasons given to explain the super-pay earned by top executives in the USA and elsewhere in terms solely of ability (pp.333–5). We return to his analysis of inequality in Chap. 4.

Yet, this massive and fast-growing role, even predominance, of finance in the advanced economies was not matched by equivalent increases in employment (pp.212–13). If anything, these have remained flat so that the capacity of the financial industries to absorb the relatively well-paid jobs lost as manufacturing shrank, especially in the UK and USA, has been extremely disappointing. Instead, the "compensatory" employment growth that has occurred mostly took place in fields such as wholesale and retail, restaurants and food, the care services, security, cleaning, distribution, hairdressing and other personal services. These are jobs where wages are low, employment conditions are insecure—characterized, for example, by zero-hour contracts and temporary agency work which preclude access to health, pension and other benefits—and liable, in some cases, to be replaced by machines in the near future (see Chap. 5).

The key point to note about the growing weight exercised by the financial industries is that it is here the largest salaries, bonuses and profits are being made not only by those working in the sector themselves but also by the world's richest individuals whose money they invest and lend out to other people. Drawing on evidence by US researchers, *The Economist* (2012: 12–15) reported that the 25 top hedge fund managers in the USA earn more than the combined incomes of the CEOs running the leading 500 companies. Piketty makes a similar point when he observes that top managers in the financial industries are twice as likely as managers in other industries to be in the highest income groups (2014: 296).

The facts relating to financialization—the ability of this sector to suck wealth out of the rest of the economy—are quite staggering as the following evidence suggests. Moreover, it also points to some of the key mechanisms through which the productivity–wage gap is taking place. *The World Wealth Report of 2015* argued that at the end of 2014 the total wealth owned not by companies but by the world's High Net Worth Individuals (HNWIs)—some 14.6 million people with directly investable assets of at least $1 million—was equal to approximately $56 trillion. According to the WB this wealth was more than three times the value of US GDP in 2015 ($17.9 trillion) and is equal to 76 percent of the entire world's GDP of $73 trillion in 2015. The numbers of such HNWIs is growing by around 8 percent each year and the overall wealth they own is predicted to reach approximately $70 trillion by 2017. This estimation of the wealth owned by the world's richest people is not the whole story because these figures are based on recorded and traceable valuables. A lot more such wealth owned by individuals is hidden away in tax havens, as we will see in the next section.[4]

The Transnational Capitalist Class—The Global Plutocrats

Freeland's work (2012) on what she calls, the 'rise of the new global super-rich', or the 'plutocrats', also throws interesting light on rising inequality. In an important sense Freeland builds on a significant stream of scholarly work in globalization theory which has explored the rise of a transnational capitalist class consisting of increasingly integrated corporate interests from many countries. This class is said to have become largely dis-embedded from national societies and collaborates to shape the policies of governments (see Sklair 2001; Robinson and Harris 2000; and Robinson 2002). Freeland argues that the rise of the global plutocracy has taken us to a second 'Gilded Age'. The first occurred in the final years of the nineteenth century in the USA when self-made industrial tycoons such as Andrew Carnegie established vast manufacturing industries, accumulated huge personal fortunes partly based on low wages and for a time dominated national politics. This transformation also encouraged rural populations to migrate to the industrial cities. However, Freeland's term 'the second Gilded Age' refers to two different sets of plutocrats whose growing personal fortunes and economic power are closely entwined through activities linked to globalization and financialization. First is the return of the super-rich 1 percent in the advanced economies to whom a disproportionate amount of the new wealth from economic growth is accruing partly as a result of the productivity–wages gap. But, second is the emergence of a new class of entrepreneurs and other wealth takers and makers in the Global South whose fortunes are derived from the industrialization of their countries and the associated socio-economic transformations taking place, including urbanization, massive building construction and the spread of large-scale

---

[4] Forbes (2016) claims that in March 2016, there were also 1810 billionaires worldwide and their collective assets were worth $6.5 trillion—slightly down on 2015.

commercial farming.[5] These changes are concentrated particularly, though not only, in the BRIC countries of Brazil, Russia, India and China but also encompass Mexico, Indonesia, Argentina, Malaysia, Thailand and others.

Freeland adds that 'today's super-rich are increasingly a nation unto themselves' (5). In addition, their talent, wealth and power in a globalizing world means it will be extremely difficult to regulate their activities or persuade them to share their wealth more widely or fairly. Even the *Financial Times* was moved to comment in June 2009 that the benefits of economic growth 'had gone into the pockets of plutocrats rather than the bulk of the population' (Funnell 2009: 1). Moreover, when we investigate the facts pertaining to current inequality in the countries of the Global South, we find that the levels are often worse than those prevailing in the West and are rising rapidly. In China, for example, supposedly a socialist country committed to ending poverty, the Gini coefficient, measuring the degree of inequality, was more than 0.46 in 2012, higher even than that of the USA at 0.45. We take up this theme in more detail in Chap. 4. For the moment, the following quote from Hardt and Negri's book *Multitude* (2004: 164) sums up Freeland's argument very well. Describing how inequality has always been regarded by some as a potential threat to 'the entire scaffolding of capitalist rule' when certain political conditions prevailed, they make the following point:

> [c]apitalist globalization, however, has managed to solve this problem .... Not by making labour relationships equal in countries throughout the world but rather by generalizing the perverse mechanisms of unevenness and inequality everywhere… between the richest and poorest neighbourhoods of Los Angeles, between Moscow and Siberia, between the centre and periphery of every European city, between the southern and northern rims of the Mediterranean… one could continue indefinitely.

---

[5] Some claim that development since the 1990s in parts of the Global South has fundamentally shifted the balance of world economic power away from Western dominance. Others are sceptical. For example, they point to China's central position: buying in huge stocks of raw materials (from Brazil and others) and components from South East Asian countries for home assembly and re-export. But this creates additional dependencies and has reduced market opportunities for other developing countries who can't compete with China. Meanwhile, China has built up huge debts and remains well behind the West in terms of developing advanced technology (see, e.g., Nolan 2004; Kiely 2007 and 2015).

2.4 Tax Matters

Huge quantities of wealth are being disproportionately accumulated by a tiny plutocratic elite and/or a few thousand global corporations and their leading shareholders. Alarmingly, a decreasing share of this wealth is being re-invested in the real, productive economy. But what about the reproduction of those societal institutions of education, health, stable family life, community safety, transport and communication and so on that necessarily underpin capitalism and help to guarantee a democratic, peaceful society? Is today's capitalism or its super-rich owners and managers making a fair contribution towards this through various forms of taxation?

Issues relating to the incidence and share of taxation and tax avoidance (legal but morally reprehensible) and tax evasion (technically illegal) are very complex so we concentrate only on key questions of relevance to vampire capitalism. First, we look briefly at recent data concerning the regressive nature of contemporary tax systems and the tax burden in most Western economies before turning to some aspects of tax avoidance/evasion through tax havens.

Going Backwards: Abolishing Progressive Tax Systems

Since the 1970s the marginal rates of income tax levied on the highest incomes have fallen rapidly across most Western economies. Writing about the USA and looking at the overall effect of all the taxes to which US citizens are subject, Stiglitz (2013: 90–1) shows how the super-rich paid an average rate of 16.6 percent in 2007 compared to around 20 percent for everyone else. This is partly linked to the fact that the top marginal rate of income tax fell from 70 percent during the late 1970s to 28 percent during the Reagan administration in the early 1980s. It rose again during the Clinton Presidency but then G. B. Bush lowered it to 35 percent (89). This lowering of the marginal rate of income tax has virtually abolished the progressive and redistributive character of taxation systems in the USA—and across the Western countries—that existed from the 1940s through to the 1970s. But taxations systems have also become regressive for two other reasons. One is that as income taxes became less progressive, taxes on consumption, employment and social security became relatively far more significant as sources of government revenue and these fall on everyone, rich and poor alike. Moreover, the poorest earners spend a larger proportion of their incomes on these regressive taxes than the wealthy—though this includes taxes on tobacco, alcohol and gambling (Quiggin 2010: 149).

Second, it is also important to remember that taxes on capital gains and estate duties or inheritance taxes fall more heavily upon the wealthy because they normally obtain a far greater portion of their wealth than other citizens from the rising value of their real estate, stocks and bonds, business and so on. Here, Stiglitz (2013: 91) shows how it has been the reduction in capital gains tax in the USA that has exercised the greatest effect in reducing the tax burden on the very rich. Thus, Clinton reduced capital gains tax to 20 percent before Bush lowered it still further to 15 percent (xxxi). In addition, during his presidency Bush reduced estate taxes but also suspended them altogether for one year in 2012. Stiglitz (2013: 91) argues that these sorts of tax measures will add to the continued concentration of wealth in the hands of a tiny elite while turning the USA into a country belonging to 'an inherited oligarchy.'

Another potentially key source of revenue for governments comes from corporation taxes. But in the era of global finance and open borders for businesses the tendency for governments to attract a larger share of inward investment by lowering corporation taxes has intensified. In the EU, Ireland's success in pulling in foreign business by offering a relatively low level of corporation tax (12.5 percent in 2015) has been widely noticed, and other countries, such as the UK under the Coalition government, have followed the same path (it was reduced from 24 percent in 2012 to 20 percent in 2015 and will fall to 17 percent in 2020). Interestingly, the USA has maintained higher rates of corporation tax than some of its competitors, at 39 percent in 2015. However, Stiglitz (2013: 92) argues there are so many loopholes and special provisions that the system has been 'eviscerated'. So much so that the contribution of corporation tax to Federal Government revenue fell from 30 percent in the mid-1950s to under 9 percent in 2012.

Inter-governmental competition to reduce tax demands on business clearly accentuates the overall tendency for tax revenues to fall, and at a time when the demands on public spending are inevitably set to rise due to an ageing population and improving health technologies and expectations, among other issues. Moreover, as in the case of wages, governments and citizen populations are locked into a race to the bottom in which it is increasingly likely that there will be far more losers than winners, particularly as this version of competition is between nations not individual businesses or workers. Certainly, Streek's (2014: 118) assessment, below, is depressing but doubtless realistic.

> Global liberalization, especially of capital markets, makes tax increases on high incomes and internationally mobile corporate profits appear so unrealistic that they are not even discussed. Tax increases would have to be pushed through against the trend of the last decade and a half… If they were in fact achieved, they would in all likelihood be limited to immobile sources—mainly in the form of social security contributions and sales taxes.

Before leaving this discussion of the diminishing contributions economic elites make to national revenues it is worth recalling that capitalism cannot survive without the support systems provided by society and by the state. This includes both the emotional and social burden of reproducing society's institutions through family and community responsibilities—un-costed and non-remunerated—but also the economic costs of funding education, health, infrastructure, law and order, research and so on. It is notable in this respect how often business spokespersons, lobbies and organizations complain about the cost of welfare provisions such as income tax credit for the low-waged, unemployment and housing benefits and so on. Such public expenditure is presented as a major financial burden that steals resources needed for business investment, dulling the incentives for innovation and enterprise. But, taking Britain as an example, Farnsworth (2013) shows that government funding for corporate welfare is not inconsiderable. This is designed to channel resources directly towards private businesses in the form of capital/investment allowances, subsidies and tax reductions and exemptions, one-off payments towards the projects undertaken by individual firms and so on.

In the financial year 2011/12, for example, drawing on government figures Farnsworth shows that businesses in the UK received a total of nearly £37 billion in various payments (62). These increased after the 2008 crisis and up until 2012. Turning to UK welfare spending for the same year, the cost of some of the benefits that are most frequently attacked as wasteful—namely Jobseeker's Allowance, housing benefits, child allowances and tax credits for low-income earners—came to a grand total of £34 billion (Milne 2013). These are the very welfare benefits that would be less necessary and burdensome if businesses paid decent living wages and if the government and the building industry produced a more effective house-building programme so that rents did not continue to rise relentlessly.

Too Big to Pay

It is important to remember that measures and systems used by pirates, shipping companies, exporters and many others, designed to evade official rules and laws concerning the payment of customs duties, taxes and so on, have been legion for centuries. Governments have long struggled to find ways to counter such tactics. As for the financial industries, the volume of global flows of capital and money and the transnationalization of corporate investment and production have all grown massively during the last 30 years. Accordingly, the opportunities for, and incidence of, numerous forms of cross-border illicit activities have multiplied. Tax Justice Network (TJN) claims that overall the global offshore tax industry has increased four times since the mid-1980s (Henry 2012: 15). To take one example, the value of the deposits held in one of the tax havens linked to Britain—Jersey—increased from less than £20 billion in 1980 to around £175 billion by 2005 (cited in Lansley 2011: 107). Government concern has grown along with the realization that only effective international cooperation over such questions as how to neutralize tax havens, harmonize mutually enforceable tax rules and better regulate systems for transferring money between countries holds out much hope of countering these excesses effectively.

The financial crisis of 2008 gave an added impetus to this search for international cooperation. At the Paris emergency meeting of the G20 nations in April 2009, future common action in respect to tax evasion was placed high on the agenda. But in the meantime governments, the EU, WB and other IGOs became more concerned with how to impose austerity regimes on their populations. Purportedly, the chief aim was to reduce the deficits contracted by bailing out the banks in 2008. Thus, according to Shaxson (2011: 24–5) despite the rhetoric, concrete actions to improve the transparency of financial flows, reduce the secrecy surrounding tax havens and so on have been limited. There are many reasons for this but one key explanation is that several leading Western economies, particularly the UK and the USA, and their financial industries, stand at the forefront of actively facilitating and benefiting from illicit global financial flows. As Shaxson reminds us, when 'the fox announces that it has done an excellent job of beefing up the security of the henhouse, we should be very cautious indeed' (25).

There are around 80 territories which offer secrecy, low or no tax obligations, a medley of '"pirate banking" services' (TJN 2012) and an army of additional professional enablers in the form of lawyers, insurers, financial advisors, accountants and others. Their job is to help tax avoiders set up anonymous shell companies, trusts and other vehicles designed for concealing wealth. Everyone has heard of the Cayman Islands, the British Virgin Islands, Singapore, Monaco, Bermuda, Panama, Mauritius, Jersey and Luxemburg and many other small islands or micro-states which specialize in providing infamous tax-evading possibilities. The financial services industry in the Cayman Islands includes 80,000 registered companies and more than three-quarters of global hedge funds. But as the fifth largest financial centre in the world it has a population under 60,000 and as of 2010, only one cinema. The nearly two trillion dollars it holds in the form of deposits is considerably larger than that held by New York's banks (Shaxson 2011: 18). What is less understood is that several highly developed nations, including the Netherlands, Ireland, Belgium and Austria, also provide tax-avoidance services.

Even more significant and perhaps surprising is the reality that the UK, through the City of London, and the USA via Manhattan and Wall

2 The Rise of Vampire Capitalism (and not a slayer in sight) 49

Street, operate right at the centre of the worldwide spider web of offshore business 'artificially manipulating paper trails of money crossing borders' (Shaxson 2011: 13). They also offer corporations and rich individuals various government-sanctioned 'arrangements' designed to assist tax avoidance and tax evasion. According to Henry's 2012 report, *The Price of Offshore Revisited,* produced for TJN, a great deal of the cash deposited in tax havens gets siphoned back to big Western banks through various links and chains where it can be 'invested' or 'cleaned' more securely than by the numerous shell banks and companies originally set up in havens such as Dubai or the Virgin Islands. Indeed, Henry explains how TJN estimated that in 2010, between them the world's 50 leading private banks were managing around $12 trillion of the total amount of private cross-border financial wealth in the offshore system. This figure had more than doubled compared to 2005, prior to the financial crash. Among these dominant world banking players are Credit Agricole, Barclays, Credit Suisse, Citigroup/Morgan Stanley, Deutsche Bank and Goldman Sachs.

Omitting terrorist groups there are four main clients funnelling money through these secretive networks. Various criminal interests launder their gains from drugs, people smuggling, slavery, arms dealing and so on, through tax havens. They then re-invest the proceeds from crime in different kinds of legitimate enterprises. Then there are the corrupt leaders of developing countries. Estimates by Global Financial Integrity in Washington DC suggest that between 2004 and 2013, nearly $8 trillion left developing countries and was secreted away either into offshore havens (45 percent) or into Western banks (Global Financial Integrity 2015). The national tax revenue lost each year to these countries as a result of the theft of such vast sums—often with the collusion of foreign companies investing in local minerals—is considerably larger than the total amount of aid these countries receive each year (Organization for Economic Cooperation and Development: OECD).

Third, transnational corporations engage in various forms of financial misconduct, especially transfer pricing. An example might involve a company under-invoicing a subsidiary operating in a second country for goods sold to the former in order to move profits from the high tax economy where it is based to the subsidiary's country, where tax rates are much lower. More important, though, is the practice whereby corporations use the process of transfer pricing to siphon their profits on a vast scale from their worldwide operations into companies registered as based in tax havens. Often this involves sending money through several complex layers of accounts and tax havens—'layering'—in order to disguise the character and origin of an income source. According to Zucman (2015: 32–3) these corporate practices are increasing all the time and to such an extent that now 55 percent of the profits made by US firms from overseas operations end up in tax havens. This not only means that a huge amount of tax revenue is lost to the US government but these arrangements also distort business competition because smaller businesses whose operations are not international need to pay the full statutory tax rates. In addition, the revenue lost to governments from the financial tricks managed by global corporations drives up the tax burdens on ordinary citizens, further increasing inequality (Zucman 2015).

Finally, private individuals, or HNWIs, make up the fourth category. Henry and the TJN's 2012 report estimated that overall the world's super-rich—less than 10 million people in total—had amassed somewhere between $21 and $32 trillion in various offshore havens. Of this, nearly $10 trillion has been secreted away by fewer than 100,000 of the very richest individuals. And these estimates only include financial assets, not property of various kinds. Consequently, and as in the case of Transnational Corporations (TNCs), each year vast sums in potential tax revenue, as a percentage of the annual interest generated by this hidden financial wealth, are lost to the governments of countries where this money would otherwise have been legally invested.

2.5 Rent-Seeking Practices

Some capitalists have always tried to enhance their profits and market share by means other than improving productivity and responding to market opportunities. Forming monopoly arrangements is one such tactic but another involves businesses engaging in various rent-seeking activities based on establishing influence over politicians and governments. The commonplace term for such situations is 'crony capitalism'. Drawing on the work of various researchers *The Economist* published a piece entitled 'Planet Plutocrat' in March 2014 which included a 'Crony- Capitalism Index'. Interestingly, in the list of 23 countries the USA came out as number 17, with Britain placed at 15—just before and after Turkey and Thailand respectively (*The Economist* 2014). Hong Kong, Russia, India and China came out in first, second, ninth and nineteenth positions.

A key aspect of crony capitalism is the 'revolving door' phenomenon noticed by many observers of contemporary global life. This is the tendency for leading figures in politics, government officials, the members of IGOs such as the IMF and former CEOs from a range of private businesses to accept key posts and cross the borders between various organizations at different times during their careers. Tony Blair is one notable example, as is the cohort of elite individuals from the business and political world who meet every January at the World Economic Forum (WEF) in Davos to debate, forge connections and exchange ideas on key matters concerning world policy. Carroll and Carson's (2003) study of the overlapping networks formed by five major IGOs engaged in formulating world economic policy, and the interlocking company directors from 350 leading corporations, revealed the existence of a powerful nexus of core individuals who move between careers and posts. They mix with each other and cement ties with governments, think tanks and powerful companies.

Case Study 1: Rent-seeking in today's India

In his lucid book, *Capital: A Portrait of Twenty-First Century Delhi* (2014), Dasgupta vividly explores many key aspects of the Indian economic 'miracle' since the economic liberalization programme began in earnest in the early 1990s. His material is further illuminated by personal case studies. One theme concerns the rise of India's middle class: the nearly 10 percent of the population whose incomes are more than $10,000 (500,000 rupees) per year. Their incomes stand in stark contrast to the rural poor who still form approximately 70 percent of the population (268) and who live on annual incomes closer to $500. Then there is the tiny economic elite. Dasgupta explores the two main paths through which the latter have accumulated their vast business wealth since the early 1990s. One lay through the massive privatization of vast chunks of state enterprise in cement, mines, oil, gas, the media and telecommunications and so on, as well as land. These

(continued)

(continued)

> state assets were built up after Independence in 1947 by governments determined to make their country less economically dependent (345). But the second path to business growth was based on catering for the leisure habits and lifestyle preference of the same rising middle class: modern housing estates, golf courses, private airports, sports facilities, private townships and the infrastructural projects to supply power, water and new road systems without which these facilities could not flourish (350). Behind most of these ventures lies the need for rural land.
>
> The crucial factor lubricating the transfer of state enterprises and/or rural land into the hands of India's millionaires and its 100 billionaires (Forbes 2016)[6] has been the alliance forged between politicians and administrators. Faced with economic liberalization since 1991 the old 'license raj' of local, state and government bureaucrats who once controlled the regulations concerning public wealth have faced diminishing power. Yet they understand and command the minutia of rules, procedures, precedents and customs regarding rural land rights and use. Thus, officials and entrepreneurial elites have become partners in the vast transfer of land into the hands of the latter in exchange for money and perhaps business shares. With privatization the bureaucrats frequently assist in deals that involve under-pricing. In the case of rural land, the officials deploy their knowledge of local land rights to either forcibly remove peasants whose land rights are unclear or unregistered or impose compulsory purchasing orders on tracts of land while legitimizing payments by businesses well below market value (pp.348–50).
>
> According to Dasgupta, two consequences followed. Millions of disposed peasants have migrated to Delhi and other Indian cities to swell the slum-dweller population. Meanwhile India's 'pool of billionaires expanded rapidly, increasing their wealth from less than 1 percent of the national income in 1996 to 22 per in 2008' (346).

---

[6] This figure compares with China's 190 and places India third in the world for the number of billionaires.

Crony Capitalism, the US Government and the Financial Crisis

In neo-classical economic theory, an orthodoxy which still dominates many university economics departments, there is very little room for the idea of crony capitalism. Rather, this branch of economics assumes that competition working through supply and demand, and the productivity levels achieved by each player—right down to the marginal productivity provided by the last person to be employed—largely determine the rewards players receive, whether as workers or entrepreneurs. Stiglitz (2013) critiques this mainstream economics with its notion of 'appropriate' levels of inequality in relation to market competition, arguing that 'American inequality didn't just happen. It was created... but it was not market forces alone' (36). Rather, 'the outsize inequality', involving the wealth accruing to the top 1 percent experienced by the USA, was a direct consequence of government policies from Reagan's presidency onwards (1981 to 1989). These shaped market forces in ways that were advantageous to the wealthy and to large businesses, especially the increasingly powerful finance industry.

There were several reasons why governments across the EU and USA were so reluctant to seriously curb, by re-regulation, the hubris of many in the financial industries. Heading the list of likely explanations was the influence of neoliberal ideology which by the early 1980s dominated UK and US politics. Indeed, it became unacceptable to challenge the almost religious fervour with which neoliberal 'market fundamentalist ideology' (Stiglitz 2013: xxv) was widely upheld in the media, among officials, many academics and elsewhere. This ongoing process was further aggravated by a number of institutional realities. One was the absence of what Stiglitz (2013: 39) refers to as 'good corporate governance laws'. Consequently, the power of corporate CEOs grew to the point where many were able to appoint their company's board of directors, perhaps filling it with their own nominees, while setting their own compensation terms. Working in parallel was a veritable army of corporate lawyers protecting the interests of corporations and their leaders. Similarly, instead of preventing individuals and businesses from behaving badly, and shaping laws to the mutual benefit of everyone, the US legal system reduced much litigation to an 'arms race' based on who could afford to spend the largest sums on the cleverest lawyers (124–5). Then there was the case of the rating agencies such as Standard and Poor's. Seemingly independent, they calculated financial risk by engaging in fantastic games of statistical probability-testing and were perceived as being staffed by near-geniuses who had doctorates in mathematics or similar 'scientific' subjects. All these people couldn't possibly be wrong.

Stiglitz goes on to argue that by following policies in accordance with neoliberal thinking and the wishes and demands of business three major consequences ensued.[7] First, any idea of income and wealth re-distribution as one solution to poverty and growing inequality and imbalances in the economy was resisted by policy-makers. Second, by progressively deregulating the economy, and especially finance, the US government under Clinton and G.B. Bush effectively colluded in restricting, rather than guaranteeing, market competition. This, in turn, permitted the banks and other agencies to engage in a range of abusive practises that earned them high returns—or 'rents'—at the expense and the risk of everyone else's savings, investments, debts, house ownership and jobs (Stiglitz 2013: 308). These abuses included: over-borrowing (leveraging assets far beyond their deposit levels) and over-lending; encouraging massive mortgage borrowing among individuals whose incomes were too low or uncertain to guarantee continued payment; over-charging for credit cards; creating and then selling on a new type of income-earning security, called 'collateral debt obligations' or CDOs, consisting of bundles of debts carrying varying degrees of risk relating to future payment default; and bidding up the volume and values of derivative trading[8] without restraint to a level estimated at $638 trillion in 2013 by the Bank of International Settlements.[9] This estimate for derivatives is approximately ten times the value of world GDP.

Third, the willingness of governments and institutions to stand back and allow financial arrogance full sway permitted banks and other financial businesses to collude in a number of illegal activities. One of these involved fixing the London Interbank Offer Rate (LIBOR) at rates that that were not justified by actual market forces at the time. Individual brokers were dragged into these activities by promises of personal gain

---

[7] In effect, the Federal Reserve at this time was under what one US economist (Stigler 1971) called 'regulatory capture' where special interests co-opt government policy to further their own ends.

[8] Instruments for managing future risks on the changing prices of currencies, commodities, shares and so on.

[9] Other estimates put it much higher—somewhere between $1000 trillion and $1200 trillion.

from various banks (see, e.g., Treanor 2012). The banks, in turn, might benefit because by underreporting their interest rate they could appear to be in a much stronger market position than they actually were. One of the wider dangers of LIBOR fixing for the global economy as a whole is that the interest rates agreed between banks and the general business confidence they are intended to inspire underpin as much as $350 trillion of trade in derivatives as well as vast loans and business contracts (Durden 2012). Of course, it isn't only firms involved in finance that act irresponsibly and with opacity—sometimes with officials and/or governments turning a blind eye—as the revelations in September 2015 concerning Volkswagen's deliberate cheating on the emission levels from its vehicles clearly demonstrated to a shocked world.

Fourth, Stiglitz (2013: 300 and 309) argues that the US Federal Reserve could have curbed or constrained some of these activities and/or intervened to limit the size of the banks and the growing interconnections between them. By not doing so it helped the banks and other financial companies to expand using their high profits. One result was that these banks were 'too-big-to fail' or too big to be allowed to fail because of their crucial role in the wider economy. This gave the larger banks a competitive advantage, in effect, a subsidy provided by taxpayers. This is because the knowledge that the government would intervene to prevent them collapsing meant they could attract funds for their various profitable ventures at lower rates of interest than would otherwise have been possible. Later, the 'too-big-to-fail' policy ensured that the US and other governments weighed in with colossal bail-outs in 2008. This left these governments with deficits to be paid for by citizens through years of austerity. Meanwhile, the executives of these leading financial and other firms continued to pay themselves huge bonuses and salaries and often emerged from the crisis even richer than before.

Privatization and Rent-Seeking in the Global South

Rent-seeking business behaviour is by no means confined to the advanced economies. Corruption involving state officials and political leaders accepting bribes from business leaders in return for access to public contracts or foreign currency, loans from state banks and much else besides is unfortunately rife across many developing countries. In the Global South neoliberal arguments played a part in many countries' privatization programmes because of the external pressures imposed by the USA through the WB and IMF—the so-called Washington Consensus in the 1980s and 90s (see Chap. 3). However, selling public assets has often been far more significant as a vehicle for boosting the bank accounts of private beneficiaries, though the assets involved vary between countries as the following few examples demonstrate.

Russia's post-1989 'sale of the century' (Freeland 2012: 191), based on 'the greatest rent-seeking windfall in economic history' (191), is perhaps the most outstanding case. Here, state factories, mines, power stations and services were sold off to political insiders and often to previous Soviet 'apparatchiks'. The rise of what Freeland calls the 'red oligarchs' (2012) in China, is slightly different. There, it has been state control over land and the ability to borrow money from state banks that has enabled leading politicians, and/or those who have built close network connections to political leaders, to obtain and invest in real estate, often on a vast scale. Research showed that in 2011 a high proportion of China's 1000 wealthiest individuals were members of the 'red dynasties': that is, the children or grandchildren of the early communist leaders from the 1940s, 50s and 60s. They also form an 'important political fraction' of the Communist Party today (Freeland 2012: 208). Moreover, the 70 richest members of the National People's Congress—the country's ruling body—possessed wealth totalling $90 billion in 2011 (204).

The close link between high wealth and political power is also commonplace across Africa. One particularly tragic and extreme case is the Democratic Republic of the Congo. Local warlords in conflict with the central government along with intervening foreign armies from surrounding countries such as Uganda and Rwanda—whose soldiers have in effect become 'business armies' (Žižek 2011: 163)—plunged the country into civil war in 2008 over control of various mineral resources and regions. Žižek argues that beneath the 'façade of ethnic warfare' as the primary explanation for the genocidal murders and chaos experienced by this troubled country lies the needs of global capitalism in the guise of various international companies. These are desperate for access to mining rights, preferably without the need to pay taxes. As such they are often willing to help the warring parties get rich in the process.

2.6 Summary and Conclusions

None of the practices and abuses discussed above are new. Yet they have all occurred, almost in synchrony, during the same short space of 30 or so years, while worsening and intensifying in their effects since the late 1990s. This seems to demand an explanation over and beyond the usual diagnoses of the workings of capitalism. At the same time their combined impact has been far reaching and *sui generis*. They are generating consequences which are more than the sum of their separate parts.

There is obviously a crucial issue to be faced here. If we believe that vampire capitalism threatens to undermine not just social life but the very survival of capitalism itself, it becomes imperative that governments and other leading agents in world affairs, urged on by ordinary citizens, reshape global institutions and rules so as to minimize its abuses along the lines advocated recently by Hutton (2016). Unfortunately, it isn't difficult to foresee serious obstacles. Not least is capitalism's 'DNA' which impels its actors to resist permanent social, ethical or democratic constraints in their drive to convert virtually all human activities into schemes for producing wealth. But this only leads to a further question, namely, why has capitalism become so 'unfettered' such that the forces that were once able to 'counterbalance' it, in the decades before and especially after WW2, have become so weakened (Sandel 2016: 29). Of course, this is not a new insight. Eventually it became evident that those years of mid-twentieth century prosperity, lower inequality and relatively high economic growth, were exceptional (see, e.g., Offe 1985)—and made possible by special events and conjunctions of factors. It has been all too tempting, and as it turned out, misleading, to regard the triple combination that was Fordism[10]—a highly effective system of production, a Keynesian-led economy that boosted consumption and a socio-political pact between

---

[10] I am indebted to Stephen Edgell for this point.

government, unions and employers—as a template or benchmark against which we could usefully evaluate all later forms of capitalism.

In Chap. 3 we argue that during the post-war era and to an extent in the years before that it was possible to exercise a degree of control over capitalism through a combination of organized political protest, government intervention, the perceived need to save it from its own contradictions and the fortuitous yet dangerous impact of geo-political forces, especially WW1, WW2 and the Cold War. We have to wonder what kinds of crises it may take before this might happen again.

Bibliography

Beck, U. (2009). *World at risk*. Cambridge: Polity.

Carroll, W. K., & Carson, C. (2003). The network of global corporations and elite policy groups: A structure for transnational capitalist class formation. *Global Networks: A Journal of Transnational Affairs, 3*(1), 29–59.

Dew-Becker, I. and Gordon, R. J. (2005). *Where did the productivity growth go? Inflation dynamics and the distribution of income*. National Bureau of Economic Research. Retrieved August 9, 2016, from http://www.nber.org/papers/w11842

Domhoff, G. W. (2016) *Wealth, income, and power*. Who Rules America? Retrieved August 10, 2016, from http://www2.ucsc.edu/whorulesamerica/power/wealth.html

Durden, T. (2012) *Manipulation and abuse confirmed in $359 trillion market*. Retrieved August 10, 2016, from http://www.zerohedge.com/news/manipulation-and-abuse-confirmed-350-trillion-market

Elliott, L., & Atkiknson, D. (2008). *The gods that failed: How blind faith in markets has cost us our futures*. London: Bodley Head.

Farnsworth, K. (2013). Public policies for private corporations: The British corporate welfare state. *Renewal, 21*(4), 51–65.

Forbes. (2016). *The world's billionaires*. Retrieved August 10, 2016, from www.forbes.com/billionaires/.

Freeland, C. (2012). *Plutocrats: The rise of the new global super-rich and the fall of everyone else*. New York: Penguin.

Funnell, B. (2009, July 30). Debt is capitalism's dirty little secret. *Financial Times*. Retrieved August 10, 2016, from http://www.ft.com/cms/s/0/e23c6d04-659d-11de-8e34-00144feabdc0.html#axzz4GvQlbNjv

Giugliano, F. (2015, July 25). BoE's Haldane says corporations putting shareholders before economy. *Financial Times*. Retrieved August 9, 2016, from http://www.ft.com/cms/s/0/7d347016-32f4-11e5-b05b-b01debd57852.html#axzz4GvQlbNjv

Global Financial Integrity. (2015). *Illicit financial flows from developing countries, 2004–2013.* Retrieved August 10, 2016, from http://www.gfintegrity.org/report/illicit-financial-flows-from-developing-countries-2004-2013/

Gowan, P. (2009). Crisis in the heartlands: Consequences of the new Wall Street system. *New Left Review, 55*, 5–28.

Hardt, M., & Negri, A. (2004). *Multitude: War and democracy in the age of empire.* New York: Penguin Press.

Henry, J. S. (2012). *The price of offshore revisited.* Tax Justice Network. Retrieved August 10, 2016, from http://www.taxjustice.net/cms/upload/pdf/Price_of_Offshore_Revisited_120722.pdf

Hutton, W. (2007). *The writing on the wall: China and the West in the 21st century.* London: Abacus.

Hutton, W. (2016, January 17). *Why are we looking on helplessly as markets crash all over the world? The Guardian.* Retrieved August 10, 2016, from https://www.theguardian.com/commentisfree/2016/jan/17/china-economic-crisis-world-economy-global-capitalism

Kiely, R. (2007). *The new political economy of development: Globalization, imperialism, hegemony.* Basingstoke: Palgrave.

Kiely, R. (2015). *The BRICs, US 'Decline' and global transformations.* Basingstoke: Palgrave.

Lansley, S. (2011). *The cost of inequality: Why economic equality is essential for recovery.* London: Gibson Square.

Lapavitsas, C. (2013). *Profits without producing: How finance exploits us all.* London: Verso.

Milne, S. (2013, January 8). There is a problem with welfare, but it's not the 'shirkers'. *The Guardian*. Retrieved August 11, 2016, from https://www.theguardian.com/commentisfree/2013/jan/08/welfare-problem-real-scroungers-greedy

Nolan, P. (2004). *China at the crossroads.* Cambridge: Polity.

Offe, C. (1985). *Disorganized capitalism.* Cambridge: Polity.

Piketty, T. (2014). *Capital in the twenty-first century.* Cambridge, MA: The Belknap Press.

Quiggin, J. (2010). *Zombie economics: How dead ideas still walk among us.* Princeton, NJ: Princeton University Press.

Robinson, W. I. (2002). Capitalist globalization and the transnationalization of the state. In M. Rupert & H. Smith (Eds.), *Historical materialism and globalization* (pp. 210–229). London: Routledge.

Robinson, W. I., & Harris, J. (2000). Towards a global ruling class? Globalization and the transnational capitalist class. *Science and Society, 64*(1), 11–54.

Sandel, M. (2016, June 10–16). The energy of the Brexiteers and Trump is born of the failure of elites. *New Statesman*. Retrieved August 11, 2016, from http://www.newstatesman.com/politics/uk/2016/06/michael-sandel-energy-brexiteers-and-trump-born-failure-elites

Sennett, R. (2006). *The culture of the new capitalism*. London: Yale University Press.

Shaxson, N. (2011). *Treasure islands and the men who stole the world*. London: Vintage.

Sklair, L. (2001). *The transnationalist capitalist class*. London: Blackwell.

Stigler, C. J. (1971). The theory of economic regulation. *The Bell Journal of Economics and Management Science, 2*(1), 30–21.

Stiglitz, J. (2013). *The price of inequality*. London: Penguin.

Streek, W. (2014). *Buying time: The delayed crisis of democratic capitalism*. London: Verso.

The Economist. (2012, October 10). *For richer, for poorer*. Retrieved August 11, 2016, from http://www.economist.com/node/21564414

The Economist. (2014, March 15). *Planet plutocrat: Our crony-capitalist index*. Retrieved August 11, 2016, from http://www.economist.com/news/international/21599041-countries-where-politically-connected-businessmen-are-most-likely-prosper-planet

Treanor, J. (2012, October 21). Twenty-two more face investigation over potential Libor rigging. *The Guardian*. Retrieved August 11, 2016, from https://www.theguardian.com/business/2013/oct/21/sfo-investigation-libor-22

Webster, F. (2002). *Theories of the information society*. London: Routledge.

Žižek, S. (2011). *Living in the end times*. London: Verso.

Zucman, G. (2015, October 11). Inequality is the great concern of our age: So why do we tolerate rapacious, unjust tax havens?" *The Guardian*. Retrieved August 11, 2016, from https://www.theguardian.com/commentisfree/2015/oct/11/inequality-will-continue-until-corporations-stop-avoiding-tax

3

The Roots of Vampire Capitalism

In this chapter we examine the structural transformations since the 1970s that have created the conditions for vampire capitalism, including the growing power of the financial industries, especially from the 1980s, and the industrialization taking place in parts of the Global South since the 1960s. Also crucial has been the acceleration of globalization processes. Globalization has greatly facilitated the increased mobility and cross-border reach not just of people, material goods, images, information and elites but also 'the movement of abstracted capital and culture through processes of disembodied exchange' (James 2005: 201). Then there is the influence of neoliberal ideology and policy-making. Although each of these transformations has underpinned and reinforced the others, some observers have argued that neoliberalism has trumped this list in respect to its causal influence. In different ways each of these forces has substantially weakened the social and workplace solidarity that played such an active role in shaping the culture and politics of Western capitalism, especially during the period from 1945 until the 1970s. The relative decline of worker and citizen power is also rooted in additional causes, not least the rise of an ethos of individualization and a culture of hedonistic consumerism. We return to this theme in Chap. 6.

3.1 Holding Capitalism to Account—Mid-Twentieth-Century Events

We begin by sketching a brief historical context. What were the key events in the first half of the twentieth century and the previous constraints on the actions of capital, the 'checks and balances' (Hutton 2007: 26), that once embedded capital more firmly in society such that the media, trade unions and governments were more inclined and better equipped to demand a degree of capitalist accountability than today?

The success of the Bolshevik communist revolution in Russia in 1917 is one such event of massive significance. Although it turned into one of the most despotic and brutal regimes in modern history, perhaps the *most* brutal, and imposed much needless suffering on millions, it did demonstrate the possibility of a credible alternative to capitalist development, at least until the 1980s. It also provided concrete support for socialist groups and parties across the world. Moreover, in its early period it seemed to give a practical reality to the imagination and hopes of millions of people living in industrial capitalist regimes who dreamed of a future transition to socialism at a time when only meagre benefits were trickling down to most ordinary people. Hobsbawm (1994), an influential observer of twentieth-century history, argued that Soviet success against the Nazi war-machine during WW2 and the Cold War era of East–West technical, economic and ideological rivalry that followed, helped to persuade some capitalist interests and Western governments of the need to accelerate a number of key reforms in order to head off or neutralize potential anti-capitalist movements. These included some tolerance for strong trade unions, the extension of welfare reforms, prioritizing full employment, and adopting Keynesian demand-management economic policies.

Secondly, as Piketty (2014: 135–8 and 271–6) has shown, before WW1 the richest 10 per cent living in a number of European countries, including France, Britain and Sweden, owned 90 per cent of these nations' wealth (261). However, three great shocks in the first half of the twentieth century hit these members of the rentier class (who were living primarily on the returns from accumulated wealth) extremely hard but also hurt capitalist interests in general. The two world wars resulted in the destruction of much property. War also led governments to introduce public policies such as rent controls and nationalization which further harmed those living on inherited or accumulated property. But the Wall Street financial collapse of 1929, followed by the Great Depression, also caused widespread bankruptcy across the West, not only of banks and of companies but also of individuals and families whose incomes were linked to share ownership and/or rents from land and property. The need to finance the war effort and pay war debts afterwards also compelled governments to impose and/or to raise much higher rates of tax on the incomes, capital, estates and inheritances of the wealthy. In France, for example, the share of income accruing to the top 10 per cent of the population fell from around 45 per cent just before WW1, recovered during the 1930s before plummeting to below 30 per cent during WW2. And as in other countries, most of this 'compression' or levelling in French income distribution was linked to falling returns on accumulated capital and higher taxes. In Britain the share of income received by the top 1 per cent, after allowing for taxation, fell from 12.6 to 4.2 per cent during the period from 1937 to 1978—after which it began a rapid recovery under Thatcher's governments (Lansley 2011: 15–16).

There is almost certainly a final aspect connected to the two world wars that contributed to rendering capitalism relatively more accountable than it has since become (Kennedy 2010: 59–60). War required the mass mobilization of citizens in the USA, UK, Italy, Japan and elsewhere, including, of course, Germany, for war work. Men, and many women, were recruited for the armed forces in vast numbers, though many remained in industry, while huge numbers of women replaced the men who had left factories and farms, albeit less so in Germany. Citizens also had to be persuaded to accept many personal sacrifices in addition to the dangers of war to themselves and their families: rationing, shortages; the suspension of leisure activities; long hours of work; and all kinds of additional disciplines. In America as much as Europe and elsewhere, few of the wealthy entirely escaped these privations and their children were often drafted into the armed forces or war work as frequently as the less well-off. In short, many ordinary people emerged from these wars, especially WW2, with high expectations of economic reform to match the promises they had been made of better times ahead, and more politically determined to fight for such changes if necessary. But the sense of shared sacrifice and common effort may have also left some of the wealthy relatively more sympathetic to the plight of the less well-off.

Of course, none of these world-shattering events that changed the balance of power between labour and capital can be repeated. Nor would we wish similar crises to occur. Moreover, it is only now these events have passed into history that we can see more clearly how this era of a more accountable and 'fairer' capitalism after WW2 was also rooted in a sense of shared national identity and belonging. Further, it was grounded in economic ownership and employment that were still fundamentally national in character and therefore more accessible to democratic and class-based political action.

3.2 Neoliberalism and the Era of Unaccountable Capitalism

The impact of neoliberal policies on the day-to-day lives of nearly everyone since the late 1970s has been overwhelming (Harvey 2005). Referring to the EU, Žižek claims (2011: 155) that its governments and institutions are faced with the task of dismantling the welfare state and the previous long-term commitment to social capitalism in order to ensure Europe's survival in 'the new global economy'—sculptured, in effect, by decades of neoliberal ideology. But the ability of these ideas to insinuate key notions about self-direction and individual blame for economic injustice into the consciousness of many ordinary citizens has been equally powerful.

The Crises of the 1970s and the Neoliberal Moment

Neoliberalism emerged originally in the 1930s among a group of thinkers from several countries. The most influential and well-known members were Friedrich Hayek and Ludwig von Mises from Austria but included such figures as Wilhem Röpke and Alexander Rüstow in Germany and later on Milton Friedman in America. The founding meeting of this group took place at Mont Pelerin in Switzerland in 1947 which also gave the group their future collective name (Turner 2008: 71–75). In contrast, Mirowski (2013: 6) refers to this group as the 'Neoliberal Thought Collective' or 'NLT'. They were disturbed by the Great Depression but rather more so by the policies of deliberate state intervention in the workings of market capitalism undertaken by governments during the 1930s and after WW2, particularly Germany, the USA and Britain. From the perspective of the political parties, governments and intellectuals who supported greater state involvement, their justification for doing so was clear: they were attempting to restore employment, reduce inequality and 'reform' capitalism in order to prevent future financial collapses of such magnitude occurring again. President Roosevelt's 'New Deal' in the USA was the most notable example but Hitler's not dissimilar policies after 1933 in Germany provides a further example, though the Nazi government's intentions were also tied up with war preparations.

Of course, the 1930s were dangerous years. In addition to mass unemployment, fascist regimes across Europe were fostering certain private businesses over others and encouraging cartels, strengthening their armament industries and abolishing democracy. Stalin's centrally planned Soviet economy was achieving rapid industrialization but had entirely crushed any vestiges of private enterprise, personal freedom or even the semblance of an independent judiciary. For Hayek and his associates, the preservation of individual freedom was the paramount goal. Any moves by the state to abolish or even to seriously regulate the operation of the free market and private enterprise—which they termed 'collectivism'—or to replace the market with planning were destined not only to undermine economic efficiency and therefore growth but would also lead, in time, to the undermining of political freedom. Von Mises, for example, critiqued the idea that the bureaucratic direction of economic life based on planning would be effective since it presupposed a degree of rationality and super-management that was unattainable and would almost certainly place powers in the hands of officials, which they had not earned and could only misuse (Turner 2008: 63). Free markets, private property and enterprise were the only guarantees of prosperity and democracy but also the moral sovereignty and capacity for self-development on the part of individuals (Hayek 1944). These, in turn, required a judiciary strong enough to guarantee the rule of law and minimal government focussed solely on providing rules and laws that would ensure the continued viability of market capitalism and the provision of minimal welfare protection for those unable to compete in economic life. Although Soviet Russia and Europe's fascist regimes were obviously operating at the extreme end of the spectrum of oppression linked to overgrown states and interference with the market, the theories developed by neoliberals convinced them that even far more modest forms of collectivism undermined individual economic and political freedom.

Despite neoliberal forebodings, and to different degrees during the period from the 1940s to roughly the mid-1970s, most Western governments of all political complexions adopted Keynesian demand-management economic policies which prioritized full employment. For the most part, too, they retained a strong commitment to extending a welfare state and to the pursuit of a social-democratic consensus between government, capital and labour in respect to prioritizing high wages linked to rising productivity and economic growth. The growth of think tanks committed to following neoliberal ideas from the 1950s onwards is an indication of their continuing influence during this period. But it was really in the 1970s—and even more so after this—that neoliberalism came to the forefront of democratic politics. This coincided with the twin crises of Fordist capitalism and growing uncertainty concerning the future of social-democratic consensus politics. We now examine the circumstances surrounding this 1970s crisis before returning to examine the leading neoliberal arguments.

The Fordist system, named after Henry Ford who first introduced it into his car factory in Detroit before WW1, gradually spread across many economic sectors and was taken up by other Western economies from the 1920s onwards—though its heyday is generally seen as during the post–WW2 era (see Edgell 2012: Chap. 5). At its core lay integrated and often very large companies which combined highly specialized labour processes and dedicated and increasingly automated machinery in the mass production of largely standardized goods based on long production runs. These goods were mostly intended for domestic sale in often protected markets. The high productivity achieved by intensive control over the largely regimented work force and the economies of large-scale production enabled employers to pay high wages to their workers. The latter could then afford to buy the goods produced cheaply by the same factories they worked for—helped by the beginnings of hire-purchase consumer credit schemes. After WW2 and through until at least the 1960s the combination of highly productive firms with the adoption of Keynesian economic policies generated sustained rates of economic growth across most countries which had rarely been experienced before. Piketty (2014: 96–97) shows how GDP per capita growth in Europe was around 4 per cent a year from 1950 to 1970, though this is partly explained by Europe catching up with the USA's higher growth achievement after 1914. Such high growth rates, in turn, allowed governments to invest extensively in public resources.

Then, from the late 1960s company profitability began to decline. Organized labour was the factor most frequently blamed for the almost simultaneous demise of much of the Fordist system and for the profit squeeze on capital. Decades of full employment and rising incomes meant that labour had become increasingly confident and organized. Meanwhile many workers resisted further attempts by managers to counter falling profits by pushing for ever higher levels of productivity since this often required increasingly tedious work and intensifying pressure for higher output (see Beynon 1973). The period of strikes and workplace unrest that followed during much of the 1970s and the tensions this created was aggravated by rising inflation which hit profits as well as the living standards of workers (Offe 1985: 59–63; Edgell 2012: Chap. 5). Inflation had several causes, including the end of world currency stability and the impetus this gave to growing waves of offshore finance. We return to this later. Nor did a general rise in government spending help. In the case of the USA much of this was related to the costs of the Vietnam War and President Johnson's spending on the 'great society' during the late 1960s. However, the fourfold oil price hike of 1973 followed by another in 1979 was especially critical.

A slowdown in the growth of output along with rapidly rising prices combined to produce 'stagflation': high inflation coupled to unemployment. This was especially troubling because the preceding 30 years of juggling the goal of full employment as against keeping inflation under control now seemed to fall apart. The crises of the 1970s provided a pretext for the major turn towards the era of neoliberal economic policy beginning with Thatcher in Britain in 1979 and Reagan in the USA from 1981. According to Dardot and Laval (2013: 152) the monetarist policy of high interest rates adopted by Britain and continued under Reagan in America were designed to deal simultaneously with pressure from trade unions and the problem of stagflation. By breaking the index between prices and wages it was possible to transfer 'the hole made in the purchasing power of wage-earners by the two oil shocks to the benefit of enterprises'. Along with this went a widespread deregulation of finance, the privatization of public enterprises, the dismantling of controls on international capital movements and tax cuts. But more than that there was an attack on the existing systems of progressive taxation as well as additional measures intended to weaken trade union power and render work practices more flexible and malleable.

The Neoliberal Argument

The standard impression of neoliberalism circulating in the media, one its proponents do little to challenge, is one of defending individual liberty from state oppression while 'freeing' market capitalism from an inefficient public sector and stifling government regulation. According to Mirowski (2013), Dardot and Laval (2013), Turner (2008), and others, however, the view that neoliberalism aims to shrink the state whenever possible in order to return to a pure, self-regulating, early nineteenth-century type of *laissez faire* economy is a myth. Indeed, there are several sources of confusion or mystification surrounding the debate concerning markets and capitalist economies and these need to be unravelled.

First, there are different kinds of markets both over historical time and within capitalism *per se*. For millennia, markets consisted mainly of different social arrangements and locations where locals regularly met to renew social bonds, usually at specific times, while exchanging their surpluses from subsistence production. During this long period of history 'encumbered markets' were 'the norm in every society' (Gray 1998: 17). Economic activity was embedded in society rather than the reverse. On the other hand, this did not mean that prices were always fixed by social ethics or religious influences or that the vagaries of supply and demand could not affect price. They frequently did in pre-capitalist tribal and peasant societies though such price changes rarely or never fed back into changes in production systems. Thus, markets can and do flourish without capitalism. But what neoliberals and everyone else mean by markets in modern capitalist economies is something quite different. Here, nearly all goods are produced solely in order to be sold for their exchange value and for profit and this operates alongside the relentless drive to accumulate capital based on investing money in harnessing the labour-power of free workers as the route to creating new value (Marx and Engels 1967; Schweickart 2002).

Second, despite the mystique neoliberals attach to 'markets'—which we discuss below—modern market economies are not natural phenomena that emerge mysteriously of their own accord. Polanyi's highly influential analysis (published in 1944) of the emergence of Britain as the first truly modern market economy challenged this interpretation. There was a *laissez faire* period between the 1830s and 60s when markets were more or less allowed to flourish without regulation. Many liberal thinkers at that time argued that whatever problems or uncertainties might emerge from the free flow of market forces they would 'resolve' themselves to the benefit of all if left alone without interference. But Polanyi shows how (a) the emergence of the free market was preceded by massive state involvement and (b) it only existed during those years because strong democratic institutions capable of resisting its consequences had yet to emerge. Moreover, (c) *laissez faire* lasted only a short time before reform movements and legislation intervened to alleviate the disintegration of family life, spread of disease and epidemics, widespread social unrest, lack of effective demand due to low wages and so on that it had brought in its wake. Writing about the risk that unrestrained markets pose for wider society Polanyi also made the crucial point that although labour, land and money 'form an absolutely vital part of the economic system' unlike all other resources they cannot be commodities. People are not created to be sold and have a life outside the economy. Land is produced by nature not by human hand and money exists because of banking practices supported by the state. More important, if the 'market mechanism' was allowed to become the 'sole director of the fate of human beings and their natural environment' we would face 'the demolition of society' (Polanyi 1944: 78–79).

In fact, British governments already had a long history of direct intervention in the legal, customary and social institutions of society especially the massive transfer of peasant and common land into the hands of large commercial farmers through the various enclosure movements—processes which simultaneously removed the source of independent livelihood from those evicted, driving them into the search for employment. Marx called these preceding political, legal and often violent changes, 'primitive accumulation'. But the Poor Law Act of 1834 and the abolition of the Corn Laws in 1846 further propelled Britain decisively in the direction of a free market economy. By removing the previous localized systems for providing relief to the destitute and unemployed and replacing them with the harsh disincentive of turning to the workhouse for charity, the Poor Law removed the obstacles to the mobility of labour. This, in turn, increased the supply of cheap factory workers. The Corn Laws had previously kept the price of grain artificially high by using a sliding scale system which minimized cheaper imports. This had protected aristocratic estates as well as tenant and other farmers from foreign competition. But in doing so it also kept the price of food—and therefore the wages of factory workers—artificially high. Thus, with all these measures the 'road to the free market was opened and kept open by an enormous increase in continuous, centrally organized and controlled interventionism' (Polanyi 1944: 142). Exactly the same kinds of deliberate state action designed to remove the obstacles to capitalist markets were later adopted by Prussia, America, France, Italy and of course Japan, among others. Capitalist markets do not emerge of their own accord.

Returning to the present, a second source of confusion surrounding the state concerns the question of how neoliberalism envisages its role in an advanced market economy increasingly 'freed' from government interference. Here, in respect to the ideal of a completely unregulated *laissez faire* capitalism, Mirowski (2013: 16) observes that neoliberals have never been particularly keen on this 'Eden of right-wing folklore, a paradise that never existed anywhere, anytime'. Neither was 'mature neoliberalism … enamoured of the minimalist night-watchman state of the classical liberal tradition' (40). Even as far back as the 1930s few saw the market as entirely self-regulating (Dardot and Laval 2013: 216). The play of supply and demand through market forces always needed to be administered. Instead, what neoliberals have pursued since the 1980s has been a project designed to 'redefine the shape and functions of the state, *not to destroy it*' (Mirowski 2013: 56, author's italics).

The most obvious way in which neoliberalism has given the state new tasks rather than diminishing its power concerns government policies such as privatization, reducing the tax burden on rich wealth creators, labour market and trade union 'reform' and deregulation. These involved the explicit use of state power as a vehicle for directly strengthening private enterprise at the expense of wage workers, welfare spending and the public sector (see Panitch and Gindin 2004). Privatizing public enterprises paid for out of citizen taxation can also be regarded as a form of deliberate theft and especially since, in the case of Britain in the 1980s and 1990s when gas, water, communications and so on were sold to private shareholders, most shares soon ended up in the hands of large investors. Chapter 8 examines the wider argument that 'enclosing the commons' (Boyle 2003) (i.e. selling shared public resources to private bodies for profit) takes many forms in addition to the sale of state enterprises. These include: finding legal pretexts for seizing open fields for commercial farming, the products of the knowledge economy or ecological resources such as forest and biodiversity. Harvey (2005), indeed, is quite clear that it is perfectly possible to point to neoliberal policies as vehicles purposely designed to restore the wealth and assets that economic elites and capitalists had foregone during the first 70 years of the twentieth century, though not everyone would agree or would push this argument quite so far.

But in addition neoliberalism facilitated a culture of constant collaboration whereby business was more or less openly encouraged to capture the ear of politicians on a whole range of macro-economic issues (Edgell and Duke 1991: Chap. 7). In the USA this included several major policies: the Federal Reserve's policy of low interest rates following the crash in 2000 and the housing bubble in the years that followed; the central priority assigned to keeping inflation low; and above all the pressure to deregulate finance and abolish the restrictions on bank practices erected during the 1930s' New Deal despite growing signs of debt and market volatility (Stiglitz 2013: 300–2 and 112–5). Given this central link between a series of specific government actions, informed by neoliberalism and designed to benefit capital and the wealthy, references to shrinking the state often amount to little more than rhetoric used by Right-wing politicians to validate their free enterprise credentials. Alternatively, it is concerned with legitimizing the sale of public enterprises to private businesses (Mirowski 2013: 57–58; Dardot and Laval 2013: 218). Where this involves welfare and other activities that the public wishes to be financed out of public revenue on the grounds of equity and fairness—such as health—the privatization of public assets amounts to little more than the transfer of tax revenues provided by citizens into the pockets of private companies. Clearly this has less to do with rolling back the state and rather more with commercializing its activities while deliberately boosting a flagging private sector or crony capitalism at the same time, frequently followed by costlier services of diminishing quality.

A Trio of Core Neoliberal Presumptions

All these policies implemented by those in thrall to neoliberalism have become pervasive during the last 30 years. Accompanying them has been the mantra: 'there is no alternative' because it is '*simply obvious* … everything in society, including healthcare and education, should be run as a business' since only neoliberal capitalism is 'real' and 'natural' (Fisher 2009: 17, author's italics). But underpinning the concrete policies we have been compelled to endure are several additional neoliberal claims. These are less well known and rarely examined either by protagonists or critics. However, several scholars have placed these claims under much closer scrutiny and have revealed some bizarre as well as disturbing notions. These are based on little else but personal preferences and untestable presumptions about human social behaviour dressed in the guise of weighty philosophical and ethical concerns (Fisher 2009; Crouch 2013; Dardot and Laval 2013; Harvey 2005; Mirowski 2013; and Stiglitz 2013, among many others). Three of these claims and presumptions are particularly crucial.

One concerns the desire to transform the state so that it becomes subject to the same competitive market forces as private businesses. The marketization of government functions—contracting out such services as the administration of prisons or the allocation of welfare payments to private companies—along with the wholesale privatization of public enterprises constitute the most obvious examples. But neoliberals also wish to construct an 'entrepreneurial society'. Mirowski argues that even politics is treated as if it was a market (2013: 58). In effect, the economy, and the need for everyone to survive and compete within its orbit, becomes the overriding structure to which all other aspects of life become subordinated. We are to live in a world of generalized competition where 'the economy is conflated with the universe of human existence' (58). Economic life becomes the supreme testing ground for each individual's personal conduct and moral choices.

A number of additional effects flow from this. For example, citizens become consumers and, in respect to government, the customers of state services. Governments, nations and entire national workforces must learn to compete in the evolving global marketplace or face decline. Preparing citizens for this fate becomes a key duty of governments (Dardot and Laval 2013: 186–7). The provision of welfare paid out of taxes then becomes a drag on 'enterprise' and 'wealth creation' and a 'disincentive' for families and individuals to contribute fully to the economy. As such, and like collective action and social solidarity—which are alleged to promote a culture of dependency and individual weakness—welfare provision undermines personal morality (pp. 163–8). In addition, public bodies and governments need to become far more subject to regular auditing arrangements to ensure their accountability to market logic and efficiency.

Underlying this conviction about market competition is a second set of arguments concerning knowledge. Much of this stems from Hayek's work and influence on neoliberal thought. Hayek believed that unlike the economy or business organizations, the market does not pursue or possess goals but is spontaneous and open. It registers the cumulative summation of all the decisions taken separately by participating individuals. As such it operates independently of the conscious will of those who interact within its realms (Turner 2008: 121–4). Consequently, the market generates a kind of superior information and knowledge that is beneficial because it creates outcomes that were not consciously intended and could not have been deliberately planned (Dardot and Laval 2013: 123–7). The prices resulting from the play of demand and supply under competitive conditions constitute the main expression of this process in that they relay all the information participants require. Attempts to surpass or replace the market usually fail because the alternative information available to bureaucrats or planners will be incapable of reflecting the conscious and unconscious desires of multiple participants and citizens (Mirowski 2013: 54–55).

The third pillar of neoliberalism concerns the motivations that induce individuals to seek continuous employment, acquire appropriate new skills and accept whatever disciplines are germane to each type of workplace. In the case of early British industrial capitalism, Marx's explanation was straightforward. Despite being legally free, economic necessity compelled the individual to sell his labour-power to the factory owner, especially after the Enclosures and the implementation of the 1834 Poor Law. Even in the age of the welfare state economic pressures and inducements continue to drive people into the capitalist fold. However, by themselves they have never been sufficient to guarantee full worker commitment. Here, Foucault's work on the disciplinary forces that bring order to capitalist economies is highly influential.

As modern industrial societies evolved, a range of specialized knowledge codes became necessary and applicable in the factory, office, hospital, clinic, law court, prison, asylum, accountancy practice and elsewhere. This technical knowledge acquired by different professionals and administrators rendered them indispensable to governments, businesses and wider society, not least because their skills facilitated government regulation. But knowledge also conferred a kind of power. This power could not easily be resisted or ignored precisely because of professionals' hard-won credentials and the indisputable benefits of their knowledge. Such knowledge fostered compliance and legitimacy in respect to capitalist economies and the operations of the modern state. Foucault's analysis also showed that power is no longer concentrated solely in the institutions of the modern state and its rulers. Nor does its exercise always involve physical coercion. Instead, it seeps into all relationships where people need access to technical knowledge.

In his later writings, Foucault (1977, 1980 and 2008) developed the concept of 'bio-power'. As the economic and military priorities of modernizing states develop—driven in part by international rivalry—they need to shape the health, work skills, readiness for future military involvement, educational attainment and demographic balance of their subject populations. Typically, therefore, governments try to regulate and control reproductive intentions in respect to family size and the spread of sexually transmitted diseases. Exercising this type of control also means governments need to acquire volumes of reliable and up-to-date information.

As with other sources of power, bio-power also involves an element of subjective internalization. Examples might be the practise of family birth control, sexual abstinence or following a healthy, balanced diet by citizens. Thus, under modernity citizens accept a third kind of control: the discipline coming from within themselves. This is what Foucault calls governmentality: the individual chooses freely to impose rules and constraints on herself because she believes these are in her own as well as society's wider interest. According to Mirowski (2013: 94–95), at a time in the later 1970s when neoliberal politics was beginning to be practised and widely discussed, Foucault realized its proponents were intending to 'recast not just markets and government, but the totality of human existence ... through the production of subjectivity in the multitude'. But the subjectivity neoliberals planned to inculcate throughout the world aimed to capture the individual's consciousness much more intensively than previous capitalist regimes. How was this to be achieved?

First, neoliberalism attempts to unify all aspects of existence—affiliations, creativity, work and performance, political involvement, skill acquisition, consumer interests and so on—around the pursuit of economic activity (Dardot and Laval 2013: 258–60). Again, the market economy provides a vehicle for self-realization and all individual experience throughout life. Second, neoliberalism raises the principle of self-government to a new level by demanding that everyone becomes an entrepreneur, a continuous manager of everything s/he does in the pursuit of personal advantage in the market. Here, human resources, as the total bundle of individual skills and orientations, replace the established idea in political economy that labour is entirely separate from the entrepreneur or capital. The intrinsic, distinctive value of the worker becomes subsumed under the general rubric of the owner/manager and is accordingly devalued (Mirowski 2013: 58–60). Third, this new entrepreneur-citizen-worker-consumer takes on the responsibility and the risks involved not only in performing her own role as an employee but also those of the enterprise. By working for others, she is working for herself. The work place becomes the site where everything necessary to the good life is achieved, not just material prosperity and security but also self-expression and self-realization.

Fourth, by becoming her own self-governing entrepreneur, the individual takes full responsibility for her own actions and for the risks that are unavoidably associated with managing her own life. Thus, by a sleight of hand—as in a conjuring trick—she only has herself to blame for any failures she experiences: redundancy, insecure employment, work that falls well below her educational attainments and so on. Living under neoliberal ideology we are all accountable for our own lives and for wider crises and catastrophes but only as separate individuals, never as collective subjects. This way of thinking about agency also gets corporations, hedge funds, oil conglomerates and indeed capitalism in general, pretty much off the hook, while the individual is held fully accountable (Fisher 2009: 67).

Critical Reflections on Neoliberal Ideology

Not surprisingly neoliberalism has been criticized (e.g. Harvey 2005 and Reinert 2007). Below, we focus particularly on the argument that the market economy can be the sole guarantee of freedom and economic efficiency and that under its auspices the individual is the sole agent of her destiny.

(1) Neoliberals seem oblivious to the reality that there are many different kinds of markets. Moreover, the players operating within them do not all wield the same degree of influence over the outcomes, and substantial distortions are likely to arise. For example, the investment required in drilling for oil, transporting it and then refining it for sale (and therefore the possibility for forming oligopolistic and price-

controlling trade agreements) is of a totally different order than that required to run a local garage repair business or small factory. Similarly, in the agricultural industry farmers who supply milk or pork may vary in size but few are as capable of determining prices as national or international supermarkets who often become the former's main buyers and then impose low compulsory prices—justified because this is what their own consumers demand. When many of the latter are low paid a vicious spiral arises where poorly reimbursed workers require cheap goods, and this then has repercussions for farm prices to the point where many smaller farmers go out of business. In other words, unequal market power generates further inequality.

(2) Irrespective of what form they take or the locality where they reside (cyber space, downtown Manchester, retail parks, a stock exchange floor), markets do, of course, bring people together in the exchange of goods and services. Notwithstanding the power of advertising, the possibility of monopoly agreements and other price-fixing arrangements, market prices mostly follow from the unplanned and unintended actions of innumerable micro-decisions made by millions of separate consumers or businesses. Yet, the market does not operate as the fount of all knowledge, even in the case of purely market questions regarding consumer choices. It cannot tell us how to live, what forms of social justice we might seek or what kind of future may be desirable. Of course, neoliberals do not make this claim. But it is an abrogation of intellectual responsibility to insist 'the market' provides the only source of freedom and valid knowledge and then disavow any other mechanism for dealing with human problems because it might lead to people other than private owners, competing workers or individual consumers exercising some influence over events. Buying potatoes, preparing for a job interview or trying to turn an annual business profit are all essential actions. But they do not prepare societies to fight wars, manage the influx of huge numbers of refugees fleeing from oppression, deal with the consequences of an ageing society, cope with climate change, prepare for global shortages of food, water or oil or manage the pending effects of vast technological change on future employment. Our lives cannot be left entirely to the vagaries of supposedly free and competitive markets.

(3) Neoliberal insistence that all individuals should become entrepreneurs in control of their lives through the miracles of the market allows the successful to take sole credit for their actions even though in many cases their success partly resulted from their parents' income, social contacts and private education. Similarly, since the less successful are entirely responsible for their own situation—and given that 'the market' has promoted abundance for some—there is no reason to help them. The removal of welfare help is legitimized. But even if everyone struggled to seek the golden path of self-entrepreneurship most would 'fail' in relative terms simply because no society, including modern capitalism, can provide well-paid professional/scientific/managerial jobs for more than a minority. By definition, only a minority of citizens can achieve those top earnings. In any case, not everyone is capable of gaining a doctorate in advanced mathematics or running a four-minute mile and this should not be held against them.

(4) Ironically, even if everyone was equally capable and diligent in struggling for the top qualifications and skills there would still be winners and losers, given the huge shortage of prizes and the need for most people to take up the low-paid jobs which form the great majority. This is the nature of competition. In business as in sport, or any arena where people are pitted against each other, the 'success' of some requires the 'failure' of the many. And the difference in ability between s/he who wins the top prize—in running the 1000 metres as much as in the competition to become the CEO—and the nearest competitors is so minute, if any, as to render the unequal distribution of rewards that follows totally unjustified. The system itself guarantees the creation of a vast pool of ordinary participants and a substantial minority of losers. The latter are the casualties of a competitive system they did not create and from which they cannot escape—especially in today's world of expensive technology, ever higher skill levels, vast corporate monopolies and global markets. Neoliberalism asks us to accept this is a valid model for our society while encouraging us to heap plaudits and wealth on the few winners.

Whether intentionally or otherwise, neoliberal regimes have strengthened the power, relative unaccountability and hubris of capitalism and its elites. At the same time, the policies supposedly justified by neoliberalism's theoretical arguments have been used by governments and capital as a stick with which to undermine the previous bases of worker power but also the very belief and confidence that collective action is valid, that people have every right to resist growing inequality and the deterioration of their employment security through taking joint action.

3.3 Financialization

Financialization refers to a series of processes whereby financial products, such as company equity stock, government bonds and derivatives, have become relatively more significant in the global economy along with the influence over other businesses exercised by the institutions which provide these services. The latter includes various kinds of dealers and brokers who buy and sell financial products for clients, individuals or companies, those who manage pension and investment funds, again on behalf of individuals or group investors, traditional/retail banks, investment banks specializing in lending to other businesses and hedge funds. For many observers the term 'financialization' also carries the implication that as the financial sector has grown—accelerating since the 1990s—so has its capacity to divert economic resources away from the 'real', productive economy and to capture a growing share of the wider profits made by capitalist enterprises. Batt and Appelbaum (2013: 1) capture precisely what is involved. 'Financialization refers to a shift from managerial capitalism, in which the returns on investments derive from the value created by productive enterprises, to a new form of *financial capitalism,* where companies are viewed as assets to be bought and sold and as vehicles for maximizing profits through financial strategies' (author's italics). They add that since the 1980s non-financial firms have also become increasingly dependent on financial investments—acquiring non-tangible assets in addition to productive ones—to the point where, by 2000, many firms possessed a roughly equal proportion of both (4).

According to Lapavitsas (2013) the contribution of the financial industries to GDP, including insurance and real estate, rose from 14 to 30 per cent in the UK between 1970 and 2009. Similar huge increases in the weight of finance occurred in other advanced economies: for example, in the USA from 20 to 30 per cent and from 15 to 25 per cent in Japan between 1992 and 2006 (211). At the same time, the share in overall pre-tax corporate profits of the financial services industries also rose markedly, reaching 45 per cent in the USA by the early 2000s (213). In contrast, the contribution of finance to employment has been rather small in relation to its huge and growing weight. How did financialization become so dominant in the world economy?

The pivotal role of London during the nineteenth century in providing a degree of financial order in an expanding world economy came under severe strain in the first decades of the twentieth century when Britain faced huge war debts, industrial decline and an overstretched empire. Consequently, sterling, as world money, was under risk, and the need to protect it for international use also constrained Britain's own attempts at recovery. Such problems were temporarily resolved after WW2 because, as part of the financial structure set in place in 1944 at the Bretton Woods conference, the USA agreed that the dollar would henceforth operate as world money in the West. This helped to generate worldwide confidence in the dollar by tying its value to US gold reserves. The Bretton Woods agreement also established a system of semi-fixed exchange rates in which the participating countries agreed to minimize their future resort to protectionist policies such as devaluation, import controls and high tariffs. These had worsened the impact of the Great Depression during the 1930s by undercutting trade. The agreement also established two IGOs, the WB and the International Monetary Fund (IMF). Their future roles were designated, respectively, as providing long-term loans for infrastructural projects that private banks might balk at financing and supplying short-term emergency assistance to governments.

Following WW2, the much stronger US economy led the way in helping to generate three decades of high economic growth by providing Marshall Aid to Europe designed to speed post-war recovery and head off support for communist parties. It also generously opened its markets to the growing exports produced by its recovering former war-time allies and enemies. The theory developed by Panitch and Gindin (2004) relating to

America's motives and role in establishing the Bretton Woods system, and in manipulating much that followed in the years after, is interesting and helpful. They argue that together both the US state and capitalist interests sought to dominate the post-war Western sphere through a form of imperialism that unlike European colonialism was informal, that is, not based on direct political rule. The primary strategy involved guaranteeing the survival and the future vitality (profitability) of capitalism and the market within the USA itself by promoting 'free enterprise and free trade internationally' (18). This meant pursuing America's national interests by acting to protect and extend capitalism globally through persuading, but also rewarding, the governments of its allies and former enemies to accept 'responsibility for managing its [their] domestic order' (17). Two additional points are worth noting here. This post-war American strategy, which, according to Panitch and Gindin has continued through various phases until now, followed a decade of New Deal policies. Although US capitalism thrived during the war years the preceding decade had been one of substantial state regulation of finance and relatively high taxation. Second, in contrast to neoliberal ideology, this analysis points strongly, not to the irrelevance of cumbersome state apparatuses to the recovery and strengthening of capitalism at both the national and global level but to the exact opposite.

By the 1970s, and with recovery and economic growth well established in Europe and Japan, international trade grew rapidly. As a result, many national companies effectively became multi- or transnational corporations (TNCs) by setting up branch plants or establishing affiliate companies in competitor and other overseas markets. This, in turn, created new business opportunities for the financial services industry since the larger banks followed national industrial companies and other clients overseas. In short, what Sassen (2000 and 2002), Taylor (2004) and others have called the 'producer service industries'—that is, not just leading financial firms but also the major companies providing support services in law, insurance, managements consultancy, advertising—increasingly went global.

The Politics of Financial Liberalization and Offshore Banking

This process gathered pace from the 1960s and gave rise to an offshore banking system. As the quantity of money swirling through the world's financial centres rose, its owners required a degree of flexibility and earning potential that national and official banks could not supply. The Eurodollar market, as it was eventually called, increasingly filled this gap. TNCs, for example, needed to juggle multiple currencies or store profits and working capital temporarily in worldwide safe havens. Additional deposits came from the world's super-rich, criminal gangs, magnates and corrupt politicians and officials across many developing countries, creaming off their nations' resources, often with the silent 'cooperation' of various Western mining and other companies. Some of the enormous dollar earnings of the oil countries were also steered in the direction of the offshore banks. These earnings quadrupled in 1973 and then tripled again in 1979 partly as a result of pressure on the Organization of Petroleum Exporting Countries (OPEC) from the Arab oil producers who demanded huge increases in the price of oil. As the reserves of the Eurodollar market increased, the capacity of those who controlled them to shape the direction of world financial affairs became increasingly evident.

In 1971 President Nixon devalued the US dollar and de-linked its value from gold. Now the stability of world money was no longer guaranteed. America's trade deficit had been growing for some time partly because of foreign import penetration into its domestic market but also because of US spending on the war in Vietnam. By ushering in an era of greater currency uncertainty, dollar devaluation added to the already growing complexity of world trade. Meanwhile, America relaxed its former controls and allowed its own banks to join the offshore global credit system of depositing and lending that had built up around the Eurodollar market. Thus, from the 1970s onwards, the path was clear for the US government and its 'allies', the WB and IMF, to play a disproportionate role in strengthening the offshore financial system.

In the mid-1970s, the IMF and the WB assumed a different role to merely helping governments deal with balance of payment problems.

They switched to assisting developing countries with their underlying economic dilemmas. Partly this involved encouraging a large splurge of private bank lending to governments in the developing countries and many responded by borrowing large amounts. However, much of this borrowing was deployed by governments on wasteful projects that were unlikely to ever generate a return sufficient to allow the original loan to be repaid. Other loans were spent on military hardware. Huge amounts were also sequestered by officials and politicians and returned to the global banking system as private accounts. Much of this was to have dire consequences for many developing countries. Meanwhile, as we have seen, by the late 1970s, inflationary pressures were building up in the world economy, including in the USA. Under Volker, Chairman of the Federal Reserve from 1979, and partly in an attempt to rein in inflation, first President Carter and then Reagan from early 1981 pushed up the main US Bank interest rate to an unusually high level. This compelled other countries to follow suit. Very high interest rates—21.5 per cent in December 1980, thereafter remaining between 15 and 18 per cent under Reagan until July 1982—were also a mechanism for taming American labour unions. What followed was a global recession which lasted for some years. This hit manufacturing industries and their workforces hard across many Western economies including in the USA itself, especially since the high dollar made US manufactures less competitive.

The collapse in world growth and trade also hurt the countries of the Global South—who had borrowed heavily only a few years earlier—particularly badly. High world interest rates pushed up the cost of servicing their debts to impossible levels while the recession reduced the demand and prices for their raw material exports. What followed was the so-called Third World Debt Crisis of the 1980s when the global banking system went into a severe crisis as several of the wealthiest debtor countries, including Argentina, Mexico and Brazil, defaulted on their loans. Only massive intervention by the WB, IMF and the US government prevented some of the leading global banks—with their inter-linked loans—from collapsing, along with confidence in world finance as a whole.

The Reagan government then exercised its direct influence over the WB and IMF to insist that policies designed to deal with their debt, or 'conditionality', were imposed on these countries. This was the so-called

Washington Consensus. Again, according to Panitch and Gindin (2004), this was a core expression of America's system of informal imperialist control over global capitalism set up in 1944. In exchange for debt relief (longer payment terms, more favourable rates of interest and fresh loans) and access to American markets, the debtor countries had to sign up to a package of the same neoliberal measures that were concurrently being imposed in the USA and elsewhere: privatizing state enterprises (which often meant selling them at knocked-down prices to Western TNCs); the abolition of controls on inward capital flows; cutting state spending and so on (see Kiely [2005a] for details). Ostensibly these 'structural adjustment policies' (SAPs) were designed to eliminate the waste and corruption associated with too much direct state involvement while giving local and foreign capitalist enterprises greater room to invest. In practice, critics such as Klein, in her book *The Shock Doctrine* (2007), and Dardot and Laval (2013), argue that the underlying purpose of the Washington Consensus was to bring the developing countries under the direct financial and political control of the US government. It also became easier for TNCs to secure greater market penetration of the affected debtor economies.

According to Gowan (2009) and others, during the 1980s the US government also attempted to out-flank its trade rivals and compensate for its relatively declining industrial hegemony by boosting Wall Street's already substantial global business advantages in financial services. This was at a time when finance and its products, along with the commercial opportunities for providing credit worldwide, were becoming steadily more crucial in an ever more interdependent global economy. Stiglitz, a leading former World Bank economist, pushes the argument concerning the relationship between government and the rise of finance a crucial step further. As we saw in Chap. 2, Stiglitz (2013: 301–11) is scathing about how bankers and financial leaders soon captured the perspectives and policies of the US government's policy-making economic agency, the Federal Reserve. In effect they determined the latter's public policies from the 1980s onwards. As a result, the Fed permitted the continued deregulation of finance which encouraged growing indebtedness and ultimately lead to financial collapse.

Dardot and Laval (2013: 155) partially agree with Stiglitz, except that in their view finance became relatively autonomous from the real economy of production and commercial trade during the 1980s and not just from the US government. They also identify neoliberal ideology, steered by the US state, as the primary strategy through which the worldwide regime of domination by the financial industries was actively constructed. In 1999, for example, the US government repealed the Glass-Steagall Act of 1933, passed during Roosevelt's New Deal government, which had separated retail and investment banking. This deregulation replaced the national protection of financial industries with a regime of competition; one that the leading economies were likely to win. Deregulation also opened the way for financial corporations to combine previously separate activities in financial consultancy, banking and insurance. Meanwhile, governments could more easily fund their domestic public spending and investment by borrowing from international investors (Dardot and Laval 2013: 157–8).

Whichever way we view the causal relationship between financial liberalization and neoliberal ideology, both were promoted through state-led political projects, with the US government taking the leading part. Like the birth of capitalism and industry in nineteenth- and twentieth-century economies, financialization did not spring into existence solely through its own momentum.

The Financial Crisis of 2008–2009 and Beyond

There is wide agreement that financialization and neoliberal policies created the conditions for the implosion that led to the most recent capitalist crisis (Elliott and Atkinson 2008; Dardot and Laval 2013; Gamble 2014; Stiglitz 2013; Quiggin 2010; and Mirowski 2013). This implosion began in 2008 with the collapse of Lehman Brothers in New York but was soon followed by the huge financial losses suffered by a series of other investment banks and financial businesses. What actions by the deregulated financial industries caused this crisis?

Banks such as Lehman Brothers were allowed to borrow and build up liabilities vastly in excess of their capital base—31 times in the case of Lehman's. Much of this borrowing had been lent to house buyers, many of whose incomes were low or insecure. Consequently, when the US housing bubble collapsed, many defaulted on their loans causing havoc for the lenders—the so-called subprime US mortgage crisis. In addition, leading banks had devised a system of securitization whereby various kinds of toxic high-risk but high-yield debts, plus their income-earning streams (mortgages, student loans, car-purchase credit and so on), were bundled together with low-yield, low-risk debts and sold to pension funds, other investors and to banks themselves—despite the toxic nature of much of their contents. Panic set in as one business after another contemplated how much they had lent to other banks but also their own dependence on borrowing in order to purchase/invest in credit derivatives. In these circumstances the collapse of one bank would pull others down in turn. Citibank in the USA provides just one example. In early 2007 its shares were valued at $55 but by the middle of 2009 this had fallen to only $3. Ultimately, its directors were forced to write off capital losses of $105 billion. Most of this had to be guaranteed by the government and tax payers. In fact, the former eventually took a 34-per cent stake in Citibank (Ford and Larsen 2009).

Dealing with this crisis required government intervention to the tune of $5 trillion (Gowan 2009) across the EU and USA in the attempt to prevent a far wider range of businesses collapsing, mass unemployment and, ultimately, the inability to draw money from banks. The financial crisis also gave rise to a period of austerity, unemployment and insecurity in the Western countries which continues till the present time. This might have been much worse had it not been for two counter-recessionary forces. One was the resort to quantitative easing on a massive scale by some Western governments, accompanied by extremely low interest rates. Between 2009 and 2015 around $12 trillion was pumped into the global economy by state banks, mostly in the USA, UK and belatedly in the EU (Mason 2015a: 2). Unfortunately most of this seems to have been absorbed by the private banks to re-build their capital bases.[1] Alternatively, in the hands of the super-rich, some of this money has contributed to rising property values. The other crucial factor bolstering

---

[1] Some also leaked into currency devaluations, especially of the dollar, thereby introducing protectionism by stealth into the global economy.

the global and especially the Western economies was the ability of the Chinese and other non-Western economies to keep demand expanding in the world economy with its astonishingly high rates of economic growth. Yet, by the summer of 2015, China's economic strength and that of the emerging markets looked increasingly fragile, as we will see in Chap. 4. In any case, the underlying strength of China's economy and its capacity to become a world technological leader on a par with countries such as the USA, Japan or Germany are in question (e.g. Starrs 2013; Kiely 2007: 209–12). Meanwhile the disorder in the world's financial system remained largely untamed (Hutton 2015: 36).

3.4 Globalization: Uniting But Also Fracturing Humanity

Globalization, as the forging of new interconnectivities and exchanges between societies and social actors, is not new. Yet since the 1980s globalizing processes have intensified, accelerated and spread into new areas and activities. Held et al. (1999: 17–26) suggest that when all three occur simultaneously we have 'thick globalization'. Globalizing processes are being driven by many factors but especially the abstract, impersonal power of money and competition (James 2005), unleashed by the opening of borders to investment and capital flows (Williams 2014) and followed by the industrialization of many countries in the Global South. But vast flows of unmoored cultural fragments, intensified through transnational migration, the mass media, international tourism, the Information Revolution, and so on, are also crucial. Evidence of these cumulative processes are apparent even in the remotest and poorest regions of the planet, whether through consumer brands and signs cluttering road sides and markets, a growing water scarcity as the climate alters, or when people use mobile phones or iPads to contact their kin who have migrated overseas (Cohen and Kennedy 2013; Axford 2013).

It is nevertheless important not to impute more influence to globalization processes than they actually possess. For one thing the local, as physical place and source of primary identity, plus the dense micro-pressures of the everyday, remain a powerful fulcrum governing most people's lives *alongside* global forces which—in any case—they may only partly recognize or understand (Kennedy 2010: 144–63). There has also been a tendency for some theory to reify the idea of the 'spatial extension' of social life, forgetting that it is people and their multiple interactions that create global processes, not an abstract scalar logic (141–4). Others argue that some globalization theorists have also tended to conflate the multiple processes they draw on and describe in order to define globalization, with its causes leading to a circular argument and a tautological theory (see Rosenberg 2005, and Kiely 2007, for a deeper analysis). Further, evidence that globalizing realities are giving rise to a 'global consciousness'—an awareness of the world as one place shared by a single humanity and deserving of our empathy (Robertson 1992)—remains thin. In large part, the dearth of subjective understanding and empathy towards globalizing processes is a reaction to the very transformations that globalization has wrought: worsening the life conditions of many and unsettling their identities, especially among the poor, marginalized and underemployed, both in the advanced countries and the Global South (Bauman 1998). Consequently, instead of sympathy for refugees fleeing from war zones, for foreign migrants or religious, sectarian and ethnic minorities living nearby we find explosions of racist, nativistic and populist movements and the widespread retreat into dangerous forms of social exclusion and localism, and even a reassertion of nationalism as we saw in Chap. 1. Writers such as Bauman (1998) and Sloterdijk (2014) also argue that globalization has enhanced the advantages enjoyed by perhaps one quarter of humanity living in the 'Crystal Palace' (Sloterdijk 2014) of economic plenty, mostly, but not entirely in the Global North. Certainly, the current workings of globalization strengthen the mobility of global elites, rendering them increasingly remote and unaccountable (Lansley 2011) as we saw in Chap. 2.

Globalizing Processes Since the 1960s

Neoliberal policies accelerated and deepened existing processes of globalization particularly through the liberalization of capital flows and markets via the imposition of SAPs. EU countries such as Greece and Portugal were also driven to swallow liberalization. Another core agent whose actions have hugely deepened globalizing processes are the TNCs, with their worldwide networks of branch plants, affiliates and partner companies and their construction of global supply chains straddling several nations. Supply chains are networks of interdependent producers, often extending right down to very small firms or even homeworkers engaged in producing minor components of a commodity. Agricultural supplies of seasonal vegetables, fruit and flowers also form supply chains. Moreover, as we have seen, the rise of an offshore, largely deregulated banking system from the 1960s onwards reinforced globalizing processes and supported the key actors involved in forging numerous cross-border interconnections. They provided not just investment capital but also a range of business services for lubricating exchanges and providing safe havens for storing profits.

The rise of TNCs and the actions of Western governments, especially the USA, in inducing the rest of the world to accept neoliberal policies are not the only reasons why the pace and depth of globalization processes accelerated, especially from the 1980s. Another important cause, one which usually receives scant attention, revolves around the determination of Japan and several governments in the Global South, from the 1960s onwards, to modernize their economies. Indeed, it has been this increasing addition of technologically advanced industrial national capacities to the world's reservoir of economic activity, albeit unevenly, that partly preceded but also underpinned the rise of an ever more globalized capitalism. China's ability from the late 1970s to progressively capture the manufacturing markets of the world—by 2010 it already topped the share of world exports (*CIA World Factbook* 2011)—is of course the outstanding case. Yet, between 1953 and the late 1990s the share of world manufacturing produced by the so-called Newly Industrializing Countries or NICs rose from around 5 to 23 per cent (Dicken 2003: 37). This surge was spearheaded not by China but by the four 'tiger' economies, South Korea, Taiwan, Hong Kong and Singapore from the 1960s onwards, along with countries such as Brazil, Mexico, Thailand, Indonesia and Malaysia. The following brief discussion singles out the main turning points in this wider process.

The re-emergence of Japan as a major exporting economy from the 1950s was a major step in this wider process, not least because it offered a model for some of the later NICs. Like that of the 'tiger' economies 90 years later, Japan's industrialization from the 1870s was born out of internal political crisis linked to the external threat to its national integrity posed by a technologically superior power perceived to hold colonizing ambitions: the USA (Cummings 1987). Following its defeat in WW2 and a decade of US occupation, Japanese governments prioritized rapid economic growth rather than military might as the future path to international status and national security. To this end, Japan's government built on a system for accelerating and deepening industrial progress established in the 1920s. Scholars of post–WW2 Japan labelled this trajectory and pattern the 'developmental state' (e.g. Johnson 1982; White 1988). Relying on the central direction provided by a disciplined and technically capable bureaucracy, coupled to the considerable exercise of state control over public savings and the national banking system, government elites assumed responsibility for setting national growth priorities and targets. Here, the intention was to progressively upgrade the nation's technological capacity into a world-class capability.

Japan's just-in-time or lean production system and the practice of tiered company sub-contracting allowed firms to minimize their supply of stocks. Japanese firms also operated a more flexible mode of deploying their workers based on multi-tasking and the practice of lifetime employment plus linking pay to performance and seniority in respect to workers in the largest companies. Such measures proved so successful that by 1980 Japanese companies were out-producing American car companies and accounted for 28 per cent of world vehicle output. They also captured a growing share of the US and European car home markets (Dohse et al. 1985: 117). Japan's worldwide competitive success constituted yet another nail in the coffin of post–WW2 Fordism across North America and Europe. Indeed, by the mid-1980s Japan was establishing branch plants across these regions to serve local markets in several key industries. This 'Japanization' of Western industry offered local workers, rival companies and suppliers the opportunity to imitate post-Fordist methods. Japanization was also an indication of accelerating globalization.

Beginning less than two decades later, in the early 1960s the Asian 'Tiger' economies—and China from the late 1970s—also adopted versions of the 'developmental state' model. Among the strategies employed were: encouraging high rates of domestic saving to finance rapid investment; prioritizing exports of high value-added commodities, through subsidies and tax advantages; and helping local firms to assimilate foreign technology. Behind these strategies, in turn, lay two key principles: foster indigenous rather than foreign companies and be prepared to interfere with market indices such as rates of interest and export prices in order to favour the most successful and technologically advanced companies (see Wade 1990 on Taiwan and Amsden 1989 for the case of South Korea). Of course, such measures are utterly contrary to the commands of neoliberal theory.

From the 1960s other countries tried to attract foreign investment while building their own future industrial capacity. Establishing Export Processing Zones (EPZs) was one key strategy for doing this. This involved government investment in creating special 'offshore' production zones offering tax advantages, cheap, non-unionized labour—mostly women workers—subsidized plant and infrastructure, duty-free imports and similar advantages. This appealed to many overseas companies who could then benefit from relocating some of their more labour-intensive and low value-added consumer operations to these EPZs. The volume of manufactured goods supplied to world markets from and by EPZs soon expanded (see Klein 2000 for a critique of EPZs). So, too, did the technical quality and range of consumer goods and parts stemming from these zones, and consequently the number of countries eager to use EPZs as a strategy for expanding their manufacturing capacity. This included China which, following its economic reforms and decision to encourage foreign investment as a key plank in its rapid industrialization project, established four EPZs, called 'special economic zones', in Shenzhen Province in the late 1970s. Mexico's *maquiladoras,* established from 1965 onwards along its border with the USA, represent another notable case.

Clearly, such measures adopted by governments in the Global South allowed TNCs to search the world for the least-cost investment and production outlets. This widening and deepening of worldwide investment by TNCs was facilitated by the revolutions in communication and transport technologies but also by the economic policies imposed on many indebted developing countries through the Washington Consensus. Many developing countries have also invested in higher education in order to improve the value-creating possibilities of their local labour (Freeman 2007: 26–27). According to Freeman, the number of college and university students rose by 400 per cent across many developing countries between 1970 and 2000. In China, the number of students who attained first degrees rose by 4 million between 2000 and 2005. Such measures improved each nation's industrial skills-base and independent business potential but also benefitted TNCs who employed such high-quality workers at wage levels considerably lower than at home. Up-grading national educational levels also makes it easier for developing countries to transfer and absorb some advanced technologies. India's ability to process and export high-quality information technology (IT) services for legal, medical, commercial, bank, insurance and other companies across the world is a case in point. Between 2000 and 2006 the value of these exports rose from $565 million to $6.2 billion (Paus 2007: 13).

Freeman (2007: 25–26) identified an additional factor contributing to the massive diffusion of capitalism worldwide and which constitutes one of the huge 'drivers' of economic globalization. This is the doubling of the supply of labour available to capitalism across the world in the 20 years between 1980 and 2000 with the numbers expanding from around 1460 million workers to perhaps 3 billion in 2000. The IMF pointed to the same reality when it suggested that the supply of global labour has probably risen fourfold since 1980 (*The Economist* 2007: 84). Part of the explanation lies in all the factors we have already outlined. But two additional, major changes were also responsible for this shift. First was China's decision to open its borders to foreign investors and its determination to hugely expand into world export markets from the late 1970s. Second, and following the end of the Cold War after 1989, the former countries of the Soviet Union and its allies also 'joined' the world capitalist system.

3.5 Summary and Conclusions

In the hands of certain political leaders and parties, who were often, in turn, the spokespersons for commercial interests, neoliberal ideology has probably contributed more to the rise a largely unfettered vampire capitalism than any other single factor, though industrialization in the Global South and the rise of an offshore banking system were well underway prior to the 1980s. Nevertheless, privatizations, moves towards a regressive tax system, attacks on trade unions, the liberalization of capital movements, and the rest have worked to strengthen corporations and capitalism generally, in addition to the various professional elites who manage their affairs. At the same time, the rise of the financial services added a virtually bottomless dimension to global capitalism's capacities to accumulate—again, hugely assisted by neoliberal policies. As we saw in Chap. 2, however, this same process also deepened capital's propensity to engage in cycles of speculative risk-taking while luring a growing proportion of finance and other kinds of capital away from productive investment.

Considered overall, a highly integrated global economy has come into being during the last 50 years. It is also vastly more complex, multipolar and difficult to manage (Gamble 2014) than anything that existed in the years after WW2—notwithstanding Panitch and Gindin's (2004) argument that America has continued to operate its informal imperialist system throughout. One of the most profound transformations brought by all these changes has been the creation of a world labour market. Here, billons of people are compelled to compete with multiple others whose skills, conditions of work, market opportunities and above all wages are often very different from their own. By weakening the once 'solidaristic conditions' (Gottfried 2013: 223) and bargaining strength that workers in many countries once enjoyed, when industry and economic life in general was far more localized, global competition, financialization and neoliberal policies have undoubtedly made it much harder to hold capitalism and its leading elites to account.

Bibliography

Amsden, A. (1989). *Asia's next giant: South Korea and late industrialization.* New York: Oxford University Press.

Axford, B. (2013). *Theories of globalization.* Cambridge: Polity.

Batt, R. L. and Appelbaum, E. (2013). *The impact of financialization on management and employment outcomes.* W. E. Upjohn Institute for Employment Research. Retrieved August 9, 2016, from http://research.upjohn.org/cgi/viewcontent.cgi?article=1208&context=up_workingpapers

Bauman, Z. (1998). *Globalization: The human consequences.* Cambridge: Polity.

Beynon, H. (1973). *Working for ford.* Harmondsworth: Allen Lane.

Boyle, J. (2003). The second enclosure movement and the construction of the public domain. *Law and Contemporary Problems, 66*(1/2), 33–74.

CIA World Factbook. (2011). Washington, DC: Central Intelligence Agency.

Cohen, R., & Kennedy, P. (2007). *Global sociology* (2nd ed.). New York: New York University Press.

Cohen, R., & Kennedy, P. (2013). *Global sociology* (3rd ed.). New York: New York University Press.

Crouch, C. (2013). *Making capitalism fit for society.* Cambridge: Polity.

Cummings, B. (1987). Northeast Asian political economy. In F. C. Deyo (Ed.), *Political economy of the New Asian industrialization* (pp. 44–83). Ithaca, NY: Cornell University Press.

Dardot, P. and Laval, C. (2013). *The new way of the World: On neo-liberal society* (trans: Elliot, G.). London: Verso.

Dicken, P. (2003). *Global shift: Reshaping the global economic map in the 21st century.* London: Sage.

Dohse, K., Jurgens, V., & Malsch, T. (1985). From fordism to toyotism. *Politics and Society, 14*(2), 115–146.

Edgell, A. (2012). *The sociology of work: Continuity and change in paid and unpaid work.* London: Sage.

Edgell, S., & Duke, V. (1991). *A measure of Thatcherism: A sociology of Britain.* London: Harper-Collins.

Elliott, L., & Atkiknson, D. (2008). *The gods that failed: How blind faith in markets has cost us our futures.* London: Bodley Head.

Fisher, M. (2009). *Capitalist realism: Is there no alternative?* Winchester: Zero Books.

Ford, J. and Larsen, P. T. (2009, November 18). How to shrink the banks. *Prospect.* Retrieved August 9, 2016, from http://www.prospectmagazine.co.uk/features/how-to-shrink-the-banks

Foucault, M. (1977). *Discipline and punish: The birth of the prison.* London: Allen Lane.
Foucault, M. (1980). *Power/knowledge: Selected interviews and other writings, 1972–77* (ed.: Gordon, C.). New York: Pantheon Books.
Freeman, R. B. (2007). The challenge of the growing globalization of labour markets to economic and social policy. In E. Paus (Ed.), *Global capitalism unbound: Winners and losers in offshore outsourcing* (pp. 23–40). Basingstoke: Palgrave.
Gamble, A. (2014). *Crisis without end? The unravelling of western prosperity.* Basingstoke: Palgrave.
Gottfried, H. (2013). *Gender, work, and economy: Unpacking the global economy.* Cambridge: Polity.
Gowan, P. (2009). Crisis in the heartlands: Consequences of the new Wall Street system. *New Left Review, 55,* 5–28.
Gray, J. (1998). *False dawn: The delusions of global capital.* London: Granta Publications.
Harvey, D. (2005). *A brief history of neoliberalism.* Oxford: Oxford University Press.
Hayek, F. A. (1944). *The road to Serfdom.* London: Routledge.
Held, D., Goldblatt, A., & Perraton, J. (1999). *Global Transformations.* Cambridge: Polity.
Hobsbawm, E. (1994). *Age of extremes: The short twentieth century, 1914–1991.* London: Michael Joseph.
Hutton, W. (2007). *The writing on the wall: China and the West in the 21st century.* London: Abacus.
Hutton, W. (2015, October 11). The world economic order is collapsing and this time there seems no way out. *The Guardian.* Retrieved August 10, 2016, from https://www.theguardian.com/commentisfree/2015/oct/11/world-order-collapse-refugees-emerging-economies-china-slowdown-recession
James, P. (2005). Arguing globalizations: Proposition towards an investigation of global formations. *Globalizations, 2*(2), 193–209.
Johnson, C. (1982). *MITI and the Japanese miracle.* Stanford, CA: Stanford University Press.
Kennedy, P. (2010). *Local lives and global transformations: Towards world society.* Basingstoke: Palgrave-Macmillan.
Kiely, R. (2005a). *Empire in the age of globalisation.* London: Pluto.
Kiely, R. (2007). *The new political economy of development: Globalization, imperialism, hegemony.* Basingstoke: Palgrave.
Klein, N. (2000). *No logo: No space, no choice, no jobs.* London: Flamingo.

Klein, N. (2007). *The shock doctrine: The rise of disaster capitalism*. New York: Metropolitan Books.
Lansley, S. (2011). *The cost of inequality: Why economic equality is essential for recovery*. London: Gibson Square.
Lapavitsas, C. (2013). *Profits without producing: How finance exploits us all*. London: Verso.
Marx, K., & Engels, F. (1967). *The communist manifesto*. Harmondsworth: Penguin.
Mason, P. (2015b). *Postcapitalism: A guide to our future*. Milton Keynes: Allen Lane.
Mirowski, P. (2013). *Never let a serious issue go to waste: How neoliberalism survived the financial crisis*. London: Verso.
Offe, C. (1985). *Disorganized capitalism*. Cambridge: Polity.
Panitch, L., & Gindin, S. (2004). Global capitalism and American Empire. In L. Panitch & C. Leys (Eds.), *The socialist register* (pp. 1–42). London: Merlin.
Paus, E. (2007). Winners and losers from offshore outsourcing: What is to be done? In E. Paus (Ed.), *Global capitalism unbound: Winners and losers in offshore outsourcing* (pp. 3–20). Basingstoke: Palgrave.
Piketty, T. (2014). *Capital in the twenty-first century*. Cambridge, MA: The Belknap Press.
Polanyi, K. (1944). *Origins of our time: The great transformation*. London: Victor Gollanz.
Quiggin, J. (2010). *Zombie economics: How dead ideas still walk among us*. Princeton, NJ: Princeton University Press.
Reinert, E. S. (2007). *How rich countries got rich… and poor countries stay poor*. London: Constable.
Robertson, R. (1992). *Globalization: Social theory and social culture*. London: Sage.
Rosenberg, J. (2005). Globalization theory: A post-mortem. *International Politics, 42*(1), 2–74.
Sassen, S. (2000). *Cities in a world economy*. Thousand Oaks, CA: Pine Forge.
Sassen, S. (2002). Introduction: Locating cities in global circuits. In S. Sassen (Ed.), *Global networks: Linked cities* (pp. 1–37). New York: Routledge.
Schweickart, D. (2002). *After capitalism*. Oxford: Rowan and Littlefield.
Sloterdijk, P. (2014). *In the world interior of capital*. Cambridge: Polity.
Starrs, S. (2013). American economic power hasn't declined—It globalized. Summarizing the data and taking globalization seriously. *International Studies Quarterly, 57*(4), 817–830.
Stiglitz, J. (2013). *The price of inequality*. London: Penguin.

Taylor, P. L. (2004). *World city network: A global urban analysis.* London: Routledge.
The Economist. (2007, April 7). Has globalization hurt workers in rich countries? The IMF wades in, p. 84.
Turner, R. S. (2008). *Neo-liberal ideology: History, concepts and policies.* Edinburgh: Edinburgh University Press.
Wade, R. (1990). *Governing the market: Economic theory and the role of government in East Asian industrialization.* Princeton, NJ: Princeton University Press.
White, G. (1988). *Developmental states in East Asia.* Basingstoke: Macmillan.
Williams, M. (2014). The solidarity economy and social transformation. In V. Satgar (Ed.), *The solidarity economy alternative: Emerging theory and practice* (pp. 37–63). Scottsville: University of KwaZulu-Natal Press.
Žižek, S. (2011). *Living in the end times.* London: Verso.

4

Living with Twenty-First-Century Capitalism

If they wish to survive, capitalists need to make profits, outwit their competitors and expand their market reach in an inherently uncertain environment. It is this compulsion to endlessly expand that cloaks capitalism with a dogged one-dimensionality. Early in the twentieth century Weber was concerned that capitalism's need for a formal rationality, 'capable of being expressed in numerical, calculable terms' (Weber 1968: 85), had diffused to, crowded out and come to dominate other spheres of modern life. As this rationalization process, underpinned by modern bureaucracy and administration, intensified, so 'material goods have gained an increasingly and inexorable power over the lives of men as at no previous period in history' (Weber 1992: 181). Consequently, modern citizens have become locked in an 'iron cage' and it is impossible to know who 'who will live in this cage in future' or whether future escape from it may become possible (pp.181–2). But there is another kind of rationality: substantive rationality. Whereas formal or instrumental rationality involves an orientation towards finding and then matching the most appropriate and technically proficient means to the attainment of a given goal, substantive rationality is concerned with what values or goals we should prioritize as essential to the human condition in the first place and how we should balance them in respect to all other possible goals (Brubaker 1984). Examples of the latter might include fostering community cohesion and fraternity, cementing family or other solidarities, deciding what constitutes social justice, equity or fairness or defining the rights and freedoms of individuals as against the loyalties to which societies are also entitled.

There is an overwhelming case for arguing that capitalism's obsessive one-dimensionality, or 'formal rationality', may now be far more dominant than it was even during the early twentieth century when Weber was writing. This was the era before two world wars, the rise of communism and before the privations of the Great Depression compelled governments, politicians, workers and citizens to demand (or accept) a partial re-balancing of rationalities. Since then capitalism has effectively broken free of the ties that once strapped it to the various modernizing projects pursued by states and societies. In Chap. 3 we identified the interlocking transformations that permitted capital to become largely dis-embedded from national economies. According to Dardot and Laval (2013: 262), these transformations—coupled to vampire capitalism—have tightened the screw of instrumental rationality more than ever. Every world inhabitant is now locked into his or her own solitary and private 'iron cage'. With these arguments in mind we now explore the most salient aspects of the current crisis of capitalist modernity facing us in the early twenty-first century.

4.1 Neoliberal Economics: The Downward Spiral

Taking our cue from the discussion of vampire capitalism and the transformations that preceded and accompanied it we scrutinize their impact on socio-economic life and ask whether we are being propelled into a downward spiral.

Wage Stagnation

As we saw in Chap. 2, wages and salaries in North America and Europe have been stagnant and even declining for several decades. According to the Pew Research Center (2014: 1–2), after allowing for inflation real average wages in the USA are no higher than in 1964, and for some workers lower. In fact, average wages peaked in 1973—during the Fordist era—at $4.03 and exercised the same purchasing power as an average wage of $22.41 in 2014. It is this, in turn, which helps to explain the escalation of consumer debt, especially since the 1990s (see below). In Chap. 5 we look in detail at another change that has aggravated the plight of many workers, namely technological change. This has also steadily reduced the number and quality of jobs across manufacturing and the services sector for some time (Rifkin 1995; Gottfried 2013: 77–78). Meanwhile the 'new' jobs left behind in its wake are mostly 'McJobs' (McMicheal 2000). These are insecure, casualized, seasonal, often in low-grade service work such as catering or retail or the care industry, and poorly paid. As additional kinds of work continue to disappear and/or are relegated to the status of 'McJobs' and as robotization and developments in AI reduce the demand for many of today's professionals, it seems likely that the highly paid work of the future will be confined to perhaps between 10 and 20 per cent of the population. These will be extremely well educated and very specialized individuals working at the frontiers of technology and science as well as computerization and finance.

In contrast, the earnings of the new and rising middle classes across much of the Global South have been rising—though this, too, is subject to the constraints just outlined for the advanced countries. But in any case, the work conditions and wage levels obtained by the mass of factory and farm workers, a high proportion of them women, as well as labourers, remain low. For many years, encouraged by governments, global corporations have been outsourcing their manufacturing processes on a huge scale to poor countries while depending at the same time on complex global supply chains, reaching down through networks of ever smaller enterprises. Clearly, one of the main reasons why Western companies have engaged in such spatial optimization strategies is the opportunity to pay much lower wages along with the prospect of resisting demands for reasonable working conditions from local employees whose bargaining power is weak. Across much of the world, then, a 'casualization and informalization of labour' has been occurring where work lacks social protection and regulation and there is minimum expectation of work becoming permanent. This is a result of the 'withering' away of the former core, and relatively safe, work once available to members of the industrial working-class, coupled to the rise of both male and female employees who find themselves confined to the 'new legions of the precariat flitting between jobs ... with little security, few enterprise benefits and tenuous access to state benefits' (Standing 2009: 110 and 2011). Gottfried (2013: 221–2) shows how 'vulnerable' employment constitutes an even less secure version of informal labour and affects women particularly badly. It encompasses people who are mainly self-employed who either have no employees or use their own family members as unpaid workers. They face extremely 'variable and unpredictable economic conditions', lack any kind of protection or safety net and often rely entirely on their own resources. Vulnerable employment is increasing and in 2008 encompassed more than four-fifths of women in Sub-Saharan Africa (SSA) and South Asia (SA) but also high numbers of men.

The Dangers of Growing Inequality

The recent and marked shift towards inequality especially, though not only, in the advanced economies, probably constitutes the most potentially disruptive aspect of global capitalism today, and one that endangers its own long-term survival. Thus, in marked contrast to the middle decades of the last century, income and wealth have been accruing much more disproportionately towards the top decile of each population. But this skewed distribution grows in intensity in regard to the top centile (1 per cent) and this disproportionality continues as the percentage of receivers gets ever closer to 0.1 per cent—or the thousandth percentile. A number of researchers have investigated this topic, most notably the French economist Thomas Piketty. Recently Piketty produced an impressive amount of data and analysis in a much acclaimed book on inequality, economic growth and capitalism (2014: 294). In it he refers to the 'explosion' of inequality in the USA since 1980. The income share of the top 10 per cent rose from between 30 and 35 per cent in the 1970s to somewhere between 45 and 50 per cent in the 2000s—a rise of at least 15 points. As already mentioned, the bulk of this inequality is explained by the growing income share accruing to the top 1 per cent with the latter's share of national income growing from 9 per cent in the 1970s to approximately 20 per cent during the decade 2000–2010 (296). This is further proof of the argument concerning the productivity–wages gap developed in Chap. 2 above, since these figures demonstrate how a very large share of America's economic growth during these years ended up in the salary and bonus packets of the richest US citizens. Further evidence was provided early in 2016 when a gamut of think tanks, NGOs, and other organizations produced new data suggesting that inequality was worsening rapidly. Oxfam, for example, claimed that the world's 62 richest billionaires owned the same amount of wealth as the poorest half of the world's population, while the wealth owned by the latter contracted by 41 per cent between 2010 and 2015 even though their numbers rose by 400 million (Elliott 2016a: 1).

Similar figures for other Western countries bear out Piketty's basic case. In Britain, for example, Lansley (2011: 44–45) shows how from the early 1980s the share of the nation's rising output from economic growth going to wage earners began to decline. This had many causes, not least attacks on trade unions and de-industrialization policies, helped by high interest rates and the over-valued pound, stage-managed by the Thatcher government. But following a brief partial reversal of this trend during the early years of New Labour, this decline resumed with real increases in wages falling further behind the growth in productivity. The trend then accelerated from 2000 onwards (54–58).

Rising inequality also gives rise to several additional and related questions. First, we ask: what was the impact of the financial crisis of 2007–2008 on the incomes of top earners? Here, and contrary to expectations that such a severe crash would at least dent top earnings, the opposite appears to have occurred. Accordingly, in 2010 the top decile in the USA still took at least 46 per cent of the national income share—in some cases an even higher figure than for 2007–2008 (Piketty 2014: 296). In fact, in general, the super-rich seem to have emerged unscathed despite the fall in stock market values, unemployment and the vast number of mortgage defaults suffered by the less well-off majority which helped to pull down the leading banks. If top incomes did fall slightly, the incomes of many CEOs soon recovered and resumed their upward rise while the wealthy continued to absorb most of the gains from economic growth (Stiglitz 2013: 3–4).

A second obvious question raised by rising inequality concerns the degree to which super-earnings are deserved. In her discussion of the 'global plutocrats' (see Chap. 2) Freedland (2012) argued that irrespective of their main arenas of economic opportunity the super-rich from both the Global North and South form a 'transglobal community of peers' (5) who share very similar lifestyles and orientations. These include, upper-middle-class family origins, a very high level of education, often a technocratic as well as commercial talent and orientation, a determination to bestow their achievements onto their children, a very highly developed sense of their own heroic significance as world leaders and a similar proclivity to exploit political connections. Equally significant, many of the super-rich are first-generation entrepreneurs or leaders in technology so that inherited wealth from their families played little or even no part in their success.[1] Piketty, too, (2014: 334–5) raises the question of whether the huge and rising incomes taken by today's super-rich represents a form of 'meritocratic extremism' (334). On balance, and in contrast to Freedland, Piketty seems doubtful that this epithet is entirely justifiable. On one hand, he describes how the inherited wealth of the 'rentiers'—though still important in explaining inequality and likely to remain so—has become secondary to the wealth accumulated by a new class of managers from their unprecedentedly high incomes (276–8). At the same time, and like other observers, he points to the strong indications that due to the failures of corporate governance many top executives across all sectors are able to set their own salaries (334).[2] He further argues that variations in pay seem to bear little relationship to the performance of companies. Indeed, the rewards received by individual executives often vary according to the external or surreptitious factors affecting a company's sales and profits rather than anything that happens internally (334–5).

---

[1] If true, this may render them formidable enemies in any future struggle to share out the world's wealth and incomes more fairly through the kinds of measures suggested by Piketty (2014)—notably, an annual wealth tax plus a much more progressive income tax.

[2] This assessment is similar to that discussed by Dew-Becker and Gordon (2005)—outlined in Chap. 2, Sect. 2.2—where they describe the mutual back-scratching taking place between senior executives from different companies.

A third and crucial question concerns the impact that the widening gap between a tiny elite and everyone else is having on global capitalism as a whole. Here, a cacophony of recent voices joining in the chorus of concern has been remarkable. Thus, even conservative bodies such as the IMF and OECD warned in May 2015 that global economic growth and progress are being threatened by inequality (OECD 2015a, b).[3] The OECD, for example, reported that the world economy had reached a 'tipping point' with levels of inequality reaching the 'highest since records began'. This included a number of countries in the Global South such as Mexico, Chile and Turkey. It warned that future world economic growth is on a 'knife edge' because of growing inequality. Again, Piketty (2014) is absolutely clear about the past and future dangers to capitalism and to economic growth resulting from growing levels of inequality. For one thing, he reminds us that the share of US national income taken by the top decile has peaked twice during the last 100 years: in 1928 and 2007. Both events immediately preceded huge crises. Moreover, he uses the word 'transfer' to describe how almost 60 per cent of the value of US economic growth in the 30 years leading up to 2007–2008 was absorbed by the top 10 per cent of income earners while the bottom 90 per cent acquired the remainder. This comes out at less than 0.5 per cent a year in increased income for the vast bulk of the population.[4] As he observes in a particularly stark comment: it is difficult to understand how an economy and society 'can continue to function indefinitely with such extreme divergence between social groups' (297).

Tax—The Forbidden Path to Raising Revenue

Drawing on data compiled by the OECD for seven nations, Streek (2014: 63) shows how from a relatively low average base of around 36 per cent of GDP in 1970, government spending leapt ahead, reaching an average of 45 per cent in 2010. The media, the business lobby and

---

[3] See also the discussion in Chap. 8, Sect. 8.1.
[4] These figures help to explain why UNICEF figures on child poverty for 2012 reveal that the USA was ranked 34 out of 35 Western countries, just above Romania (UNICEF 2015).

neoliberal politicians usually argue that this crisis in public finances is a consequence of the ever-rising demands of citizens on democratic governments who then respond by increasing public spending in order to remain in office.[5] In fact the fiscal crisis has rather more to do with falling tax receipts in relation to economic growth (66). When government borrowing rose in the 1970s revenues from taxes were already falling behind spending. This gap between spending and receipts, the 'debt surge', and the rise of what Streek calls 'the debt state', accelerated markedly in the 1990s and again after the crisis of 2007–2008. One explanation for declining tax revenues was the growing ability of businesses to re-locate to countries with less onerous tax systems, helped by globalization (66–67). But in addition, government willingness to reduce the tax burden on capital and the wealthy was fuelled by neoliberal influence on politics and policy. Thus, as we have seen, not only were income tax rates on the rich hugely reduced but the principle of progressive taxation was more or less abandoned. Instead, a disproportionate share of the tax burden now falls on the less well-off, particularly in respect to higher taxes on consumption.

In effect this was tantamount to subsidizing the wealthy since they were the main winners from the boom years between the mid-1990s and 2007 while their incomes and assets increased rapidly, partly due to falling taxes (Streek 2014: 74–75). It perhaps goes without saying that the very idea of taking a leaf out of the mid-twentieth century policy of substantial wealth and income redistribution simply does not appear anywhere on the agendas of neoliberals or, indeed, of most other political parties. At the same time as governments were reducing the tax burden on the wealthy, they were also cutting back on welfare spending and those public services that mostly benefitted the less well-off. This has continued through the austerity policies widely adopted across Europe and elsewhere since 2008.

Three additional points follow from Streek's analysis of the crisis of the contemporary neoliberal debt state. One is that the embargo on tax increases is occurring at a time when public expenditure needs are

---

[5] In reality, of course, much of this public debt was due to governments stepping in in 2008 in order to 'nationalize' the financial losses created by the private banking system.

rising. This is linked to a number of present and future costs, which we consider elsewhere in this chapter. Particularly crucial, however, is the reality of an ageing society and therefore the burgeoning costs of health and social care at a time when technological advance is extending life expectancy. Second, while individual citizens are coping with stagnant or falling incomes, largely through accumulating increased private debt, governments are borrowing from international financiers by launching state bonds as the main lever for staving off the further collapse of public finance. But this only places governments and citizens at the mercy of global financial lenders—frequently the very same global plutocrats discussed in Chap. 2, as part of vampire capitalism, who secrete their wealth in tax havens and avoid paying even modest official tax rates. Streek (2014: 79–80) fears there is a danger these global creditors will demand economic policies that favour their interests rather than those of national electorates. As such they form a second and external 'constituency' of the debt state beyond the control of democratic politics. Recent years have certainly revealed many instances across the EU countries, for example in Italy, Greece and Spain, where massively onerous austerity policies have been imposed by governments on desperate populations in order to prevent borrowed foreign debts rising too far and triggering cripplingly high interest rates.

A third consequence of the taboo on raising taxes concerns the intergovernmental competition to reduce the fiscal demands on incoming business investment. Clearly this further accentuates the tendency for overall tax revenues to fall. As in the case of wages, governments and labour forces are locked into a race to the bottom in which it is increasingly likely there will be far more losers than winners. Considered overall, Streek's assessment concerning the prospect that future governments will succeed in winning additional revenue contributions to public spending by taxing the super-rich and corporations more effectively is depressing but doubtless realistic:

> Global liberalization, especially of capital markets, makes tax increases on high incomes and internationally mobile corporate profits appear so unrealistic that they are not even discussed. Tax increases would have to be pushed through against the trend of the last decade and a half. … If they

were in fact achieved, they would in all likelihood be limited to immobile sources—mainly in the form of social security contributions and sales taxes. (Streek 2014: 118)

Debt as a Way of Life (and the remaining driver of global growth?)

Paraphrasing Marx, Žižek (2014: 41) captures the widespread anxiety concerning the dimensions of debt in today's world among many economists, politicians and other informed observers, when he suggests that a 'spectre is haunting capitalism today—the spectre of debt'. He goes on to add that under neoliberalism debt has become a way of life for individuals just as much as for governments and private and public enterprises. As we saw in the previous chapter, alongside its virtual deification of market competition, neoliberalism has converted the citizen/worker into a personal capitalist-entrepreneur responsible for her own economic destiny. This 'individualization of social policy'—coupled to widespread privatization—means that everyone is expected to take out private insurance against unemployment or illness in place of shared welfare provision, to speculate in accumulating a private pension portfolio as state pensions fail to rise, or even fall, to take on debt in order to pay for higher education and, above all, to seek compensation for shrinking wages by using credit cards as the primary path to consumerism.

But like other observers (e.g. Streek 2014; Fisher 2009), Žižek points out that under neoliberalism the individual is expected to assume responsibility not only for herself but also for the environment, the economic system in general and national debts (43). Fisher (2009: 63) pushes this argument even further, pointing to the 'centerlessness of global capitalism' and the seeming absence of any 'overall controllers' except, perhaps, 'nebulous, unaccountable interests exercising corporate irresponsibility'. This situation leaves us desperate to find the missing centre (65), so we blame easily identifiable targets for crises, namely, individuals, whether these are particular citizens, politicians or company directors. In reality, of course, there is a centre and it exists in the shape of capitalism and its systemic failures. Unfortunately, and as presently constituted, 'what is there *is* not capable of exercising responsibility' (Fisher 2009: 65) and so we return once again to the individual.

Recent concrete data demonstrating the sheer quantity of different kinds of debt worldwide seem alarming. *The Economist's* 'Global Debt Clock', which concentrates on public or government debt, gave a figure worldwide of more than $57 trillion on 23 November 2015. Japan's approximate contribution to this overall figure was $12 trillion while the figures for India and the USA respectively were $1.5 trillion and nearly $16 trillion (*The Economist* 2015). Da Costa (2015), writing in the *Wall Street Journal*, provided figures measured in terms of overall national debt from all sources as a percentage of GDP. These figures gave China's overall debt in mid-2014 as equal to 282 per cent of its GDP, or $28 trillion. The same piece also observed that China's debt to GDP had risen from 121 per cent in 2000 to 158 per cent in 2007 before reaching 282 per cent in 2014. In actual figures China's economy had added almost $21 trillion in new debt since 2007. Clearly these figures verify the claim previously outlined that much of China's growth in the last few years has been augmented by a deliberate policy of spend and borrow (see also Hutton 2016: 40). However, nearly half of this debt was clocked up not by the government or the state banks but by non-financial corporations and included a huge volume of private investment in real estate.

A number of other countries also demonstrate ratios of overall national debt to GDP that are as high or nearly as high as China's. For example, the figures for Australia, USA and Germany respectively in mid-2014 were 274, 269 and 258 per cent. Turning to the question of government spending *per se*, as a proportion of these overall figures we find that in the USA, Germany and Canada, in contrast to China's 19 per cent, governments contribute the single highest amount: approximately one-third of the total in the case of America, 30 per cent for Germany and almost a quarter in Canada.

Given the neoliberal emphasis on the entrepreneurial self-made individual it is also necessary to consider the role of consumer spending. Certainly, as Streek (2014: 39–41) shows, household debt rose sharply from the 1990s in Italy, Sweden and other Scandinavian countries as well as in the USA and UK. One set of figures for the USA suggests that overall household debt was not far short of $12 trillion in October

2015, up by nearly 2 per cent from the previous year (Chen 2015). The largest proportion of this came from mortgage payments (more than $8 trillion) but nearly $1 trillion was linked to credit card debt—surely an indication of the extent to which workers' earnings have stagnated. For those households that were carrying debts, the average amount owed specifically on their credit cards was $16,140 in 2014. The average credit card debt for all households was rather less at $7259. Apparently, average US household debt peaked in early 2009 when it reached $19,000 for indebted households. Thereafter and for two years it fell back but this was due less to reduced consumer borrowing than to the credit card companies writing off some of the debts and restricting their lending.

Perhaps the most telling item in this story of American household and individual debt—one repeated across many other Western countries—is the steadily rising loan burden among future workers: namely students. The same study showed that the average US student's loan was nearly $32,000 in October 2015 and that in total such loans reached $1. 9 trillion. Thus, even before they have begun their lifetime career path most young adults have already embarked on a parallel trajectory whereby debt becomes an inescapable fate for all but those with very wealthy parents. Writing about why so many recent protest movements, from the Arab Spring to the Occupy Movement across many countries, have involved young people, Mason (2013: 66) pointed to the 'graduate with no future' forced to accept that she will most likely be poorer than her parents as one of the major explanations.

Student debt, however, is not the only obstacle youth are facing today. There is also a host of additional, future costs that did not encumber their parents or their 'baby boomer' grandparents to the same degree. Mason also outlines some of these (66–67). Depending on the nation in question, these include: the rising and high cost of rented accommodation and the exorbitant price of housing; the need to contribute a growing share of their future incomes to pay towards the care costs of an ever larger population of ageing people, hooked on ever more expensive health technologies; the reality of shrinking family and other welfare benefits as neoliberal austerity policies bite; the need in many instances to work longer for less while saving for their own pensions without the generous contributions once provided by many employers; and the future costs of cleaning up the damage to seas, forests, land, flora and fauna while dealing with climate change and the likely costs of absorbing millions of future environmental migrants.

The Failure to Re-regulate Finance

In his erudite book Gamble (2014) recently argued that the ability of Western governments to cope with the aftermath of the 2008 financial crisis was severely hampered by two main realities. One was the grip of neoliberal economic policies with their legacy of stagnant and falling living standards coupled to the insistence on dealing with public debt by continuing cuts to government spending and imposing austerity regimes. But alongside this, globalization has given rise to a more multipolar world of competing states. This renders attempts to improve international cooperation on issues relating to trade regulation, the flows of money, currencies, investments and so on more difficult, especially given the recent relative withdrawal of the USA from its former role as the world's hegemonic military and economic power. The result has been a slow and uneven recovery among the Western economies while domestic, government and private debt remain high and austerity policies continue to keep living standards and spending low.[6] All this risks the onset of a long period where economies stagnate, consumer spending stalls and prices begin to fall so that consumers respond by holding off their spending even more. Ultimately, all this risks slowing down economic growth in China and some other southern countries.

Gamble's fears of contagion, as deflation in the West undermines growth in the emerging southern economies, were borne out by the events of summer 2015. During the years after the 2007–2008 crisis, continuing high rates of economic growth in the emerging economies, particularly China, partly offset falling growth in the West. Indeed, Jayati Ghosh (2015) has argued that China's economic model since the early 1990s of low wages and export-led growth not only generated

---

[6] On the other hand, and throughout the recent period, cheap imports from China and elsewhere in the Global South have partly compensated for falling living standards in the West.

huge employment and development at home but also helped to drive growth in other emerging economies, as well as older Western ones such as Australia. This was because vast quantities of oil, raw materials, components and spare parts were needed to feed China's factories. But China did not escape the wider consequences of the 2007–2008 financial crisis altogether. In response to diminished demand for its manufactured goods from the West and in the attempt to retain its high rate of economic growth, the government encouraged provincial governments and public enterprises to increase their borrowing and investment. Consequently, as we have seen, debt in China increased fourfold between 2007 and 2014, fostering various speculative bubbles and a huge rise in property values. Ghosh (2015) concludes that China and the other emerging economies need to urgently find a different growth strategy, one less dependent on exports and rising debt (Ghosh 2015).

Meanwhile, by the late summer of 2015, China's growth had slowed to 7 per cent along with its exports of manufactures. Falling output from China's factories and slower economic growth fuelled a huge slide in the value of shares on the Shanghai stock market partly in response to the government's attempt to boost growth by devaluing the renminbi. Almost one trillion dollars flowed out of the emerging market economies, not just China, between June 2014 and July 2015 (Ryan 2015: 25). Then, in October 2015 the IMF picked up on this and other indications of world financial disorder and expressed concern that far too much credit was surging around the world. It went on to suggest that the emerging economies of the Global South, such as China, were particularly vulnerable to excessive borrowing as their main remedy for slowing growth (Inman 2015: 24).

Indeed, taking an overall view, one respected and seasoned observer, Will Hutton (2015: 36), summarized the continuing crisis by saying that the global financial order 'has gone rogue'. It continues to resist most attempts at reform in the aftermath of 2007–2008. Central to this is the reality that global banks 'now make profits to an extraordinary degree from doing business with each other' rather than by investing in directly productive enterprises. Meanwhile, money-capital continues to flow around the world unchecked with the constant risk that it will generate further speculative booms in commodities or real estate, followed by the financial collapse of entire national economies when hot money leaves as quickly as it came, as in the Asian economies in 1997, or lead to larger meltdowns on the scale of 2007–2008. But there is a much deeper problem, as Žižek (2011: 168) argues: namely, the 'structural impossibility of finding a global political order which might correspond to the global capitalist economy … that would match it'. Despite globalization we continue to live in an international system of sovereign nation states, each trying to guard its own borders, citizens and security systems from outside interference. Yet, looming overhead, largely disengaged from the geo-political system of governments and states, sits a mostly unregulated and interconnected globalized economy.

> **Case Study 2: Economic Discontent but Populist-Cultural Protest**
>
>> A large constituency of working-class voters feel that not only has the economy left them behind, but so has the culture, that the sources of their dignity, their dignity of labour, have been eroded and mocked by … globalisation, the rise of finance, the attention … on economic and financial elites. (Sandel 2016: 28–29)
>
> **Trumpism** By summer 2016 Donald Trump had emerged as the clear victor in the primary elections for the Republican Party presidential nomination. Many in the USA and worldwide were dismayed that someone who had expressed blatantly misogynistic, anti-immigrant, anti-Islamic and racist comments during his campaign could nevertheless win. Much of Trump's support came from working-class men who might normally have voted Democrat. Apparently they were attracted not just by Trump's obvious disdain for Washington elite politics but by promises to protect US industry from foreign competition and to discourage further 'offshoring'. These promises strongly appealed to people whose jobs have long been threatened by de-industrialization and globalization and who have endured decades of stagnant or falling real wages. Bernie Sanders's socialist agenda during the same contest for the Democratic presidential nomination, and his apparent appeal particularly to young, possibly better educated voters, also surprised political observers.[7]
>
> **Britain votes to leave the EU** During the referendum campaign in June 2016, Yougov, an international market research organization, compared the social characteristics of voters in each camp. The differences between

---

[7] Interestingly, Trump's share of the Republican vote in the industrial state of Michigan was 37 per cent, well ahead of Hillary Clinton.

(continued)

(continued)

the Brexit 'leavers' and the 'remainers' were revealing. The former were markedly older, less well educated and likely to hold manual jobs, or were casual workers, unemployed or state pensioners living in towns and rural areas. Regional differences were also evident. Londoners, people living in Scotland and Northern Ireland were strongly for 'remain' while people living in the North, Midlands and East of Britain—areas affected by decades of de-industrialization and by a strong presence of EU immigrants working in agriculture for low wages in poorly regulated working conditions—leaned heavily towards 'leave' (Yougov 2016). Indeed, the perception that EU immigrants were taking jobs, houses and school places from native Brits was blatantly evident. One academic commented that 'the referendum is a battle between the cosmopolitans and those who have had a less good deal from an increasingly global economy and the decline of Britain's manufacturing base' (Jennings 2016: 14). Other observers fleshed out these insights. One journalist declared that Britain was 'in the midst of a working-class revolt' by people who when interviewed on doorsteps said 'no one listens to us' (Harris 2016: 33). Following the narrow victory for Brexit on June 24 the post-election consensus regarding actual voting patterns bore out these deep divisions, particularly those around class and education.

Crises of cultural identity In both these instances economic deprivation has morphed not into a demand for stronger left-wing policies but rather a leaning towards populist/nationalist political leaders. The latter promise to prioritize the needs and cultural identities of the native population and reassert national autonomy in the face of globalization. A similar pattern is evident across the EU with the rise of right-wing populist parties in France, the Netherlands, Austria, Italy, Germany, Poland and Hungary, among others, especially since the late 1990s (Mudde 2007). Their ability to win a growing proportion of votes has contributed to the fracturing of democratic party politics. These parties are also highly critical of the EU and some are committed to leaving it, as with the UK Independence Party (UKIP) and Marie Le Pen's Front National in France. These parties regard political elites and mainstream parties as disinterested in the needs of ordinary citizens. Above all they are opposed to immigration policies. The recent study by Fieschi, Morris and Caballero (2012) looked at 'reluctant radicals' in eight EU countries. It found that these make up around 50 per cent of populist voters but they do not join particular parties. A relatively low level of educational attainment emerged as the single most 'consistent predictor' (11) of reluctant radicalism. Further, the reluctant radicals' dissatisfaction with the cultural impact of immigrants—particularly Muslims—on their sense of national belonging often outweighed their economic discontent linked to unemployment, de-industrialization and globalization (41).

4.2 Privatization, the Shrinking State and the Occluded Society

The battle between labour and capital over the distribution of rewards from productive enterprise is not the only long-term struggle generated by market capitalism. There is also the conflict and contradiction between what Streek (2014: 58) calls *market justice* and *social justice* (author's italics). This is a dichotomy not dissimilar to that outlined above in connection with Weber. Here, the one-dimensionality of capitalism compels its protagonists to progressively subordinate society, the state and its political processes, including democracy, to the overwhelming need to capture every activity and then shape these into forms capable of creating wealth through profit. Castoriadis's (2007: 93–94) take on this same theme is especially revealing. He insists that unlike previous historical regimes which mainly sought mastery over the politics of foreign societies, the striving for domination under capitalism is notable for two additional and unique features: the drive to subjugate and invade the 'totality of society' and not just production and consumption, and to do so through extending 'rationalization'—calculability—to every sphere of human affairs. Neoliberalism follows exactly this path. Indeed, it seeks to 'eliminate the very category of value in the ethical sense' (Fisher 2009: 16–17). Instead it 'has successfully installed' a business-only model while claiming that transferring all activities into the hands of capitalism is the only feasible and possible way forward.

Two familiar themes arise directly from this craving for endless new profitable opportunities. One concerns the neoliberal goal to shrink the state's involvement in the economy, though it is far from clear exactly what this involves. This was placed explicitly on Reagan's political agenda in his inaugural presidential address to the world in January 1981.[8] The other involves the demand to privatize public activities in order to 'free' private capitalism from stifling bureaucracy and allow it to engage in the kind of 'real' innovation and enterprise which will lead to economic

---

[8] Recall, though, the discussion in Chap. 3 which pointed out that neoliberals knowingly deploy the state in order to push and protect their marketization agenda. Outsourcing essential public functions to private firms while continuing to fund this out of taxation is quite different.

growth for all. Britain's Conservative Government in 2015 committed its supporters to just such a programme, which it legitimized in exactly these terms. Its stated intention is to reduce the state's share of national GDP from around 45 per cent in 2010 to about 36 per cent by 2020.

Following from this, and during the 1980s and 1990s, governments in many countries privatized certain public utilities completely. In doing so, however, they often backed the new private owners by continuing to provide sizeable state subsidies, as in the case of the fuel and power industry and rail networks in the UK—in contradiction to the ostensible logic behind privatization of reducing the burden on the public purse (Bowman et al. 2014: 11). Alternatively, governments outsourced an increasing number of public amenities, such as school meal services and prisons. In effect, such actions provide capitalism with 'soft' guaranteed commercial opportunities for profit since states usually remain committed to funding these activities from tax revenue. Though begun several decades ago and continued by the last Labour government, Britain's Conservative Coalition after 2010 pushed downsizing, selling-off and 'outsourcing' almost to an art form. Recently this even included selling the nation's Royal Mail at a seriously undervalued price. According to Jones (2014: 18–19), in 2012 alone the British government spent £4 billion on paying Serco, G4S, Atos and Capita for 'servicing' a number of Britain's public agencies, from prison management to administering and distributing welfare benefits including to disabled people. In effect, according to Jones, much of Britain's public sector has become a major source of profit for private companies. However, there is extensive evidence that the companies involved in this process have often done little to improve the services.

Meanwhile, and following the increase in public deficits after the 2008–2009 crisis, governments in the EU and elsewhere continue their budgetary struggles to cut welfare and other kinds of public spending while operating austerity policies. How successful these strategies will prove to be and with what consequences is not clear. Nevertheless, several critical reflections are necessary. First, the official justification for these policies is the importance, especially at a time of national indebtedness, of reducing the tax burden on citizens while cutting out the unnecessary and inefficient practices that were allegedly rife when these services were publicly owned. Some have suggested these inefficient practices included: the wasteful process of paying decent, living wages to workers while providing permanent work, appropriate training and reasonable pension prospects—and this at a time when many private sector employees had to increasingly accept zero-hours contracts. The savings on labour costs, made possible by privatization, is mostly code for lower wages and reduced employment security. In contrast, however, the following are not usually included in the plan to reduce labour costs: the new or additional salaries and bonuses paid to managers and CEOs, dividends to shareholders, payments to PR advisors, marketing and advertising companies, the cost of acquiring smart brand images and logos plus various consultants—and all the other inevitable adjuncts of private enterprise.

A second concern is that the long-run intention of many governments and political parties, and certainly the British Conservatives, is to engage in much deeper attempts to downsize the state through privatizing far broader swathes of the public sector. Here, for example, government obligatory services, including the British National Health Service (NHS), would not only be put out to private tender but sold off entirely to private capital. At a stroke, such policies would reduce government spending and create new arenas available to the market.[9] But at the same time, if current experience is any guide—including the story of private medicine in the USA—such privatized public services will mean citizens end up paying a lot more in private insurances, fees and prices than they ever paid in tax. At the same time, they are likely to receive medical services that, except in the case of the wealthy who can afford them, are mostly of lower quality.

Lastly, Mazzucato's *The Entrepreneurial State* (2011) fundamentally challenges the standard neoliberal argument that private business is always more lean, efficient and above all innovatory and entrepreneurial than the state and public activity. In common with other researchers Mazzucato argues that a number of major new technologies were not only funded by governments, but state agencies played the leading role in advancing

---

[9] Such 'real' tax cuts will also leave the rich substantially better off, since—unlike everyone else—many already fund their educational, health and other services out of private funds so falling taxes will provide a bonus.

Schumpeterian-type innovations based on the 'creative destruction' that generates increased growth and wealth vastly in excess of the processes destroyed by the same change. Frequently it is governments rather than private companies that take on the most risky innovative projects with uncertain outcomes but which lead to 'general purpose technologies' (GPTs). These are later diffused across the economy as a whole. The large-scale, very long-term perspective required for such developments, in addition to the vast sums of investment they require, often place such GPTs beyond the capacity of private firms who have to keep shareholders and rival businesses at bay while constantly bringing a stream of both old and new products onto the market with proven or testable marketable qualities.

Mazzucato (2011) lists the following as examples of recent technological developments where the state was the lead investor: various aviation technologies; space technologies; nuclear energy; the Internet; much of the bio-technology industry; some pharmaceutical products; and nanotechnology. In addition, governments or their agents took a targeted and highly proactive role in bringing these innovations to a point where they were ready to be marketed by private companies, often based on networks which the state had also prepared. Writing about Silicon Valley, she observes that it was 'built upon decades of state-led vision around the power of the Internet, decades of investment in the riskiest research, and decades of nurturing regional innovations systems and new company start-ups' (3). Unfortunately, it is private capitalist companies that usually reap the long-term financial rewards from the wider deployment of these technological breakthroughs. They also generally receive most of the praise from politicians and media people who either do not understand the essentially collective nature of innovatory activity or who choose not to do so in case it undermines the public's faith in the 'magic' of the market. Partly, however, this misunderstanding of the entrepreneurial state is also due to the fact that the public agencies largely responsible for such innovations are kept hidden from view.

The wider implication of this and the previous points is clear. By insisting on shrinking the state and endlessly trumpeting the virtues of cutting public spending, capitalism and its political and other protagonists are in serious danger of exposing economic life—and therefore the rest of us—to a series of self-destructive reactions.

4.3 The Twin Treadmills: Perpetual Competition and Economic Growth

The United Nation Development Programme (UNDP) has been committed for some time to pursuing notions of human development that move away from the sole emphasis on material improvement. Accordingly, in assessing the quality of life different people experience, its *Human Development Index* (see Therborn 2013: 103–7) incorporates measures of life expectancy, education and the effects of inequality in differentially shaping the quality of people's lives in addition to income. Despite this, the goal of economic growth measured in terms of GDP remain the dominant concern of most governments. The primary evidence sought after and picked over by rival politicians, economists, journalists, trade union leaders and other national and international observers invariably concerns changing rates of economic growth, budget and trade deficits or surpluses, changes in per capita GDP, the prospect of increasing the numbers living on more than $2 per day and so on—all rated against international comparisons.

In this mind-set, the possibility of thinking along entirely different lines concerning the task of improving the lives of most humans is frequently blocked out. As we saw in the previous section, debates on economic policy 'have been gripped by an imaginary about competition and markets' (Bowman et al. 2014: 1) in which these are the cure for all economic woes. Moreover, it is assumed that 'the universal prescription of greater competition can be applied confidently to economic problems at the level of the individual worker, consumer, firm, sector, city, region or nation' (9–10). When it comes to larger questions of social justice, the survival of the planet, the social as well as economic dangers of inequality, or whether economic growth led by private business is always the most efficacious path to overcoming poverty, we are more likely to encounter deafening silence than serious debate by most politicians and business representatives. The exception to this occurs when economic and political leaders are temporarily facing the full gaze of the world's media, as at the World Economic Forum at Davos each January or during UN-sponsored international forums such as the Paris environmental conference of December 2015. What are the main dangers and contradictions implicit in capitalism's one-dimensionality, considerably toughened by decades of neoliberal policy-dogma, and the insecurities brought by globalization?

(1) Seductive voices promise us that once the current period of faltering growth is past the new technologies coming 'on-stream', along with the benefits of neoliberal 'reform' and the rise of economic vibrancy across the Global South, will usher in a new 'growth cycle'. This will propel several hundred million more people over the $1.25 or $2 per day poverty threshold.[10] However, there are several difficulties with this argument. One is that neoliberal policy proscriptions seem to have produced an economic model which runs along very narrow tracks while excluding alternative policy agendas. Certainly, without a general raising of wage levels—so that effective demand increases along a wide front—it is difficult to see how growth can be sustained or sufficiently high to make substantial inroads into world poverty. In any case, even if economic growth does occur, despite these built-in constraints, much or even most of this new wealth seems destined to end up in the secret bank accounts of vampire capitalist elites rather than being re-cycled into productive investment. There are few indications that many perceive and acknowledge growing inequality and the predatory character of much contemporary capitalist activity, in general, as problems requiring urgent resolution.

(2) As we have seen, many respected observers have questioned the prospects for long-term economic growth in the absence of major policy changes and reforms (e.g. Stiglitz, Freedman and Lansley). However, additional voices paint a more serious, long-term and restrained picture of world growth prospects notwithstanding the current situation. The sheer weight of historical and contemporary data and the

---

[10] The latter is obviously to be welcomed but less so when the same growth allows many who currently own two cars to purchase a third or if it means the very rich invest in yet more scenic properties in various global cities.

acuity of the analysis recently presented by Piketty (2014) lend his argument particular force. He shows how the economic growth which accelerated in Europe during the nineteenth century was driven both by a rising population and technological change. As the latter became more sophisticated it simultaneously required that human capital or labour be better trained and educated. Eventually, the share of economic growth accruing to labour increased while that of capital fell, particularly during the period from 1914 to the 1970s. Interestingly, during these same middle decades of the twentieth century average world per capita output growth rates were also considerably higher than the long-term average: 2.8 per cent from 1950 to 1970 compared to 0.9 between 1820 and 1913 and 1.7 from 1980 to 2012 (94). Looking to the future Piketty argues that although further technological change will continue to permit economic growth the latter is unlikely to increase much beyond the long-term average of around 1 to 1.5 per cent. Beyond 2050 this percentage may turn out to be even lower. This is partly due to the fact that the rate of world population growth is gradually slowing, though it continues to rise in absolute terms. But there is also another aspect. Although advancing technology upgrades the skills of some humans,[11] it also creates more capital in the form of buildings, equipment, robots, infrastructure, patent rights and so on. Piketty suggests that this has two profound long-term implications. One is that because 'technology, like the market, has neither limits nor morality' a continued rise in 'economic and technological rationality' does not necessarily mean there will be a parallel and equal improvement in human well-being and the evolution of a fairer, more democratic society. His second conclusion forms one of the main theses of his entire book. Whenever economic growth is stagnant or low, and falls below the average return on capital stock—whether land, buildings, minerals, factories, stocks and shares, and so on—the latter will increase in value faster than society's overall income. The owners will therefore not only maintain their stock of wealth but new savings and

---

[11] As we well see in the next chapter, there is a growing debate suggesting that this future skill enhancement is likely to require and therefore benefit only minorities of highly educated people.

returns on this wealth will allow them to acquire more and become even richer. Thus, capitalist industrialization and the technological revolutions of the last 200 years have transformed the material conditions of life for many but they have not 'altered the deep structures of capital or … truly reduced the macroeconomic importance of capital relative to labour' (234).

(3) A major rationale for economic growth is that it provides the only or the most promising path to reducing poverty. Among the reasons for doubting this assumption are the following. First, overcoming poverty has always depended just as much, if not more, on successful collective and organized resistance by trade unions and worker's parties, on unique events such as major wars and on the redistributive policies deliberately imposed by governments, currently outlawed by neoliberal politics. Second, poverty is invariably associated with and partly caused by different kinds of extreme inequality. In the USA, still one of the richest countries in the world, the income of the poorest decile is below the average for all such groups across the 30 member states making up the group of OECD nations (cited in Therborn 2013: 42–43). In a very real sense, then, the incidence of poverty exists in relation to the wider facts of wealth and income distribution in a given country. Indeed, using the same OECD data for 2008, Therborn shows that the rates of poverty were highest in the three most unequal countries: Mexico, Turkey and, again, the USA.

(4) There is increasing evidence that economic growth is also coming up against certain limits as indicated by climate change and environment destruction. Chapter 7 examines this theme in considerable detail. For the moment, however, we point to the growing consensus that economic growth and industrialization have already harmed the planet's bio-system and natural diversity and is giving rise to climate change. As this escalates the poorest and least protected people, living in countries with weak, failing states, will generally be the worst affected. Rising sea levels are already driving millions of Bangladeshis away from their farms in the tributaries of the river Brahmaputra and

its delta and threatening the future of many small island states.[12] Such distress will be accompanied by mass environmental migration to the richer countries. There are also fears that conflicts over dwindling resources, particularly water, are likely to trigger wars over the control of shared river systems.

(5) Several demographic time bombs also complicate the prospects for future economic growth. The rate of world population growth has slowed in recent decades as birth control programmes and the gradual empowerment of women, especially through education, have reduced the birth rate, excepting the very poorest countries. Nevertheless, demographers predict that by mid-century the world's population will reach around nine billion people and may continue rising to perhaps 11 billion later in the century. It is currently just over 7 billion. Finding sufficient jobs, water, food and living space for so many people, especially given the other problems outlined in this and previous chapters, constitutes only one dimension of this scenario. There are least two others. First, across much of the Global South—China is a key exception because of its earlier 'one child per family policy'—at least 50 per cent of the population is under the age of 25. This proportion is particularly high in SSA and in the Middle East and North Africa (MENA). This additional youthful labour power is potentially good for economic growth but only if viable employment incomes are available for most. But, to give one example, IMF figures for 2010 revealed that this was not the case in MENA in 2009 where youth unemployment was 25 per cent—higher than in any other world region (Ahmed 2012: 1). Second, in the Western countries, and also China, the opposite situation exists: an ageing population whose elderly people require ever more expensive care and advanced medical treatment. However, the same demographic transition towards an ageing society is also taking place quite quickly across the Global South. It is estimated that by 2050 there will 1.5 billion people over the age of 65, equal to 16 per cent of the

---

[12] These have now formed their own environmental interest group—the Alliance of Small Island States (AOSIS)—and worked to shape the discussions and agreement at the Paris COP conference in December 2015.

world's population, whereas it was only 5 per cent in 1950 (Population Reference Bureau 2011: 2). Projected figures for some European countries, including Germany, Italy and UK are particularly high. However, with static or declining populations, as birth rates fall, and as the relative proportion of younger working people capable of generating sufficient wealth to fund the needs of the elderly declines, the question arises as to the affordability of an ageing society. Increased inward migration offers one solution. Indeed, the UK and other health systems already depend on foreign trained nurses and doctors from the Global South. But as in the case of environmental migration will such large flows be tolerated? Populist hostility or wariness across the EU countries towards the inflow of Syrian refugees in summer 2015 were not encouraging.

(6) The treadmill of non-stop economic growth, along with all its risks and dangers, is not all we have to fear. Neoliberalism demands that we must also factor generalized competition into our situation. Until the end of time, we are to be locked into a scrabble for advantage by constantly up-grading our individual skills in the hope of minutely out-performing every worker who shares the same skills or level of education across the world. Images of small caged rodents, trapped in a whirling wheel whose exit they have forgotten, readily come to mind. Similarly, each of the world's 200 national economies will endlessly strive to raise productivity and/or reduce costs and wages, or stage a technical leap by some minute fraction in the attempt to push up their nation's slice of world markets before another economy catches up and takes the lead or snatches their earlier hard-won advantage back again. In any case, as Mattel (2012: 313) argues, it is difficult to view the obsession with economic growth as anything other than a 'merely quantitative function (production for the sake of production)'.[13] These scenarios sound more like nightmares than rational future projects for intelligent people.

---

[13] Matei's next sentence continues as follows: 'The need for private goods is created (or invented) by manipulating demand by means of specific and massive investments called marketing'.

4.4 Summary and Conclusions

Governments and politicians seem in thrall to neoliberal market-babble with its endless hymn to the wonders of competition, public sector retrenchment and reverence towards wealth 'makers'. Together with globalization and financialization, the changes brought by neoliberalism have effectively placed capitalist economies, especially in the West, into a gridlock. Any reform that falls outside neoliberal-speak or which is predicated on placing constraints on the finance industry and/or moderating the impact of extreme global openness is effectively banned. The result is a growth model which calls for growing extremes of wealth and inequality, a constant squeeze on the real wages earned by the vast majority of citizens, rising personal debt, the central role of the 'debt state' (Streek 2014)—because governments are not permitted to raise taxes—and constant demands to allow private enterprise to invade and commercialize every aspect of human endeavour.

But there are obvious contradictions embedded in this array of policy commands. The lack of effective demand worldwide, except among the very wealthy and the new middle classes in the Global South, hits profits and deters growth-producing investment. Even influential IGOs such as the IMF and OECD have recently begun to doubt the wisdom of their own previous conservative policy pronouncements, as we will see in Chap. 8. Second, without direct state support some long-term innovations with a potential to foster wider economic growth will either not take place or will prove too fragile to make much difference. Third, there is no guarantee that shrinking the state and creating more space for private capitalism will generate faster growth. Partly this is because vampire capitalists siphon off a disproportionate share of growing wealth into non-productive ventures or tax havens, rather than re-investing it in the real economy or permitting it to raise general living standards. But in addition the ability of the financial industries to divert savings and wealth into speculative investments associated with the stock market, derivatives and so on further undermines the prospect of real job creation through an expanding economy.

Fourth, if an expanding private capitalism takes over the area left vacant by the shrinking state, but in the process further reduces average wages and raises the costs of the services it provides, then inequality will increase further and welfare compensation will contract. How falling wages, rising living costs, disappearing welfare and the mass poverty and distress that results is supposed to help capitalism and modernity to survive remains a mystery. Even if the world suddenly charges forward onto new uplands of economic growth, driven, perhaps by unfolding technological paradigms and the long-awaited advantages of freer market forces, it is difficult to believe that the rewards will reach most people or will be sufficient to outweigh the current brakes pressing down on whatever wheels of economic recovery there may be.

Certainly, we are entitled to question the necessity and the wisdom of condemning humanity to tread the mills of economic growth and endless competition for ever. This is particularly the case when we remember two key points. One is that wealth redistribution and evening out income flows is at least as effective in reducing poverty among the world's poorest people as economic growth. But second, we now understand that human material wants have no natural limits. Unless replaced by a different social ethos 'the machinery of want-generation will carry on' relentlessly, despite the many dangers and risks it brings (Skidlesky and Skidelsky 2012: 70).

Bibliography

Ahmed, M. (2012). *Youth unemployment in the MENA Region: Determinants and challenges.* International Monetary Fund. Retrieved August 8, 2016, from https://www.imf.org/en/News/Articles/2015/09/28/04/54/vc061312

Bowman, A., Froud, J., Johal, S., Law, J., Leaver, A., Moran, M., & Williams, K. (2014). *The end of the experiment: From competition to the foundational economy.* Manchester: Manchester University Press.

Brubaker, R. (1984). *The limits of rationality: An essay on the social and moral thought of Max Weber.* London: Allen and Unwin.

Castoriadis, C. (2007). [electronic publication date] *Figures of the unthinkable.* [Anonymous translation.] Retrieved August 9, 2016, from http://www.notbored.org/FTPK.pdf

Chen, T. (2015) *American household credit card debt statistics: 2015*. Retrieved August 9, 2016, from https://www.nerdwallet.com/blog/credit-card-data/average-credit-card-debt-household/

Da Costa, P. N. (2015, February 4). China's total debt load equal 282 per cent of GDP, raises economic risks. *Wall Street Journal*. Retrieved August 9, 2016, from http://blogs.wsj.com/economics/2015/02/04/chinas-total-debt-load-equals-282-of-gdp-raising-its-economic-risks/

Dardot, P. and Laval, C. (2013). *The new way of the World: On neo-liberal society* (trans: Elliot, G.). London: Verso.

Dew-Becker, I. and Gordon, R. J. (2005). *Where did the productivity growth go? Inflation dynamics and the distribution of income*. National Bureau of Economic Research. Retrieved August 9, 2016, from http://www.nber.org/papers/w11842

Elliott, L. (2016a, January 1). Richest 62 people as wealthy as half the world's population, says Oxfam. *The Guardian*. Retrieved August 9, 2016, from https://www.theguardian.com/business/2016/jan/18/richest-62-billionaires-wealthy-half-world-population-combined

Fieschi, C., Morris M. and Caballero, L. (2012). *Recapturing the reluctant radical: How to win back Europe's populist vote*. Online: Counterpoint. Retrieved August 10, 2016, from http://counterpoint.uk.com/wp-content/uploads/2013/02/E-version-Recapturing-the-Reluctant-Radical-September-2012.pdf

Fisher, M. (2009). *Capitalist realism: Is there no alternative?* Winchester: Zero Books.

Freeland, C. (2012). *Plutocrats: The rise of the new global super-rich and the fall of everyone else*. New York: Penguin.

Gamble, A. (2014). *Crisis without end? The unravelling of western prosperity*. Basingstoke: Palgrave.

Ghosh, J. (2015, August 23). Is the game up for China's much emulated growth model? *The Guardian*. Retrieved August 10, 2016, from https://www.theguardian.com/commentisfree/2015/aug/23/china-growth-model-brics

Gottfried, H. (2013). *Gender, work, and economy: Unpacking the global economy*. Cambridge: Polity.

Hutton, W. (2015, October 11). The world economic order is collapsing and this time there seems no way out. *The Guardian*. Retrieved August 10, 2016, from https://www.theguardian.com/commentisfree/2015/oct/11/world-order-collapse-refugees-emerging-economies-china-slowdown-recession

Hutton, W. (2016, January 17). *Why are we looking on helplessly as markets crash all over the world? The Guardian*. Retrieved August 10, 2016, from https://www.theguardian.com/commentisfree/2016/jan/17/china-economic-crisis-world-economy-global-capitalism

Inman, P. (2015, October 7). Risk of global financial crash has increased, warns IMF. *The Guardian*. Retrieved August 10, 2016, from https://www.theguardian.com/business/2015/oct/07/risk-global-financial-crash-increased-imf-emerging-economies-eurozone-stability-report

Jennings, W. (2016, July 5). North v south, young v old—The new political faultlines. *The Guardian*. Retrieved August 10, 2016, from http://www.theguardian.com/politics/2016/jun/04/eu-referendum-campaign-polls-fault-lines-politics

Jones, O. (2014, August 9). "It's socialism for the rich and capitalism for the rest of us in Britain." *The Guardian*. Retrieved August 10, 2016, from https://www.theguardian.com/books/2014/aug/29/socialism-for-the-rich

Lansley, S. (2011). *The cost of inequality: Why economic equality is essential for recovery*. London: Gibson Square.

Mason, P. (2013). *Why it's still kicking off everywhere: The new global revolutions*. London: Verso.

Mazzucato, M. (2011). The entrepreneurial state. *Renewal: A Journal of Social Democracy, 19*(3/4), 1–11. http://www.renewal.org.uk/articles/the-entrepreneurial-state/

McMicheal, P. (2000). *Development and social change: A global perspective*. Thousand Oaks, Ca.: Pine Forge.

Mudde, C. (2007). *Populist radical right parties in Europe*. Cambridge: Cambridge University Press.

Organization for Economic Cooperation and Development. (2015a). *Improving job quality and reducing gender gaps are essential to tackling poverty*. Retrieved August 9, 2016, from http://www.oecd.org/social/reducing-gender-gaps-and-poor-job-quality-essential-to-tackle-growing-inequality.htm

Organization for Economic Cooperation and Development. (2015b). *In it together: Why less inequality benefits all*. Retrieved August 11, 2016, from http://www.oecd.org/social/in-it-together-why-less-inequality-benefits-all-9789264235120-en.htm

Pew Research Center. (2014). *For most workers real wages have barely budged for decades*. Retrieved August 11, 2016, from http://www.pewresearch.org/fact-tank/2014/10/09/for-most-workers-real-wages-have-barely-budged-for-decades/

Piketty, T. (2014). *Capital in the twenty-first century*. Cambridge, MA: The Belknap Press.
Population Reference Bureau. (2011). Retrieved August 8, 2016, from http://www.prb.org/Publications/Articles/2011/agingpopulationclocks.aspx
Rifkin, J. (1995). *The end of work: The decline of the global labour force and the dawn of the post-market era*. New York: Putnam Publishing.
Ryan, F. (2015, August 18). China's flight of capital causes global ripples. *The Guardian*. Retrieved August 11, 2016, from https://www.theguardian.com/world/2015/aug/19/chinas-flight-of-capital-causes-global-ripples
Sandel, M. (2016, June 10–16). The energy of the Brexiteers and Trump is born of the failure of elites. *New Statesman*. Retrieved August 11, 2016, from http://www.newstatesman.com/politics/uk/2016/06/michael-sandel-energy-brexiteers-and-trump-born-failure-elites
Standing, G. (2009). *Work after globalization: Building occupational citizenship*. Cheltenham: Edward Elgar.
Standing, G. (2011). *The precariat: The new dangerous class*. London: Bloomsbury Academic.
Stiglitz, J. (2013). *The price of inequality*. London: Penguin.
Streek, W. (2014). *Buying time: The delayed crisis of democratic capitalism*. London: Verso.
The Economist. (2015). *The global debt clock*. Retrieved August 11, 2016, from http://www.economist.com/content/global_debt_clock
Therborn, G. (2013). *The killing fields of inequality*. Cambridge: Polity.
Weber, M. (1968). *Economy and society, Volume 1*. New York: Bedminster Press.
Weber, M. (1992). *The protestant ethic and the spirit of capitalism*. London: Routledge.
Žižek, S. (2011). *Living in the end times*. London: Verso.
Žižek, S. (2014). *Trouble in paradise: From the end of history to the end of capitalism*. London: Allen Lane.

5

The Juggernaut of Science and Technology: Friend or Foe?

In this chapter we turn to questions concerning the involvement and the culpability of science and technology in forging both the advantages and the risks confronting us today. As we saw in Chap. 1, the contemporary world was not made by capitalism alone, even though it has largely hijacked science and technology in the pursuit of profit. Nor does the instrumental rationality that dominates capitalism spring solely from relentless wealth accumulation. The drive to modernity carried its own overwhelming obsession with pursuing material and other kinds of progress. Lying at the core of modernity's precepts and ambitions, too, was an emphasis on scepticism and critical reflection, and the need to question knowledge and test it against independent truth criteria. These powerful orientations originated primarily in the Scientific Revolution and the Enlightenment.[1] Given this background, the central role of science and technology in the origins and trajectory of modernity is hardly surprising. In countless ways, too, science has also facilitated the relentless march of capitalism, and of course, the latter has been a major funder

---

[1] These are discussed more thoroughly in Chap. 1 along with notions of modernity and modernization and their intersections with capitalism.

of scientific development. Thus, when we try to weigh the innumerable gains from science—in medicine, food production, energy and transport, global communication systems and much else besides—against the little understood future dangers we may face from genetic technology, climate change, AI and so on, it is not always clear whether we should hold science or capitalism accountable or both.

We explore the recent but also the contemporary role of science and technology in our lives in respect to three central themes. First, we look at the evidence exploring the impact of technological change, particularly the digital revolution, on current and future employment and income opportunities. Then, we focus on the more general claim that science's contribution to capitalist modernity has generated the world risk society. Here, the principles of modernity now threaten the very institutions that capitalist modernity created. Last, and partly because of technological change, we consider the condition now faced by a growing number of people of being structurally irrelevant to capitalism, rather than simply unemployed, and argue that a workless future now beckons billions of world citizens.

5.1 Technology and the Future of Employment

Throughout most of history technological development was not driven solely by the needs of profit or the intellectual curiosity and technical skills of inventors. Instead, tools and technical knowledge were held in common by extended families or communities for use in agriculture, hunting and the construction of symbolic projects such as Stonehenge. Later, the needs of state systems as determined by their political and military rulers were paramount in determining whether and how technology was produced or deployed. At times this took the form of suppressing certain inventions in order to prevent social distress among artisans whose livelihoods might be harmed by their free operation. The refusal by Queen Elizabeth I to grant a patent for the stocking frame-knitting machine in 1589 on these grounds is an interesting case in point (Frey and

Osborne 2013: 6). In stark contrast, capitalism transformed the course of technological change because of its need to capture the improvements taking place in large areas of science and technology. This was a key part of its drive to create value and 'reduce the collective power of work and transfer returns from workers to capitalists' (Evans and Tilly 2016: 653). This was possible because whether in the form of machinery or control over the intellectual patent rights of the ideas and systems that made it possible, technology is a form of capital buttressed by legally enforceable rights in private or public property ownership, recognized and protected by the state. At the macro-level, economists have always recognized that creating and harnessing more advanced technologies and so raising the workforce's productivity lies at the heart of long-term growth in the economy as a whole.

In contrast, some observers have hoped that technical advances would one day enable humanity to overcome scarcity to such an extent that work time could be reduced, perhaps to a few hours a week. People would then be empowered to spend more time engaged in creative leisure and social activities. Writing in 1930 Keynes famously predicted this outcome for his grandchildren. However, as Skidelsky and Skidelsky (2012: Chap. 1) observed, Keynes failed to take into account that the majority of citizens would not be satisfied with fulfilling their material needs but would be highly susceptible to pursuing an endless spiral of wants manufactured both by their own imaginations and by the creative inventiveness of capitalism. Indeed, left to its own devices capitalism's 'machinery of want-generation will carry on churning, endlessly and pointlessly' (70) while penetrating and commoditizing ever more areas of social life in the search for profitable accumulation. At the same time this perpetual growth based on tempting consumers to desire new products helps to ensure that there will be sufficient employment for workers despite the constant replacement of human labour with machines (Frayne 2016: 623).

Technology Until the 1970s: A Respite for Employment

Paradoxically and despite growing fears that technological change has been reducing employment in a number of occupations, there has been a huge increase during the last 50 years or so in the numbers of people who are either in paid employment or seeking it. In the Global South this is mainly due to population increase coupled with the rural migration of distressed farmers and agricultural workers into the cities—often in the face of land loss, competition from large capitalist farms, or falling prices for their products. The most notable force swelling the demand for paid employment in the advanced countries—though this has also been happening in countries such as Brazil and Egypt—has been the huge rise in female employment: for example, from 49 to 69 per cent in the USA between 1970 and 1990 and from 48 to 61 per cent in Japan (Beck 2000: 39). In the USA rising employment is also linked to legal and undocumented migration flows, mainly from Hispanic peoples and who then tend to have bigger families. Similarly, the EU's agreement on free labour movement has made it possible for many skilled and unskilled people to move from the poorer regions of Eastern Europe—and from regions outside the EU, whether as refugees or as economic migrants—towards the most prosperous nations, such as Germany, in search of employment. As with much earlier inflows of ex-colonial labour migrants into Britain from the Caribbean and South Asia, and into France from North Africa, during the 1950s and 1960s, some of the more recent EU and non-EU migrants tend to have higher birth rates. Their larger families compensate for falling family size among native Europeans. Of course, within this overall rise in the economically active population looking for work there are also some casualties caused by heightened competition for the best-paid and most secure jobs. This has caused resentment across the EU among those native citizens who end up either unemployed or compelled to accept insecure, poorly paid 'McJobs'. These are often young males with limited education, or older workers whose skills are no longer required. In turn, such resentments are strongly linked to the rise of populist, right-wing, nationalist parties (Fieschi, Morris and Caballero 2012; Mudde 2007; and Liang 2007. See also Case Study 2 in Chap. 4).

As already indicated, since at least the mid-nineteenth century, capitalists have used advancing machine technologies of different kinds not only as a device for improving worker productivity but also in order to replace human workers with units of capital. These were the property of the entrepreneur and shareholders but that wasn't their only advantage. Machines do not require or demand training, tea breaks, holidays, pensions, health benefits and so on. Nor do machines tend towards acts of protest or subversion. When Marx was writing about British industrial capitalism it was skilled craftsmen and artisans that capitalists were most concerned to replace with machinery. But for some time, their ability to perform highly specialized tasks, a result of long periods of training, and their central role in manufacturing products but also as tool makers and repairers, as men who could maintain machines and so on, at a time when many factories were still only partially mechanized, made them indispensable. Their skills also meant they were quasi-independent and able to demand relatively high wages. Indeed, the rise and adoption of Taylorist work practices across many industries in the early twentieth century was partly motivated by the desire to capture the shop-floor knowledge and skills possessed by craft workers and then incorporate them into an increasingly mechanized production system (Montgomery 1987).[2] Replacing the craftsman were machines, designed, invented and supervised by a growing class of professional technicians and managers. The worker who then became the mainstay of Fordist production was the deskilled machine operator, slotted, as a very tiny specialized cog, into a vast, integrated production system. In principle and often in practice the Fordist system considerably enhanced capitalist and management control over a largely semi-skilled workforce while it also hugely increased worker productivity and therefore the ability to pay higher wages.

Fordist manufacturing techniques spread through a number of key industries, including wider car production, but also into many industrializing economies as the twentieth century wore on (see readings in Amin 1994). Several additional socio-economic changes were either directly linked to the Fordist industrial era, or else helped to underpin its success. One of these was increased social mobility as middle-class occupations expanded rapidly and far beyond the capacity of existing upper-middle-class families to provide enough children to fill the vacant and growing occupational niches. As we have seen, a key strand in this

---

[2] Writing about factories in late-nineteenth-century America, Montgomery (1987) wrote how very often skilled workers at this time possessed 'the manager's brain' under their workmen's caps.

process of upward social movement involved the rise of professional engineers, designers, scientific researchers, technicians and others, both in the private and the expanding public sectors, along with the expansion of secondary and tertiary education. Higher wages among manual workers also spurred the demand for new products and services and therefore for additional professionals and businesses engaged in the media and entertainment industries, leisure and tourism, as well as the production of consumer goods. Meanwhile, the increased significance of administration, banking, shopping, wholesale distribution and so on also created an expanding need for clerical, office, retail and other employees, recording, communicating and checking an ever-growing volume of minute business and other transactions. In short, technological change in the first half of the twentieth century generated a wide range of additional and complementary employment both within and outside the factory.

Following from this, Rifkin (1995) and others point to a second important process that continued until the 1970s. Thus, despite the increased mechanization of industry and rising worker productivity, as machines were refined and improved, job losses in manufacturing did not generally lead to technical unemployment. This was because higher productivity and wage savings either encouraged businesses to increase their investment in existing plant or to seek new business ventures. Moreover, the combination of falling prices as productivity rose along with the higher wages earned by those workers who kept their jobs increased the money in consumers' pockets. This then created a demand for new kinds of goods and services and therefore additional jobs while fuelling economic growth. Rifkin (1995) further argued that this benevolent spiral, whereby technological advance and rising productivity created widespread compensatory employment, was buttressed by additional changes that also generated positive effects on employment, though these proved to be of a temporary or one-off nature. These included: the adoption of Keynesian demand-management policies across the Western economies, a vast expansion in the public sector, including building or extending a welfare state, and Cold-War military spending by the USA from the 1940s.

From the 1970s, however, observers were confronted with declining or disappearing textile, mining, steel, ship-building, car and other industries across vast swathes of once affluent regions in North America and Europe.

At the same time, evidence of the rapid industrialization underway in some parts of the Global South became increasingly evident. Faced with these transformations academics and others suggested that the advanced economies were in the throes of a transition to a new kind of economy. This gigantic switch from an industrial to an advanced service economy, it was claimed, constituted a qualitative leap, paralleling that undertaken in the nineteenth century from an agricultural to an industrial society. In this newly emerging economy, value and wealth would come less from energy, raw material inputs or physical labour and rather more from knowledge, information and the networking made possible by computerization. Among the early forecasters and analysts of the transition were Drucker (1993) and Scott and Urry (1994). Similar arguments were developed and refined by Reich (1992), with his discussion of the symbolic knowledge economy, led by the creative designers and knowledge generators ('symbolic analysts') and by Castells in his magisterial book: *The Rise of the Network Society: The Information Age: Economy, Society and Culture* (1996). Perez's (2009) work on the origins of technological revolutions in key innovations and how these then diffuse and provide the basis for new infrastructures and markets is also highly relevant here. Perez sees the current information and communication era as the fifth technological revolution since industrialization began in the late eighteenth century.

Other commentators on this transformation such as Rifkin (1995), Martin and Schumann (1997) and Beck (2000) drew more guarded inferences or even rather pessimistic conclusions from these same arguments. More recently, other writers and scholars have built on this theory of the symbolic knowledge economy or the rise of 'cognitive capitalism' (DeLong and Summers 2001; Benkler 2006; Vercellonne 2010; and Mason 2015b). They have also considered its future implications for work, citizen rights, capitalism's future, the prospect of radical political and social change and the emergence of what Rifkin (2014) calls the 'collaborative commons'. This is where networked individuals pool and share information and skills outside the realm of work and profit dominated by capital. In Case Study 3, on the 'gig', or self-employment economy, we briefly outline some of the features attributable to this emerging service economy where they relate to information technology—but we reserve a more thorough discussion until Chap. 8.

Technological Change and the New Economy: Jobs Under Threat

Technological unemployment became increasingly evident from the 1970s. In part, job losses were driven by economic rather than purely technical influences. In particular, intensifying competition from Japanese and other non-Western economies highlighted the increased importance of price in international competitiveness and underlined the problem of rising domestic wages relative to other countries. Technologies which could reduce the wages bill and enhance competitiveness became crucial. But they also reinforced the impetus towards increased investment through the semi- or total automation of factories and the installation of integrated and continuous production lines. In the process they simultaneously signalled the onset of robotization. Accordingly, plant size in major industries in respect to the numbers employed began to fall, including steel, rubber, mining chemicals, oil, textiles and a range of consumer goods industries.[3] Rifkin (1995: 134) describes the case of US Steel, America's largest integrated steel corporation. The company employed 120,000 workers in 1980 but by 1990 only 20,000 people were needed to produce the same output, and the numbers were set to fall further. Meanwhile, middle management jobs also began to decline as computers reduced the need for steep vertical hierarchies of communication and control (see also Sennett 2006, and Chap. 6 of this book). Simultaneously, technological advance also began to affect non-industrial, lower white-collar workers.

According to Frey and Osborne (2013: 13), already by the 1960s the falling cost and increased technical sophistication of computers had led to their commercial use by private companies. In fact, between 1945 and 1980 the cost of using computers declined rapidly each year by an average of 37 per cent. Summarizing the findings of other researchers, Frey and Osborne go on to explain how 'telephone operators were made redundant, the first industrial robot was introduced by General Motors

---

[3] This turn towards technological unemployment in the 1970s obviously reinforced the wider changes discussed in Chap. 3, that were also beginning to alter work experience in the advanced countries, and which were undermining the bargaining power and job security of a growing number of workers.

in the 1960s and in the 1970s airline reservations systems led the way in self-service technology' (11). The cost of computers fell further, and at an accelerating rate, during the 1980s and 1990s, along with 'a surge' in their power. Consequently, a widening range of computerized systems were either substituted for workers altogether or enhanced their efficiency wherever work involved routine and repetitive calculations and activities. Examples include: the introduction of bar-code scanners in retail, cash machines in banking and the replacement of some typists and typing operations through the growing use of personal computers (11). Not surprisingly, many kinds of workers, including bank tellers, warehouse distributors and retailers, discovered that their jobs were susceptible to computerization.

In the case of office and administrative work after 1970 the transformation encompassed much more than computerizing the repetitive typing undertaken by innumerable clerks through word processing, memory storage and spread sheets. By 2000 computers were also linked to the Internet and the web. As a result, workers could engage in instantaneous networking, access and download material of varying content and undertake calculations very rapidly (Gordon 2012). The rate at which computerization was occurring between 1970 and 1995 is also revealed by a study which examined the relative increase in demand for graduates across the USA at this time compared to the preceding decades. Research by Autor, Katz and Krueger (1998) revealed that the highest uptake of graduates occurred in those industries where the relative share of investment in skill upgrading through computerization was prominent compared to other kinds of investment. They concluded that somewhere between 30 and 50 per cent of the increased relative company demand for more skilled workers was due to this growing rate of computerization.

Manning's (2004) study tested the hypothesis that technology increases the need for skilled workers but tends to reduce the relative demand for less skilled or unskilled people. In common with other researchers Manning pointed out that computers work best when they are confronted with a programme consisting of a list of instructions which say: 'if this, then do that' (5). To deal with such situations, programmers construct algorithms, that is, sets of instructions that define precise sequences of operations for computers to follow and that cover all the possible actions appropriate to the operation in question. It transpired that the kinds of jobs most at risk from computerization were not so much those requiring little skill but rather those involving the performance of routine and repetitive tasks. This point is now firmly established in the literature. Drawing on Manning's earlier research, Goos and Manning (2003) examined the changing distribution of UK employment from 1979 to 1999 as between the different deciles defined in terms of the median wage for each job. Although, as expected, there was a considerable increase in employment for jobs included in the top two deciles, employment also rose significantly in the case of work included in the bottom decile in terms of median earnings. Among the occupations falling into the top ten according to job growth were computer analysts and programmers, management consultants and business analysts, software engineers and financial managers. Included in the bottom ten occupations in terms of employment loss, in contrast, were jobs such as foundry labourers, coal miners, railway signalmen, print compositors, machine setters and drillers and electrical operatives (pp.31–33).

As Manning's research clearly shows, most of the latter earn above-median wages and are based in manufacturing where companies which have replaced workers with new technology generate considerable gains in productivity. But of equal interest is that employment growth was also robust for hairdressing, cleaners, shelf-fillers, bar staff, care assistants and attendants and hospital ward assistants. Such work is often described as technically low-skilled as well as low-paid. Here, computers and robots are currently unable to substitute for the mobility, multi-tasked activity, dexterity and need to interface sympathetically and sensitively with clients/patients/customers required of such workers.[4] Manning (2004) inferred from this UK data that technological change may constitute rather less of a threat to unskilled workers than was previously suspected. Employment projections undertaken by the US Bureau of Labour Statistics support this conclusion, reporting that for the decade from 2002 to 2012 among the top ten occupations for employment growth five fell in the bottom quarter ranked in terms of median earnings. Clearly what we are seeing

---

[4] Manning observed that in the case of care and health workers' employment, growth is also explained by an ageing population.

in these and other such findings is the appearance of a 'U' shaped curve which points to the polarization of work experiences in relation to technology (see also Frey and Osborne 2013: 12). Median income and often quite skilled but routine jobs are replaced by robots and are computerized while employment expands both at the top and bottom end of the job continuum. Manning (2004: 21–22) further refined his findings by reporting on US research which discovered that the demand for low-skilled workers, even in the case of those who were high school drop-outs, is often stronger in cities where there is a concentration of highly skilled and relatively well-paid workers who require a range of personal and domestic services and who live in close proximity to the low-skilled.

5.2 Towards a Digitalized and Jobless Future?

As we have seen, until recently technical advances in the range of tasks accomplished by computers and robots have mostly been restricted either to routine manual/physical labour or to work requiring some cognition but which is again fundamentally routine (Autor 2011; Acemoglu and Autor 2011). Yet, as the cost of computerized technology falls and the range of tasks it can successfully perform expands, so capital will have the incentive to replace labour with machines over a widening array of tasks. Frey and Osborne's (2013) explanation concerning this transformation is particularly useful. The extension of computerization to non-routine tasks requiring cognitive capacities is strongly linked to the arrival of 'Big Data'. This involves the possibility of making sense out of ever larger and more complex sets of information as computers with a vastly enhanced memory, or networks of linked machines, can manage much larger volumes of data more quickly and effectively than humans (16–17). Algorithms can be devised that facilitate the more effective storage and analysis of such data sets and are also better than humans at discerning underlying patterns. In addition, unlike human interpretation involving cognitive work, algorithms are 'free of irrational bias' and their 'vigilance need not be interrupted by rest breaks or lapses of concentration' (17).

Technological Advances Coming Your Way Soon

Frey and Osborne (2013: 17–20) discuss several further advances. One such improvement concerns sensory technology which can monitor and detect visual information and sometimes sound effects. This enables machines to register minor changes or faults more accurately and consistently than humans. Examples include, watching CCTV in factories or streets, assessing the loss of moisture in fields or irrigation systems and screening the minute changes in the condition of patients in intensive care units. The possible application of the latter to systems for diagnosing various health problems is obvious. Another improvement involves computers responding to human speech and reacting to behaviour in interface situations. The potential applications here are also considerable. Speech recognition is one such area but teaching and student assessment could also benefit from the streamlining and resource-saving that such advances can generate. Even occupations requiring careful judgement and the ability to reach complex decisions based on assessing a large number of variables are becoming susceptible to computerization. The authors give the examples of financial companies where the automation of decisions relating to flows of financial data via AI has been standard procedure for some time. Additional activities where AI can operate far more rapidly than humans include: dealing with news items, press releases, business details and interpreting financial and legal documents. Even software engineers are not exempt from discovering that some of their roles can be better achieved by sophisticated algorithms—including the automatic detection of bugs (p.19).

A wide range of non-routine manual work is also likely to be taken over by robots in the very near future and indeed this is already happening. Much of the advance in this area is associated with the growing mobility of robots and their enhanced sensory and manipulative capacities, including machine vision. This means they can replace not just repetitive factory operations but also manual jobs demanding flexibility, dexterity and mobility (Frey and Osborne 2013: 20–22). The age of the driver-less car is also arriving because vehicles can easily be fitted with a range of sophisticated sensors and communication equipment that will permit 'an algorithmic vehicle controller' (20) to simultaneously coordinate information coming from all directions, from cameras and from Google maps of entire road networks stored on board. It is predicted that such drivers will be safer and more reliable than even highly experienced humans and will certainly not be subject to the same distractions. Robots are also being developed which can learn from humans and recognize patterns. Meanwhile the cost of producing robots possessing all these and additional capacities continues to fall quite rapidly and is set to decline even faster in the coming years. The work relating to transport Frey and Osborne (2013: 20–21) list as already within the capabilities of these latest versions of robots include the following: fork lift driving; mining vehicles; hospital transport systems; and farm vehicles. Some Chinese factories are already replacing workers with robots for certain manufacturing operations as a strategy for retaining local and global market share as national wage levels rise (see also Brynjolfsson and McAfee 2014: 184). This includes Foxconn, a major sub-contractor for Apple products with a factory staff of 1.2 million workers. Soon, too, the authors suggest low-wage service work, including domestic service, which has been an area of job creation till now, will also succumb to substitution by robots, especially as their relative cost falls.

Frey and Osborne (2013) conducted their own research project with a view to pinning down more precisely the ways in which computerization will affect employment in the twenty-first century. This involved formulating a model which allowed them to assess the likelihood of 702 occupations being computerized in respect to three risk categories: high, medium and low. On this basis they estimated that nearly half of total employment in the USA (47 per cent) is at high risk of being replaced by various forms of computerization over the next two decades. The occupational areas included in this high-risk category are: office and administrative work, a good deal of transportation, most routine production jobs in manufacturing, some construction work and many of the services including sales—despite the degree of social responsiveness to customers that much service work requires. They also suggested that the substitution of human labour by computerization will pass through two waves.

The first will encompass the occupations outlined above. In between the two waves there will be a period where the rate of human job replacement slows down and reaches a 'technological plateau' (39). Here humans will retain a temporary advantage in certain areas requiring superior manual dexterity, work involving the perception of irregularities or the ability to undertake repairs and maintenance operations. Gradually, however, the authors believe that technical advance will remove some of these human advantages and these kinds of middle-risk jobs will also become susceptible to computerization. In contrast, the kinds of work which remain at low risk of computerization (39–41) are jobs where creativity, social intelligence, perceptiveness, negotiation skills and the ability to care for others are essential elements. These are qualities that presuppose the ability to understand and respond to social relationships and changing feelings—what Hochschild (2003) calls 'emotional labour', that is, the ability to interpret body language, demonstrate humour and sympathy, collaborate with others and produce new ideas. Consequently, a large part of the operations involved in management, finance, the arts, teaching, law, health and the media are unlikely to be computerized any time soon.

Brynjolfsson and McAfee (2014) adopt a more openly enthusiastic view of what they call 'thinking machines' or AI, which can work on advanced cognitive tasks (90–96). In their view the latter are far more significant for our future than machines that merely replace physical labour. Indeed, the latter 'pale against the life-changing potential of artificial intelligence' (91). They also cite a number of benefits stemming from recent developments in AI including improved wheelchair control for quadriplegics, enhancing implants that restore hearing to the deaf and helping doctors to diagnose illnesses by analysing vast volumes of medical histories matched against patient symptoms. In respect to health, they insist that digitalization will 'augment', not replace, the expertise of medical professionals (92–93). Above all, they seem certain that the age of digitalization—which they depict as the 'second machine age'—makes possible 'countless instances of machine intelligence and billions of interconnected brains working together to better understand and improve our world' (96).

5 The Juggernaut of Science and Technology: Friend or Foe?

Case Study 3: The 'gig' economy and ICT: blessings and misgivings

On 29 November 2015, Tim Adams reported in *The Observer* on 'The Future of Work'. Adams's article was based on interviews with people working in the emerging 'gig' or temporary/self-employment economy and observations drawn from several scholarly writers, including Frey and Osborne (2013) and Rifkin (2014). In relation to jobs connected to ICT the gig economy, Adams argued, is all about combining three elements: (1) the IT skills people have already acquired, (2) the under-utilized capacities and opportunities ignored or neglected by the capitalist market and (3) the exponential growth of possibilities for sharing information and many other kinds of resources—from jobs to cheap travel possibilities—via the Internet. In recent years a number of IT-savvy entrepreneurs, seeing the gaps in the market, have invested in establishing the infrastructure or Internet platforms which allow consumers or those seeking work to benefit from using their systems. One such platform is *BlaBlaCar*. For a small fee car owners and would-be travellers can find each other in order to share driving costs. Currently, *BlaBlaCar* employs a tiny core of people worldwide but locates car seats for at least two million passengers each month who then save on the cost of train journeys. Other such platforms include: *Airbnb's* system for allowing owners to let out their spare bedrooms to temporary visitors, *YouTube's* sharing of media and other skills and *Uber's* capacity to offer low-cost taxi rides between strangers while providing part-time driving work.

Underpinning the emerging 'gig' economy lies the reality of dwindling prospects for lifetime careers and the need to juggle with a series of part-time micro-niches in the real economy. But this also means low wages and insecurity, meagre pensions and perhaps limited prospects for a stable family life. For those employed in more traditional workplace situations, too, the technical 'advances' of digitalization bring additional dis-benefits: intensified workplace monitoring, subjection to GPS systems, extreme company pressure to meet targets, the invasion of privacy as employers demand health and other checks and business exploitation of personal data for profitable value as with Facebook. Yet, for many of the young 'millennial generation', who are totally familiar with the digital world, the 'gig' economy provides alternatives they value: more autonomy and self-direction, less hierarchical and more flexible workplaces and the chance to deploy their extensive social networking inclusivity. Thus, in addition to the sheer numbers of people who possess IT skills and a widening range of apps at their fingertips, what supports the gig economy is the willingness to share resources through relationships with strangers built on trust and common need. The digital economy is also creating new forms of employment that some young people find attractive. The 'human cloud', for example, consists of online firms that find freelancers—or e-lancers—who seek work in

(continued)

(continued)

> digital companies. They are invited to bid for the jobs available worldwide where employers need to hire temporary workers. One estimate suggests that within ten years there will be around half a billion such e-lancers moving from job to job and country to country.
> But with intense competition between equally IT-skilled e-lancers, including those from India and other low-wage economies, all bidding for such work, there is a risk of yet another race to the bottom whereby levels of remuneration are dragged down. New research on the 'sharing economy' is also casting doubt on some of the claims made for its advantages. For example, *Uber's* algorithm is said to reflect market conditions and helps demand and supply to operate effectively and to everyone's advantage. But it has been suggested that this representation of an impersonal market is often a mirage designed to persuade drivers to remain in areas where real demand for rides is low while prospective riders see more cars on their app looking for business than actually exist. In reality, demand and supply can be 'mobilized' to coincide with periods when prices surge (Hwang and Elish 2015; and O'Connor 2015).

Technology and Employment in Future—Some Gains and Losses

Considered overall, we find that unlike the nineteenth century where it was skilled workers in manufacturing who found themselves being replaced by mechanization, the equivalent occupations designated as 'highly skilled' today are the ones least likely to be taken over by machines. But to what extent does the relative employment security enjoyed by those falling roughly within the top two deciles of the occupational system compensate for the impending job losses faced by nearly everyone else? The adoption of ever cheaper computerized machines in the advanced countries will bring down production costs without necessarily giving rise to compensatory employment. At the same time international competition will surely compel businesses in the developing world to follow suit. This is already happening in China as we have seen.

Given all this it becomes extremely difficult to see how the billions of rural dwellers, along with the urban unemployed living in the shanty towns of India, Latin America, the Middle East, SSA and even China, who have not yet been absorbed into the burgeoning middle-class modern capitalist economy, will find the kinds of employment that will enable them to provide a better life for their families. Even some of the optimism that bubbles through the pages of Brynjolfsson and McAfee (2014) book seems dented at times. Writing about the enormous advantages that digitalized technologies will bring humanity, particularly the reality of a 'different economics' where 'abundance is the norm rather than scarcity' (10), they nevertheless concede that this same digitalized economy will also bring 'thorny challenges' and widespread economic disruption. Here, they are mainly referring to the advanced economies:

> [T]here's never been a better time to be a worker with special skills or the right education, because these people can use technology to create and capture value. However, there's never been a worse time to be a worker with only 'ordinary' skills and abilities to offer, because computers, robots and other digital technologies are acquiring these skills and abilities at an extraordinary rate. (11)

The authors suggest that as in the past the ability of human workers to survive in competition with technology will depend largely on their willingness to seek higher levels of educational attainment: education becomes the answer to the technological unemployment hastened by digitalization. This theme is repeated later in their book even though they also insist that rapid developments in the various fields of AI—such as machine learning, machine vision and complex computation—will increasingly invade many of the highly skilled and non-routine occupations currently regarded as 'safe' from digital advance.

Manning (2004) also articulates doubts concerning this relatively positive view of technological change and the situation faced by unskilled workers. For one thing, as educational levels rise at a time when many middle-level jobs are declining, the low-skilled are likely to face increasing competition from people with higher levels of education who are prepared to downsize rather than remain unemployed (see also Frey and Osborne 2013: 13). Employers are happy to recruit better educated workers for the same low wages they would otherwise pay to those with little education (9). This is already happening and its incidence has risen since the financial crisis of 2008 as graduates and others across North America and the EU have faced no, or low-growth 'austerity' economics, university debts and high unemployment. Second, there is a wider problem faced by many other kinds of workers in addition to the relatively unskilled. This is the dilemma that as the cost of computers and robots continues to fall while their skills and general competencies improve, workers may be forced to choose between accepting ever lower wages and little work security or else permanent unemployment. As Manning (2004: 25) argues: 'if wage inequality is large enough the rich will always want the poor to do mundane tasks for them'. Here we see that technological change provides yet another key factor reinforcing the deepening inequality we discussed in Chaps. 2, 3 and 4.

Finally, and following from the previous point, technological change intersects at many points with the needs and drives of capitalism. Not least, the reality that it is corporate interests that pays the salaries of many scientists and technologists. One of several major dilemmas that arises for capitalism from its drive to control technological development is that the resulting mass unemployment, inequality and falling wage levels likely to follow will undermine its ability to sell many kinds of products despite the parallel potential for prices to fall. Nearly 30 years ago Gorz (1989: 6) pointed presciently and with acuity to the problem for capitalism and those it purports to serve:

> [A]utomation is able to produce a reduction in price *because it reduces wages costs* or, in other words, the number of paid workers. Obviously the people who will enjoy this additional purchasing power as a result of prices coming down will be the ones who can retain well-paid employment and not the workers who will be expelled or excluded from production. (author's italics)

5.3 Science-Technology and the 'World Risk Society'

For Beck, 'modernity's belief in itself' meant 'an unstoppable victory march' in the interests of human progress through the 'boundless plasticity of modern technology' (2009: 212). Similarly, Gray (1995: 266) argued that what ultimately survived from the Enlightenment Project—later, to be 'transmitted' to most of the world by the West—was 'the radical modernist project of subjugating nature by deploying technology to exploit the earth for human purposes'. What both authors stress is the unshakeable belief held by moderns in the inevitability, necessity and importance of the self-perpetuating thrust for 'linear progression' (Beck 2009: 212). This, in turn, meant that the original Enlightenment quest for critical reason mutated into Weber's (1992: 181–2) prison of formal or instrumental rationality where the obsession with calculating means smothers all possible substantive, moral and political choices (Weber 1968: 85–86 and Brubaker 1984).

We now explore Beck's argument (2009) that released from any possible restraint by radical modernity, science and technology have led us into the 'world risk society' and therefore, perhaps, towards a perilous future. Moreover, in doing so, their practitioners have sometimes demonstrated little evidence of drawing on the tool-kit of scepticism and doubt in respect to the practical implications of their work, even though this forms the bedrock of scientific methodology itself. In examining this argument, we also consider the responsibility of scientific and technological researchers, as individuals and as groups of professionals, for our predicament, as against the immensely powerful agencies that inevitably sponsor much of their research, particularly private corporations and/or military/state bodies.

Modernity and the Rise of the Risk Society

In his path-breaking book, *The Risk Society: Towards a New Modernity* (1992), Beck distinguished between two eras of modernity. In the 'first' or 'simple' modernity, overcoming material scarcity and the drive to create wealth through industrialization was the absolute priority. During the more recent era of 'high', 'late' or 'reflexive' modernity, however, we have increasingly been compelled to grapple with the vast dangers and risks generated by the 'first'. Several core, almost endemic, features of this earlier modernity led to this state of affairs including the unquestioned belief in material progress and the harnessing of science and technology to the service of capitalism. Yet, industrialization, capitalism and the application of science to production also made possible the generation of previously unimaginable wealth. But in bringing the vicissitudes of an untamed nature gradually under control—famines caused by extreme weather conditions or unreliable harvests, the diseases associated with poverty and unhygienic living conditions, the perils and costs of slow transport and communications and so on—modernity also released an escalating torrent of new human-made risks that were the direct result of industrialization and technological advance.

These included: thousands of new chemical compounds, many of which were highly toxic and which spread silently into rivers, seas, water tables and through the food chain; the massive pollution of the environment by oil spills and vast volumes of waste effluent, including plastics; the constant risk of nuclear, chemical and bio-chemical leakages into the environment, whether deliberately through warfare or because of neglect or accident; and the growing threat to the biosphere both from diminishing biodiversity and from greenhouse gas emissions. Beck points out that unlike those stemming from nature, all these risks and dangers demonstrate similar and terrifying characteristics. They are impersonal, often hidden, invisible and very hard to detect. Building up cumulatively, they diffuse widely and affect all life forms and generations indiscriminately—though the poor will always be harmed first and probably the hardest. They are unbound by time and space, are often irreversible and uncontrollable and frequently exercise a 'boomerang effect' in that the waste and toxins exported elsewhere seep back to their place of origin through poisoned food, polluted air, sea currents and the rest.

Beck attributes a high degree of culpability for all these risks to science and scientists and not just to those who find ways to operationalize its discoveries in practical and profitable ways. This scientific failure to foresee, avoid or manage the adverse results of their research can be explained by a number of practices and orientations. For one thing, some scientists are not only trapped in a self-reinforcing belief in the virtues and inevitability of material progress, considerably bolstered by the certainty of their own objectivity and purely disinterested approach to knowledge, but unintentionally they also mutually validate each other's technical rationality and its supposed neutrality. Second, their contempt for lay-persons who lack a scientific training, and who they suppose can have no understanding

5   The Juggernaut of Science and Technology: Friend or Foe?

of scientific methodology, often leaves them convinced that the public's apparent ignorance renders their objections irrelevant: they can be largely ignored. Another factor concerns the over-specialized nature of scientific disciplines and sub-disciplines. This sometimes means that the identification and analysis of risks falls through the gaps between different areas of knowledge. On the question of scientific method Beck further criticizes scientists because their research often results in what he calls 'end-of-pipe' solutions. Instead of developing engineering, chemical or other practical solutions from the very onset of a project which are designed to operate for the entire cycle of a product or process, many scientists allow themselves to be content with damage limitation exercises. They look for solutions when problems have been revealed rather than work to avoid the possibility of contamination from the outset.

Perhaps most damaging and dangerous of all these failures, suggests Beck, is the willingness of many scientists to be seduced by corporate power and the prestige—or sense of patriotic duty—associated with agreeing to work for teams undertaking military research for governments. The Manhattan Project on the development of the atom bomb in the USA during WW2 is probably the most notable example. This project absorbed 130,000 people including innumerable young and older scientists from the UK, USA and elsewhere, in the name of democratic values and the defeat of fascism. But it also unleashed a military precedent in the bombing of Japan in 1945 and an East–West race for Cold-War supremacy of immense danger. In addition it alienated and created divisions between many scientists. In the case of capitalism, it is of course private firms who today provide the bulk of the research funding and professional career opportunities that many scientists need in order to develop their intellectual interests and utilize their knowledge—although universities, increasingly locked into a global race for supremacy, provide similar inducements. By hiding their personal career interests behind professionalism and the mystique of expert knowledge, while blaming their employers for misuse of their research findings, scientists have increasingly alienated the public's trust in their objectivity. To an extent, this has also undermined the credibility of science itself. Far from believing science to be the solution to human problems we have come to see it as a major cause and reason for concern.

The Twenty-First-Century World Risk Society

In Chap. 6 we explore Beck's theory that the cumulative risks and unintended side effects of the first modernity have compelled individuals to become more reflexive. We are learning to continuously monitor the impact of our own actions both on others but also on the world around us: a kind of relentless self-confrontation. In part, this reflexivity creates the possibility of moving towards a more positive and less dangerous future as we take more personal responsibility for our actions. In his more recent work *World at Risk* (2009), however, Beck seems to have become less optimistic concerning the possibilities of reflexive modernity. First, the very successes of modernity and the colossal dangers it has spawned have weakened the confidence that modernizers once held in their capacity to control whatever risks might be released. This is because even though new knowledge seems to offer the promise of rendering previously unpredictable risks into risks that can be calculated, this very same process only lets loose further and new un-predictabilities. The belief that we can always control the 'manufactured, self-inflicted insecurity' (8) produced by modernity is giving way to chronic uncertainty. Second, what makes this situation even more uncertain and perhaps alarming is that while science continues to make us more aware of risk, its very impotence in coping with the uncontrollable and unpredictable nature of modernity's side effects also threatens the legitimacy of scientific research in areas such as genetics, nanotechnology and robotics where there may (or may not) be good prospects of winning safer benefits for human life.

Third, we are increasingly aware of being threatened, not just by modernity's failures, but also by its 'triumphs' (22). For example, medical advances have raised life expectancy but have also led to the rising costs and demographic imbalance of an ageing society. Immense improvements in human productivity through technological development (216) also create unemployment and worsen inequality as we have seen. Fourth, although globalization and spreading industrialization means that the world is united in sharing vast mega-risks this is a forced unity grounded in common fears and insecurities. If anything, the dangers of climate change, nuclear war, terrorism, the spread of global pandemics through air travel and so on exacerbate the old conflicts of religion and culture that pre-date modernity (12). Fifth, unlike environmental and economic risks where faith in our ability to control risks proved to be misplaced and we did not intend our actions to be destructive, certain new kinds of global risks are of a very different nature. Here, Beck suggests that various forms of contemporary terrorism, particularly Islamic fundamentalism, are aggressively malicious and forward-thinking in their intentions (204 and 227). They are empowered by information technology, rapid travel, globalization and technical advances in small-scale warfare on a scale not possible before. All this renders them highly dangerous and fearsome. In particular, we have little defence against suicidal terrorist attacks motivated by religious hopes of entering an unearthly paradise. Because of these new, even less calculable risks, future scientists will need to justify and account not only for the possibility of unforeseen side effects from technological 'progress' but also for the potential purposive and malicious abuse of their discoveries by as yet unknown others.

Thus, like earlier critics and doubters, including Weber and Durkheim but also more recent theorists, Beck believes that modernization is overwhelming and undermining its own social, cultural, economic and political achievements. In fact, he distinguishes between the basic principles of modernity and its institutions. But the latter, as we have seen, are in crisis: declining welfare protection, unemployment, ageing societies, our loss of confidence in science and professionalism, environmental distress and the growing pressures on marriage and family life (231). To this we could add the current concerns briefly outlined in Chap. 1: namely, widespread disillusionment with democratic politics and politicians and a fear of globalization's impact on the solidity of national loyalties. As Beck summarizes the situation: 'the *continuity* of the basic principles (their loss of definition and their increasing reflexivity) leads to *dis*-continuity in the basic institutions' (231).

But for Beck, two elements of the basic principles of modernity are paramount in this core contradiction. One concerns the continuous rationalization expressed through industrial modernity's relentless obsession with exploiting the natural world. Armed with this realization we are tempted to listen to the siren voices which insist that just as the only cure for a failing market capitalism lies with more markets and more competition, so, equally, when confronted with the dangers of modernity in the shape of relentless technological change, the only answer is yet more modernity and yet more advanced technology. The second contradiction Beck seems to single out is the individualization process which many believe has merely broken down into 'self-centredness and the ego-centric society' (231).[5] But more modernity along the dimensions of rationalization and individualization promises only further disenchantment, societal disintegration and perhaps conflict. We have reached a moment where a fundamental re-think of what modernity is, and what its possible alternative formations might be, needs urgent attention—a project to which we attempt to make a modest contribution in Chap. 9. Failure in this regard opens the door to anti-modernization movements which might bring even more destructive and dangerous consequences (223).

Towards Dangerous Extremes of Rationality: Science or Capitalism?

In Beck's analysis it is the scientists and technologists who seem to be loaded with the chief blame for the obsession with mastering nature and allowing rationality to dominate all aspects of life, thereby taking us dangerously close to the abyss of the world risk society. But is this entirely fair? In this section we consider other thinkers and examples in an attempt to evaluate Beck's assertions.

Rustin (1994), for example, argues that Beck gives too much causal weight to the role of ideas and knowledge exercised by self-conscious agents in explaining both the rise of the risk society and the capacity for reflexive individuals to act in order to avert further dangers. The dominant techno-scientific rationality which Beck sees as so central is not an abstract system capable of thinking for itself. Rather, it has been directed by powerful corporate forces eager to harness its vast potential for profit. Moreover, the ideas and morality exercised by networks of reflexive

---

[5] This is discussed in detail in Chap. 6 along with Beck's analysis of the individualization process, which he and others regard as crucial to understanding contemporary society. For an excellent evaluation and critique of Beck's work on individualization and the economy see Mythen (2005).

citizens alone will be insufficient to bring this behemoth under sociopolitical control. The ability of capital to dominate science and technological development is also emphasized by Hardt and Negri (2004). Writing about the growing field of bio-genetics they describe how the knowledge derived from research into plants and animals is being transformed into private property by companies taking out international patents (181–8). The same has already happened in respect to the human genome. They argue that essentially not only are the world's fauna and flora common property belonging to everyone but we are moving into an era where increasing quantities of goods and labour are immaterial in character: they are based on various kinds of knowledge and creative invention and are produced through cooperative, shared activity. The collaborative scientific research involved in bio-research constitutes a very obvious example.

Growing attempts by corporations to privatize the 'commons' (see also Boyle 2003 and Benkler 2006, and the discussion in Chap. 8) 'thwarts' such creativity since it is the very openness to ideas, to mutual learning and the ability to stand on the shoulders of the many who produce such knowledge that leads to new knowledge. This openness, indeed, is what originally fuelled the cybernetic revolution and the development of the Internet in Silicon Valley and elsewhere until business moved in and took possession of the 'electronic commons' (Hardt and Negri 2004: 185). In general, scientists working in these and related fields are not personally 'driven to innovate by the potential of riches from patents' (186) and they are aware of the danger that private ownership of knowledge will inhibit further development. One notable example is demonstrated by Tim Berners-Lee, regarded as the inventor of the World Wide Web, who did not wish to commercialize this advance for personal financial benefit.

In contrast, it is certainly not difficult to discover clear indications of scientists, engineers and other practitioners who seem to be almost unquestioningly enamoured of the virtues of economic growth and perpetual technological 'progress'. Moreover, in some instances their remedies for dealing with global problems such as global warming seem deliberately designed to avoid jeopardizing either of these goals. We say much more about environmental issues in Chap. 7. But in her recent book on climate change, Klein (2014) provides abundant examples of hubristic and—in her view—misplaced, even dangerous forms of scientific endeavour. Two such cases are: the development of fracking in the USA and elsewhere and the technology being developed which is designed to dim the sun through geoengineering. The development of hydraulic fracking was partly a response to growing criticism of the fossil fuel industry as scientists and some members of the public became more aware of global warming and its causes. Natural shale gas is regarded as a lower emitter of greenhouse gases than coal and oil and largely on this basis it gained support and investment funds—especially in the USA where its sheer scale meant additional benefits for the economy from self-sufficiency and lower energy costs for industry. A number of adverse consequences have followed from the growth of this form of 'extractivism'. The most dangerous in respect to global warming is the reality that fracking tends to release larger quantities of methane into the atmosphere than other forms of gas extraction and methane is over 80 times more effective than carbon dioxide in trapping the sun's heat (Klein 2014: 143).

While the great majority of scientists around the world are committed to reducing global warming through measures aimed at cutting the emissions of greenhouse gases, for example, the members of the Intergovernmental Panel on Climate Change (IPCC), a minority, have become embroiled in vast projects often requiring unimaginably huge investments. Among these schemes are sun-blocking, by constructing a vast shield in the sky, seeding the oceans with particles designed to reflect the sun's rays back into space or spraying sulphur into the atmosphere via helium balloons or planes in order to create more cloud cover or more reflective clouds (Klein 2014: 258–63). The point about geoengineering projects such as these is that they are regarded by many as preferable to adopting anti-pollution measures and renewable energy systems that might slow economic growth. In addition, and usually for the best possible motive of helping to solve a major world problem, they are often supported by highly reputable institutions and individuals whose backing renders them more popular and acceptable in the eyes of the wider public. Thus, in 2011 the highly prestigious and long-established UK Royal Society convened a conference of world experts on the prospects for geoengineering. Earlier, in 2009, it had also approached the UK government requesting that more resources were made available for research in this area (256). Klein describes how the debate on geoengineering is usually confined to a small group of inventors, scientists and funders who are engaged in promoting each other's work. However, there is often a clique of famous academics and celebrity business people, such as Richard Branson and Bill Gates, either providing funding behind the scenes or lending their support (263–4). Some of the scientists involved may also be hoping that research funding, future patent rights or business opportunities will result from their activities.

In Sect. 5.1 we discussed the book by Brynjolfsson and McAfee (2014), both employed at the MIT's (Massachusetts Institute of Technology) Center for Digital Business. They describe the present historical moment as characterized by 'brilliant technologies'. They also make no secret of their delight concerning the ability of 'mechanical power' first to enhance human life from the time of Britain's Industrial Revolution onwards and now the promise that human mental as well as physical power will experience another massive leap forward through the technologies of the second machine age and particularly though digitalization. They are aware of the challenges that lie ahead—especially for those who are less well educated—and how much the future depends on the choices we make. Yet, overall they see a future which promises an 'increase in volume, variety, and quality and the decrease in cost of the many offerings brought by modern technological progress' (12). They trumpet the advantages of two changes in particular: the rise of 'true machine intelligence' and the connectivity of all humans across the planet through digital networks (251). In the case of the former, they envisage a doubling of the storage capacity possible in the case of the human brain and the prospect of machines becoming 'self-aware'. When this happens things could become highly 'unpredictable' (258) including the likelihood that humans and computers 'could merge seamlessly' (258) into some kind of cyborg—though they do not use that term. We may also be glad to discover that this will not mean machines will become like humans who will 'still have vital roles to play' (188).

In Chaps. 11 and 12 of their book the authors do take on the concern raised by many economists and others to the effect that the technological changes they are discussing will eradicate the work prospects for a growing number of people. After much soul searching on this key issue, however, they take refuge in the following arguments. One is that humans will retain a lead over even the most advanced robots for some time to come particularly in respect to creativity. As they put it, the game is not over yet (188–94). But this does not offer much in the way of practical policy solutions or hope for the majority, even perhaps, those who are highly intelligent and educated. Second, digital advances and robotization will reduce the cost and therefore the price of many goods and this might lead to a growing demand for workers as the economy expands (176–7). Brynjolfsson and McAfee could be proved right on this point but as we saw in Sect. 5.2 some observers take a very different and more pessimistic view. Third, they point out that much current and future technological unemployment is also caused by globalization and therefore the ability of Western companies to offshore industrial production to lower paid workers across the Global South. Unfortunately, this does not help the advanced countries and their citizens to cope with unemployment unless it is being suggested that wages in the latter should be brought down to even lower levels. Last, they ultimately suggest that the problem of growing unemployment for those who lack high levels of education should be left to politicians and others. Hopefully they 'can do more to invent technologies and business models that augment and amplify the unique capabilities of humans to create new sources of values, instead of automating the ones that already exist' (182). Undoubtedly, society and government do need to take up this challenge. Yet at the same time such pronouncements also emphasize the difficult path that has to be trodden while simultaneously getting scientists such as the authors off the hook of personal responsibility.

Moreover, in making this point they also draw our attention to their own unbounded certainty of, and relish in, perpetual and unrestrained scientific advance. It always brings immense material gains for humanity which will and must inevitably outweigh any costs or pain: the advantages it generates are 'progressive'. By the same token, the economic growth necessary to the funding of scientific enterprise is always justified and remains key to human happiness, though we can hope that future policies will take account of growing inequality and other disadvantages of technological advance. As such there can never be any question of placing scientific research or the drive for economic growth under the slightest

5 The Juggernaut of Science and Technology: Friend or Foe?

restraint beyond taking steps to minimize their most obvious dangers. In fact, as Bauman (2002: 144) powerfully argues:

> Technology is not pulled forward by needs protesting neglect and clamouring for satisfaction, but pushed from behind by assets clamouring for profitable use and protesting unemployment of resources. Technology develops *because it develops:* all other explanations come dangerously close to ideological adornment or wishful thinking. (Author's italics)

Similar concerns and criticisms are evident in the writings of a number of contemporary observers of advancing technology. Carr (2014), for example, worries that, in effect, we are handing over the running of large areas of human activity and even our daily lives and social relationships—through our reliance on iPhones and the social media, such as Facebook—to algorithms. In the case of the latter we lose control of the personal information we make available to Google and Facebook. This is then deployed in order to (a) build up profiles of our consumer preferences for sale to the advertisers who then target us with commercial inducements while (b) allowing governments and security services to scrutinize our comments and thoughts as a form of domination.[6] Soon, it is predicted, search engines will know what we are thinking and what we may need before we do ourselves. But the likelihood that many highly skilled professionals such as medics and lawyers will find large parts of their work have been handed over to robots is only one kind of dilemma (see Garside 2014: 30; Meltzer 2014: 9–11; and Carr 2014: 112–20). Carr also suggests that when much of our decision-making is given to machines we risk 'automation complacency' where we are persuaded the machine is flawless and we can relax our attention. Worse, we may lose the skill and capacity to take control back when things go wrong (67–68). He gives the example of an ocean liner in 1995 cruising with passengers from Bermuda to Boston and using GPS navigation signals to stay on

---

[6] Many observers have expressed alarm at the innocence and alacrity with which most people have greeted the cyber-age and jumped into using the social media. Morozov (2011 and 2015), for example, criticizes the ability of governments to exploit the social media as a path to increased surveillance of populations, among other dangers, while Dean (2009) balks at the 'technology fetishism' (38) bred by the communications revolution which engenders a shallow if not false sense of social solidarity and agency.

course. But when the cable came loose and the readings were no longer accurate none of the crew noticed for 30 hours that the ship was drifting off course until it finally ran aground on a sandbank miles from its destination (68). Similar incidents, some involving passenger deaths, have occurred with airliners whose crews handed control to the computer in the cockpit, something which is commonplace on most flights (44–45).

In addition, key ethical questions concerning who is entitled to decide when and how a new algorithm is designed and for what purpose, are increasingly ignored. 'Who gets to program the robot's conscience?' asks Carr (p.186). Should it be the manufacturer, the owner, the software coders, government regulators, insurance underwriters? As ever more human activities are handed over to computers, dilemmas over ethics will become more pressing. Carr rightly questions the wisdom of leaving such decisions entirely to corporate plutocrats and the tiny cliques of self-referential scientists they employ. Neither of these ever seem to ask why humanity would wish to hand not just our entire work activity but our very future over to machines.

5.4 Surplus to Requirements

The ILO report, *World Employment and Social Outlook—Trends 2015*, claims that at the end of 2014 200 million people worldwide were unemployed—up by more than 30 million on the pre-2008 figure. More significantly, 280 million new jobs will be required by the end of 2019 given new entrants to the labour market (International Labour Organization 2015: 11). The ILO further predicts that young people, especially women, will be hard hit by any future employment deficit, and even more so if they live in Latin America, China, Russia or certain Arab countries. The worry concerning youth unemployment is rendered worse by the fact that despite continuing improvements in educational attainment, including at the tertiary level, young people have been hurt far more by the recession than older workers and this trend seems likely to continue. Those in 'vulnerable employment'—mostly self-employed women working in family micro-enterprises—remains constant at around 45 per cent of the total global work force: more than 1.4 billion people (see also Gottfried 2013:

221–2). They are disproportionately found in SSA and SA. The nature of their employment renders improving productivity difficult, so most remain very poor, slowing down the rate at which poverty can be reduced.

Industry now provides around 22 per cent of global employment including 12 per cent in the advanced economies. But this percentage is falling and will not provide a key element in any strong future world economic recovery except for highly skilled, non-routine jobs. Everywhere, most future employment growth will emerge in the private services sector with all the disadvantages already discussed. Other commentators believe the ILO's definition of unemployment is too narrow (Roberts 2016: 471–2) and that in some instances the actual rates are much higher. In the UK, for example, the official figures indicate that 2.5 million people were out of work in 2013. However, if those who wished to work but who were not claiming benefits or registered as unemployed are added to this figure—mostly students and older workers—then the number of unemployed doubles. This is before a further million people are added who are under-employed because they work part-time and would like longer hours.

In recent years, others have also questioned the usual ways in which we consider unemployment. Davis (2006: 15–16), for example, commented on the unprecedentedly rapid urbanization that has occurred during the last 50 or more years. In doing so he drew on the findings of an international research team: *Understanding Slums: Case Studies for the Global Report on Human Settlements* (UN-HABITAT) (2003). Predicting that by 2015 there will be around 550 cities with populations of more than 1 million, compared to 86 in 1950, Davis points out that most of these were in the Global South and will include the world's mega-cities of over 8 million people. However, the majority of rural-urban migrants end up in slums and shanty towns with their inadequate facilities and vast informal economies where families compete against each other for minute shares of work and micro-business opportunities. The numbers worldwide living in this way are around 1 billion people—or one-third of the world's entire urban population. There are many reasons why millions end up in this predicament but one stands out. Everywhere, apart from the economies of South East Asia, rapid urbanization, driven by population growth and rural distress, involves 'the reproduction of poverty, not the supply of jobs' (Davis 2006: 16). Moreover, as a rising number of the roughly 40 per cent of humanity who still work the land move to the cities this problem could get much worse.[7] De Rivero (2001: 4–7) argued that it is technological change in the form of computerization and automation that is leaving around 30 per cent of the world's working population—many concentrated in the poorest and least developed countries—unemployed and bereft of the same possibilities of being absorbed into the low-skill service work still available in the advanced countries (6–7). A recent report by the Swiss Bank USB also pointed to the potential loss of competitive advantage that some developing economies in Latin America and India will face when automation and AI are widely adopted in the Global North, as this will lower production costs and undermine the former's current cheap labour advantage (Treanor 2016: 21).

Such evidence calls to mind the aphorism which suggests that the only thing worse than being exploited by capitalism is not being exploited by it: having captured virtually all other possibilities of earning a living there is no prospect of living on its outside (Hoogvelt 1997). Accordingly, growing numbers of people—not all in the Global South—have become structurally irrelevant. Here, Jameson (2011: 149) reminds us of 'the fundamental structural centrality of unemployment' for capitalism and how it is 'inseparable from the dynamic of accumulation' (149). Much of this is directly related to the drive to raise productivity. However, Jameson also argues that the situation today in respect to 'those massive populations around the world who have … "dropped out of history" … deliberately excluded from the modernizing projects' of the Global North and South is very different from earlier crises of unemployment. Previously, as in 1919, for example, governments could still send excess workers to the colonies or back to the countryside where farming was far less mechanized than now. But today the rise of the financial industries and the creation of a global market along with the absence of world wars, with their potential for re-building and re-stocking capital, as in the early 1950s,

---

[7] In this context, any large-scale moves to replace the South's agricultural workforce—whose members enjoy few if any alternative work opportunities—with robotized machinery seems politically dangerous. Thus, there is room to doubt their ability to afford the food they once produced for themselves, but which will then be churned out by high-tech, digitalized farming, once they have re-located to a more or less jobless life in the cities.

mean that the destitute masses across the world whose predicament is put down to ethnic conflict, weak states or famine, and who are often looked after by international charities, are, in reality victims of unemployment for which capitalism has no solution (147–8).

5.5 Summary and Conclusions

The evidence that technological change is likely to threaten a vast numbers of jobs in the near future seems rather overwhelming. Without radical political steps designed to either curtail or compensate for this in some way a future of worsening inequality and poverty for many who currently inhabit the wealthier nations seems unavoidable and piled on top of the existing forces fuelling this scenario. Similarly, the failure of promised economic improvement to reach huge numbers in the Global South, who are still extremely poor, looms before us. At the same time, and not only in respect to environmental issues, two centuries of sweeping and largely un-regulated industrial and technological change have left our planet massively polluted, dangerously bereft of its once teeming life forms and threatened by chemical, nuclear and biological disasters on a scarcely imaginable scale—triggered either by natural disasters or geopolitical conflicts between nations. In general, Beck's critique of scientific endeavour (1992 and 2009) as perhaps the main cause of these threats seems unwarranted particularly when we recall the worldwide work of the IPCC. In addition, as Hardt and Negri (2004), among others, have pointed out, it is capitalist needs and interests that exercise the greatest weight in steering the directions of scientific work and technological innovation while reaping the largest rewards. And when the research costs of developing new products throws future profitability in doubt, as in the current situation in respect to the desperate need for new anti-biotics in the pharmaceutical industry, competition renders company collaboration unlikely, leaving some form of state intervention as the only solution.

In any event, as Carr (2014) suggests, it is not just a minority of scientists in hock to corporate interests who risk allowing the juggernaut of technology to roar out of control and endanger our future. All too often what lies behind the handing of power and responsibility to the interested few is a boundless but misplaced faith in technological 'progress' upheld by politicians and ordinary citizens. Here, we return once again to the dual monsters of a now uncontrolled one-dimensional capitalism riding the horse of a modernity obsessed with dominating nature and the right to pursue human material advance interminably, and at whatever cost. Brower (2010)—a writer and environmentalist—wondered why nearly half the US public in 2009 still refused to believe the evidence for global warming. Like Carr, and others, he decided that part of the explanation lies in a belief in the 'technological fix' and the idea that 'science will save us' (22). But equally or more dangerous is the parallel justification that follows from such ideas: the inference that we are perfectly entitled to use up all the resources we need in order to feed our material cravings and as if there were no generations to follow. Placing our faith in science also allows us to avoid the 'real solution, which will be the hard, nontechnical work of changing human behavior' (23).

Bibliography

Amin, A. (1994). *Post-fordism: A reader*. Oxford: Wiley-Blackwell.

Autor, D. (2011). The polarization of job opportunities in the US labor market: Implications for employment and earnings. *Community Investment, 43*(2), 11–18.

Autor, D. H., Katz, L. F., & Krueger, A. B. (1998). Computing inequality: Have computers changed the labor market. *The Quarterly Journal of Economics, 113*(4), 1169–1213.

Bauman, Z. (2002). *Society under siege*. Cambridge: Polity.

Beck, U. (1992). *The risk society: Towards a new modernity*. London: Sage.

Beck, U. (2000). *The Brave new world of work*. Cambridge: Polity.

Beck, U. (2009). *World at risk*. Cambridge: Polity.

Benkler, Y. (2006). *The wealth of networks: How social production transforms markets and freedom*. New Haven, CT: Yale University Press.

Boyle, J. (2003). The second enclosure movement and the construction of the public domain. *Law and Contemporary Problems, 66*(1/2), 33–74.

Brower, K. (2010). The danger of cosmic genius. *The Atlantic*. Retrieved August 9, 2016, from http://www.theatlantic.com/magazine/archive/2010/12/the-danger-of-cosmic-genius/308306/

Brubaker, R. (1984). *The limits of rationality: An essay on the social and moral thought of Max Weber*. London: Allen and Unwin.

Brynjolfsson, E. and McAfee, A. (2014) *The second machine age: Work, progress and prosperity in a time of brilliant technologies*. New York: W.W. Norton and Company.

Carr, N. (2014). *The glass cage: Automation and US*. New York: W. W. Norton and Company.

Castells, M. (1996). *The rise of the network society*. Oxford: Blackwell.

Davis, M. (2006). *Planet of slums*. London: Verso.

De Rivero, O. (2001). *The myth of development*. London: Zed.

Dean, J. (2009). *Democracy and other neoliberal fantasies: Communicative capitalism and left politics*. Durham: Duke University Press.

DeLong, J. B. and Summers, L. H. (2001). *The 'new economy': Background, historical perspective, questions, and speculations*. Federal Reserve Bank of Kansas City. Retrieved August 9, 2016, from https://www.kansascityfed.org/publicat/econrev/Pdf/4q01delo.pdf

Drucker, P. (1993). *Post-capitalist society*. Oxford: Butterworth Heinemann.

Evans, P., & Tilly, C. (2016). The future of work: Escaping the current dystopian trajectory and building better alternatives. In S. Edgell, G. H., & E. Granter (Eds.), *The sociology of work and employment* (pp. 651–671) . London: Sage.Public policies for private corporations: The British corporate welfare state

Fieschi, C., Morris M. and Caballero, L. (2012). *Recapturing the reluctant radical: How to win back Europe's populist vote*. Online: Counterpoint. Retrieved August 10, 2016, from http://counterpoint.uk.com/wp-content/uploads/2013/02/E-version-Recapturing-the-Reluctant-Radical-September-2012.pdf

Frayne, D. (2016). Critiques of work. In S. Edgell, H. Gottfried, & E. Granter (Eds.), *The sociology of work and employment* (pp. 616–633). London: Sage.

Frey, C. B. and Osborne, M. A. (2013). *The future of employment: How susceptible are jobs to computerisation?* Oxford University Engineering Sciences Department. Retrieved August 9, 2016, from http://www.oxfordmartin.ox.ac.uk/downloads/academic/The_Future_of_Employment.pdf

Garside, J. (2014, April 20). The age of artificial intelligence may be getting closer." *The Guardian*, p. 30.

Goos, M. and Manning, A. (2003). *Lousy jobs and lovely jobs: The rising polarization of work in Britain*. Centre for Economic Performance. Retrieved August 10, 2016, from http://eprints.lse.ac.uk/20002/1/Lousy_and_Lovely_Jobs_the_Rising_Polarization_of_Work_in_Britain.pdf

Gordon, R. J. (2012). *Is U.S. economic growth over? Faltering innovation confronts the six headwinds*. National Bureau of Economic Research. Retrieved August 10, 2016, from http://www.nber.org/papers/w18315

Gorz, A. (1989). *Critique of economic reason*. London: Verso.

Gottfried, H. (2013). *Gender, work, and economy: Unpacking the global economy*. Cambridge: Polity.

Gray, J. (1995). *Enlightenment's wake*. London: Routledge.

Hardt, M., & Negri, A. (2004). *Multitude: War and democracy in the age of empire*. New York: Penguin Press.

Hochschild, A. R. (2003). *The managed heart: Commercialization of human feeling*. Berkley: University of California Press.

Hoogvelt, A. M. (1997). *Globalization and the post-colonial world: The new political economy of development*. Basingstoke: Macmillan.

Hwang, T. and Elish, M. C. (2015) *The mirage of the marketplace: The disingenuous ways Uber hides behind its algorithm*. Slate. Retrieved August 10, 2016, from http://www.slate.com/articles/technology/future_tense/2015/07/uber_s_algorithm_and_the_mirage_of_the_marketplace.html

International Labour Organization. (2015). *World employment and social outlook—Trends 2015*. Retrieved August 10, 2016, from http://www.ilo.org/global/research/global-reports/weso/2015/lang--en/index.htm

Jameson, F. (2011). *Representing capital: A reading of volume one*. London: Verso.

Klein, N. (2014). *This changes everything: Capitalism vs the climate*. London: Allen Lane.

Lash, S., & Urry, J. (1994). *Economies of signs and spaces*. London: Sage.

Liang, C. S. (2007). Europe for the 'Europeans': The foreign and security policy of the populist radical right. In C. S. Liang (Ed.), *Europe for the Europeans: The foreign and security policy of the populist radical right* (pp. 1–32). Aldershot: Ashgate.

Manning, A. (2004) *We can work it out: The impact of technological change on the demand for low-skilled workers*. Centre for Economic Performance; Discussion Paper No. 640. London School of Economics.

Martin, H.-P., & Schumann, H. (1997). *Global trap: Globalization and the assault on prosperity and democracy*. London: Zed Books.

Mason, P. (2015a, November 2). Apocalypse now: Has the next giant financial crash already begun? *The Guardian*. Retrieved August 10, 2016, from https://www.theguardian.com/commentisfree/2015/nov/01/financial-armageddon-crash-warning-signs

Meltzer, T. (2014, July 16). Computer says go. *The Guardian, G2*, pp. 9–11.

Montgomery, D. (1987). *The fall of the house of labour: The workplace, the state, and american labour activism, 1865–1925*. Cambridge: Cambridge University Press.

Morozov, E. (2011). *The net delusion: How not to liberate the world*. London: Allen Lane.

Mudde, C. (2007). *Populist radical right parties in Europe*. Cambridge: Cambridge University Press.

Mythen, G. (2005). Employment, individualization and insecurity: Rethinking the risk society perspective. *The Sociological Review, 53*(1), 129–149.

O'Connor, J. (2015, October 8). The human cloud: A new world of work. *Financial Times*. Retrieved August 11, 2016, from http://www.ft.com/cms/s/2/a4b6e13e-675e-11e5-97d0-1456a776a4f5.html#axzz4H1SfS8MS

Perez, C. (2009). *Technological revolutions and techno-economic paradigms*. Tallinn University of Technology. Retrieved August 11, 2016, from http://technologygovernance.eu/files/main/2009070708552121.pdf

Reich, R. (1992). *The work of nations*. New York: Knopf.

Rifkin, J. (1995). *The end of work: The decline of the global labour force and the dawn of the post-market era*. New York: Putnam Publishing.

Rifkin, J. (2014). *The zero marginal cost society: The Internet of things, the collaborative commons, and the eclipse of capitalism*. Basingstoke: Palgrave/Macmillan.

Roberts, K. (2016). Unemployment. In S. Edgell, H. Gottfried, & E. Granter (Eds.), *The sociology of work and employment* (pp. 469–484). London: Sage.

Rustin, M. (1994). Incomplete modernity: Ulrich Beck's risk society. *Radical Philosophy, 67*, 3–11.

Sennett, R. (2006). *The culture of the new capitalism*. London: Yale University Press.

Skidelsky, R., & Skidelsky, E. (2012). *How much is enough? Money and the good life*. London: Penguin.

Treanor, J. (2016, January 20). Automation will hit poor nations and the unskilled. *The Guardian*.

UN-HABITAT. (2003). *The challenge of slums: Global report on human settlement*. London: Earthscan.

Vercellonne, C. (2010). The crisis of the law of value and the becoming-rent of profit. In A. Fumagalli & S. Mezzadra (Eds.), *Crisis in the Global Economy: Financial Markets, Social Struggles, and New Political Scenarios* (pp. 85–118). Los Angeles: Semiotext(e).

Weber, M. (1968). *Economy and society, Volume 1*. New York: Bedminster Press.

Weber, M. (1992). *The protestant ethic and the spirit of capitalism*. London: Routledge.

6

Individualization and the Cultures of Capitalism

The Enlightenment thinkers believed that human intentions and actions make society, not God or nature. In turn, the institutions that emerged from the interactions between individual actors shaped their goals, values and behaviour. Within the constraints set by societal membership and the obligations it demanded in exchange for protection and belonging, the individual had the right to personal freedom through exercising reason. Enlightenment thinkers mainly understood this idea of reason as a kind of consciousness that had previously been repressed because of the dominance of religious thought and institutions, the superstitions endemic to poverty-stricken, uneducated populations, and the social rigidities, formulaic practices and unquestionable respect for the past, dominant in traditional societies (Giddens 1994). Henceforth, reason would flourish through scientific knowledge. Because science also demanded critical thinking and a commitment to observation, experiment and openness to factual information, its growing importance would simultaneously reinforce wider commitments to democratic government, social tolerance and the ability of individuals to express self-determination (Seidman 1998:

© The Author(s) 2017
P. Kennedy, *Vampire Capitalism*, DOI 10.1057/978-1-137-55266-2_6

20–25). In short, all roads led to a future where social actors would shape nature while enjoying the personal freedom to express their individuality as a consequence of education and scientific understanding but expressed within a societal framework governed by increasingly humane, democratic and rational rules.

In the previous chapter, and in Chap. 1, we briefly considered some criticisms levelled against the ideas and assumptions that come from the Enlightenment. Yet, in the face of doubts and critiques, two issues concerning the individual have remained paramount, and their thematic presence weaves in and out of twentieth century and more recent academic and public debate. One concerns the nature, causes and trajectory of individuality within modernizing and industrializing societies. The other refers to the desire to preserve the goal of individual freedom and to protect it from various dangers. Yet, modernization has always been inherently transforming and subject to disruption and restless change. From the perspective of individual agents, modernity has meant never being satisfied with our achievements or experiences: the future always beckons.

Not surprisingly, our understanding of individualization processes is subject to debate and much of this is examined below. Focussing on the contemporary socio-cultural situation, this chapter explores some of the main contrasting interpretations of individuality. In doing so, and, following in Durkheim's footsteps, we ask whether the current trajectory of individualization is leading humanity towards an ever more fragile and fractured social solidarity where a social existence, splintered into a 'syndicate of egoisms' (J. Roman, cited in Bauman 1998: 36), precludes the capacity to cope with future crises.

6.1 Individualization and the Disappearing Society

There is a strong perception in the writings of many sociologists and others that since the 1960s or so, the individual social actor has moved very much to centre stage. When UK Prime Minister Margaret Thatcher famously commented during an interview in 1987 that 'there is no such thing as society ... only individual men and women, and their families', she was primarily engaged in justifying her party's neoliberal commitment to reducing state involvement in the economy. Nevertheless, her remark reverberated and remained as a stock part of the popular political repertoire. Perhaps, too, it echoed what some serious observers were contemplating at that time. In this section we dissect this claim and explore some of its dimensions.

Of particular interest is the rise of an increasingly prevalent form of individualism, primarily within the advanced societies, such that social actors expect, demand and indeed insist that each citizen has the absolute right to live a life of his/her own dominated by 'an ethic of self-fulfilment' (Beck and Beck-Gernsheim 2002: 22). Self-realization becomes not only our primary goal but also a duty. Further, the pursuit of self-fulfilment requires 'the self-organization and self-thematization of people's biographies' (24). To this argument, Bauman (2000: 31) added the suggestion that individualization along the lines indicated by Beck and Beck-Gernsheim (2002) amounts to a situation where constructing our identities becomes a 'task' and is no longer a 'given', or a choice. In a similar vein, Giddens (1991: 5) argued that the pursuit of 'self-actualization' within the 'tightly confined personal realm', and constructed around lifestyle choices, has become the key resource for engaging in 'life planning and daily activity'. Closely tied into Giddens's idea of individualization in contemporary society is his claim that it has given rise to the 'pure relationship' (1992) between the partners in romantic relationships. Unlike traditional and earlier modern societies where marriage was supported by law, religious sanction and clear notions of duty and obligation to wider families and communities, in 'high' modernity such relationships are based on the closest possible intimacy and sharing of emotions and feelings solely between the two partners involved (1992). This, in turn, requires and engenders trust and equality. If and when these break down so, very likely, will the relationship as it is only the particular voluntary and individual exchange of emotional support which each gained and demanded that held the relationship together.

So ubiquitous and pervasive have the needs, desires and actions of the individual become to our understanding of how social and cultural life works, relentlessly thrust into our daily consciousness by media exposure, that it is sometimes difficult to believe that something we once referred to as 'society' exists at all. It is as if society functions only as background context or as a rather vague arena whose space exists merely to facilitate each individual's daily live performances. Sociologists such as Touraine (1995) and Bauman (2000) seem to bear out this idea. Touraine's comment below (1995: 373) is especially apposite:

> There no longer seems to be any correspondence between actor and system. … Whilst the market is replacing social norms and cultural values with competition, an obsession with identity is replacing involvement in society at the personal level and our societies are becoming increasingly uncoordinated sets of collectivities, sub-cultures and individuals.

Both suggest that social actors now run their lives as if society—in Durkheim's sense of an entity in modernity that still provides moral order and demands certain restraints despite increasing social differentiation and the greater autonomy granted to the individual—had delegated its former capacity to generate shared meanings and normative regulation almost entirely to the individual.

In his book *Liquid Modernity* (2000: 3) Bauman reminds us how Marx and Engels insisted long ago (1848) that nothing in modernity stays still for long. Instead, there is a strong melting tendency tied up with the intrinsic restlessness and unfinished nature of modernity as a set of forward-moving processes. Nevertheless, in confronting pre-modern systems, and given the goals of material progress and national survival, the elites who pushed through the reforms and policies associated with early modernity strove to construct a set of institutions. The intention was to make the world 'manageable' by eliminating the 'accidental and contingent' as far as possible from the lives of citizens, partly by extending control over nature (Bauman 2002: 28). In this long era of early to mid-modernity, until well into the twentieth century, 'society' remained a useful and revealing metaphor for 'solid modernity'. In effect this society built 'tough frames and enclosures meant to last' which fused together the scattering of diverse businesses, industries and economic interests along with local/regional customs and dialects into one language and one national community through education, law, the mass media and government regulation (42). In this context, Foucault's argument that modernity required the rise of the disciplinary society, constructed around different kinds of specialized professional knowledge coupled to the regulatory demands of factory, barracks, prison, clinic, school, workhouse and so on also has a strong resonance.

During this era of 'solid modernity', when state welfare systems were fragmentary or mostly absent, ordinary citizens also engaged in political struggles and community engagements on their own account.[1] These were designed to make collective provision for individual accident and other misfortunes. They did this through forming or joining such organizations as trade unions, mutual societies, cooperatives or mechanics' institutes. Through these experiences and practices, individuals became re-embedded into the emerging urban industrial society following their initial social dislocation after migrating from village life and following their early encounters with the chaos, impersonality, poverty and complexity of the industrial city.

Yet, the 'permanent' melting tendencies of modernity inevitably resumed and became particularly evident and powerful during the second half of the twentieth century. Thus, liquid modernity means that every aspect of human life, economic, cultural, political, the personal and intimate and so on, is liable to dissolve and flow in any direction. But especially noticeable is the reality that the individual social actor's behaviour and goals are no longer guided by wider social norms but by the concerns and needs specific to his/her own situation (22). Here, Bauman adds a proviso (29): we no longer believe in modernity as a project that can lead to an ultimate condition of human, social perfection. Nevertheless, what remains of this idea of improvement has been transferred decisively from collective action or society, in the guise of government legislation, onto the shoulders of the self-assertive individual. This also explains why discourses relating to modernity now revolve around notions of 'human rights' rather than the 'just society' (29). Nor, as presently found, does liquid modernity provide much prospect for social

---

[1] E.P. Thomson's classic and renowned book *The Making of the English Working Class* (1963) captures these processes brilliantly.

re-embedding into new social collectivities, as happened in an earlier era. Rather, and metaphorically speaking, all that is on offer for individuals today are 'motel beds, sleeping bags and analysts' couches' (22).

Touraine (1995) offers a very similar prognosis. Economic and technological changes in particular have pitch-forked society into a struggle for international survival. This condition threatens to sever the connection between human subjectivity and the real world of work, economics and science, thereby fostering a 'widespread obsession with identity', but one that is divorced from a societal framework (5). In the poorer countries, such developments risk fermenting a new and growing communitarianism while in the advanced nations we are likely to see the growth of 'narcissistic individualism'. Neither family, religion, the demands of different social allegiances, nor even democracy, can be permitted to obstruct the individual's freedom to express his/her personal behaviour and need for self-realization—except for one restriction. This is the taboo on not hurting the 'other' as a result of exercising one's own private pursuits. Unfortunately, however, this loose and flexible constraint on the exercise of personal freedom is subject to different interpretations because it is not grounded in societal norms reinforced by clear sanctions. Consequently, it is liable to slip in many directions. By the same token, it still offers an individualism that defines 'man as a non-social being' (262).

It is also worth recalling the claims of neoliberalism outlined in Chap. 3. Here, the market economy replaces society as the primary arena where individuals can and should play out their daily lives as private, self-driven entrepreneurs. By responding to market signals, rather than social obligations, loyalties and affiliations, individuals maximize their personal freedom. Their actions and priorities, along with those of many others, will also keep the oppressive tentacles of the state at bay and provide the opportunity to achieve economic success through competition. Meanwhile, in a system where the knowledge signals coming from the market are all-pervasive and all-knowing, everyone's economic fate lies in their own hands. Accordingly, the burden of carrying the less diligent and least successful citizens will cease to be so onerous. After all, their personal failures and miseries cannot be laid at the door of a non-existent society but only at their own feet. Extending them 'too much help' will merely reinforce the same behaviour and personal attributes which led them astray in the first place. Thus, from an entirely different route we return to the thinning, even vanishing, society, no longer capable of holding individual social as opposed to economic behaviour to account. Meanwhile, the mass of self-governing individuals gets on with separately building their personal share portfolios and/or busily constructing their own chosen DIY life courses.

6.2 'Who Do You Think You Are?'

Since at least the 1980s there has been a growing interest in the salient characteristics of the individual who inhabits late modernity, high modernity, postmodernity, liquid modernity, second modernity and so on. Sociologists, students of consumer behaviour, popular culture and the media along with post-structural cultural theorists have been at the forefront of these investigations into individualization, while offering various explanations for its rise to dominance. As we have seen, neoliberalism has also tried to hijack this domain as have a number of public spokespersons in the media and politics. Drawing mainly on recent sociological theorizations, we now pinpoint a sample of some of the most clearly defined and insightful but also contradictory of these individual 'prototypes'. Together they demonstrate the extreme complexity and evolving nature of social life and culture but also lay bare the frailty of society in the early twentieth century.

The Reflexive Individual—Taking on the World

Giddens (1990 and 1991), Beck (1992) and Beck and Beck-Gernscheim (2002) all see contemporary social actors as compelled to take responsibility for their own lives through continuously monitoring their impact on other social actors and on the wider environment around them. As Giddens (1994) argues, people in all societies reflect on their situation in the light of incoming knowledge. However, freed from the prescriptive demands and formulaic nature of customs and rules in pre-modern societies, and confronted with the sheer increase in the flow of knowledge, modern individuals both can and must continuously reinterpret information and redirect their own actions instead of merely following traditional guidelines. Consequently, the need for self-confrontation, as we monitor and respond to the way our actions affect others, becomes inescapable. These same authors also agree that this is rendered even more essential given that modern social actors exist in a globalizing world—one that in any case results from the inherently diffusing and expansive nature of modernity (see also Bauman 2002). Driven by the twin engines of science and capitalism and riven with geopolitical rivalries, this 'runaway world of enormous power' is fraught with uncertainty. While it promises an exhilarating ride it is liable to swerve off in unexpected and dangerous directions (Giddens 1990: 139). Here, we see that for these sociologists the micro-life of the perceptive individual, repeatedly re-constructing his personal lifeworld, is brought into close conjunction with the vast, bursting macro-world of global modernity.

In addition to throwing up immense cumulative hazards the continuing scientific and technological advances of capitalist industrialization throughout the twentieth century led to several further social transformations culminating in 'reflexive' modernity (Beck 1992). On one hand, the penetration of commercialization into more and more areas of social life combined with rising living standards and the establishment of welfare systems, at least in the advanced societies, released individuals far more significantly than before from the demands and pull of social structures. Thus, we see the rise of new kinds of communities based on (online) communication and shared lifestyle interests instead of locality, social class and workplace solidarity. Women achieved greater independence through paid employment and education and were therefore able to experience marriage and even permanent partnership as a personal choice rather than the primary path to economic security and social recognition. Coincidentally, divorce became far more common. Growing generational differences in cultural interests and social ties also became far more noticeable and pronounced.

On the other hand, and bound up with this, the individual desires to live a life of her own, to construct her own DIY biography and lifestyle as we have seen. This is her preferred option and both its possibility and desirability are trumpeted every day in films, pop music, on reality TV, in magazine advice columns, on Facebook, through the pronouncements of celebrities and much else besides. Yet increased distance from family, locale, community, ethnic and other primary bonds, coupled to recent neoliberal attacks on welfare provision, have also given the individual little choice but to do so (Beck and Beck-Gernscheim 2002). Berking (2000) pushes this argument further by suggesting that reflexive individuals are expected not only to manage their pensions and career prospects but also to take responsibility for their bodies and everyday appearance and presentation. We are expected to be slim and fit, amusing, stylishly dressed, a virtuoso in managing our online apps and social media connections, willing to cultivate a green footprint and so on.

But Beck, Beck-Gernsheim and Berking also argue that the reflexivity always present in human interactions takes on a new dimension. We increasingly monitor and modify the impact of our daily actions on the physical and economic environment and not just in respect to those with whom we interact. This is even more necessary and unavoidable given the cumulative weight of our own personal lifestyle actions and demands as they ceaselessly contribute to the side effects of capitalist economic growth: car possession, air travel, our demand for hot water and air-conditioned residences, our consumption of foreign and unseasonable foods, the waste and effluence we generate, our relentless craving for an endless stream of new signifiers embedded in consumer goods and so on.

The 'Neoliberal Individual': Living for Market Gain

In Chap. 3 we interrogated the thinking behind the neoliberal projection of the contemporary individual as both able and needing to exercise an 'entrepreneurship of the self'. Here, the market economy promises that providing individuals develop the technologies of the self—enhanced training, delayed gratification, a single-minded devotion to thrift and industriousness, a determination to compete—anyone can become successful, or at least comfortably well-off and capable of exercising control over their own destiny. For those individuals committed to the neoliberal path to economic stardom, failure is not an option. If failure does occur, it will be the individual's own fault. Despite the sheer banal, underlying self-congratulatory justification of wealth and power here, there is no denying that neoliberalism appears to have been thoroughly internalized by many ordinary citizens. Even some who are poor and who exist in highly marginalized situations of multiple socio-economic deprivation seem to prefer blaming other equally destitute citizens—who also depend on welfare or low wages—for their country's ills rather than the elites who decide economic policy and manage the world's institutions, surely an instance of Foucault's concept of governmentality or self-policing.

Interestingly, there is a certain overlap between the neoliberal and Giddens/Beck/Beck-Gernsheim versions of the contemporary individual in the sense that both must monitor and take responsibility for their actions. Of course, the reflexivity exercised by the former is directed towards tracking and responding to market signals rather than the environmental, political and social consequences of their actions. Presumably, too, the neoliberal individual's responsiveness to social events and relations veers primarily towards building connections with potential economic patrons. Nevertheless, both types of individual deal with endless streams of incoming knowledge and are driven to adapt their performance in the light of what they have learned from the results of their own previous actions.

The Postmodern Fragmented Self, Floating in Hyperreal Space

Attempts to identify and depict the realm of the 'postmodern' began in the 1960s and were boosted by the political disillusionment which followed the events of France in May 1968. Then, student revolts and workers' strikes virtually paralysed that country for several weeks but eventually broke down. By the 1980s the discourse of the postmodern was in full swing across the Academy and was being widely taught to students. The vast and growing sphere of topics, themes and issues subsumed within its orbit soon 'stretched in all directions across different debates, different disciplinary and discursive boundaries'. To such an extent that according to Hebdige (1998: 78–79) the term became a 'buzzword'. The discourse surrounding the postmodern encompassed everything from architectural style, new art forms, popular culture, fashion and the power of images, to the rise of transnational corporations in a globalizing economy and concerns with bureaucracy and the failings of democratic and totalitarian politics. Nevertheless, underpinning all this lay two crucial philosophical and epistemological breaks with the previous presumptions that had dominated Western thought as well as the ideologies and theories that had grown out of it, including Marxism.

One involved Lyotard's (1984) attack on the belief in the possibility and the legitimacy of pursuing grand projects or metanarratives since the claims to valid knowledge, on which their credibility rested, were highly questionable. This included scientific knowledge which cannot provide a logic or matrix from which we can deduce a morality or politics: it cannot tell us how to live or what constitutes justice. Along with this went a scepticism concerning the belief in material or any other kind of progress, particularly when linked to the idea of a universal human nature (see also Gray 1995). The legitimacy of pursuing vast projects in the name of collective subjects such as the working class, advancing technological development or the spirit of the fatherland also lacked justification. But this undermining of previous certainties was accompanied by a second kind of scepticism: the idea that meaning—in spoken or written texts, films, songs, social actions or projects and so on—is manifest and can be readily accessible and brought into everyday understanding if we use the appropriate knowledge techniques. Thus, Derrida (1978), and other poststructuralists, rejected the idea that meaning is somehow always present and emanates from some cause or presence while waiting to be retrieved from hidden underlying structures. Meaning is not a given but exists only in everyday processes conducted by social actors. Like icons, images, adverts and so on, written spoken words and sounds are the signifiers or signs which we clumsily use to try to convey an underlying meaning. And invariably if we try to pin down the meaning of a signifier we find that it only leads us to yet further signifiers or words. Because meaning is always deferred it tends to constantly allude us so that we never quite arrive at what is signified or the referent.

Every forum and technique of cultural participation and communication is affected by this escalating uncertainty about meaning. This is particularly so in societies where higher living standards and a proliferating variety of media outlets and forms of leisure and consumption become affordable and desired by citizens. In this context Baudrillard (1988) argued that advertising, including packaging of all kinds, but also celebrity culture, TV soaps, entertainment parks and much else besides become vehicles for carrying all kinds of subtle and not-so-subtle messages. Much of the time we become so seduced by the representations of power, status or sexual attractiveness built into these messages that it is these that we really wish to acquire rather than the goods which supposedly embody them. As Sennett (2006: 161) observed, we find the actual possession and use of the things we buy less 'arousing' than contemplating our desire for goods prior to their purchase. Moreover, under postmodern conditions the sheer volume of swirling signs bombarding us from all sides and the tendency for these to become free-floating, detached from the medium conveying them, and liable to mutate in bewildering ways, has two further consequences.

First, lacking a stable frame of reference against which to measure reality or make sense of what is happening around us, and despite the attempt by advertisers and media experts to attract our attention and entice us with meanings, meaning eludes us. We cannot find ourselves or realize our dreams, as we had hoped, on the clothes racks in the arcade, on the supermarket shelves or by visiting eBay. Life takes on a shallow or depthless quality (Jameson 1992: 9–12). Second, Baudrillard argues that this glossy and ever-present world of messages, images and dreams seems to shrink the importance of the practical, social, everyday world. Instead, the world of fantasy, of dream parks, of TV soaps, of advertising and corporate brands, becomes more real than 'reality'. When this happens we reach out for the fake, hyperreal world promised by the simulacra—cultural inventions that have no reality of their own and which are only copies of themselves. We may even construct our lives around such simulacra so that the practical world of real things imitates and expresses the unreal and the fake rather than the reverse. In the extreme case, images, detached from life fuse together into a series of spectacles which seem to affirm social life but in fact transform it into 'mere appearance' (Debord 1983: 10).[2]

Under the condition of postmodernity, what happens to the individual, apparently lost in a swirl of shifting signifiers and bereft of either moral, knowledge-based or everyday cultural meanings? The figure that emerges is one whose self has become fragmented and de-centred. Certainly the autonomous bourgeois individual, projected by the Enlightenment, supposedly capable of exercising reason and acquiring independent knowledge through science, has disappeared into the vortex of the postmodern. Jameson (1992) further suggests that 'the liberation, in contemporary society, from the older *anomie* of the centred subject' brings relief from the anxiety and loneliness suffered by this self-sufficient figure. But it may simultaneously bring 'liberation from every other kind of feeling as well, since there is no longer a self present to do the feeling' (15). What emotions may remain are 'free-floating and impersonal' (16). There is, though, another aspect to the postmodern self that tends to receive less attention. This is the reality that whatever feeds into the postmodern experience, very little of it is possible without money. The penetration of capitalism into every crevice of social and cultural experience is central to the flourishing of postmodernity, not least in respect to the possibility of individuals experimenting with signs and constructing and re-constructing their identities through lifestyle. Popular culture—including all the welcome diversification, plurality and reversal of the previous hierarchies that once revolved around elite sensibilities—is also a thoroughly commercialized culture, a capitalist culture.

The 'Free' Individual—Imprisoned Within His/Her Own Little World

Bauman's contributions to our understanding of the contemporary individual are especially compelling. Like Beck, Giddens and others, Bauman

---

[2] Postmodern theory covers far more ground than can be discussed here: for example, the claim that social life is aesthetized in the kaleidoscope of shifting surfaces, the collapse of any distinction between 'high' bourgeois and popular 'low' culture and the rise of pluralistic cultural experiences which bring the previously excluded and marginalized—women, racial and ethnic minorities, LGBTs and so on—into the centre.

argues in his book *Society Under Siege* (2002) that society has retreated, leaving the question of personal identity largely up to the individual's own choice. Now, we are told, 'look inside yourself' (2000: 30) for answers to that question and this normally accords exactly with our expectations and wishes. But various consequences follow from this scenario and they tend to detract somewhat from the emancipation we desire. One is that the continuing and underlying restless dissatisfaction endemic to modernity, where nothing is ever finished, leaves the individual believing that there is no limit to their capacity for self-improvement. But because modernity keeps moving on, so do the definitions, challenges and potentialities confronting the lone individual. This may leave people with a sense of personal failure in a culture that reminds us society is no longer our mentor and protector (34).

Second, the reality that we must blame ourselves for our own weaknesses and failures leaves us disinclined to forgive others for their peccadillos. In the first modernity when most shared the same harsh obstacles to self-improvement, we saw the frailties of others in the same light as our own. Now we are tuned into a mind-set that makes such mutual tolerance more problematic. Indeed, third, Bauman (2000: 36) further suggests that setting us free from social control may leave us indifferent, or certainly sceptical, concerning the sufferings of others as well as disinterested in public issues, citizenship and politics. Individualization diverts our attention onto our own performance and away from the 'social space where the contradictions of individual existence are collectively produced' (38).

Bauman (2000: 23–25) provides a fascinating metaphor for the condition of individuals today. They are driven to be reflexive, self-promoting but also responsibly concerned with their own lifestyle management and convinced that they are entitled and indeed duty-bound to express opinions and offer criticisms whenever the private needs they have paid for are unmet. Thus, our self-contained individual and his family own a caravan which they park at various caravan sites during their vacations and travels. This allows them to bring their own home with all its private comforts and unique aesthetic preferences with them when they are on the move. Each driver also brings along and possesses 'his or her own itinerary and time schedule' (24). At the caravan site, they pay the manager for all the additional services they have been informed are available in exchange for rent while insisting on the right to be left alone. Because they have paid to occupy the site they feel completely justified in complaining and demanding that the manager correct any faults in the promised services or to be reimbursed if this is not possible. Indeed, they have a very strong sense of their personal rights. Although they are prepared to argue in this way with the manager and even, perhaps, offer advice concerning how to improve the site's facilities 'it won't occur to them to question and renegotiate the managerial philosophy of the site' as a whole (24). Nor will they feel any responsibility for its long-term or permanent improvement despite the opinions they may have expressed.

After a few days they leave to resume their itinerary and what remains behind them is a situation where nothing has changed; the site continues as before and then the next lot of caravanners arrives. Thus, no shared actions occur or are possible and each individual continues to be contained within his/her lifeworld. All that is left of his/her visit is waste packaging and effluence. At the same time, the kind of criticism that is both possible and allowable in the contemporary situation is quite different—in its narrowness and personal specificity—from the much broader kinds of shared public criticism that were commonplace and expected in an earlier era of modernity. As Bauman (2000: 25) suggests, 'we may say that a "consumer-style critique" has replaced its "producer-style" predecessor'.

Living in an Ever-Changing Present: Lost and Incomplete Identities

In two books Sennett (1998 and 2006) explores the rise of what he calls the 'new capitalism' and the changes it has wrought in the work lives of many employees but also in re-shaping the wider cultures of everyday life. We examine this in detail in the next section. For the moment we focus briefly on the impact of change on the individual's sense of self. One obvious effect of changing work practices has been the decline of craftsmanship (2006: 105–15). In an age of rapid technological and market change where the shelf-life of skills is short, what firms are looking for is an employee's potential to add value to future company operations, not the accumulation of proudly guarded past skills. It is younger, less expensive workers who are most likely to possess the right degree of adaptability and who neither expect nor wish to remain with the same firm throughout their work life as an older generation often did. Similarly, 'mental superficiality' is the new value: knowledge that scratches surfaces, and that does not depend on background context and is quickly discarded when no longer needed. What all this adds up to, Sennett (2006: 86) suggests is 'the spectre of uselessness'. This is most likely to challenge the identities of older, highly skilled workers, trained for an earlier era but it also closes the door on those younger workers who are not equipped or inclined to follow the path of higher educational attainment into the flexible, high-tech workplace.

Sennett sees a further loss and danger. If people no longer feel needed and/or their pay and lack of job security preclude the possibility of rearing a family, they are liable to feel thoroughly demoralized. Possessing and sharing 'a connection to the world' and 'being necessary to others' are crucial attributes of what Sennett calls character (1998: 146). These attributes also allow the individual to construct a sustained story concerning their life path. Yet, the short-term, future-oriented nature of the work required in the new capitalist enterprises, with their demand for multi-skilling and 'indifference' (1998: 146) towards employees, coupled to the latter's constant mobility between jobs, renders this extremely difficult. Even younger and more educated workers, perhaps, are likely to be damaged by demands from the new capitalism for a series of shallow, fragmented and partial identities that undercut the possibility of developing a life narrative.

6.3 The Rise of Consumer Culture and the Decline of Work Identity

Consumer behaviour is inextricably bound up, both as cause and effect, with the massive change in work practices that began to sweep through economic life from the 1970s but also with the rise of a postmodern culture of signs and spectacles. In this section we begin our discussion by considering the ways in which consumer behaviour and aspirations contributed to the rise of Sennett's (1998 and 2006) 'new capitalism'.

The Consumer as Co-Conspirator in the Decline of Work Security

As we saw in Chap. 4, several macro-economic transformations gathered pace from the 1970s. In different ways their cumulative impact on employment and work conditions across a growing number of industries and economic sectors was considerable. Streek (2012: 29–30) argues that the gradual collapse of much Fordist industrial practice had additional causes other than factory struggles over wages and productivity, capital's counter-attack against labour through neoliberal policies from the late 1970s and Japanese import penetration. Already in the 1950s a consumer youth culture was emerging fed by a generation who, unlike their parents, had no memory of pre-war poverty and who benefitted from joining the workforce at a time of abundant jobs, economic optimism and rising wages. More generally, by the 1960s older workers too were beginning to take growing prosperity for granted, while technical advances in the dissemination of TV, cinema and music at a time of growing leisure and a rising desire to resist elite presumptions concerning appropriate cultural styles, all combined to fuel the demand for a more popular, often low-brow culture through which individuals could sculpt their personal lifestyle desires (Featherstone 1992). Post-war prosperity had allowed citizens to satisfy their basic wants. Now, rising expectations were creating a desire for a choice of products customized to meet individual desires. Characteristic of this new consumerism, too, was its freedom from traditional social obligations and constraints. When selecting a commodity and choosing a style that resonated with the self-perception of the purchaser there was no compulsion to express a collective identity linked to social class or locality or any other social category. Only fashion identities mattered as businesses strove to create and respond to various niche markets. Even then, the consumer was free to change such identities while selecting from a vast and changing range (Streek 2012: 35).

But the necessity to satisfy the proliferation of consumer wants placed growing pressure on factories to allocate more space, time and resources to decisions regarding the design, appeal and presentation of their products. The standardized commodities produced by Fordist factories were becoming redundant. According to Streek, firms responded to this challenge in several ways: employing more women as a means of gaining relatively low-cost, amenable labour; re-locating some industrial processes to low-wage countries; but also re-engineering their products so that they could run shorter production cycles, build in greater flexibility, adapt to changing fashions and customize goods to better match the idiosyncrasies of individual purchasers. Commercial responsiveness and evolving consumer culture, aided and abetted by media and entertainment cultures, further undercut workplace bargaining power and social cohesiveness by creating consumerist diversions targeted at individuals and their personal dreams.

Sennett (2006: 144–5) elaborates Streek's analysis in an interesting way. The product re-engineering in which many firms increasingly engaged was akin to a kind of 'gold plating', dependent on giving greater free rein to product designers and advertisers in addition to deploying machines which could be rapidly adjusted to make small product changes. Firms manufactured a range of variations on their original product and/or endlessly re-decorated models in order to magnify what were really quite minor, stylistic or visual differences. Of course, technical advances in communication around the same time in regard to such things as bar coding and the increased deployment of electronic point of sale systems (EPOS) by shops hugely facilitated re-engineering by manufacturers since they were able to receive constant and immediate information from retailers and their own warehouses regarding the changing flow of consumer tastes. Branding an entire range of company products around a carefully constructed and projected theme also reinforced this process of making rather superficial modifications seem like markedly different products. As Sennett (148–9) suggests, the good purchased by the consumer remained almost or basically the same. Nevertheless, the consumer invested their desires and dreams in their favourite possessions. Consequently, it was not too difficult to believe that the product s/he had just bought really was different and truly reflected his/her shifting taste and choice.

Case Study 4: The changing character of sport consumption

Most modern sports were codified and became key aspects of local and national pastimes in the nineteenth century, particularly in Britain. They were then widely diffused through colonization and Westernization. During the twentieth century governments worldwide encouraged sport as 'patriot games' (Maguire 1999): a way of inculcating nationalist identities (see Cohen and Kennedy 2007 for a comprehensive analysis). Further, until the 1970s the Olympic Games, for example, remained largely the domain of amateurs driven by a sense of patriotic duty or personal ambition to attain high standards. Yet, Streek (2012: 34) describes how within 30 years the 'austere ethos of strict discipline and self-control' was transformed into 'hedonistic entertainment' and 'consumerist narcissism' for fans, and a vehicle for 'celebratory self-presentation' for leading professional sports personalities who also enjoyed huge opportunities for amassing personal fortunes from earnings and sponsoring products. In fact, the Olympics (and other sports) have become a 'giant money-making machine' that attracts sponsors, the advertisers of corporate merchandise (often manufactured using child or other cheap labour in poor countries), tailored to meet the hopes and aspirations of millions of fans, expanding global TV satellite and the 'global media-sport complex' (Maguire 1999)—but also vast live gate audiences of enthusiastic fans, loyal to particular clubs. Swept along by this same commercialization, local companies such as Adidas and Puma in Germany became multi-billion dollar companies selling sport fashion products, not just running shoes, worldwide to eager consumers (Streek 2012: 34–35). Meanwhile, many highly successful players appear to have lost any sense of loyalty to particular teams, national or otherwise. Instead, they play for the highest bidder.

Throughout this process of ratchetting up the commercial and media hype surrounding national and global sports contests, capitalism has seemingly played by far the leading role. But capital has not just lead audiences. It has also been partly driven by the insatiable demand from them to watch ever more spectacular contests and virtuoso performances from players (Miller et al. 2001: 68). Consequently, by 2012 total global sports revenues reached $130 billion: including, $40 billion from sponsorship, $32 billion from media/TV rights and fees and $18 billion from merchandising. With so much money involved it is not surprising that there is growing concern across the various international federations, in football, cricket, tennis, athletics, cycling and several other sports, that corruption of various kinds (money laundering, match-fixing, kickbacks for player transfers, rigging of arena construction contracts, the large-scale doping of competitors) is rife. The alleged human rights abuses committed against migrant workers engaged in building the World Cup stadiums in Qatar for 2022 constitutes a further dimension.

Work, Flexible Specialization and the Decline of Work Culture

In *The Culture of the New Capitalism*, Sennett (2006) dissects with admirable clarity a catalogue of changes that replaced earlier work processes and experiences during the last decades of the twentieth century, particularly in the larger global manufacturing and other sector companies. As Sennett suggests, many who had constructed and benefitted from the social capitalism of the mid-twentieth century had believed that it would endure. However, a series of changes coming on-stream from the 1970s onwards dismantled much of the previous edifice of collaboration and worker protection. As we saw in Chaps. 2, 3 and 4, they included: the shift of power to shareholders and 'empowered investors' (40) looking for short-term gains; the gush of vast money flows through the global financial system, exposing firms to the demands of fickle investors worldwide; and the increased adoption of automation so that the wide 'employment base' (44) of factory and office was no longer necessary. The neoliberal attack on the public sector and a supposed welfare dependency culture, added to rising international competition, further legitimized the switch by many businesses to leaner and often meaner production systems.

A number of consequences soon followed and we considered some in earlier chapters and in the previous subsection. But what needs additional emphasis is the widespread simultaneous adoption of enhanced communication technologies. On one hand, top managers gained a far more panoptic view of the entire span of company operations and this enhanced their surveillance power over all workers (Sennett 2006: 51–55). On the other, they were able to 'thin down' the bureaucratic chain of command. The overall result has been a considerable centralization of power and control at the top of many organizations. Along with the other changes, all of this promoted company flexibility, increased the speed with which firms could respond to changing consumer demand or competition from other companies and boosted company profitability. But it also further widened the gap between the firm's centre and periphery.

6 Individualization and the Cultures of Capitalism 189

Top management power expanded while the employees' ability to exercise much influence over shaping the agendas which set their own work tasks usually diminished.

Other observers have commented on this centralization of power and intensified surveillance of employees—including among professionals such as school and university teachers. Deleuze's (1992) idea of the 'society of control' is highly relevant. Deleuze contrasted today's corporate capitalism with Foucault's delineation of the disciplinary society of an earlier modern era organized around enclosed environments, particularly the factory, and where activities were concentrated in ordered spaces and time periods, each governed by its own fixed rules. Now, however, control is 'free-floating' and modulating as in the case of markets. Those in charge continuously declare the need for 'necessary reforms', while 'perpetual' training replaces examinations and nothing is ever complete. Further, every condition exists in a state of 'metastability' operating 'through challenges, contests, and highly comic group sessions' such that individuals are constantly motivated to compete against each other (4–5). Following this line of argument, Fisher (2009) argues that it is the combination of neoliberal economic priorities and the 'cybernetization' of work environments through digitalization and the rise of the flexible economy that have led us to the society of control. Here, the worker must demonstrate his/her emotional commitment to the firm and not merely submission to the myriad systems of surveillance and regulation. Meanwhile, the formidable presence of the communication system means that there is literally nowhere for employees to hide (40).

Among the control techniques used by managers that are now ubiquitous across much of the private and public worlds of work are targets and auditing procedures. The former tend to become ends in themselves rather than ways of measuring real performance. This is because the teachers or medical staff, for example, who are obliged to adopt them, are driven to find safe and easy ways to tick the relevant boxes, thereby guaranteeing their success rates. But in the process they may avoid the more important tasks which they would likely fail, given the resources and time available to them if they prioritized these instead. Declining educational standards are probably one consequence because the targets governments set for students dispose teachers to concentrate on how to pass exams rather than the acquisition of deep knowledge—which is also harder to assess properly (43–44). Where the creation of auditing cultures is concerned, what tends to transpire is that the auditing process itself becomes more important than actual performance. Thus, 'a short-circuiting occurs, and work becomes geared towards the generation and massaging of representations rather than the official goals of the work itself' (Fisher 2009: 42).

Sennett (2006: 63–80) further argues that the work practices of the new capitalism have led to long-term 'social deficits'. One consists of each employee's sense of loyalty to the company. A number of experiences are likely to test this including: the frequent imposition of fresh targets without discussion; the demand for multi-skilling, often unsupported by appropriate training; constant monitoring and surveillance; and seemingly arbitrary changes to hours of work and pay. A second likely casualty is the decline of informal trust since it requires time for interpersonal relationships and understandings based on an intimate knowledge of other people's skills and idiosyncrasies to form. But temporary or irregular employment and strong pressures towards immediacy and constant disruption undermine the possibility of such close relationships gelling. Sennett's (2006: 69) third social deficit refers to the accumulation of knowledge concerning a company's past record, how it is organized and the various relationships that make it work. Again, such institutional knowledge is likely to be thin or even absent when employee turnover, particularly among the low-skilled, is high, as machines constantly replace workers and contracts are irregular and temporary.

Consumerism to the Rescue? Contrasting Views

The literature on consumerism and its implications for social life and for individual lives is vast. Some have criticized consumerism for generating vapid, hedonistic self-obsessions and de-politicization, while others have celebrated consumers as creative heroes, sturdily pursuing life-enhancing practices which enrich social experience. While, for example, Kenway et al. (2006) offer a rather positive view within a global perspective, Ritzer's (2004) analysis is distinctly critical. There are, however, many positions in between, often ambivalent, with the majority of theorists providing a fairly neutral, balanced assessment of consumerism's impact, along with useful analysis (e.g. Bourdieu 1984; Featherstone 1992; Slater 1997; Tomlinson 1999; and Humphrey 2010).

We now look briefly at the work of three recent scholars whose ideas on consumerism are especially relevant to the theme of individualization and society. For Sennett (2006), consumerism and leisure practices have probably replaced the world of work as many people's primary source of identity and self-value, helping to fill the vacuum left in the individual's diminished sense of self-worth following the changes to work life outlined above. Advertising and branding, for example, capture the imagination of consumers and offer the individual a kind of potency even though this is partly buried beneath a less than rational belief in the life-enhancing properties of material goods. Similarly, consumerism stimulates responsiveness to carefully orchestrated and seductive signifiers thereby offering an invitation to fantasize about our lives and identities (150–4). Consumers enjoy their emotional investment in goods and welcome the endless new forms of stimulation that a store such as Walmart provides with its vast cornucopia of goods, all readily available in one location. In fact, the individual achieves a certain freedom by 'dreaming of something beyond the routines and confines of everyday life' (161) and this is not unlike being in a theatre. Consumerism also complements the changing work situation because like the latter it operates on the play of temporary and short-lived experiences and alliances, the need for constant alertness to change and new challenges. Neither as contemporary citizens, workers or consumers do most people act or think like craftsmen. If the craft worker was engaged, committed, full of concentration and in thrall to his/her hard-won expertise, today's individual is inattentive, disinterested in acquiring a deep understanding and relatively uncommitted to permanent attachments (171). Finally, Sennett stresses that most consumers are actively involved in their own lifestyle construction. The adverts and brands do not simply shape our desires without our participation.

In one sense, Touraine's (1995) analysis is very similar. The decline of the 'productivist society' (142) built around work has been accompanied by societal fragmentation but also the increased significance of consumerism. Yet, consumerism does not provide some kind of countervailing support in the face of society's disintegration. This is because it further divorces the individual from the social order since it is governed by the libido, or seduction, by a 'retreat in to tribalism and narcissism' (143) rather than the call of the nation or obligations to social institutions. Putting this another way, involvement in consumer practices takes us away from our social roles and leads us into a search for the self (143–4). Indeed, the power of consumerism means, in effect, that modernity is now primarily associated with 'the liberation of desires and the satisfaction of needs, rather than the reign of reason' (257).

Dean's (2009) concept of 'communicative capitalism' (4)—that is, the ascendancy of highly commercialized, intensive and proliferating forms of access to information, entertainment and communication—provides insights into consumerism similar to Touraine's. Capitalism, argues Dean, increasingly targets its commodities on the single and unique individual rather than broader market categories such as 'housewives'. This individualization permits consumers to 'star' in their own YouTube or Facebook show: it intensifies and legitimizes their narcissism. But it also magnifies the isolation of consumers as they sit at home in front of their laptop, stare at their iPhone on the train or walk the streets listening through their headphone to their personal tracks. Like Sennett, Dean notes that this repeats and reflects the isolating nature of the 'flexible' arrangements typically confronting the employee at work. A second and more insidious process, Dean claims, is the fact that some academics, including those on the Left, have echoed the business and mass media lobbies in suggesting that consumerism should be celebrated because of its creativity and ability to enhance individual freedom. But there is a neoliberal subtext at play here: we should 'let the market decide' (22). In this 'neoliberalised' view, the market is not only 'right' in social and economic senses, but also the proper forum for expressing individuality and attaining 'freedom'. After all, Walmart's goods, Disneyland's shows and rides, McDonald's burgers and reality TV are all popular. Hordes of people visit these sites all the time. It follows that they, and other commercial offerings like them, must be providing 'what people want'.

6.4 Individualization and its Deficits

The Lonely Powerlessness of the Late Modern Individual

The five types of individual depicted in Sect. 6.2 share at least one key feature in common. They may be comforted and distracted by the delights of consumer self-realization, mesmerized by postmodernity's glittering signs, diverted by the market's promise of future personal advantage, and share some of their aesthetic and lifestyle preferences with like-minded others. However, when it comes to dealing with the economic, political, environmental and wider social elements that fundamentally shape their life course and prospects for long-term security, our five individuals mostly swim alone in the cold seas of neoliberal globalization. The sturdy raft of society which once provided a sense of social belonging and continuous support seems to have drifted well out of reach. They can draw on only minimum support, if any, from fellow citizens. In part, of course, this scenario is an artefact of the way in which their prototypes have been defined. Nevertheless, the discourses that have tended to dominate not just sociology but also political economy and various political ideologies over the last 30 years or so, in addition to popular magazine and other media cultures, all point in this direction. Working briefly through the nuts and bolts of these five individual cases it quickly becomes evident that although part of their loneliness is explicable in terms of personal choice, wider factors outside their control play the larger role.[3]

Our neoliberal entrepreneur functions alone primarily because this is the only kind of economy available or allowed. In any case, the deal on offer is the promise of private economic aggrandizement in exchange for accepting personal responsibility for the individual's own fate in a perpetually competitive market environment. Assailed by multitudes of swirling signals and socialized into seeing that reality only exists in the form of endlessly fluctuating representations, the postmodern individual is presumably bereft of guidelines, perspectives and parameters. S/he seeks only those choices that celebrate fluidity and aesthetic diversity while remaining unaware, perhaps, that this exposes her/him directly to commercial targeting by the branding strategies of corporate advertising (Dean 2009: 8). The diminishing scope and solidity of the new workplace culture described by Sennett leaves the individual lacking in continuity and exposed to intensifying surveillance, isolation and rampant job insecurity. As a compensatory alternative, consumerism offers many attractions—but it also leans the individual towards a fascination with material possessions, some of which may prove less life-enhancing than s/he had been led to expect. Both Bauman's (2000) caravan family and the reflexive individual of the second modernity described by Giddens, Beck and Beck-Gernsheim seem to enjoy and express more choice. Attuned, also, to the cumulative side effects of capitalist modernity, which s/he is determined to tackle, and strongly attracted by the possibility of constructing his/her own 'do it yourself' lifestyle and biography, this individual, again, appears to exercise a good deal of choice. Moreover, we assume that the caravanner also relishes the freedom to cherish their private domain even though this same action leaves them isolated.

Yet, there is a compelling, if not overwhelming, reason why even our highly reflexive and self-confrontational individual can do little either to resolve his/her own personal insecurities or contribute towards healing the world's frightening divisions simply by their willingness to assume

---

[3] Some recent observers are convinced that the digital revolution, along with the rise of the social media and networked sociality, are changing individualization processes to the extent that new forms of social solidarity are emerging (e.g. Mason 2013 and 2015a and Rifkin 2014). In Chaps. 8 and 9 we examine this argument in detail.

a stance of reflexivity and personal responsibility. As Bauman reminds us (2000: 34–35 and 2002: 68–69) there are powerful forces constraining the choices open to our reflexive individual and, of course, everyone else. None can avoid the regime of economic insecurity, austerity politics and diminishing welfare protection which has been extensively imposed during the last 30 or so years, and intensified since 2008. Indeed, it is precisely the running down of previous systems of collective security and protection that have left people with no alternative but to try to assume more responsibility for their own lives. Partly, as we have seen, this is due to globalization, which has shrunk each society's autonomy. Bauman's observation that globalization has reduced the state to little more than an 'enlarged and ennobled police precinct' (2002: 82) obsessed with keeping law and order and rendering its territory attractive to overseas investors may be an exaggeration. But it does highlight the central reality that the capacity of most democratic governments to exercise 'sovereign power' either in respect to its citizens or globalizing processes has diminished compared to the recent past. In any case, and whatever the cause or situation, the fact remains that as citizens 'we cannot refuse to participate in the individualizing game' (Bauman 2000: 34) of taking responsibility for our own fate. Certainly, the business world, the neoliberal state and its politicians, among others, remind us of this through regular lectures. The reality, though, is that the individual alone cannot take on this task because the great majority of us lack the necessary resources to do so. Powerful pressures to believe in self-destiny, and the shrill arguments persuading us that any resort to collective solidarity in search of common causes is unlikely to work, are both strong. But their ubiquity and noise cannot cancel the reality that our 'life choices are not matters of choice' (69). Rather, the constraints and threats that confront us are not produced by individuals operating alone but by the many brought together in vast impersonal structures and systems. To paraphrase Vonnegut's words in *Slaughterhouse Five*, we seem to be little more than 'the playthings of enormous forces'. It follows that 'a gap is growing between individuality as fate and individuality as the practical and realistic capacity for self-assertion' (Bauman 2000: 34). As Bauman suggests, very few are equipped to bridge that gap. The risks and privations we experience are 'socially produced' but the responsibility and need to cope with them have been individualized.

Arguably, therefore, reflexivity by itself is too fragile as a resource to allow the individual to take on the heavy burden of confronting his/her own personal and encircling dangers. Nor can it help to achieve wider global change to the extent seemingly envisaged by Giddens, Beck and Beck-Gernsheim.

The Corruption of Politics and Weak Social Solidarity

The consequences for democratic political systems of the rise of postmodern consumer culture have been widely debated, including by several scholars whose work is examined in this chapter. By far the most obvious and disturbing consequence is that the role of the citizen has become elided with that of the consumer. In this process the latter became the dominant player. Voters and citizens have come to expect that politicians and governments will woo them and pander to their particular needs and concerns in the same way that advertisers and branded goods offer them endless variety and choice, including goods customized to suit their individual tastes, dressed up in engaging packaging. In effect, commercial culture teaches the citizen to become a consumer of politics. In this process the citizen-consumer begins to ask herself what policy-product, currently on the political agenda, or in the news, she might or might not wish to buy, and which particular party or politician seems to be offering her the best deal to fit her particular requirements in return for her vote-purchase (Streek 2012 and Sennett 2006).

Dean (2009: 22) reminds us that consumerism is basically about catering for people's actual or supposed needs through money and the market. In effect, though, the power of consumerism means that 'commercial choice' becomes the 'paradigmatic form of choosing'. This, in turn, leads to a major source of confusion involving a careless—or perhaps not so careless—merging of two very different things. Thus, highlighting the freedom of choice provided by capitalism diverts attention from the reality that 'the market is not a system for delivering political outcomes'. Commercial advertising campaigns for lipstick, a new gadget or a holiday package are not the same as political campaigns, and the kinds of 'truths' and promises each offers are qualitatively different. Here, communicative capitalism in alliance with neoliberalism undermines democratic politics.

Several further consequences have followed. One is that a fundamental distinction became established between the kinds of goods provided by the state via the public realm and those sold by private companies (Streek 2012: 36–39). The former catered for people's needs, social housing, welfare provision, schools and so on, while citizens turned to the private sector in order to satisfy their individual wants. This division was accentuated by the vast expansion of niche marketing from the 1970s onwards, coupled to the rapid growth of TV and telecommunications. The rising profusion of channels tended to down-play the educational content of programming, replacing it with a huge emphasis on entertainment value.[4] Over time the public sector and its goods came to be regarded not only as dull and uniform but also inefficient since unlike private companies its institutions were inept at making themselves attractive to their users, and catering for individual preferences. In response, UK governments—particularly Thatcher's and Blair's—began trying to personalize public institutions such as hospitals, while introducing management systems based on internal markets that imitated the commercial world. Streek (2012: 39–42) argues, however, that public services cannot be equated with private consumer goods since the former are based on collective and universal provision compared to a mass of personalized and changing desires. Similarly, it is not only fallacious, but actually dangerous, to equate the citizen with the consumer. If 'citizenship' is to be meaningful, it requires elements of duty, sharing, discipline and compromise over matters that affect everyone. It cannot be about pleasing the fickle, transient identity fantasies of innumerable separate individuals.

Another consequence is that politics has been trivialized as different parties and politicians vie with each other to offer or spin policies that they hope will appeal to voters, while being perfectly prepared to switch to another if the first fails to attract (Sennett 2006 134–5 and 157–73). Yet, politics also takes on theatrical aspects where presentation, appear-

---

[4] Streek (2012: 37) shows how Germany had only two national television channels in the 1970s but now that are over 100 across many cities.

ance and performance become all important: voters prefer their leading figures to be lean, witty and stylistically dressed. Sennett also suggests that politicians forget that today's consumers are not like craftsmen: their attention spans are short; they are inattentive and more impressed by surfaces than deep arguments.[5]

In short, politicians play these games but in the end they fail to convince or win the serious attention of voters. Like Dean, Sennett argues that it is misleading to equate political goods/policies with consumer goods. Decisions in the former domain cannot be decided and implemented in the same way that faddy and temporary choices and demands are expressed in respect to dress accessories or kitchen appliances by multitudes of individuals, day by day. Overall the result is, at best, a widespread disinterest in politics and, at worst, a loss of trust in the political process.

Despite the constant and weighty emphasis on individualism—which diverts our attention to the sphere of the private and away from public issues—Bauman (2000: 35) suggests that we are capable of seeing the sufferings and privations of others. Often this happens through reality TV shows and similar media events where people relate their individual stories of personal misfortune. Unfortunately, a particular person's specific losses and problems tend to be *non-additive* with our own and those of other individuals. Sometimes, the audience, and we as silent viewers at home, may feel drawn into sympathizing with the sufferings of those who bravely or unashamedly present their problems to the public. However, partly because of their highly individual nature the grievances of others and societal fragmentation means that our own misfortunes 'lack the interfaces allowing them to dovetail' and form commonalities on which we might be persuaded to collaborate in joint actions (35).

This surely is the crux of the dilemma. To bring about meaningful and effective change away from the current insecurities that plague all our lives we need to find some way of returning to actions involving collective solidarity—though not necessarily along the lines of earlier

---

[5] Perhaps, though, politicians are only too aware of this reality—and this explains the soundbites they frequently employ in attempting to shape public opinion. I am indebted to Ray Kiely for this observation.

forms—so that we no longer rely solely on lone, personal practices. Nor does this encompass Giddens's (1991) notion of 'life politics' since the latter is separate and different from seeking emancipation from societal oppression and massive inequalities through participation in large political and other movements and organizations. These, supposedly, belonged to an earlier era, whereas life politics is oriented towards the individual's project of self-actualization around issues of identity and interpersonal relationships.

6.5 Summary and Conclusions

Despite differences of emphasis, the individualization processes that many see as central to contemporary social life, particularly in the advanced countries, all point towards a condition of relative isolation and disempowerment in respect to the possibility of engaging in collective action designed to transform the wider parameters of socio-economic life. Indeed, so central is the emphasis on the individual and his/her task of self-realization in today's culture that the very idea of returning to earlier forms of social solidarity seems, at best, eccentric and unreal, and at worst, reprehensible and probably anti-democratic. Earlier chapters argued that several interwoven transformations have been crucial in weakening those earlier assemblages of class, citizenship and community cohesion that once contributed to holding capitalism to account: neoliberal policies, globalization, financialization and the industrialization of much of the Global South. Yet, in part, what prevents us from activating and joining contemporary forms of large-scale collective action is precisely our own relentless efforts at self-promotion and the pursuit of private individual identities. These leave us without much social support from fellow social actors, not just because our private emotional needs and circumstances do not gel around shared common problems but because prioritizing self-regard also tends to divide rather than unite. It leaves us with the disunity of 'self-centredness and the ego-centric society' (Beck 2009: 231).

Further, as Touraine observes (1995: 257), from the wider perspective of societal concerns and dangers that encompass many people and not just single individuals, individualism 'has no content of its own'. It leaves us too obsessed with the outcomes of our own actions rather than with actions and consequences that are manifestly harming others as well. Thus, there is a strong sense in which individualization is a chimera, a fake. It leaves us alone and disempowered. We are unable to shape the substance of our lives because by ourselves, and through solitary, micro-actions revolving solely around our own private dreams, idiosyncrasies and lifestyle preoccupations, we cannot confront the systemic structures and overwhelming inequalities that actually prevent us from pursuing a more meaningful, real individualization. Meanwhile the illusion of individualization closes our eyes to the potentially alternative paths to that same end but which require collective action.

Bibliography

Baudrillard, J. (1988). *Selected writings* (ed. M. Poster). Cambridge: Polity.
Bauman, Z. (1998). *Globalization: The human consequences*. Cambridge: Polity.
Bauman, Z. (2000). *Liquid modernity*. Cambridge: Polity.
Bauman, Z. (2002). *Society under siege*. Cambridge: Polity.
Beck, U. (1992). *The risk society: Towards a new modernity*. London: Sage.
Beck, U. (2009). *World at risk*. Cambridge: Polity.
Beck, U., & Beck-Gernscheim, E. (2002). *Individualization*. London: Sage.
Berking, H. (2000). Solidary individualism. In S. Lash, B. Szersynski, & B. Wynne (Eds.), *Risk, environment and modernity: Towards a new ecology* (pp. 185–201). London: Sage.
Bourdieu, P. (1984). *Distinction: A social critique of the judgement of taste*. Cambridge, MA: Harvard University Press.
Cohen, R., & Kennedy, P. (2007). *Global sociology* (2nd ed.). New York: New York University Press.
Dean, J. (2009). *Democracy and other neoliberal fantasies: Communicative capitalism and left politics*. Durham: Duke University Press.
Debord, G. (1983). *Society of the spectacle*. Detroit: Black and Red.
Deleuze, G. (1992). Postscript on the sociefised control. *October, 59*(winter), 3–7.
Derrida, J. (1978). *Writing and difference*. London: Routledge and Kegan Paul.
Featherstone, M. (1992). *Consumer culture and postmodernism*. London: Sage.
Fisher, M. (2009). *Capitalist realism: Is there no alternative?* Winchester: Zero Books.

Giddens, A. (1990). *The consequences of modernity*. Cambridge: Polity.
Giddens, A. (1991). *Modernity and self-identity: Self and society in the late modern age*. Cambridge: Polity.
Giddens, A. (1994). Living in a post-traditional society in Beck, U., Giddens, A. and Lash, S. [Eds.] *Reflexive modernity: Politics, tradition and aesthetics in the modern social order*. Cambridge: Polity, pp. 56–108.
Giddens, A. (1992). *The transformation of intimacy*. Cambridge: Polity.
Gray, J. (1995). *Enlightenment's wake*. London: Routledge.
Hebdige, D. (1998). Postmodernism and 'The Other Side'. In J. Storey (Ed.), *Cultural theory and popular culture: A reader*. Dorchester: Pearson/Prentice Hall.
Humphrey, K. (2010). *Excess: Anti-consumption in the West*. Cambridge: Polity.
Jameson, F. (1992). *Postmodernism or the cultural logic of late capitalism*. London: Verso.
Kenway, J., Kraack, A., & Hickey-Moody, A. (2006). *Masculinity beyond the metropolis*. Basingstoke: Palgrave-Macmillan.
Maguire, J. (1999). *Global sport identities, societies, civilizations*. Cambridge: Polity.
Mason, P. (2013). *Why it's still kicking off everywhere: The new global revolutions*. London: Verso.
Mason, P. (2015b). *Postcapitalism: A guide to our future*. Milton Keynes: Allen Lane.
Miller, T., Lawrence, G., McKay, J., & Rowe, D. (2001). *Globalization and sport: Playing the World*. London: Sage.
Rifkin, J. (2014). *The zero marginal cost society: The Internet of things, the collaborative commons, and the eclipse of capitalism*. Basingstoke: Palgrave/Macmillan.
Ritzer, G. (2004). *The globalization of nothing*. London: Pine Forge.
Seidman, S. (1998). *Contested knowledge: Social theory in the postmodern era*. Oxford: Blackwell.
Sennett, R. (1998). *The corrosion of character: The personal consequences of work in the new capitalism*. New York: W. W. Norton and Company.
Sennett, R. (2006). *The culture of the new capitalism*. London: Yale University Press.
Slater, D. (1997). *Consumer culture and modernity*. Cambridge: Polity.
Streek, W. (2012). Citizens as consumers: Consideration on the new politics of consumption. *New Left Review. 76* (July–August edition), pp. 27-48.
Thompson, E. P. (1963). *The making of the english working class*. London: Victor Gollanz.
Tomlinson, J. (1999). *Globalization and culture*. Cambridge: Polity.
Touraine, A. (1995). *Critique of modernity*. Oxford: Blackwell.

7

Global Capitalism and the Biosphere: Our Future in Jeopardy

This chapter investigates three linked themes. First, we consider the scientific evidence and explanations of climate change. In doing so it also explores the underlying dependence of modern life and material affluence on fossil fuels. Until very recently, governments, capitalist interests and ordinary citizens have treated unrestrained access to a carbon-based economy as if it was somehow a human right, like democratic freedom, which should never be taken away. Many continue to think in these terms. Second, we examine some of the examples which point to the impact climate change is already having on societies but also the various inequalities it is likely to accentuate further as the planet continues to warm up. Last, the discussion is framed within a larger, key question of whether global neoliberal capitalism can provide the primary route to countering climate change, as most commentators claim. Closely tied to this is a discussion concerning the possible contribution of various promised technological 'fixes'.

7.1 Welcome to the 'Anthropogenic Age'—of Climate Change

The past, approximately 11,700 years (i.e. since the last ice age), is known as the Holocene era. Human influence in re-shaping the natural and geological environment has been considerable. But some scientists argue that we have moved into an entirely new era: the 'Anthropocene Age'. This is the period where there is overwhelming evidence that human activity is exerting a cumulative, global and often adverse effect on the earth's geology and biosphere,[1] such that these are being altered, perhaps irretrievably. Changes include habitat loss; the massive erosion and transportation or loss of soils; a deterioration in the long-term viability of global water systems; and atmospheric and climate change, among other transformations. Of these, the most compelling is climate change.

In December 2015, the Paris Agreement on Climate Change was reached. Representatives from 196 nations signed up to actions (in force from 2020) intended to limit emissions of greenhouse gases (GHGs) to levels that would prevent global temperatures from rising above 2 degrees centigrade (2C). Below this level it is believed that the risk of temperature increases triggering further damaging and unmanageable climate changes will be minimized, though many would prefer action to keep temperature rises within the 1.5C band. The Paris Agreement followed 23 years of international conferences held under the auspices of the UN. This began with the Earth Summit at Rio in 1992. All attempted to achieve international accord on action to slow global warming, but with only minor successes until Paris.

GHGs and the Scientific Evidence

Carbon dioxide (CO_2), nitrous oxide and methane are the main substances emitted through human activity and which contribute to GHGs, although ozone is a further component. They arise particularly during

---

[1] The biosphere consists of the atmosphere, the oceans, lakes and rivers and their tidal systems plus plant life and other living organisms—from bacteria to insects, fish and animals, including humans.

fossil-fuel combustion and cement production.[2] Slightly less than a third of all CO_2 emissions result from agriculture and deforestation. Throughout the history of human life, relatively slow population increase coupled to the pre-industrial character of economic life, based primarily on animal, water and human power, meant that CO_2 levels remained fairly constant and were mostly absorbed by natural processes—oceans and lakes, forests and other vegetation. However, industrialization, with its power stations, oil wells, massive transport, distribution and heating systems, factories, industrial agriculture, proliferating cities and the colossal expansion of vehicles, among other causes, drastically disrupted these previous systems of approximate balance. The Worldwatch Institute (2016) reported that 87 per cent of world energy sources in 2012 came from fossil fuels: coal supplied 30 per cent, oil 33 per cent and natural gas 24 per cent, respectively. It also cited the International Energy Agency's prediction that by 2017 coal will become the leading primary energy source. This means that energy sources that emit only tiny or no GHGs accounted for barely one-tenth of the total, with renewables (wind, solar and geothermal) providing less than 2 per cent, though this has been rising since 2010 as we will see later.

Between 1751 and 2011 around 555 billion metric tons (or gigatons)[3] of CO_2 were dumped into the Earth's atmosphere, an amount beyond the natural absorbing capacity of the biosphere. According to the IPCC[4] approximately one-third of these 'surplus' GHGs are absorbed by the oceans, giving rise to a huge increase in acidification and de-oxidation, both of which harm marine life (IPCC 2013: 11). Some is also absorbed by the world's remaining forests, particularly those in the tropics. So far the biosphere has absorbed more than half of GHG emissions. Yet, the rising volumes of remaining gases are trapping some of the sun's radiation within the Earth's atmosphere, preventing it from escaping back into space. Consequently, average temperatures are rising, a phenomenon

---

[2] When limestone, used in the manufacture of cement, is converted to lime, it emits CO_2.

[3] One gigaton = one billion tons.

[4] The IPCC was formed in 1988 by the United Nations Environment Programme (UNEP). The IPCC is made up of around 2500 scientists worldwide whose research traces the links between GHG emissions and climate change. They have submitted a number of major reports and are widely respected by governments, most think tanks, IGOs and NGOs.

known as global warming. These emissions will remain in the Earth's atmosphere for thousands of years. Even if the world undertook concerted action to reduce GHG emissions from now, their effects will continue to operate far into the future. CO_2 provides around 80 per cent of these GHG emissions; hence it is the huge increase in CO_2 emissions that causes the most concern. However, methane, currently a marginal contributor, has a capacity to heat the atmosphere by a factor perhaps 80 times greater than CO_2 (Klein 2014: 143). Should temperature rises trigger the release of the methane currently locked in the ocean bed and in the Siberian semi-frozen tundra, rising temperatures might spiral beyond our control.

According to IPCC research (2013: 11) atmospheric concentrations of GHGs have increased to higher levels than at any time for which measurements are available, that is, during the last 800,000 years. Scientific ability to provide such measurements have been enhanced by the improving technology that enables them to examine the CO_2 atmospheric content deposited in ice-cores drilled in the Antarctic and Greenland ice caps. These samples have revealed that CO_2 values fluctuated during the last 800,000 years and prior to industrialization reached their highest level of nearly 300 parts per million (ppm) around 330,000 years ago. In 1750 atmospheric levels of CO_2 were approximately 280 ppm. They reached 316 ppm in 1960 and were then measured at 386 ppm in 2010, but had edged up further to 400 ppm by 2014 (Carbon Dioxide Information Analysis Centre [2012: 1–2]). From this we can deduce several startling conclusions. First, atmospheric levels of GHGs appear to be rising every year despite measures to mitigate CO_2 emissions and the global economic down-turn following 2008. Indeed, the IPPC (2014: 6) reported that the rate at which anthropogenic emissions have grown, accelerated from about 2.2 per cent a year on average from 2000 to 2010 compared to 1.3 per cent annually from 1970 to 2000 (2014: 6). This helps to explain the IPCC's calculation (2014: 7) that approximately half the cumulative rise in CO_2 emissions since 1750 took place between 1970 and that 2010. Second, overall CO_2 levels are 40 per cent higher than they were in the pre-industrial era (IPCC 2013: 11).

Taking into account all sources and allowing for margins of error, the IPCC (2014: 8) estimated the CO_2 equivalent emissions in 2011

7 Global Capitalism and the Biosphere: Our Future in Jeopardy

at approximately 430 ppm. This gave a baseline from which to evaluate global scenarios concerning likely future rises in temperature if serious strategies are not put in place to mitigate emissions. They conclude that the combination of world population growth, the continuing dependence on fossil fuels and efforts to increase economic growth will result in atmospheric concentrations of GHG equivalents of at least 450 ppm by 2030—that is, without mitigating measures. The IPCC further predicts that on the same basis atmospheric emission levels could reach between 750 to 1300 ppm by 2100. These would drive temperatures to anywhere between 3.7C and 4.8C above pre-industrial levels—possibly much higher if warming triggers the release of methane from Siberia's melting permafrost, among other sources (49–50). Accordingly, any overshoot of emissions beyond the 530 ppm level renders the possibility of keeping the global rise in temperature within the 2C band increasingly unlikely.

The same IPCC report (2014: 53) argued that remaining within this 2C band ideally requires the world to ensure emissions do not rise beyond 450–500 ppm, or a level scarcely higher than they are today. The report's warning is unequivocal: nations must triple or quadruple their 'global share of zero- and low-carbon energy supply' coming from renewables such as wind and solar, nuclear power, bioenergy and geothermal sources. In addition, any continued dependence on fossil fuels will require the development of technologies that capture and safely store carbon emissions (53).

The Impact of Climate Change: Extreme Weather and Deepening Poverty for Many

Ever more extreme weather conditions constitute the most obvious effects of climate change. For example, in March 2016 media stories, gleaned from data released by the USA's National Aeronautics Space Administration (NASA), explained that February's average global surface temperatures broke all records and by a wider margin than any previously seen (Carrington and Slezak 2016: 6). January's long-term average temperature also set records. In any case, 2015 had broken the previous record, set in 2014, for being the hottest year since data collection began in 1850, while the UK Met office expected 2016 to exceed even this. Reliable measurements that can distinguish between normal variations and freak weather patterns and the growing incidence of extremes are crucial. Recorded climatic changes, such as rising temperatures, are usually presented as global averages. However, their impact can vary across world regions. For example, rising average global temperatures are showing up more markedly in the Arctic than other regions.

The World Meteorological Office (WMO) provides regular data on weather patterns derived from such careful scientific records and measures. Here are a few examples of extreme weather incidents reported for 2015 in *Status of the Global Climate* (12–13). In addition to being the hottest year on record, with global average surface temperatures reaching 0.76C above the average for the years 1961 to 1990, the WMO also registered that average ocean heat broke all records. At its maximum, the 2015 summer Arctic sea ice covered the smallest area since data collection began in the 1970s and the rate of summer melting is accelerating. Heatwaves occurred in many locations during 2015 but were particularly bad in parts of Southern India where approximately 2000 people died. Extreme rainfall, sometimes giving rise to exceptional floods—as in North West Britain and Southern Scotland during December, where more than 341 millimetres of rain fell in one location—was widespread across the world. In Marrakesh, Morocco, the equivalent of 13 months of rain fell in one hour during August. In contrast, parts of Southern Africa experienced their driest season since records began in the early 1930s, while the drought in California continued until rain and snowfall on the Sierra mountains—linked to the Pacific's El Niño—in early 2016 finally broke the run of four dry years. In October, Cyclone Patricia hit Mexico and proved to be the strongest storm ever to occur in either the Atlantic or the North East Pacific region. Its wind speeds are reputed to have reached 346 kilometres per hour.

Such extremes are likely to occur more frequently as land and sea temperatures rise, causing ever more volatile weather cycles. Thermal oceanic expansion coupled to melting glaciers and sea ice are already raising sea levels and threatening island states. Bangladesh's coastline is being threatened every year, not just by 'normal' monsoon floods, but by inundations of greater extent and duration (see Reeves and Jouzel 2010: 52–91).

Much farm land is also under threat from salination. It is predicted that a future sea level rise of 45 centimetres will flood around 11 per cent of Bangladesh's land area and will displace up to six million inhabitants. The capital, Dhaka, is already heavily over-populated with migrants who have fled from rising rivers and coastal areas, while the neighbouring countries of India and Myanmar face their own population problems and difficulties caused by global warming. One view, therefore, is that international organizations need to plan for a future whereby huge numbers of environmental refuges will need to be transferred to other countries facing fewer stresses from climate change (64–65). Of course, some less populous states, such as Tuvalu, with its reefs and atolls in the Pacific (270–3), and the Maldives' archipelago in the Indian Ocean—1200 islands spread over 300 square kilometres—where the sea level is now rising by 5 millimetres each year (124–7), are already confronting climate change. But flooded islands, coastlines and estuaries and the accompanying loss of farmland and threat to cities such as London and New York, represent only one dimension of climate change. At the opposite end of the spectrum declining rainfall, prolonged droughts and desertification are creating their own hardships. One such case is Chad in Africa where Lake Blarigui has lost 90 per cent of its area during the last 40 years as the African monsoon rain has diminished. Once 6 metres deep, the lake bottom is now only 1.5 metres from the surface. The water is muddy and often dangerously unsanitary, while boats lie rusting on the lake-side as local fishing becomes more difficult (Reeves and Jouzel 2010: 92–97).

The IPCC report of 2014 pointed to the highly unequal per capita responsibility for emission levels across different parts of the world. Thus, in 2010, the median contribution of low-income countries was ninetimes lower than that of high-income countries and was mostly a result of farming and forestry. In fact, ten countries together accounted for 70 per cent of all CO_2 emissions from fossil fuels (IPCC 2014: 46). In terms of absolute emission levels, and using figures for 2011 supplied by the World Resources Institute, China emerges as by far the highest emitter, with over ten gigatons of gasses, followed by the USA, the EU, India, Russia, Indonesia, Brazil, Japan, Canada and Mexico respectively. This alignment clearly demonstrates that while the Global North is largely responsible for the greater part of cumulative emissions the balance of responsibility is also shifting to parts of the Global South as some countries experience rapid industrialization and urbanization.[5]

The impact of climate change will also fall disproportionately on some people and areas rather than others. The UN's *Human Development Report 2007/8* declared unequivocally that global warming represents a particular threat to the world's poorest people and those yet unborn. Both groups lack any or no political influence (6). Similarly, in *The Economics of Climate Change* (2007: 27–28), Stern observed that global warming is a huge 'externality' in the sense used by economists. Not only will those whose actions largely caused climate change never be required to pay the full costs of the pollution they have dumped on the biosphere, but the burden of coping with the consequences will fall hardest on those who bear little or no responsibility: namely, poor people and future generations (33). In the case of the former, Davis (2010) adds that climate change will also inflict the greatest damage on countries which possess the least resources for coping.

A recent World Bank publication, *Shock Waves: Managing the Impacts of Climate Change on Poverty* (2016: 2–5), explores the future conflict that is likely to arise between reducing world poverty and mitigating the effects of climate change. Poor people tend to enjoy less access to family and community support and fewer opportunities to obtain financial loans or garner support through government or local safety nets. Yet climate change will result in diminishing yields to their own farm output from drought—perhaps as much as 30 per cent by 2080—while the urban poor and farm labourers may face food price spikes. In general, by 2080 the growing incidence of drought may affect somewhere between 50 and 90 per cent of the world's poorest and most vulnerable people especially in South Asia and SSA. Equally worrying, huge tracts of agricultural land and/or ecologically marginal areas may be compulsorily sequestered by governments and corporations as ways of combatting climate change through developing bioenergy resources. However, this will massively diminish the amount of land available to poor farmers for food cultivation. We return to this later.

---

[5] It is important to note that in terms of *per capita*, rather than overall, emissions China comes out seventh in this list.

7.2 Capitalist Modernity and Fossil Fuels: An Easy Ride

The connection between fossil fuels and capitalist modernity seems so obvious as to be scarcely worth mentioning. However, once we lift up this stone we uncover a catalogue of compelling issues.

Carbon: The Bad Fairy's Curse at Modernity's Christening

Sloterdijk (2014) reminds us that Britain's industrial revolution depended not just on the harnessing of a proletariat fuelled by their own biological energy—and compelled to sell their labour-power in return for wages—but also on 'mechanical substitutes' for humans and the rise of new 'human-machine co-operations' (224). Very soon these machines needed to be driven by sources of energy that could only be supplied, first by coal, and later oil. Thus, notwithstanding the previous use of water and wind, steam engines began 'the epic of motors' which, 'as perfect slaves' requiring no human rights, liberated society from the limitations of animal and human energy. And these new energy sources provided a power that even the most efficient deployment of highly skilled wage labourers, through collective endeavour, could not attain alone. In short, the world's still unexhausted 'fossil stores' (226), beginning with coal as the 'first great agent of relief' (229), allowed 'the principle of abundance' to find 'its way into the hothouse of civilization'. Much else that we have come to take for granted has followed from humanity's largely unacknowledged and underlying debt to fossil fuels (as well as to nature as a free dump for our waste). This includes our conviction that we have a right to exploit nature in perpetuity (227–30). Sloterdijk (230) gives the example of industrial factory farming powered by 'oil floods', where we exterminate livestock on a massive scale for our culinary delight.[6] Another example

---

[6] Sloterdijk (2014: 230) gives the example of the German Government's Animal Welfare Report for 2003 which lists the slaughter of almost 400 million chickens, more than 44 million pigs and 4.3 million cows, among other animals, in the previous year. This figure does not include animal imports for human consumption.

of human arrogance in respect to the conviction that not just the world but indeed the entire universe is available to satisfy our material desires is demonstrated by the belief the minerals available on the nearest planets forming our solar system are also 'fair game' and it will soon be there turn for exploitation.

If measures to counter climate change prove to be absolutely necessary, then there is widespread consensus that they can and must remain within the envelope of economic growth and the primary commitment to enhancing GDP. Here it is argued that without further economic growth there will be insufficient revenue to pay for the new technologies required in order to reduce emissions or to compensate developing countries for the expense involved in adopting such carbon-reducing techniques as they industrialize. Similarly, many regard it as essential to counter climate change by relying on market-remedies such as carbon trading and carbon pricing, with a minimum resort to government regulation. We examine these claims later. It is also important to note that the huge expansion of international trade has reduced national economic self-sufficiency and massively increased GHG emissions. Thus, we find an increased reliance on seasonal produce along with the massive shuffling of components, finished goods, foodstuffs as well as minerals and oil across the world, particularly as imports into the Western economies. Yet, according to Eckersley (2012) an accord was reached at the 1992 Earth Summit between the international climate lobby and the then *General Agreement on Trade and Tariffs* or 'GATT' (later the WTO) whereby the former more or less accepted a 'neoliberal environmentalism' in which the benefits of an open trading system should not be jeopardized by environmental measures to mitigate GHG emissions. This prioritization of unrestricted international trade has allowed businesses to continue using the biosphere as a free resource in respect to pollution from economic activity. We see here the unquestioned assumption that avoiding further global warming may require a number of strategies and changes. But for most observers—including some IPCC and other scientists, most economists, the WB and other IGOs, plus many leading political and academic figures such as Al Gore in the USA (*An Inconvenient Truth* 2006) and Professor Nicholas Stern in the UK (*The Stern Review* 2007)—radically cutting GHG emissions now, by moving to a simpler, less materialistic and more self-reliant economy, is not one of them. We will encounter other versions of this position below.

The climate-denial movement includes some of the most prestigious organizations in the USA such as the Cato Institution, the Heritage Foundation and the Ayn Rand Institute. Klein (2014: 38) discusses a recent study which found that when self-publicized books are included nearly 90 per cent of those denying climate change are associated with Right-wing think tanks. Like many others who remain sceptical concerning the evidence of climate change, including some scientists, such views are likely to be associated with the claim that the demands of environmentalists are really a cover for reversing the moves towards neoliberalism and the miracle of the market. They are just another excuse, it is protested, for government intervention and regulation coupled to an attack on private wealth.

Case Study 5: Biodiversity, marine life and urban air quality—in question

Diminished biodiversity Scientists lack a clear picture of the numbers of living species. However, *The Living Planet Index* compiled by the World Wildlife Fund for Nature suggested that between 1970 and 2000, 40 per cent of the 1143 terrestrial, freshwater and marine creatures they tracked had disappeared (Millennium Ecosystem Assessment, quoted in Greenfacts 2016: 1). Some experts estimate the rate of species extinction as 1000 to 10,000 times higher than what occurred naturally before the Anthropocene (World Wildlife Fund 2016: 1). Given the vast quantities of GHGs absorbed by the world's oceans and the increasing acidification and de-oxygenation that this is causing, the worsening plight of living species is clearly high on the list of environmental concerns.

Plastics in the oceans According to Ocean Conservancy, an NGO advising the US government, as much as 8 million tons of plastics are washed by rivers from chemical, industrial and waste management systems into the oceans each year, particularly from economies in Asia (Donoso and

---

(continued)

(continued)

> Merkl 2016). Scientists from five countries found that in 2014 the oceans contained an estimated 5.25 trillion pieces of plastic weighing around 270,000 tons (Milman 2014). Much ends up as tiny pieces eaten by marine creatures before passing up the food chain. It often accumulates in five vast rotating oceanic patches. The largest, in the Pacific, is estimated as equal in area to the state of Texas. Twenty-nine sperm whales were stranded on North Sea shores during winter 2016 (Hoare 2016). Autopsies in Germany conducted on 13 of them revealed that their stomachs contained quantities of plastic debris. It is likely the whales confused plastic with squid which provides their main diet. We (mostly) no longer hunt whales for oil or food but may be starving them to death from plastic ingestion because of our demand for perpetual economic growth.
> **Urban air pollution** In 2014, the World Health Organization (WHO) reported that only 12 per cent of the urban dwellers living in 1600 cities across 91 countries enjoyed the air quality it recommended for good health. Around half of urban dwellers were exposed to air pollution—from domestic cooking, coal-fired power stations, vehicles and so on—at levels 2.5 times higher than recommended. The WHO argues that around 3.7 million people died in 2012 alone from heart disease, strokes and severe lung ailments linked to air pollution. According to a German-based research team led by Lelieveld (Lelieveld et al. 2015), more people now die from air pollution than malaria and HIV together, and this includes nearly three-quarters of a million people in India and 1.4 million in China.

Carbon and the Twentieth-Century Consumer Binge

Urry's fine and impassioned book, *Climate Change and Society* (2011), also places fossil-fuel burning and consumption at the core of his argument. Urry asserts that we do not need a 'Post-Fordist or post-modern sociology' (16) but a post-carbon one. This will give centre place to the necessity to re-cast all institutions and social life into an entirely new frame, based on minimizing or doing without carbon-based resources. Urry sees the carbon economy that was increasingly given free rein during the twentieth century—much of it 'unleashed' on the world as a result of a 'novel cluster of powerful high carbon systems' emerging in the USA from the early decades including the motor car—as leaving a legacy of GHG emissions and environmental damage that will prove extremely difficult to counter (51). Particularly in the Global North, but now spreading rapidly, our lives 'have been premised upon increasing incomes, wealth, security, movement, wellbeing and longevity', while 'High carbon modern production and consumption seemed to have "no borders" and no "limits to growth"' (48). Underpinning the carbon economy, too, was the assumption that the physical world, or nature, was separate from the economy and always 'available' to be shaped in the pursuit of profit. Now, all of this urgently needs to be challenged (49).

Urry (2011) describes how from the 1950s, and earlier in the USA, most people's lives spread outwards from neighbourhoods where family, work and leisure life had mostly been played out. As this occurred, ordinary individuals sought a range of specialized leisure services further afield. They became dependent on multiple forms of mobility,[7] whether through the family car or air travel, and quickly responded to a gamut of consumer and lifestyle choices on offer through the power of advertising and corporate brands. They also acquired the habit of frequently upgrading their domestic life, accommodation and leisure practices with numerous gadgets and accessories. All of this was underpinned by the growth of worldwide trade, led by corporations and the industrialization of some countries in the Global South, giving rise to a further massive proliferation of commercial choices.

The advent of neoliberalism from the 1980s accentuated and further popularized a culture and way of life predicated on growing volumes of carbon consumption (60). Among other things it helped to banish thrift, turn consumerism into a social duty, further legitimized planned obsolescence and propelled firms and households into amass-

---

[7] Urry (2011: 67) cites research claiming that by 2011 around 23 billion kilometres were travelled each year by world citizens. In the absence of restraints this is likely to quadruple by 2050.

ing credit card and other forms of debt. But Urry insists that just as the financial collapse of 2008 demonstrated that left to themselves markets have no way of avoiding crisis and even collapse, so, a solely market-driven approach to climate change will lead towards environmental catastrophe. In future, capitalism can only provide a solution to 'climate change and energy security' if it moves rapidly towards prioritizing a resource-based approach.

7.3 'Fixing' Climate Change Through Technology

Scientific research and technological advance lie at the heart of our knowledge concerning environmental change. Space exploration provided powerful images of planet earth and its lonely orbit through dark space but also helped scientists to begin imagining the connectedness between the earth's many systems, including its climate. Then from the late 1970s satellite data provided regular information concerning annual Arctic ice shrinkage, the retreat of glaciers, ocean pollution, the extent of deforestation and much else besides (Giddens 2009: 20–21). Alongside this, the measurement of annual CO_2 emissions that had begun in 1959 were intensified while in the 1990s computer advances allowed scientists to feed incoming data into complex models which could simulate the interactions between emissions and changes in climate (Urry 2011: 27). Since 1988, the IPCC has been at the centre of all this research, which has involved 'the organized actions of thousands of scientists' (28). Yet, and continuing a theme from Chap. 5, there has also been a parallel suspicion that some scientific research and proposed technological answers offer 'fixes' that are either impractical or create as many problems as they solve. They may also permit those who have most to lose from de-carbonization to perpetuate their privileges. We now outline some of the main options but also dilemmas relating to technology.

7 Global Capitalism and the Biosphere: Our Future in Jeopardy

Fossil-Fuel Reserves Versus a Carbon Budget

Based on various computer simulation models, most scientists estimate that keeping global temperature increases within the 2C level requires CO_2 emissions to stabilize at around 550ppm by 2050. (In fact, the IPCC 2014 suggested that the lower figure of 450 to 500 would be preferable). This 550ppm figure translates approximately into a reduction of the annual emission of CO_2 measured in billions of tons (gigatons) from 24 in 2002 and nearly 32 in 2011 to around 18 gigatons per year by 2050 (Stern 2007: 260). On this basis scientists argue that the world can afford to emit no more than 565 to 900 extra gigatons of CO_2 into the atmosphere before 2100—and the lower estimate is much safer. However, as McKibben (2012: 7) reminds us, emissions are still rising at the current time. Also, given that average global temperatures are already 0.8C above pre-industrial levels, and roughly the same amount of further temperature increase is yet to work itself through because of previous emissions, even the lower figure of 565 gigatons looks dangerously high. And this still gives only an 80 per cent probability of keeping within the 2C envelope.

This scenario needs to be set against another crucial set of figures. Carbon Tracker is a not-for-profit financial group working in close conjunction with a research institute at the London School of Economics. In recent years it has produced data which illustrates the known reserves of fossil fuels—coal, oil and natural gas—and their market value for the 200 main companies dealing in these resources. Their figures (2013: 4–5) indicate that in 2013 companies already had interests in fossil fuels which were equivalent, if utilized, to around 1540 gigatons of CO_2. These companies had a market value of around $4 trillion, in addition to substantial debts. But the known reserves of fossil fuels around the world are nearly double this amount—equivalent to 2860 gigatons (though estimates vary slightly). In addition, in 2013 the companies with interests in fossil fuels were planning to invest more than $6 trillion in further developing their reserves and had allocated

$674 billion during 2012 alone.[8] Clearly, as both McKibben (2012) and Carbon Tracker (2013: 10–11) observe, there is a huge mismatch between the figure of 565 gigatons and those indicating current, pending and future company investments. McKibben (2012: 12) states the situation bluntly: we 'have five times as much oil and coal and gas on the books as climate scientists think is safe to burn'. He also refers to the calculation provided by a major US financial organization: namely, that at 2012 market values the total possible emissions from the 2800 or so gigatons of CO_2 were equivalent to approximately $27 trillion. Clearly, around $20 trillion of fossil-fuel assets would need to be left as 'unburnable carbon' (5) assets.

This gap prompted Carbon Tracker (2013) to point to the need for a 'carbon budget' whereby no more than 900 of fossil fuel gigatons can be burned before 2050—giving an 80 per cent probability of keeping to the 2C target—followed by a far stricter carbon budget to be implemented after 2050 of no more than 75 gigatons. This is equivalent to only two years' emissions as measured by the current rate. Since the existing coal, oil and natural gas assets already being developed by private companies are very close to their carbon budget limit, a high proportion of their current reserves constitute 'stranded assets' (15). This obviously has huge implications for shareholders, and investment and pension fund holders who will be left holding savings of dwindling value. But an economic system driven by profit and competition offers little or no provision for companies to leave their already market-listed reserves in the ground while desisting from developing future known reserves (McKibben 2012 and Klein 2014). Harris (2016a, b) is surely right to question whether any corporation would be likely to turn away from such assets and simply leave them lying in the ground.

Complicating this further is the reality that governments such as China, Saudi Arabia, Kuwait, Venezuela and Ecuador own around 90 per cent of oil and perhaps two-thirds of coal reserves. The GDPs of some

---

[8] Canada's Alberta tar sands alone contain nearly half the CO2 limit (around 240 gigatons) and the Orinoco tar sands in Venezuela would likely emit even more gigatons than Alberta (McKibben 2012: 18–19). Despite falling coal consumption in 2014, Boren (2015) reports that China had completed 155 new coal-fired power plants in the first nine months of 2015, adding to its already huge number.

countries are highly dependent on revenues from these products, especially oil. According to Adams (2015a, b: 11–12) China presents a particularly difficult constraint on global goals to cut emissions. Its economy is the largest consumer of energy and currently relies on fossil fuels for 90 per cent of its energy (nearly two-thirds from coal)—though there are serious moves to reduce this to 80 per cent by 2030. Further, the communist leadership is strongly committed to continue growing the national economy in order to retain popular support for its regime. Some observers further argue that China's system lacks the legal and governmental structures to enable its leaders to enforce regulation over greater fuel efficiency and in the face of almost endemic corruption by local officials many of whom either will not or cannot implement government policies.

Carbon Capture and Storage (CCS) Systems

CCS is a key technology currently being developed which is regarded as one of the most powerful solutions to CO_2 emissions. CCS involves the use of technologies which capture CO_2 as and when it is produced during fuel combustion and energy generation processes, for example in industry. Carbon is then transported by ships and pipelines to destinations around the world where it can be securely stored in perpetuity in suitable underground geological formations from which leakage is hopefully highly unlikely. CCS processes, together, will increase energy costs overall but will, as the Global CCS Institute (2015) points out in its *Summary Report*, also provide the only technology which can 'significantly reduce' (3) GHG emissions from fossil-fuel burning. The report explains that in 2015 15 projects were fully operational with seven more under construction—a doubling of capacity since 2010. In total these were capable of capturing around 28 million tons of CO_2 each year. However, achieving the 80 per cent probability target of keeping the temperature rise at or below 2C requires an expanding CCS storage capacity of around 6 gigatons per year by 2050. Scaling up from the existing 15 units with a 28 million ton capacity means that somewhere in the region of 32,000 additional CCS units will be needed by 2050. Carbon Tracker's (2013) estimate is even higher: that 8 gigatons will need to be stored per year by

2050, requiring almost 38,000 new units. Whether or not the cost and technical capacity for such a colossal investment is feasible over the next 35 years remains to be seen.

Nuclear Energy

The multiple, risks associated with nuclear power generation are well known, as is the public opposition to nuclear power across many countries. Among the most salient reasons for this are: a history of terrible accidents such as the explosion at the Chernobyl plant in the Ukraine in 1987; the huge costs and long delays frequently involved in constructing reactors—Finland's Olkiluoto 3 nuclear power plant was due to become operational in 2009 but is now not expected until 2018, while its actual cost of 3 billion euros has tripled (The Intergenerational Foundation 2016: 34); the vast costs of de-commissioning old reactors; the risk of waste falling into the hands of terrorists; and the dangers associated with safely disposing of radioactive nuclear waste which remains toxic for thousands of years. Despite these issues, some have suggested that nuclear energy's carbon neutral nature means that an expanded nuclear contribution to the long-term strategic growth of renewable energy sources might be desirable. Giddens (2009: 132–3) carefully explores the argument that nuclear energy could help to fill the energy gap as carbon is phased out, and while the technical problems of renewables, such as their intermittent character and storage difficulties, are resolved. The Intergenerational Foundation (IF) (2016) claims that 441 nuclear reactors were active across 30 countries in 2016. The IF cites a report published by scientists at MIT in 2009 which calculated that if governments sought to virtually triple nuclear capacity by 2050 this would require building somewhere between 1000 and 1500 large new plants (2016: 33). However, the report also stated that given the need to replace old plants, population expansion and economic growth, even a vast project on these lines would only increase nuclear power's share of electricity generation by around 2 per cent.

The IF's own report, *Toxic Time Capsule* (Simms 2016), argues strongly against the further expansion of nuclear power on several grounds, but two are particularly convincing. One is that claiming nuclear power is carbon-free ignores a range of fossil-fuel processes involved in mining and converting uranium, constructing nuclear reactors and then dealing with its waste (36). Second, there is a major issue relating to the multiple intergenerational costs of investing in further nuclear reactors which will fall squarely on people living in the future. These include not only the problems of safe waste storage and the huge costs of building and then de-commissioning reactors but also the reality that the cost of generating electricity from nuclear sources over the long term is much higher than industry spokespersons and sympathetic governments normally claim—and certainly higher than from renewable and carbon sources. The UK government's proposal to commission the new Hinkley Point C nuclear reactor in Somerset with French and Chinese financial investment—still not finally agreed in August 2016—revived similar arguments and opposition including from some scientists. Critics argued that UK taxpayers will need to provide a subsidy of £40 billion and in addition will face a further liability of £22 billion payable to the investors if it becomes necessary to close down the plant at any time before 2060 (Carrington 2016). The company is also guaranteed a price for its electricity three times the current one and for the 35 years following the estimated date of coming on-stream in 2033.

Negative Emission Technologies

In its 2014 report, the IPCC discussed a range of strategies for mitigating the accumulation of CO_2. In the case of what they call 'overshoot' (52), or the failure by 2050 to cut GHG emissions sufficiently, they stress the possibility of introducing a range of additional methods for CO_2 removal and storage after 2050. A major contribution to this process would come from increasing the world's natural carbon 'sinks' (116). In effect, this requires 'the widespread deployment of bioenergy' (52) to capture CO_2 through measures that utilize 'alternative land transformations' (55). Here, the IPCC is talking about two processes. First, it wants to reduce deforestation and hugely expand the rate and extent of re-afforestation while increasing the 'sustainable management' of forests in order to enhance 'forest carbon stocks' (131). Second, it is calling for changes to certain agricultural practices including 'cropland management' and 'grazing land management' (133). Together, this expanded cultivation of trees and plants capable of absorbing larger quantities of CO_2 will create 'negative emissions' to counter the failure to reduce GHG emissions by other methods. The IPCC concedes that such measures may create further problems especially the increased 'competition for land between food, feed and energy uses' (55).

Although this approach is scarcely recognized in the Paris Agreement, Anderson (2015) argues that the decisions reached were 'fundamentally premised on the massive uptake' (2) of future biomass expansion systems. He also suggests that as such this existed as a fall-back strategy in the minds of some IPCC scientists, ready to be implemented if serious cuts to GHG 2050 were resisted. But bioenergy and expanded biomass carbon capture proposals are 'future techno-utopias'. These allow the world to postpone the transition to a 'zero-carbon energy' (3) system but will bring dangerous implications. For example, the huge areas of land that will have to be turned over to cultivating bioenergy crops will probably require an area between one and three times that of India. Similarly, Fuhr and Hällström, two ecologists working in established environmental institutes in Germany and Sweden, estimate (2016) that the 'land grabs' required to offset a substantial share of CO_2 emissions, mostly from poor people in developing countries, would be between 219 to 990 million hectares. This is equivalent to between 14 and 65 times the land area currently used in the USA to cultivate corn for producing ethanol. Anderson (2015: 2) adds that growing, harvesting, processing, shipping and combusting these crops before capturing the CO_2 they have absorbed will demand huge amounts of energy in their own right.

Meanwhile, the plight of those removed from small farms in order to plant bioenergy crops, when the food supplies needed to feed the world's population as it approaches nine billion may be critical, seems to have received much less attention. As McAfee (2012: 124) explains, in one example the World Bank's *Forest Carbon Partnership Facility* has lined up a number of tropical forested countries, including Indonesia, Peru and the Democratic Republic of the Congo, among others, as candidates for forest conservation through the 'the reduction or elimination of smallholder agriculture and pasture as the least-costly carbon sequestration' strategy. More expensive approaches to the same end would involve such things as reducing illegal logging even though conservation finance is limited and such transnational investment projects are driven by profit. Consequently, the most likely result will be projects that cut back on subsistence farming and small-scale ranches thereby accelerating the 'dispossession of rural populations, especially indigenous peoples'.

7.4 Capitalism as the Answer to Climate Change

Most commentators on environmentalism and climate change, including many scientists, regard the market economy, neoliberal capitalism and the continued pursuit of economic growth and competition as not only perfectly compatible with the project of averting dangerous levels of climate change but indeed as essential to that endeavour. Following in the deep footsteps left by key commentators, such as Urry, Klein and many others, we now critically explore two versions of this majority view.

Having it All: Market Competition, Continued Growth and Managed Climate Change

Since the 1990s, many governments and business consortiums have become seriously engaged with the problem of climate change. This includes the USA's Business Council for Sustainable Development and the European Business Council for a Sustainable Energy Future (Sapinski 2016) but also United Nations' agencies, such as the UNEP and the Global Environmental Facility, the WB and other IGOs. This concern has, if anything, steadily intensified. Indeed, the Paris Agreement of December 2015 seems to have further reinforced a widespread environmental consciousness. This is now evident even among the world's leading capitalist elites, economists and business advisors. Thus, at the 2016 World Economic Forum in January, the possible failure of climate change mitigation measures was listed as the top-risk impact for the next ten years, as selected by an annual survey of 750 experts (Cann 2016).

Following the Paris Agreement there was also a flurry of responses by various large investment funds. In some cases these demanded greater transparency from coal and oil companies concerning exposure to stranded assets, insisting that the companies concerned should begin the transition to low-carbon practices. Among the companies experiencing these demands were: Anglo-American, Rio Tinto and Glencoe—three of the USA's coal giants; Shell; and BP—98 per cent of whose shareholders had also made similar demands earlier in 2015 (Darby 2015). Meanwhile, Exxon Mobile, which issued a company report in 2014 declaring that climate change was 'highly unlikely' to deflect it from selling fossil fuels in the future, was faced with demands from leading investors to reveal its exposure to climate risk. This included Britain's Church of England and the New York State government. In the case of Peabody, the world's largest coal company, major investors, including the Norwegian government and two of California's largest pension funds, sold some of their multi-billion-dollar company holdings. In general, it seemed that a large-scale move by investors to divest their stock in fossil-fuel companies might be underway (Darby 2016). How far this proceeds and with what, if any, useful effects, remains to be seen.

For the most part this rising concern has revolved around a thoroughly neoliberal market-based approach to dealing with climate change, albeit taking different forms. First, in the case of the WB, its commitment to countering climate change has been accompanied by a longstanding parallel project: reducing world poverty. As we have seen, this is clearly evident in its publication *Shock Waves: Managing the Impact of Climate Change on Poverty* (2016). However, underlying the WB's approach—and that of the UN—is a neoliberal environmentalism or a 'green developmentalism' (McAfee 1999) which assumes that every aspect of nature can be assigned a monetary value in relation to potential market buyers—especially 'ecosystem services' that are useful to humans, such as preserving biodiversity and natural habitats and storing carbons (McAfee 2012: 105). This 'pricing of life *offers to nature the opportunity to earn its own right to survive in a world market economy*' (McAfee 1999: 134, author's italics). In practice, schemes based on 'Payment for Ecosystem Services' (PES) have been widely introduced across Latin America and are being pushed into Africa and Asia, supported by UN agencies, some NGOs and various governments (McAfee 2012: 106). In this way of thinking, by allocating market values to natural resources such as tropical forests and their products, international capital will be prepared to invest in conserving them, and in ways that reduce carbon emissions. Encouraging businesses to intervene in this way will be helped if governments and citizens, mostly in the Global North, effectively subsidize the costs to capital though agreeing to provide tax breaks and other advantages. McAfee argues that in effect such policies privatize nature while socializing the costs of pollution. At the same time, they sustain profitability and reduce the risks to capital of pursuing greener technologies (1999: 135).

The WB and other IGOs argue that 'marketing nature'—or 'ecosystem services'—in this way will simultaneously help to reduce rural poverty and promote economic development across many countries in the Global South. But research conducted by McAfee (2012: 115–6) and others suggests a very different outcome linked, in turn, to a fundamental contradiction between the two projects of reducing poverty and combatting climate change. In the case of forest conservation projects in Mexico, Costa Rica and elsewhere, for example, those involved anticipated that native Indian communities would benefit from selling medicinal plants and other biological materials such as genetic resources. The resulting transfer of wealth to local people would simultaneously give them an incentive to conserve endangered ecosystems. But several insufficiently understood local socio-economic factors ended up undermining these goals. In particular, poor communities often lack political clout; they may occupy land without clear legal rights to possession, and their communication and negotiation skills are likely to be at a significant disadvantage. In contrast, PES projects involving the commodification of nature require a degree of multi-layered organization, a system for arranging financial support and a series of rules that everyone understands. At the same time, the 'interests' which buy the biological products enjoy considerably more bargaining power than poor sellers and this is reflected in the low prices received by the latter. Meanwhile, larger and wealthier land owners are often better informed about PES opportunities and more capable than their poorer counterparts of seeking formal property rights and understanding how to comply with the scheme's rules. In short, poverty reduction and local development projects based on marketing nature end by deepening local wealth divisions. They also achieve little or nothing in respect to poverty reduction but 'leverage private carbon investments and ensure their profitability' (123).

A second market-based approach to countering climate change is also based on the idea of pricing environmental resources, but here it involves creating carbon markets and trading schemes applied to GHG emissions. Such schemes have been widely adopted in the EU but also in California, Australia and New Zealand. Governments impose caps on what they regard as the appropriate emissions levels for each organization and then create a market in these by selling them to businesses (Urry 2011: 114; McAfee 2012: 111–3). In principle, those businesses which have used up their allowance can buy permits allowing them to discharge more GHGs from other businesses that still have spare emission capacity. Alternatively, they can compensate for their excess pollution by financing conservation schemes elsewhere. Supposedly the latter, and the trade in carbon permits, create incentives for everyone to reduce their own emissions so they can benefit from the opportunity to sell their unused permit capacity rather than paying out to acquire more. Carbon trading also precludes the necessity for governments to impose carbon taxes or cap emissions directly. Clearly, the latter is unacceptable given neoliberal policies. The European Union Emissions Trading System (EU ETS) is by far the largest such scheme and has allowed some businesses and sectors to enjoy profits. According to the EU Commission's *Climate Action* report, 31 countries, more than 11,000 power stations and industrial plants, and also many airlines, are incorporated into the EU ETS (European Commission 2008). In total the scheme covers approximately 45 per cent of GHG emissions—although the economic retrenchment associated with the 2008 recession and its aftermath led to a fall in emissions and a surplus of permit allowances. The EU anticipates a 21 per cent decline in emission levels by 2020 in the economic sectors so far included—yet the actual net reductions so far have been disappointingly limited, leaving many observers to doubt the validity of the EU's claim (McAfee 2012: 111; Sapinski 2016: 90).

Towards a Green or Climate Capitalism

Another version of the capitalist agenda for heading off serious climate change comes in the form of 'green capitalism' (J. Harris 2016a, b) or what Sapinski (2016) describes as 'climate capitalism'. Harris shows how during the last ten years or so, a growing but loose consortium of both liberal and conservative US interest groups have seemingly taken on-board the threat that climate change poses for future corporate business costs and profits. Part of this involved forming the 'Risky Business Project', which includes Hank Paulson (former CEO of Goldman Sachs and Secretary of the Treasury) and Michael Bloomberg (a former mayor of New York) among its leading spokespersons. However, it also extends to the Pentagon and CIA who fear the 'possible social and political chaos' (8) that is likely to result from global warming because of widespread flooding in countries such as Bangladesh, and issues relating to growing water shortages in already arid regions. These and other crises, in turn, are likely to generate massive flows of environmental migrants.

Harris explains how this project for de-carbonizing economic life has also become the central concern of an emerging transnational block of corporations from many countries. Backed by politicians with transnational outlooks (see Robinson 2002), these seek to lead and shape a new era of green capitalist economic growth and accumulation (Harris 2016a, b). Like all previous cycles of expansion it will stimulate further technological innovation and the creation of entirely new products but will also create new jobs. Simultaneously, every aspect of the economic system from the design of buildings to transport will need to be reinvented so that GHG emissions are cut along with all other forms of pollution and environmental destruction. Along similar lines, the UN Secretary General Ban Ki-moon called for a 'Green New Deal' in June 2009. In January 2016 he urged a meeting of around 500 businesses and investors, organized by the CERES Sustainable Business Network, to double current investment in 'clean energy growth' to $600 billion per year (Goldberg 2016: 1–2).

Sapinski's (2016) climate capitalism draws attention to very similar processes. Since the early 1990s a coalition of corporate, political and civil society interests have mobilized in order to push for a 'climatically benign' economy based on energy efficiency but one that also seeks to turn 'climate change mitigation into an instrument of capital accumulation' (89–90). Actions to save the environment become a way of enhancing profits and promoting capitalism. All this is to be achieved primarily though using market mechanisms, especially carbon trading. At the same time the biosphere's ability to absorb emissions and pollution will be priced so that new technologies designed to lessen emissions will become more cost-effective and competitive and thereby foster the replacement of fossil fuels. Sapinski (2016: 92–93) describes how the various 'corporate-funded climate and environmental policy groups' (CEPGS) he investigated all lobby governments and UN agencies wherever these are involved in international negotiations relating to climate change. They also meet together in order to plan strategies, seek a consensus on climate policy, endeavour to gain the legitimizing support of scientists and promote a neoliberalist approach which influences wider public discourses.

7.5 The Obstacles to Capitalist Solutions

We are confronted here with highly confident assertions that neoliberal market capitalism and the technologies associated with it can not only prevent climate catastrophe but also represent the least-costly path to achieving this goal while maintaining economic growth. Given all that is at stake, these claims deserve to be rigorously scrutinized along two fundamental axes. In view of its recent and current record, how realistic is it to suppose that a capitalist path can avert climate catastrophe by 2050 and beyond? Second, as the WB (2016) insists, such a project must be equally capable of protecting the world's poorest people from the worst effects of climate change while simultaneously building the goals of social justice—including poverty reduction—and democratic accountability into the equation. We now raise a series of doubts about the ability of neoliberal 'green capitalism' to address these concerns.

7 Global Capitalism and the Biosphere: Our Future in Jeopardy

Issues Relating to Markets and Phasing Out Fossil Fuels

(1) Twenty or more years of neoliberal market-driven attempts to counter dangerous levels of GHG emissions have demonstrated a poor record, whether in respect to carbon pricing and sales of emission permits or fostering carbon-saving environmental actions in tropical forest areas that both create profits and help the poorest people.

(2) The transition to a low-carbon economy presupposes many things, but the most crucial by far is whether the extremely powerful fossil-fuel lobby, with its ability to buy political support on a massive scale—and especially in respect to the US Republican Party—will willingly forgo future profits by leaving its already scaled-in investments in the ground. Similarly, how far will the divestment process, out of fossil-fuel industries on the part of innumerable investors, proceed in actual practice? With so many pension schemes and commitments tied up in carbon-based financial investments this will not be easy. In any case, Sapinski's research (2016: 104–6) on the worldwide networks of influential business leaders ostensibly committed to combatting climate change showed that the main clusters of companies and organizations were actually connected by a very small number of leading figures. Many had simultaneous business interests in industries highly dependent on carbon energy and saw divestment out of these and fossil fuels as a long-term project.

(3) There is a problem of time. The window of opportunity for making the transition to a de-carbonized world is extremely limited. More so when we recall that the Paris Agreement does not come into force until 2020. Reducing GHG emissions to the level recommended by the IPCC—to between 550 and perhaps 900 gigatons in total by 2050—and given the Chinese, Indian and other governments' commitments to pressing ahead with an economic growth still based primarily on coal and oil (though China is also rapidly expanding its solar capacity) looks highly problematical, to say the least.

(4) Then there is the question of relying on future technologies such as nuclear power, perhaps as a stopgap measure, and carbon capture and

storage as a mechanism for compensating for whatever shortfalls may occur in operating carbon budgets. Both are controversial, especially the former, and both presuppose unimaginably vast investments being made across the world. Will the market generate these amounts without a good deal of government support—something that neoliberal economics may find difficult to accept? And how confident can we be that CCS will not give rise to problems on its own account, both technical, such as leakage, and political, in terms of operating in world regions that may become unstable, partly due to climate change?

(5) In democracies, citizens enjoy the means to vote governments out whose measures they do not like. But likely public reactions to fundamental changes towards de-carbonized economies also need to be built into future scenarios. Will the promise of long-term benefits for future generations be experienced by some—for example those who are childless—as sufficient compensation for forgoing certain material and lifestyle inconveniences and constraints? This might include: rationed airline and other forms of transport and travel; the reduced availability and certainly higher costs of buying unseasonal foods; more expensive forms of leisure; the need to make goods last longer; higher living costs linked to various carbon levies, caps and even taxes; hugely reduced lighting in cities and so on. Giddens's (2009: 2) comments on public attitudes towards global warming are revealing: '[p]eople find it hard to give the same level of reality to the future as they do to the present', while the scale of climate change and its future consequences are neither 'tangible, immediate or visible'. Also, and despite Beck's theory of reflexive modernity (see Chap. 6) many individuals are reluctant to take personal measures to counter climate change if others are unwilling to do the same (3).

Issues Relating to a Shift to Renewable Energy

(1) Developing renewable energy sources is clearly central to any serious strategy of averting dangerous levels of climate change. Solar and wind power are rapidly being developed across the world. During

2015 $160 billion was invested worldwide in solar power, with China and India centrally involved (Macalister 2016: 44–45). In Britain, for example, clean energy has surged since 2010. A total of 4 per cent of national energy needs were met by solar power in April 2016 and investment in wind power is also growing fast. Yet when set against the scale of what needs to be achieved this progress still seems dangerously slow.

(2) Indeed, despite recent encouraging signs, it remains uncertain whether the market can mobilize the scale of investment needed if renewable energy is to come on-stream on a scale sufficient to make a difference and in time. As Urry (2011: 118) reminds us: '[t]he events of 2008 made abundantly clear that markets on occasion destroy the very conditions of the market economy: they do not *necessarily* generate the solution to economic crises' (author's italics). We could add that the same reality applies to the transformation required for a shift towards renewable energy. Left to its own dynamic of profit first, capitalism cannot be relied on to solve long-term human problems. Nor can it avoid sometimes being snarled up by its inner contradictions, or desist from pushing the world into 'black holes' which benefit the super-rich at the cost of nearly everyone else (see Chap. 3). Urry adds that, 'there are some seeds of a new mode of capitalism, beyond neoliberal or disorganized capitalism' (118) but as yet these are weakly connected. We have a long way to travel.

(3) Given the mountain to climb, substantial amounts of government support to help develop and subsidize renewables—at state, regional and local levels—seem absolutely necessary. But will neoliberal market policy doctrines allow this to happen even though, according to IMF figures, worldwide the fossil-fuel industries presently receive around $5.3 trillion in various kinds of subsidies—equal to approximately 6.5 per cent of global GDP? In America alone this amounts to $700 billion a year (Dabla-Norris et al. 2015: 1). Partly, this figure consists of direct payments to companies, but it also includes tax breaks and price cuts for consumers. The bulk of this subsidy is also derived by calculating all the unpaid costs, such as air pollution and the effects on climate change, which governments and taxpayers pick up instead of the actual polluters. Recent evidence on this is not

encouraging. In Britain the government withdrew the subsidies for onshore wind farms and for solar panels in April 2016 at the very time when the industry was moving towards becoming self-sufficient. The UK government claimed that it was duty-bound to help ordinary families reduce their energy bill even though the previous subsidy to the renewable industry was only equal to £10 per year per family and might have been unnecessary after 2020 (Mathiesen 2015).

(4) Harris's survey (2016a, b) of businesses engaged in manufacturing solar panels in a number of countries, including the USA, China, Japan, Germany, Malaysia, Mexico, Taiwan and South Africa, reveals a number of critical problems confronting this new industry. First, the post-2008 recession hit many solar firms hard, and they have either gone out of business or else their growth has slowed. Second, many of the largest solar companies operate in exactly the same way as other businesses: they out-source much of their production to low-wage economies and extend their assembly lines and supply chains across several countries. The 'green' commitment of these companies does not stop them from operating with a neoliberal outlook towards labour. Third, the renewable industries are not exempt from the need to compete both within their national economy and internationally. Hence the support, or otherwise, provided by different governments—such as the 'tax holiday' in Malaysia—can make a difference to the success of individual companies. Further, China's huge government-promoted solar expansion led to global overproduction following the recession and led to setbacks for the industry globally at a time when, arguably, governments everywhere should have been supporting renewables for more important reasons than narrow definitions of company profitability. In short, Harris (2016a, b: 139) suggests that the 'fast approaching tipping point for planetary warning may also be the tipping point for capitalism. Unfortunately green capitalism will offer too little too late'.

(5) The diffuse nature of wind and solar energy (and perhaps tidal and hydro power) brings the possibility that decentralized community and/or cooperative schemes could also contribute to this process. This is already happening in some parts of Europe and the USA

where local not-for-profit schemes are flourishing. Running in parallel is the spread of domestic rooftop solar panels with feed-in tariff schemes. By October 2014 half a million US households were generating their own electricity (Mitchell 2014: 5). This localized diffusion of renewable energy helps to educate the public about climate change and broadens the scope of clean energy production. But they also directly conflict with the drive by corporations to maximize profits by investing in large-scale wind and solar farms rather than dealing with self-sufficient producer-consumers. This conflict between corporate interests and decentralized energy was highlighted by Walmart which, between 2010 and 2013, and despite trumpeting its commitment to environmental sustainability, gave funds to a large number of think tanks engaged in attacking clean energy (Mitchell 2014). Moreover, Walmart's company, First Solar, is one such large-scale business investing in solar farms. In 2013 it participated with other solar companies in placing political pressure on the Arizona government—in addition to other states including Colorado, Texas and Florida—to impose fees on households using rooftop energy systems (Mitchell 2014: 13).

7.6 Summary and Conclusions

The growing weight of scientific evidence demonstrating a rise in average global temperature seems irrefutable. Recently, too, current manifestations of climate change and our understanding of its likely drastic future consequences have been more widely understood by governments, businesses and the public—particularly as shareholders and domestic energy users. There are also encouraging signs of an upsurge of investment during the last five years in renewable energy across a number of countries. Two very crucial questions nevertheless remain uppermost in any serious analysis of climate change and this chapter has tried to critically assess some of the possible responses to them.

First, until now, modernity, capitalism and industrialization have been built on 250 years of reckless and un-costed fossil-fuel use. But can the West and the developing societies make the gigantic leap required in order to drastically reduce our carbon addiction and do so quickly, before climate change spins out of human control? The answer is that at present we cannot know except that as currently constituted the goal of permanent worldwide withdrawal from the drug of fossil fuel is tied to a second agenda. Here, the orthodox view insists that neoliberal capitalism provides the only viable vehicle for rescuing humanity from carbon-dependence while simultaneously generating the economic growth needed to fund the transition and overcome world poverty. As we have seen, however, there are many reasons for doubting that a market-only approach built around competition and the pursuit of profit can fulfil the promises its adherents make. Certainly, the financial crash of 2008—a partial result of decades of deregulation—the lacklustre economic recovery worldwide since then, and the reality that most of this was supported by huge amounts of government intervention, as much in China as in the West, do not provide convincing grounds for taking this 'orthodox' position very seriously.

Rather, the discussion in this chapter suggests that capitalism and market solutions are unlikely to bring about the transition to an environmentally safe world without considerable government intervention. Among the likely measures might be the following: direct emission and other controls over sections of industry, including aviation and shipping which are currently exempt from the provisions of the Paris Agreement (Anderson 2015); taxing carbon production so that it impacts directly on ordinary consumers too (McKibben 2012: 24); longer-term subsidies to renewables and removing those currently available to the fossil-fuel industry; incentives for households and communities to invest in wind or solar power; and much greater financial support to poorer countries to assist in their adaptation to climate change than has so far been agreed. Determined government measures to tackle the rising inequality and economic insecurity, discussed in Chaps. 2, 3 and 4, and currently experienced by ordinary citizens, may also help to ensure the latter's willing acceptance of the lifestyle inconveniences necessary during the transition. More important than anything else is the need to ensure that the world's poorest people, who bear so little responsibility for climate change and who will likely be at the forefront of coping with its consequences, do not also find that their lands, communities and livelihoods are to be sacrificed after 2050 by the imposition of vast 'negative emissions' schemes designed to compensate for our failure to deal with global warming by other methods.[9]

Bibliography

Adams, P. (2015a). *The truth about China: Why Beijing will resist demands for abatement.* Global Warming Policy Foundation. Retrieved August 9, 2016, from http://www.thegwpf.org/content/uploads/2015/12/Truth-about-China.pdf

Adams, T. (2015b, November 29). The future of work. *The Observer.*

Anderson, K. (2015) *The hidden agenda: How veiled techno-utopias shore up the Paris Agreement.* Retrieved August 9, 2016, from http://kevinanderson.info/blog/the-hidden-agenda-how-veiled-techno-utopias-shore-up-the-paris-agreement/

Boren, Z. D. (2015) *China's coal bubble: 155 coal-fired power plants in the pipeline despite overcapacity.* Retrieved August 9, 2016, from http://energydesk.greenpeace.org/2015/11/11/chinas-coal-bubble-155-new-overcapacity/

Cann, O. (2016). *What are the top global risks for 2016?* World Economic Forum. Retrieved August 9, 2016, from https://www.weforum.org/agenda/2016/01/what-are-the-top-global-risks-for-2016/

Carbon Tracker. (2013). *Unburnable carbon: Wasted capital and stranded assets.* Retrieved August 9, 2016, from http://carbontracker.live.kiln.digital/Unburnable-Carbon-2-Web-Version.pdf

Carrington, D. (2016, March 18). Hinkley Point C nuclear deal contains £22bn 'poison pill' for taxpayer. *The Guardian.* Retrieved August 9, 2016, from https://www.theguardian.com/uk-news/2016/mar/18/hinkley-point-c-nuclear-deal-22bn-poison-pill-taxpayer

Carrington, D. and Slezak, M. (2016, March 15). February broke global temperature records by 'shocking' amount. *The Guardian.* Retrieved August 9, 2016, from https://www.theguardian.com/science/2016/mar/14/february-breaks-global-temperature-records-by-shocking-amount

Dabla-Norris, E., Kochhar, K., Suphaphiphat, N., Ricka, F. and Evridiki, T. (2015). *Causes and consequences of income inequality: A global perspective.*

---

[9] We return to issues concerning small farmers and their potential contribution to attaining global environmental sustainability in Chap. 9.

International Monetary Fund. Retrieved August 12, 2016, from https://www.imf.org/external/pubs/ft/sdn/2015/sdn1513.pdf

Darby, M. (2015) *Investors pressure mining giants to phase out coal.* Climate Home. Retrieved August 9, 2016, from http://www.climatechangenews.com/2015/12/17/investors-pressure-mining-giants-to-phase-out-coal/

Darby, M. (2016) *Shareholder activists target ExxonMobil on 2C climate risk.* Climate Home. Retrieved August 9, 2016, from http://www.climatechangenews.com/2016/01/19/28330/

Davis, M. (2010). Who will build the ark? *New Left Review, 61* (January–February edition).

Donoso, D. and Merkl, A. (2016, September 9). By 2025, our seas may be filled with one ton of plastic for every three tons of fish. *The Guardian.* Retrieved August 10, 2016, from https://www.theguardian.com/sustainable-business/2015/sep/30/dow-chemical-the-ocean-conservancy-ocean-plastics-pollution

Eckersley, R. (2012). Understanding the interplay between the climate and trade regimes. In *Climate and trade in a post-2012 world* (pp. 11–18). Geneva: United Nations Environmental Program.

European Commission. (2008). *The EU emissions trading system (EU ETS).* Retrieved August 10, 2016, from http://ec.europa.eu/clima/policies/ets/faq_en.htm

Fuhr, L. and Hällström, N. (2016) *The myth of net- zero emissions.* Retrieved August 10, 2016, from https://www.project-syndicate.org/commentary/net-zero-emissions-not-enough-by-lili-fuhr-and-niclas-h-llstr-m-2014-12

Giddens, A. (2009). *The politics of climate change.* Cambridge: Polity.

Global CCS Institute. (2015). *The global status of CCS: 2015, summary report.* Retrieved August 10, 2016, from https://www.globalccsinstitute.com/publications/global-status-ccs-2015-summary-report

Goldberg, S. (2016, January 27). UN urges business leaders to double investment in green energy by 2020. *The Guardian.* https://www.theguardian.com/environment/2016/jan/27/un-urges-business-leaders-to-double-investment-in-green-energy-by-2020

Greenfacts. (2016). *The living planet index, 1970–2000.* Retrieved August 9, 2016, from http://www.greenfacts.org/en/biodiversity/figtableboxes/1037-living-planet.htm

Harris, J. (2016a). Green capitalism and social justice. *Global Capitalism and the Crisis of Democracy, 4*, 103–142 Atlanta, Georgia: Clarity Press, chapter 4.

Harris, J. (2016b, June 17). Britain is in the midst of a working-class revolt. *The Guardian.* Retrieved August 9, 2016, from https://www.theguardian.com/commentisfree/2016/jun/17/britain-working-class-revolt-eu-referendum

Hoare, P. (2016, March 30). Whales are starving—Their stomachs full of plastic waste. *The Guardian*. Retrieved August 10, 2016, from https://www.theguardian.com/commentisfree/2016/mar/30/plastic-debris-killing-sperm-whales

Intergovernmental Panel on Climate Change. (2013). *Climate change 2013: The physical science basis, summary for policy makers*. Cambridge: Cambridge University Press.

Intergovernmental Panel on Climate Change. (2014). *Climate change 2014: Mitigation of climate change: Summary for policymakers and technical summary*. Cambridge: Cambridge University Press.

Klein, N. (2014). *This changes everything: Capitalism vs the climate*. London: Allen Lane.

Lelieveld, J., Evans, J. S., Fnais, M., Giannadaki, D., & Pozzer, A. (2015). The contribution of outdoor air pollution sources to premature mortality on a global scale. *Nature, 525*, 367–371.

Macalister, T. (2016, April 17). Clouds gather over the solar power sector after golden years of success. *The Guardian*. Retrieved August 10, 2016, from https://www.theguardian.com/environment/2016/apr/16/solar-power-clouds-gather-six-years-success-uk

McAfee, K. (1999). Selling nature to save it? Biodiversity and green developmentalism. *Environment and Planning D: Society and Space, 17*(2), 133–154.

McAfee, K. (2012). The contradictory logic of global ecosystem services markets. *Development and Change, 43*(1), 105–131.

McKibben, B. (2012, July 7). Global warming's terrifying new math. *Rolling Stone*. Retrieved August 10, 2016, from http://www.rollingstone.com/politics/news/global-warmings-terrifying-new-math-20120719

Milman, O. (2014, December 10). Full scale of plastic in the world's oceans revealed for the first time. *The Guardian*. Retrieved August 11, 2016, from https://www.theguardian.com/environment/2014/dec/10/full-scale-plastic-worlds-oceans-revealed-first-time-pollution

Mitchell, S. (2014). *How the Walton family is threatening our clean energy future*. Institute For Local Self-Reliance. Retrieved August 11, 2016, from http://ilsr.org/wp-content/uploads/2014/10/ILSR-WaltonSolar-Report-Final.pdf

Reeves, H., & Jouzel, J. (2010). *Climate refugees*. Paris: Massachusetts Institute of Technology.

Robinson, W. I. (2002). Capitalist globalization and the transnationalization of the state. In M. Rupert & H. Smith (Eds.), *Historical materialism and globalization* (pp. 210–229). London: Routledge.

Sapinski, J. P. (2016). Constructing climate capitalism: Corporate power and the global climate policy-planning network. *Global Networks, 16*(1), 89–111.
Simms, A. (2016) *Toxic time capsule: Why nuclear energy is an intergenerational issue.* The Intergenerational Foundation. Retrieved August 11, 2016, from http://www.if.org.uk/wp-content/uploads/2016/04/Toxic-Time-Capsule_Final_28-Mar.pdf
Sloterdijk, P. (2014). *In the world interior of capital.* Cambridge: Polity.
Stern, N. (2007). *The economics of climate change: The stern review.* Cambridge: Cambridge University Press.
United Nations Development Program. (2007). *UN Human Development Report 2007/8: Fighting Climate Change, Human Solidarity in a Divided World.* Basingstoke: Palgrave.
Urry, J. (2011). *Climate change and society.* Cambridge: Polity.
World Wildlife Fund. (2016). *How many species are we losing?* Retrieved August 9, 2016, from http://wwf.panda.org/about_our_earth/biodiversity/biodiversity/
Worldwatch Institute. (2016). *Fossil fuels dominate primary energy.* Retrieved August 11, 2016, from http://www.worldwatch.org/fossil-fuels-dominate-primary-energy-consumption-0

8

Does Capitalism Have a Future?

The introductory discussion in Chap. 1 questioned the presumption held by most social scientists (especially economists), and also political leaders, that the dynamics and trajectory of capitalist modernity are irreversible, universal and timeless. In returning to this overall theme we note that some observers view the present condition of global capitalism and its likely trajectory as dystopian (see e.g. Frase 2011; Evans and Tilly 2016). An alternative perspective might argue that capitalism is facing future collapse, encumbered as it is by the sheer weight of the contradictions buried within its DNA, particularly in its current neoliberal form.

Building on the detailed analyses developed in previous chapters, but adding some new material, we now pose two questions which are mirror-images of each other. First, can capitalism take humanity forward to a fairer and safer future despite the syndrome of intersecting dilemmas and crises facing the world in the early twenty-first century but which also confront capitalism itself as an economic system? Far more is at stake than whether capitalism can survive and outlast the tsunamis of change bearing down on everyone. Thus, second, we wonder what kind of future our societies face should capitalism in its current form be allowed or enabled to continue. Like the optometrist's eye-testing lenses, does our vision of the future on the chart ahead look safer, freer and fairer, with or without one kind of capitalism or another, or even none at all?

As we have seen in earlier chapters, unfettered capitalism—flanked by the obsessions of modernity—is unquestionably linked to a number of troubling current and impending dilemmas. But these, in turn, are tied to escalating conflicts between classes, ethnicities and nations over competition for jobs and lifetime security, not to mention land, water, food and other resources.

Further, we are witnessing the virtual worldwide resurgence of populist, nativist, sectarian, nationalist, even racist, tensions coupled at times to the demand that various fundamentalisms must be defended, sometimes with the weapons of oppression and violence. Against this troubled background this chapter considers the issues surrounding the following dilemmas:

1. The present world condition of low- and even zero-growth currently feared by the leading IGOS and following years of falling incomes and precarious working conditions for many, exacerbated by the austerity imposed by governments after the 2008 financial collapse.
2. The bifurcation and worsening divisions lying at the heart of global capitalism, especially in the USA and UK, whereby the separate and super-charged almost autonomous economic world of the super-rich heads away from the capitalist mainland into an outer space of its own making.
3. The rise of the knowledge economy and 'cognitive capitalism', where businesses either resort to enclosure and monopoly in order to preserve profitability—thereby stifling innovation—or confront a new economy uncoiling itself at capitalism's centre that is governed by falling prices and a not-for-profit, sharing economy.
4. The need to cope with climate change and its attendant dangers while finding the political means to persuade the industries, workers and consumer lifestyles built around fossil-fuel consumption to accept the inconvenience required for switching to renewables and localized economies.

5. The equally pressing need to compensate for the vast job losses and social dislocation that many predict will arrive as robotization and artificial intelligence become increasingly salient and to do so without endangering social cohesion, economic stability, and ultimately democratic politics.
6. Warnings of future food shortages, and therefore price spikes like the one in 2007/8, are increasingly commonplace despite the growing prevalence of energy and chemical-intensive factory farming and agribusiness while, in tandem, the environmental costs of the global food industry continue to mount. In Case Study 6 we consider whether governments, IGOs, experts and farmers can meet these challenges without jeopardizing the interests of 'big' capital.

8.1 Prospects for Economic Growth—Doubts by Global Elites

Chapter 4 argued that decades of neoliberal policies have produced deepening economic marginalization and a sclerotic capitalism stuck with slow economic growth. Stagnant or declining earnings alongside rising and even rampant inequality, intensified by vampire capitalism, an overdependence on debt, and the diversion of vast funds into risky speculative activity have undermined effective demand and long-term investment. After eight years of exceptionally low interest rates and quantitative easing, growth remains stagnant in the West and has been falling in China and the emerging economies. Alternative policies are mostly outlawed by neoliberal dogma. Attempts to implement such policies risk retaliation including disinvestment and higher interests rates from bond markets.

Yet, since the end of 2014, and particularly during the first six months of 2016, there has been a barrage of doubts from leading Intergovernmental Organizations (IGO) speculating whether neoliberal capitalism might be running out of momentum. In early June 2016, Catherine Mann, chief economist at the Organisation for Economic Cooperation and Development (OECD), suggested that the world economy was locked into a 'self-fulfilling low-growth trap' where business 'has no incentive to invest given insufficient demand' (quoted in Elliott 2016b: 3). Mann also urged governments to concentrate less on austerity and to borrow in order to invest in infrastructure.

This message followed in the trail of several troubled OECD reports. For example, a report in May 2015 observed that inequality 'in OECD countries is at its highest since records began' (OECD 2015a, b: 1) and this was holding back economic growth. It added that more than half of all the new jobs created in member countries between 1995 and 2013 were part-time, temporary or involved self-employment and the resulting low pay was worsening inequality.

The ILO's report in May 2016—*World Employment Social Outlook, Trends 2016*—also made for grim reading. Global growth slowed in 2015 compared to 2014 and was expected to fall further in 2016 and 2017. Consequently unemployment rose to 197 million in 2015 and remained 27 million below the figure for worldwide employment prior to 2008. The worsening job situation was especially bad in the emerging economies. Here, among other causes, the slow-down in China as its government tries to reduce its dependence on export-led growth and high rates of borrowing was bringing down China's imports of raw materials and manufactured components (3). Among ILO explanations for slowing trade and economic growth were declining investment, an ageing population in the rich countries and the fact that the incomes of the richest 1 per cent have grown much faster than everyone else's and 50 per cent of global wealth is owned by this same top 1 per cent (10).

Given years of economic orthodoxy and a history of 'persuading' many countries to adopt neoliberal policies, the recent epiphany demonstrated by leading International Monetary Fund (IMF) researchers seems all the more remarkable. In *Neoliberalism Oversold?* (2016) Ostry, Loungani and Furceri argue that while some previous IMF policies had helped to generate growth, removing the restrictions on capital flows across national borders and insisting on cuts to government spending in order to reduce deficits have been problematic if not actually harmful. The authors distinguish between long-term capital investment and short-term inwards flows of 'hot' money which are frequently speculative in nature and expose economies to severe economic risks including considerable falls in output and growing inequality when such capital leaves just as quickly as it arrived. They explain that between 1980 and today there were 150 instances of such capital 'surges' affecting emerging economies. Contrary to neoliberal policy stipulations, therefore, some national controls on short-term capital flows may be beneficial to economic growth and financial stability. It is surely telling that China has long operated controls over capital flows across its borders. The fact that this may have at least some bearing on its much-lauded economic success is rarely acknowledged. The authors also suggest that imposing austerity as a path to attracting potential foreign investors makes little difference in the case of strong economies since investors rarely care very much about fiscal stringency in such situations. We might add that austerity policies weaken demand and therefore employment so that policies designed to reduce public debt often end up increasing public spending and borrowing rather than the opposite.

8.2 The Two Capitalist Universes of the Twenty-First Century

Freeland (2012: 5) suggested that for American investors, a 'bifurcation of the world' is taking place between the field of operations where the big banks, large corporations, the US stock exchange and the super-rich deploy their wealth and the wider US economy. This deep division has become a received aspect of the thinking displayed not only by fund managers but also by leading officials such as Alan Greenspan, the 'high priest of free markets' and chairman of the Federal Reserve who presided over US economic policy for 19 years until 2006. In the first sphere reside the highest income earners and wealth owners whose financial spaceship seems to be carrying them into an entirely separate existence of increasing enrichment, unrestrained by any laws of economic gravity, with their fortunes barely curtailed by the 2008 crisis. Existing in a parallel universe we find a low-, slow- or zero-growth economy marked by declining opportunity and widening inequality where potentially available investment lurks in the shadows created by the fragile character of global mass effective demand. This is the 'other' world economy which is apparently giving so much concern to IGOs such as the IMF. The extent to which this gigantic skewing of global capitalism may be occurring is also highlighted in the Citigroup Research report published in October 2005.

Citigroup provides advice to would-be investors concerning which securities its clients would be well-advised to purchase. It is a division of Citigroup Global Markets Inc., a provider of banking and financial services including the international broking, dealing and underwriting of bonds and equities. Citigroup was the world's largest corporation until 2008, in terms of its total assets,[1] and in 2015 it still remained the USA's third largest bank holding company despite the losses incurred during the 2008 crisis. The document, published in October 2005 by three of its employees, and followed by a second the following March, argued that the world was divided into the 'Plutonomies' and the rest (Kapur et al. 2006). The former consisted of the USA, UK and Canada but also included the rising wealthy classes in the emerging economies such as China many of whose richest citizens often prefer to invest in the asset or share markets of the Plutonomies rather than their home country markets.[2] The 'rest' encompasses most of Continental Europe and Japan, countries that are generally inclined towards more egalitarian economies, though in some instances this is changing.

Capitalism Splitting Apart at the Seams

The authors of Citigroup argue that in the Plutonomies economic growth is 'powered by and largely consumed by the wealthy few' (Kapur et al. 2005: 1). It follows that in a Plutomomy such as the USA, there is no such thing as an average or typical national consumer because the shape and direction of the economy is fired by rich consumers. These are the top 1 and 10 per cent, who take a 'disproportionate' and 'gigantic slice of income and consumption' (2). In 2004, for example, official statistics showed how the richest 10 per cent earned 43 per cent of income and possessed a net worth of 57 per cent. However, in 2000 the richest 1 per cent—or

---

[1] Citigroup had to be bailed out by the US government in 2008 to the tune of around $70 billion, but this was paid back by 2010.

[2] The authors included the following in their list of emerging market entrepreneurs/ plutocrats; 'Russian oligarchs, Chinese real estate/manufacturing tycoons, Indian software moguls, Latin American oil/agricultural barons' (Kapur et al. 2005: 21).

roughly one million households in the US—enjoyed one-fifth of overall income, almost the same share as the bottom 60 per cent of households in terms of income, or 60 million households. At that time the top 1 per cent also accounted for two-fifths of the total net financial wealth or roughly the same amount as the bottom 95 per cent of households. Recall that we encountered very similar figures from other sources in Chaps. 2 and 4.

So disproportionately large and crucial is the impact of the wealthy upon the 'Plutonomy' countries that many wider economic imbalances are largely explicable in terms of their actions. According to Citigroup the marked tendency for the national savings rate to fall, for example, occurs as a direct result of the higher share of overall income accruing to the wealthy. The two—growing inequality and falling rates of saving—are directly but inversely correlated. What happens is that in a 'plutonomy', the rich drop their savings rate, consume a larger fraction of their bloated, very large share of the economy' and this behaviour 'overshadows the decisions of everyone else' and drives 'the national numbers' (14). The wealthy also tend to increase their purchase of financial assets at the same time, so fuelling bullish stock exchange markets while their luxury spending binges massively contribute to growing trade deficits. The authors also demonstrate how the price of the products purchased by the wealthy tends to exercise little influence over their consumption: their elasticity response to price changes is low. According to the report, and by the same token, the share values of the leading companies providing for their luxury consumption have considerably out-performed most other companies and created average returns of nearly 18 per cent each year between 1985 and 2005 (30). Not surprisingly, the Citigroup authors' advice to their clients is to buy shares in exactly these companies.

Like Freeland (2012) the Citigroup document further argues that various sports, TV, music, designer and other superstars form one element in the super-rich. Their ability to reach the financial heights was helped by the Internet, cable and satellite technologies which have hugely expanded their audiences. Citigroup claim, however, that the accumulation of vast wealth by the super-rich in the Plutonomies, and the enormous influence they now exercise over the wider economy, are closely linked to the now familiar factors we examined in Chaps. 2, 3 and 4. They include: the growing share of economic growth taken by profit; the 'favourable treatment' metered out to the wealthy by 'market-friendly governments'; and the ability of the 'tech whizzes', lawyers, bankers and corporate CEOs, to turn globalization to their advantage by raising the share of new wealth that accrues to profit 'at the expense of labour' (Kapur et al. 2006: 1). In a diagnosis that is remarkably similar to Piketty's (2014) the authors continue by suggesting that not only are these Plutonomies dominated by the very rich but the latter are likely to become even wealthier in the future if no actions is taken to prevent worsening inequality. This is because none of the counter-forces that might be potentially wielded against them—more progressive tax systems, government seizures of private property or serious resistance by revived trade union-type organizations—seem likely to be imposed by governments or mobilized by workers in the foreseeable future. Indeed, globalization and the competition between governments for inward investment are tending to drive tax rates lower every year, especially in the EU economies. Equally, globalization makes it easy for companies to drive up profits by outsourcing or offshoring much of their production to low-cost countries. Only growing political demands for trade protectionism and resistance to further globalization might be capable of denting the continued rise of the super-rich.

The awesome implications of the Citigroup reports seem clear and inescapable. In the Anglo-Saxon countries and the major emerging economies—and to a lesser but changing extent in Europe and Japan—capitalism is increasingly dominated by the needs of a tiny elite though buttressed by perhaps another 10 to 20 per cent of highly skilled and well-paid technicians/professionals. As such, we are faced with an entirely new capitalist scenario whereby the role in the economy of perhaps 80 per cent of citizens is being progressively marginalized as their influence and significance as consumers and investors becomes largely redundant, while the super-rich continue to augment their wealth and influence. Moreover, as automation and robotization gather pace a far greater number of citizens will become irrelevant as a source of value-profit. Smart robots will cater for the domestic, health and personal needs of the rich but also for much of the productive input into their businesses.

Case Study 6: Issues in world food security and corporate–industrial–agriculture

The global food crisis of 2007–2008 led to steep price rises for staple foods such as rice and corn. Food riots occurred in Egypt, Bangladesh and elsewhere and 44 million were pushed into severe poverty while millions more were harmed. Likely causes were: extreme weather conditions, high oil prices (peaking at $147 per barrel in 2007) and therefore fertilizer costs, financial speculation and rising meat consumption in Asia, especially China. But an internal WB report (2008) argued that the conversion to biofuels was mostly responsible (one-third of US corn production was diverted to ethanol and a half of EU vegetable oil farming to biodiesel).[3]

A new farm agenda is needed. As a form of renewable energy and alternative to oil, biofuels were regarded as a step towards environmental safety. But the food crisis also placed environmental problems at the heart of the agenda and created new priorities. This view has been reinforced by the following.

- Chemical fertilizer use has risen hugely but relative crop output is either flat-lining (Fleming 2016) or falling while soil texture deteriorates. (China uses three times more chemical fertilizer per hectare than Brazil: two-thirds end up in rivers or the atmosphere).[4]
- Worldwide, agriculture causes 11–15 per cent of GHG emissions. But a global food system increasingly dominates agriculture. According to UNCTAD (2013) this creates between 43 per cent and 57 per cent of GHG emissions when deforestation (mainly for expanded cereal or meat production), processing, transport, packaging, retailing and refrigeration are included plus mountains of food waste.
- This global food system is built around huge corporations such as Cargill and Unilever and is helped by the EU and other governments imposing trade restrictions on food imports while subsidizing home farmers and dumping artificially cheap food on developing countries. The food corporations employ many local workers—69 per cent of these in SSA and 62 per cent in EA are women ('Agriculture at the Crossroads', IAAKSTD

---

[3] A. Chakrabortty (2008), 'Secret report: biofuel caused food crisis', *The Guardian*, July 3.
[4] http://www.grain.org/article/entries/5373-is-industrial-farming-a-tech-fix-or-dead-end-for-tackling-climate-change

(continued)

(continued)

> 2009: 11–12 and 21). But low wages, damage to health from pesticide use and the imposition of 'flexible' work conditions takes them away from their own small farms while agro-industrial methods add to environmental pollution (Food Justice 2010: 13).
>
> *Further considerations.* (a) Global population is set to continue rising so future food security is a huge issue. (b) Two-fifths of the world's population still depend on farming for their livelihoods and nearly a million of these are currently malnourished. Raising their farm output would contribute to easing their own and wider world poverty if they were helped to produce and sell more produce locally. The effectiveness of this project would also increase if:
>
> (1) Government policies in the rich countries persuaded consumers to eat less meat along with their dependence on imported and unseasonal foods and if measures are taken to reduce food waste in transport, storage and retailing;
> (2) Widespread changing land use in the direction of continued de-afforestation was reduced; and
> (3) The current 'land grabbing' practised by large investors and TNCs (backed by corrupt local government elites and the policies of Western governments) currently going on in India, Mozambique, Malawi and elsewhere were resisted so that the mass displacement of small farmers from their land ceased (GRAIN 2015).
>
> *All this has led to new interest in the future role that small farmers could play in world food production, especially given their less environmentally damaging agricultural practices. We expand this theme in Chap. 9.*

8.3 The ICT Revolution: End Game for Capitalism?

The rapid rise of information and communication technology, the accelerating range of products this has generated, and the innumerable ways that these products have penetrated and transformed how business, public, political, domestic and everyday interpersonal relationship are conducted has been astonishing. For a great many recent thinkers of different disciplines and backgrounds (e.g. Drucker 1993; Reich 1991; Castells 1996; Benkler 2006; Hardt and Negri 2009; DeLong and Summers 2001; Rifkin 2014; Mason 2015b), the rise of ICTs constitutes a third industrial revolution, promising to unleash yet another vast material leap forward in productivity and efficiency. It also contains the potential to alter the ways capitalist economies operate, simultaneously improving human life in innumerable non-material ways.[5]

Rifkin's contrast between the second and this new industrial revolution brilliantly captures this optimism. The second, which 'peaked and crashed in July 2008' (54), was based on vast infrastructural investments in fossil fuels (oil, electricity generation) and transport, as well as huge 'vertically integrated companies under centralized management' which, because of the scale at which they operated, 'lowered the price of goods and services to consumers, allowing the company to flourish' (55). In stark contrast the third industrial revolution constructed around ICT is based on connecting 'everyone and everything in a neural network' which 'brings the human race out of the age of privacy, a defining characteristic of modernity, and into the age or transparency' (73). This section thus examines three overlapping themes: what is distinctive about this 'third industrial revolution', how is the market and business responding to it, and in what ways might capitalism be undermined by the impact of ICTs now and in the near future? In examining these topics the discussion will also uncover an additional dimension of the economic vampirism examined in Chaps. 2, 3 and 4.

---

[5] Some doubt whether even in purely material terms the ICT revolution will prove to be as transformative as the second. Thus, Gordon (2012) argued that the former may have exercised its maximum impact on productivity by 2004 after 40 years of innovation in such things as mobile phones, the Internet, ATM banking, word processing and so on. He also sees a continuing US slow-down in both productivity and economic growth linked to formidable 'headwinds' such as rising inequality but also the intrinsic technological and productivity limitations of the third industrial revolution.

The Knowledge Economy or 'Cognitive Capitalism'

A bewildering number of terms have been coined to capture what is quintessentially distinctive and transformative about the ICT revolution: the knowledge or information economy; the symbolic knowledge economy; the network society/economy; cognitive capitalism; biopolitical labour and production; the zero-marginal-cost society; info-capitalism; the Internet of Things and so on. Despite the variety of terms, each of them points to the same or very similar phenomena.

The first defining feature of cognitive capitalism is the sheer centrality of information, knowledge, codes and ideas to contemporary economic life, whether as scientific discoveries and applications, designs and the blueprints for machines, clothes, household goods, buildings and so on, every kind of symbolic, cultural and media imagery and text, planning procedures, multiple forms of educational learning and much else besides. DeLong and Summers's (2001: 35) description of the knowledge economy is graphic. They explain how in the 40 years from roughly 1960 onwards, the world's 'computational power' (35) increased by a factor of four billion and at an average yearly rate of more than 50 per cent. Similarly, they observe how in the new economy the most significant knowledge we need is no longer 'how to create a useful, physically embodied good' such as an iron ingot, but one where the 'canonical source of value is a gene sequence, a line of computer code or a logo' (35). It is important to note, however, that much of this knowledge and information emanates from sources other than the market but is forged and diffused through family, community and everyday social life or, in modern societies, is produced as a result of state investment in public institutions such as schools and universities (Benkler 2006).[6]

Hardt and Negri (2009) offer a slightly different version of this when they argue that biopolitical or immaterial labour becomes hegemonic

---

[6] Hardt and Negri (2009) remind us that societies, including capitalist ones, only survive because most of social life flourishes outside the market and the realm of private property through language, gestures, myriad shared cultural meanings and long-established and sanctioned social interactions and practices that guarantee 'normal' behaviour, conflict resolution and so on.

in modern capitalist economies. This refers not just to the increasing range and importance of commodities that are symbolic, aesthetic and cognitive in content or to the fact that the value of material goods such as cars and clothes also depend far more on the input of immaterial labour. Rather, they argue that affective or emotional labour, whether as various forms of commercialized caring and service work or the dependence of economic activity on the human social capacity to forge understandings and cooperation in innumerable everyday social interactions, have also become much more crucial to economic life. Throughout history and the capitalist era, affective labour has always been ubiquitous and pivotal to all social and economic activities, and it was frequently expected that women would provide this as unpaid carers, wives and mothers.

The point about affective as well as cognitive labour, however, is that it can be, and frequently is, generated by individuals as autonomous human beings both inside the commercial factory or office and outside in the non-commercialized lifeworld of the everyday as a natural part of social interaction and human life. More often than not, and whether 'flipping burgers, fixing computers, or serving passengers on an airplane', immaterial labour 'engages workers' bodies and emotions in a kind of performance' (Gottfried 2013: 76). Immaterial labour thus feeds into modern capitalism as a component essential to its viability. Yet, whereas human actors do not necessarily need capitalism in order to provide a necessary framework and vehicle before many kinds of work and other activities and relationships can take place effectively, capitalism can only function because society already flourishes both outside and within capitalism's boundaries. We return to this idea in Chap. 9.

Second, the costs of communication and the diffusion of all kinds of knowledge and information—massively enhanced by digitalization—have fallen and continue to do so. Indeed, the relatively low cost of laptops, mobile phones, iPads and so on has brought them increasingly into the realm of ordinary citizens who then use them in order to create and transmit their own ideas, images and everyday thoughts to their friends through emails, smartphones and the social media. Much of this information is free and equally available to everyone while the cost of transmitting much of it is almost or nearly zero. Further consequences follow from this. Thus, third, the huge and escalating number of users contributing to the volume of messages pulsing through the communication channels gives rise to a degree of interconnectivity which is unparalleled. Increasingly people and things are linked together by ICT. The result is the rise of what Benkler (2006: 3) calls 'the networked information economy'. Here, a new epoch of communication brings with it far greater diversity in the sources, content and means of information that are available to users. YouTube and the blogosphere are just two examples. But, fourth, there is also the possibility of information flows becoming far more decentralized, such that the neither the market (i.e. businesses making profit out of knowledge dissemination) nor the state remain the sole contributors, much as they might prefer, and try, to be. The Internet is especially crucial here since it allows and invites everyone to contribute to non-commercialized cultural and informational flows drawn from their own repertoire of thoughts and feelings.

Fifth, according to Benkler (2006), Rifkin (2014), Mason (2015b) and others, all this, in turn, creates the prospect of far more independent collaboration taking place between people who are equals and who are connected through these vast horizontal communication networks spreading in all directions. In Chap. 9 we take up this idea and explore its wider implications for replacing capitalism in part or whole. In the meantime we consider the ways in which capital has reacted to the rise of cognitive capitalism and the implications this has for the argument that it has increasingly assumed vampire-like propensities.

Capitalism and the Knowledge Economy

Many observers have pointed to certain adverse consequences associated with the way capitalist interests have responded to the rise of the knowledge economy and the increased role of biopolitical labour. Chief among these have been (a) the drive to privatize and declare ownership of a number of scientific and intellectual discoveries—even though these originate in shared actions pursued by many over long periods of time—and (b) to extend monopoly control over various common resources generated by the Internet and networked economy. Boyle (2003) describes today's moves by capitalism to impose intellectual property rights on knowledge as tantamount to a second enclosure movement. In doing so he draws on an analogue with the British state's legal support, in the eighteenth century, for the drive by many large farmers and aristocrats to privatize and enclose large areas of common land and farms rented by peasant smallholders. The argument in favour of British land enclosures at the time—and since on the part of some historians—was that turning previously open and common land into privately owned and enclosed farms would give incentives and opportunities for landowners to introduce more efficient and productive farming practices than had been possible before. It also helped pave the way for the industrial revolution.

In short, it has been widely claimed, not least by neoliberalism, that private property, supported and enhanced by state action, is often the *sine qua non* for moving economic practises to new levels of productivity. Here, it is worth alluding to Hardin's article published in 1968, *Tragedy of the Commons*, which appears to lend some intellectual support to this claim. Hardin argued that where resources such as forests or grazing lands are held in common none of those involved has an interest in avoiding their over-use. This is because, whereas private property rights allow each owner to exercise restraint and control over their own portion, the reality of shared free resources means that anyone who does exercise restraint will simply lose out in the short run as they are unable to prevent others continuing to scramble for gain to the point where the resource in question suffers permanent damage.

It is worth noting that, arguing against this view, Ostram's (1990) careful and acclaimed research demonstrated that people can and have constructed social agreements that ensure the long-term survival of shared economic resources and without state intervention or privatization. Among the societies Ostram investigated were: Swiss farmers and villages, who in certain areas shared around 80 per cent of the alpine territory for summer cattle grazing; certain Japanese villagers who still cultivate around three million hectares of common forests and meadows; and the sharing of irrigation canals for farming in the arid region of the Turia river valley in Eastern Spain. In all these and other cases local farmers, villages or communities had evolved self-managed social arrangements which are still in operation after centuries of use. There were several reasons why reports of individual infringements to the agreed rules were extremely rare. For example, the sanctions applied in these instances tended to be graduated and were assessed by accountable and appointed 'officials'; previously agreed procedures for settling conflicts were readily available; and the participants appointed some kind of agreed external arbitrator to monitor and audit the arrangements (Ostram 1990: 89–101). These were small communities where everyone not only knew everyone else and had family and personal reputations to protect but situations where everyone's actions were open to scrutiny.

Returning to Boyle, his concern in referring to the first enclosure movement is neither to justify nor to validate the debates that have grown up around it. What he does, instead, is to challenge the line of argument concerning the alleged need for a second enclosure movement by capitalist interests in respect to the products and processes emerging through ICT industries as a precondition for efficiency, innovation and high productivity. His counter position focuses mainly around the argument that material resources such as land, timber or minerals are different from knowledge, ideas, cultural themes and information in a number of crucial respects and are therefore not directly comparable. First, the latter are created and disseminated in fragments or bits. These may accumulate, mutate, blend, merge, disappear and then reappear in a slightly different form, and so on. It is often very difficult or impossible to point exactly to the time, place or author from which a particular idea or the theme for a piece of music, dress design, art genre or recipe originally came, given that such influences are taken up by innumerable others who then selectively embellish, syncretize and add to them in some way. The classical composers Tchaikovsky and Dvorák, among others, drew on local folk music for their masterworks, and Shakespeare's propensity to build freely on the classical themes and myths of ancient Greece and Rome is often noted. In the case of the multiple influences feeding into the cumulative development of scientific knowledge over several generations as it changed and spilled in different directions, it is even harder to point decisively to a single creator (see also DeLong and Summers 2001: 32). Most scientists are acutely aware of the collective and collaborative nature of their work.

Second, when someone uses a piece of land, a microwave oven or a pair of shoes, their use precludes someone else from doing so. But as Boyle goes onto argue: 'a gene sequence, an MP3 file, or an image may be used by multiple parties; my use does not interfere with yours' (Boyle 2003: 41). This quality of being available to many people at the same time is designated as being 'non-rival'. As an extension of this, non-rival goods also offer the possibility of being used repeatedly. In most cases, and unlike our planet's biosphere, there is little or no possibility that they will be over-used to the point of severe damage or destruction. Third, in principle, scientific knowledge, facts, blue prints, melodies, images, texts and so on are eminently transferable, repeatable and therefore shareable whether through education, libraries, the Internet or other means. And in the age of digitalization and cheap, accessible down-loading many such goods are copied repeatedly and handed on to other users at low or zero cost. We return to this last point below.

Some scientists such as Tim Berners-Lee, inventor of the World Wide Web, and many in the educational and cultural world, have argued strongly in favour of preserving an open commons and an 'Open-Source' knowledge that should remain unenclosed and freely available. As Benkler, Mason, Boyle and others observe, the burgeoning of a vast new world of experimental peer-to-peer cultural interaction and shared production is something we should cherish and protect. One powerful example of the open commons is shown by Wikipedia, a non-profit-making e-company which demonstrates how the creative commons can work in practice. Since it was established in 2001 it has become almost indispensable to millions of researchers and Internet users. Mason (2015b: 128) shows how it employed 208 people in 2015 in addition to 24 million registered contributors of whom 12,000 regularly edit its pages. More than three-fifths of its employees claim they are committed to the principle that information should be freely available. Another is the Internet which we discuss below.

But at the very time when a veritable cornucopia of potentially free or almost free knowledge goods has become available, and when global networking, photocopiers and digital techniques make it almost impossible to distinguish between 'listening, editing and recreating' (Boyle 2003: 40), corporate interests, with state backing, are engaging in a second enclosure movement: in effect the privatization of the commons. This is designed to either retain, re-capture or gain new ownership—and therefore control—of the growing range of both cognitive goods (the 'electronic and creative *commons*') (Hardt and Negri 2004: 186) and the goods provided by nature that have been 'discovered' and/or modified through various kinds of labour. Key and highly contested examples here are the human genome, certain seeds, plant varieties and bacteria. In the case of the latter, much of the work conducted in this area results from the shared research of scientists but also draws on folklore and the long-held knowledge of peasants and other rural dwellers. Not only is such knowledge derived from the natural world and so belongs to no one and everyone, but it grows out of the communal and shared immaterial labour described by Hardt and Negri (2004) as outlined above. It is for this reason that many scientists and others are opposed to situations where, for example, research involving genetic modification transfers the control of seeds from farmers to agribusinesses through 'a flood of patents' (184) that then allow the latter to sell monopoly products back to farmers and others for considerable profits. There are many additional aspects of this privatization process. What follows is a highly selective summary of a few additional but key cases and the arguments surrounding these aspects.

It seems perfectly sensible to argue that those who produce intellectual goods would have little or no incentive to engage in the creative process without the promise of some payment for their efforts, however small, or the existence of a process for preventing others from endlessly pirating their products. This, in turn, supposedly justifies the imposition of intellectual property rights, licensing procedures and extensions, patents and so on. Yet Boyle counters this argument in several ways. For one thing, the growing profusion of intellectual goods characterized by ever falling costs of production and transmission implies that there needs to be a corresponding and parallel increase in the volume and intensification of legal protection by way of compensation and so as to reward and foster creativity and innovation. But this will raise the price of intellectual goods and therefore hold back their market expansion. This may be self-defeating from the perspective of innovation. The imposition of regulations, controls and such things as discriminatory pricing and licensing systems will also discourage further innovation rather than encourage it in the case of ordinary users engaged in inter-peer communications (Boyle 2003: 42–44 and 48). Second, the essentially fragmentary and mutually supportive nature of much creative activity, particularly in the case of science, has always depended on the possibility of open communication: the gradual piecing together of ideas and evidence gleaned through mutual cooperation and the accumulation of knowledge partly shared with many others. There is little or no evidence that attempting to extend property rights to compilations of facts, research experiments, individual papers or new discoveries that take place outside the private research laboratories funded by private corporations will enhance further innovation and the efficiency with which future discoveries are made (49).

From its inception, the Internet has constituted the example *par excellence* of a communal, shared resource with global reach and forged out of the revolution in ICT. Rifkin (2014: 195–7) explains how it has been supported and managed as a global facility (a) by the three stakeholders of government, private business and civil society, (b) by a gamut of non-profit-making organizations, such as the World Wide Web Consortium, which provide technological support and maintenance, but also (c) by various private cable and telecom providers in individual countries. The latter have paid to finance the infrastructure of Internet provision for which consumers pay. All of this operates under a UN umbrella organization which permits each state to participate but also to introduce their own concerns into issues around international Internet governance. Rifkin then explores how in recent years, various pressures emanating from these and other organizations have tried to make inroads into the previously open character of Internet provision thereby threatening its independence. Among these are the following. Some national governments, such as Russia, China, India, South Africa and Saudi Arabia, have introduced legislation designed to increase their control over the Internet, undermining its openness and transparency. Protecting national security against terrorism is one pretext for this but others include the desire to counter internal political dissent and extract tax revenue from the commercial activity taking place in cyberspace (197). In addition, certain commercial network providers such as Deutsche Telekom have tried to squeeze more revenue from the infrastructure they provide by increasing their control over the flows of information taking place and their content. This would enable companies to use their monopoly in order to introduce such policies as charging different rates for various classes of consumer or imposing limits on consumer downloads (198).

Perhaps most notable of all has been the behaviour of the big social media and web-based companies such as Facebook, Twitter and Google. As is well known, these sell the free information provided by and about millions of individual users to advertisers and marketing organizations. The latter then use it to develop new products and/or in order to amass information about those same consumers. In effect, the social media giants are 'providing a treasure trove of valuable personal data that is being mined, rebundled and sold to profit-making firms for targeted commercial leveraging' (201). These companies have also recently acquired huge numbers of patents. Thus, Microsoft bought 925 patents from AOL in 2011 worth over a billion dollars while Facebook purchased $550 million worth of patents from Microsoft in the same year. Meanwhile Google obtained 17,000 patents when it bought Motorola for $12.5 billion (Rifkin 2014: 202). As Rifkin concludes, these corporations, and others such as eBay and Amazon, are investing such vast amounts because they wish to create 'impenetrable enclosures'—or monopolies—protected by intellectual property rights that will enable them to increase the profits they earn from the 'global social Commons' (205).

Rent Versus Profit—Vampirism Hijacks the Cognitive Economy

In Chap. 2 we examined the turn towards vampire capitalism, whereby the world's wealthiest elites are siphoning an often unearned and disproportionately large share of the wealth generated by existing resources and economic growth into their own bank accounts. Crucial to this process has been the alliance forged between leading business interests and governments. In Stiglitz's words (2013: 39), the result has been a political system that has given 'inordinate power to those at the top'. The privileged have then used this power to widen 'the inequality of outcomes and reduce the equality of opportunity' and oppose calls for income and wealth distribution. Similarly, they have used the backing of political elites to seek monopoly business arrangements that are hidden from the public by the transparency provided by lawyers and the diversionary tactics of the Right-wing media. As we also saw in Chap. 2, Stiglitz argues that such practices are tantamount to rent-seeking behaviour. Here, as with feudal and other landowners, a reward or price is extracted based solely or primarily on rights of ownership rather than any kind of active participation in economic activity on the part of the 'landlord'. Stiglitz listed additional activities that fall within this 'rent' category today: for example, seeking trade restrictions, forging agreements with rival companies to over-charge governments or consumers for scarce, valued products—such as access to credit—or seeking special and often hidden government subsidies or favourable tax rates that other smaller businesses are not eligible to receive (Stiglitz 2013: 48–54). As we have seen, observers of cognitive capitalism—such as Boyle (2003), Benkler (2006), Hardt and Negri (2004), Rifkin (2014) Mason (2015b) and others—argue that some ICT corporations have introduced various licensing arrangements as well as intellectual property rights and patents in the attempt to squeeze additional profit out of the networking economy. They insist that much of this should also be designated as rent-seeking behaviour.

Vercellone's (2010) version of this thesis is especially helpful. He explains how the typical nineteenth- and early-twentieth-century owner-entrepreneur actively participated in organizing much of his own company and probably contributed to technical, product or market innovation as well: Schumpeter's classic function of the entrepreneur. Consequently, the profits entrepreneurs extracted from their workforce were largely deserved as a reward for their own work and for risking their capital. This profit was created at the workplace and during the production process. In contrast, much of the knowledge essential to capitalism today is far more significant for output and productivity than ever before in nearly all industries and a substantial proportion is created outside companies. Rather, it is imported into business from the sphere of public education, paid for by taxpayers, and the shared learning activities in which collaborating scientists, professionals and workers frequently engage. Further, a proportion of this productivity depends on interpersonal interaction: Hardt and Negri's (2004) immanent labour.[7]

---

[7] The growing tendency towards the intellectualization of labour and its future likely significance was anticipated and understood by Marx (see Vercellonne 2010: 100–2; Mason 2015b: 164–7).

In effect, with the relative decline in the directly productive role of capital ownership and active management in wealth creation, though much less so in the case of the hired managerial team, a resort to rent rather than profit is becoming increasingly paramount (Vercellonne 2010: 90). Here, profit maximization increasingly involves external financial manipulation, imposing intellectual property rights or other forms of monopoly control over company products and forcing conditions of precarious employment and low wages on employees—or some combination of these. Thus, we are witnessing 'the exhaustion of the progressive role of capital and its increasingly parasitical character', at least in the advanced economies. Capitalism has always depended upon the social economy: family, community, class alliances, religion and so on. Yet, the growing significance of knowledge in all industries, not just cognitive capitalist enterprises, provides capital with a largely free public good: a positive externality. Here, capital gains access to yet another source of partly or wholly unearned 'profit' to feed its vampire appetites.

The Threat to Capitalism from the Networked Economy

Coming more from the perspective of economics, DeLong and Summers (2001) coin the term 'the new economy' as a way of capturing the character of cognitive capitalism. They suggest that the new economy does not fall within the theorization of a decentralized 'Smithian' economy (after Adam Smith), where numerous firms compete and prices consequently tend to move towards their marginal costs. In contrast, the economy of the future is likely to demonstrate more 'Schumpetarian' characteristics in that innovation, particularly in technology, becomes the main source of wealth. But innovation frequently engenders high fixed costs, large-scale investment and the economies of scale, plus government subsidies. These, in turn frequently lead, at least temporarily, to monopoly power and high rewards for businesses, and it is the latter which provides the incentives for innovation. Here, DeLong and Summers point to similar conclusions concerning the monopolistic leanings of businesses involved in cognitive capitalism as those we discussed above. Nevertheless, in theory, and in the longer term, as the productivity gains from such innovation and technological developments diffuse through the economy, so prices may gradually fall, thereby creating further demand for the products concerned.

But the new economy also brings with it looming dangers for capitalism. As we have seen, the Internet, the World Wide Web and the networked economy mean that many products can be produced at minimum or zero cost through imitation and transmission to multiple others. At the same time in the growing economy of shared goods and peer-to-peer communication many consumers are likely to become less and less swayed by advertising, brand loyalties and so on as they create and copy their own products. Accordingly, 'more markets will be contestable' and competition 'will become swifter, stronger, more pervasive, and more perfect' (43). Only those companies able to retain cost advantages based on the economies of large-scale production will be able to maintain healthy profit margins. Consequently, economic principles very different from those that have governed capitalism for two centuries and which have been understood and taught by economists for generations are coming into play in respect to the knowledge economy. DeLong and Summers (2001: 52) even declare that if information goods are distributed at their marginal cost of production, or zero, then 'they cannot be created and produced by entrepreneurial firms' because under capitalism businesses need the revenue from selling their products in order to cover their costs and continue in production. On the other hand, charging prices above low marginal costs and trying to maintain a monopoly based on intellectual property rights will undermine innovation, reduce efficiency and centralize decision-making over time. Businesses operating in the knowledge economy are therefore caught between the devil and the deep blue sea: either they face competition from the low- or no-cost peer-to-peer commons—and the prospect of going out of business—or by seeking protection from monopolistic practices they stifle market growth and face increasingly antagonistic customers.

8.4 Capitalism and Impending Problems

Both climate change and robotization are inextricably bound up with the current and future trajectory of capitalism, whether in its current neoliberal form or some possible future alternative version. It is capitalism's relentless pursuit of economic growth, supported by state-led modernization projects and national rivalry that have brought the world economy to the point where GHG emissions are creating climate change, urban pollution, the loss of biodiversity and so on—all based, till now, on fossil fuels. Similarly, the drive for ever-increasing levels of productivity, propelled by profit and competition and empowered by science, have propelled technological advance towards a situation where increasing numbers, and perhaps the majority, are likely to become redundant as workers.

Climate Change and the Market Economy

In keeping with the economic zeitgeist of the times, it has been widely assumed and claimed, by the WB and other IGOs along with most governments and political parties in the advanced economies, that a market economy configured around profit-seeking constitutes the most efficacious agent for tackling the solutions to climate change. In Chap. 7 we discovered that the capitalist market 'case' was constructed around three claims: allocating market value or prices to environmental resources such as the care of forests, or what McAfee calls 'neoliberal environmentalism' (1999 and 2012); creating carbon markets, or pricing GHG emissions, and developing a trade in buying and selling the licences to emit; and the role that TNCs can and are playing in investing in clean energy as a major path towards hastening de-carbonization while generating profits for investors. One difficulty with the first two approaches is that despite considerable investment so far their results have been limited. In the case of neoliberal environmentalism, there were also unanticipated and undesirable consequences, particularly the accentuation of local inequalities rather than their diminution, as the WB and others had intended. In the case of the third approach the companies involved found themselves caught in the usual capitalist binds of needing to compete with rival businesses and countries and cope with the 2008 global economic downturn both of which endangered and delayed their projects.

But there is a further difficulty. Essentially all these market approaches to resolving environmental threats involve handing over the future care of an endangered biosphere to one of the key agencies, if not the main one, responsible for harming it in the first place. The question of whether capitalism can be trusted to rescue us from dangerous levels of climate change, given its own past culpability, is further complicated by yet another issue: the problem of time. The window of opportunity to cut GHG emissions sufficiently to avoid crossing the 2C temperature rise is extremely narrow and it is doubtful whether left to its own devices capitalism can rise to this challenge in the few decades that are left. In addition, government involvement has already been critical at nearly every step so far in the attempts to establish systems for reducing GHG emissions: facilitating world conferences, establishing carbon markets, passing legislation to reduce factory and car pollution, subsidizing green companies and so on. Much more such action, primarily led by governments, will be required in future as the following short list suggests: easing the transition from fossil fuels to renewable energy and perhaps resisting the power of the former lobby to sabotage or slow down this transition; persuading the public to reduce their consumption or switch to less environmentally damaging forms—such as eating less meat or buying more seasonal produce—through vast educational programmes and fiscal manipulation; capping and taxing carbon emissions and certain goods and services or even prohibiting some altogether; and compensating those hit hardest by such policies or by the damage brought by climate change.

Finally, avoiding further climate change cannot be left either to government or market capitalism. The public as ordinary consumers, investors and savers, voters for green solutions, participants in green debates and as protestors against interests whose actions blatantly endanger nature or accelerate global warming have already played a central role in helping to change opinion, prevent damaging practises and shape government policies. Their continued and increasing involvement in the environmental movement may prove even more critical in future. In any case, we need to remember that environmental problems represent only one of the challenges facing the world at the present time.

Robotization and AI

Technological change and scientific development have been constant companions of capitalism, either helping to drive it forward or pulled along by the power of profit and competition. Each wave disrupted previous skills and employment patterns. Yet till recently, higher productivity and falling costs improved living standards, expanded markets and so created opportunities for new businesses as well as more and often better-paid employment. As we saw in Chap. 5 though, there are fears that this largely benevolent upward spiral is losing momentum. The ICT revolution spreading through the economy has brought the knowledge economy along with the networked individual and undreamt of access to information, but it has also destroyed millions of routine jobs. In the coming decades it will dispense, in whole or part, with many more including some in the professions. Similarly, although the robotization of manufacturing has continued now for several decades, this, too, is accelerating and may soon spread to other areas including farming—which, in the West, already employs barely 2 per cent of the population. Rapid advances in AI pose further threats, perhaps even to employment in scientific research.

None of this is without benefit. Nor is it inevitable that mass future un- and under-employment will follow. Nevertheless, it does evoke several frightening and likely prospects. One is that perhaps only the top 10 to 20 per cent of people with very high and expensive educational levels will gain well-paid employment. In contrast, most may face insecure, poorly paid service work which does not allow them to save for their old age or rear a family—unless income and wealth redistribution policies return. Second, only a tiny minority of the remaining nearly two-and-a-half billion small farmers and rural dwellers and those currently living in urban slums (around one billion according to Davis 2006: 18) seem likely to be absorbed by further rapid spates of industrialization whether as factory workers or as members of the new middle class. Robotization is already replacing people in China's factories. Meanwhile the imperatives of global competition and economic growth are unlikely to divert governments from deploying the same technologies as those being adopted in the West.

Recently, and partly in response to the prospect of a near workless society, there has been a growing discussion, albeit a rather unsystematic one, around the topic of providing everyone with a citizen's income. It is not clear whether this would be added to existing welfare benefits or would replace them but include an additional amount to compensate for a possibly permanent loss of employment earnings, self-reliance and dignity in respect to making a contribution to society. One sociologist who has outlined a scheme relating to the citizen's income is Beck in T*he Brave New World of Work* (2000). Beck envisioned a situation where the growing reality of technological unemployment—already well underway at the time of his writing—will reduce permanent jobs to the point where society could, in effect, institute two socio-economic sectors and the concept of 'work' would apply equally to both. The capitalist-market-public sector would provide full-time and productive jobs whereas the second, parallel, social economy would be preoccupied with family life, education and skill acquisition, caring for the elderly and disadvantaged and looking after the environment. Citizens would be paid for their services to this second economy so they could purchase the commodities produced in the first. They would also be able, if they chose, to move between the two economies at different stages in their life course—perhaps moving into the social economy when they were undergoing education and then returning to it later to rear a family. But most citizens would not expect to remain all of their work life within the market sector.

Switzerland held a referendum on the idea of a citizen's income in 2016, though they called it a guaranteed basic income. Part of its rationale was the need to cope with the growing prospect of automation destroying jobs. More than three-quarters of voters rejected the idea mainly, it seems, because the question of how to fund the scheme was unclear. In fact, the issue of cost and funding sources is obviously crucial. It is also tied into wider questions relating both to societal morality and existing inequality. Thus, in respect to the first issue: how wedded are citizens to the belief that (a) everyone is morally obliged to be self-supporting and

(b) their incomes and wealth are entirely the result of their own efforts or lack of them? As we saw in Chap. 3 neoliberalism has certainly tried to reinforce that kind of notion and may have strengthened previous quasi-religious-cultural ideas along the same lines. This may also partly explain the disdain with which even some of the less well-off now seem to view welfare recipients, regarding most as undeserving parasites—for example in Britain. Accordingly, dislodging the hold that such entrenched perspectives have on large sections of the population in order to win acceptance for a guaranteed citizen's income may prove problematic and will certainly require a political climate sympathetic to extended debate. But second, a far more potentially intractable obstacle to change concerns the degree of inequality that already exists and how much power the wealthy are either prepared to wield in order to resist demands for wealth redistribution or are capable of wielding for this purpose.

Of course, the likely reactions of the wealthy to the introduction of a guaranteed citizen's income is merely part of the much wider problem of how to redistribute wealth and income in the pursuit of any one of a number of desired goals. These might include: a fairer society less prone to inter-class and workplace conflicts and populist demands that veer towards fascism; a more buoyant capitalism less flattened by a lack of effective demand linked to extreme inequality and a corresponding fragility in terms of achieving high economic growth; or a desire to avoid Piketty's (2014) scenario of the long-term socio-political impact of slower economic growth coupled to rising inequality. Nor can we know whether such future conflicts will even take central place in the politics of the future and, if so, how they will be resolved. The discussion in Case Study 2, Chap. 4, suggests that at present those marginalized and even excluded in the Western economies are expressing their discontent. However, they are doing so through a strong veil of cultural disaffection surrounding issues of immigrants and the loss of a familiar and once vibrant national way of life. Of course, this may change, as is suggested by the rise of populist parties of the Far-Left, such as Podemos in Spain and Syriza in

Greece, and the May–June 2016 nationwide French workers' strike.[8] The latter was strongly opposed to the government's attempt to reduce workers' current wage and employment protection rights, in particular the 35-hour week (Willsher 2016: 26). Worried by continued high rates of unemployment of around 10 per cent, Hollande's socialist government argued that employers needed to introduce the same kind of neoliberal flexibilities into their businesses as are evident in rival economies.

Alternatively, such protests and counter-protests may move in very different and far more dangerous directions. Frase (2011) points to a future where the increasing pace of automation leads to an economy 'that does not require human labour at all' (3). He then presents four possible scenarios constructed around the two variables of hierarchy versus equality and scarcity as against relative resource abundance. In one of his scenarios, which he designates as socialist, environmental despoliation and resource depletion are real but they co-exist within a workless economy alongside the equitable sharing of what benefits there are—though this requires a degree of central government planning (14–15). Another of Frase's possible futures, however, is far more dystopic and, indeed, even grimmer than the story presented in such recent films as *The Hunger Games*. Here, scarcity linked to a legacy of environmental destruction co-exists with a highly unequal and hierarchical society dominated by a powerful global elite; perhaps the perfidious '1 per cent' so often mentioned and even pilloried in recent years ever since the Occupy Movement swept across the word's cities, or the plutonomy discussed above. Yet, inequality deprives all but a tiny minority—such as the 'private military contractors' who guard the 'fortresses' of the rich—of access to incomes through employment and therefore the possibility of purchasing scarce commodities. A terrifying and stark possibility then comes into view. Frase (2011) calls this 'exterminism' or the 'genocidal war of the rich against the poor' (p.19). This is brought on by the irrelevance of the latter to the economy and therefore the possibility that the 'immiserated hordes' must be prevented from one-day rebelling against their awful situation.

---

[8] Podemos came second in the December elections of 2015 in Spain with 21 per cent of the national vote. It then allied with the United Left Party but failed to increase its share of seats at the June follow-up election in 2016. Podemos is an anti-austerity and anti-inequality pro-socialist party, popular with the young.

8.5 Summary and Conclusions

Capitalism's increased dependence on rent dressed up as profit exposes it and its leading agents to the risk of a gradual or even sudden loss of legitimacy—though any such possibility looks meagre and distant at the moment. Certainly, much of the current disillusionment and discontent with conventional politics and economic inequality across Europe and the USA mainly takes the form of cultural disaffection around perceptions of lost national identity—as is suggested by the material in Case Study 2, Chap. 4. Yet, it is difficult to ignore or fail to be concerned by the sheer weight of current and impending problems facing humanity.

Several points can be made in relation to this potentially dystopic syndrome of issues. First, capitalism in its present 'unfettered' form (Sandel 2016)—characterized by 'the absolute failure of the neoliberal Project Few', with its priority of supporting a capitalism that has been 'hijacked to serve the rich' (Winterson 2016)—is deeply implicated in all of the above as either one important factor or the primary cause. Second, these problems are directly interconnected: as with climate change and food insecurity, or the fact that without major counter-measures job losses from robotization can only crystallize the gap between the two economic worlds of the super-rich and 'the rest'. Alternatively, attempts to resolve one threat incurs the risk of deepening others. For example, improved economic growth may reduce world poverty but worsen GHG emissions, accelerate climate change and further undermine world food security.

Third, dealing with any one of these threats—never mind several of them simultaneously and in combination—will require not only a huge amount of public involvement, pressure and cooperation but also, of course, the need for different kinds of intervention by national governments. Political action will count far more than markets and profitability. Increased collaboration conducted through the infrastructure and institutions of global governance will also be key. But none of this will be straightforward given (a) the system of international relations based on 200 sovereign nation-states, (b) the distrust many states harbour towards the decades of interference exerted by various US governments in the attempt to shape the world in accordance with their own preferred values and needs and (c) the hold over policy-making and politicians that neo-liberalism continues to exercise. In fact, without countervailing pressures from organized public protest and/or government intervention, and if left free to shape the drift of events, the compulsions of the competitive market, the priorities of profit and the overwhelming power of plutocratic elites are far more likely to distort and intensify these threats and hinder their resolution than assist in attempts to overcome them. Last, as the knowledge economy becomes ever more dominant and if scholars and observers such as DeLong and Summers, Benkler, Rifkin, Mason and others are correct in seeing the stirrings of a viable, alternative social, not-for-profit economy, then the capitalism we have known may be set to lose much of its momentum and even power. In Chap. 9 we consider how the same transformation may be strengthening the prospects for an emerging autonomous not-for-profit social economy.

In short, from whichever direction we come, and considered against the big screen of history, the claim that only capitalism can provide a proven and effective vehicle for human material betterment is looking increasingly threadbare. Perhaps, instead, it represents a system that is running down, and is in danger of taking us, if we allow it to do so, towards a frightening nowhere-place we neither need nor wish to go.

Bibliography

Beck, U. (2000). *The Brave new world of work*. Cambridge: Polity.
Benkler, Y. (2006). *The wealth of networks: How social production transforms markets and freedom*. New Haven, CT: Yale University Press.
Boyle, J. (2003). The second enclosure movement and the construction of the public domain. *Law and Contemporary Problems, 66*(1/2), 33–74.
Castells, M. (1996). *The rise of the network society*. Oxford: Blackwell.
Chakrabortty, A. (2008, July 3). Secret report: Biofuel caused food crisis. *The Guardian*. Retrieved August 9, 2016, from https://www.theguardian.com/environment/2008/jul/03/biofuels.renewableenergy
Davis, M. (2006). *Planet of slums*. London: Verso.
DeLong, J. B. and Summers, L. H. (2001). *The 'new economy': Background, historical perspective, questions, and speculations*. Federal Reserve Bank of Kansas

City. Retrieved August 9, 2016, from https://www.kansascityfed.org/publicat/econrev/Pdf/4q01delo.pdf

Drucker, P. (1993). *Post-capitalist society*. Oxford: Butterworth Heinemann.

Elliott L. (2016b). Brexit could spread shockwaves through global economy, says OECD. Retrieved August 9, 2016, from https://www.theguardian.com/business/2016/jun/01/brexit-could-spread-shockwaves-trough-global-economy-says-oecd

Evans, P., & Tilly, C. (2016). The future of work: Escaping the current dystopian trajectory and building better alternatives. In S. Edgell, G. H., & E. Granter (Eds.), *The sociology of work and employment* (pp. 651–671). London: Sage.Public policies for private corporations: The British corporate welfare state

Fleming, N. (2016, June 2). Farming innovators nurture seed capital. *The Guardian*.

Frase, P. (2011, December). Four futures: Life after capitalism. *Jacobin*. Retrieved August 10, 2016, from https://www.jacobinmag.com/2011/12/four-futures/

Freeland, C. (2012). *Plutocrats: The rise of the new global super-rich and the fall of everyone else*. New York: Penguin.

Gordon, R. J. (2012). *Is U.S. economic growth over? Faltering innovation confronts the six headwinds*. National Bureau of Economic Research. Retrieved August 10, 2016, from http://www.nber.org/papers/w18315

Gottfried, H. (2013). *Gender, work, and economy: Unpacking the global economy*. Cambridge: Polity.

GRAIN. (2015). *The land-grabbers of the Nacala Corridor*. Retrieved August 10, 2016, from https://www.grain.org/article/entries/5137-the-land-grabbers-of-the-nacala-corridor

Hardt, M., & Negri, A. (2004). *Multitude: War and democracy in the age of empire*. New York: Penguin Press.

Hardt, M., & Negri, A. (2009). *Commonwealth*. New Haven, CT: Harvard University Press.

International Assessment of Agricultural Knowledge, Science and Technology for Development (IAASTD). (2009). *Agriculture at the crossroads: Synthesis report*. Retrieved August 12, 2016, from http://www.unep.org/dewa/agassessment/reports/IAASTD/EN/Agriculture%20at%20a%20Crossroads_Synthesis%20Report%20(English).pdf

Justice, F. (2010). *The report of the food and fairness inquiry*. Brighton: Food Ethics Council.

Kapur, A., Macleod, N., & Singh, N. (2005). *Plutonomy: Buying luxury, explaining global imbalances.* London: Citigroup Global Markets.

Kapur, A., Macleod, N., & Singh, N. (2006). *Revisiting plutonomy: The rich getting richer.* London: Citigroup Global Markets.

Mason, P. (2015a, November 2). Apocalypse now: Has the next giant financial crash already begun? *The Guardian.* Retrieved August 10, 2016, from https://www.theguardian.com/commentisfree/2015/nov/01/financial-armageddon-crash-warning-signs

McAfee, K. (1999). Selling nature to save it? Biodiversity and green developmentalism. *Environment and Planning D: Society and Space, 17*(2), 133–154.

McAfee, K. (2012). The contradictory logic of global ecosystem services markets. *Development and Change, 43*(1), 105–131.

Organization for Economic Cooperation and Development. (2015a). *Improving job quality and reducing gender gaps are essential to tackling poverty.* Retrieved August 9, 2016, from http://www.oecd.org/social/reducing-gender-gaps-and-poor-job-quality-essential-to-tackle-growing-inequality.htm

Organization for Economic Cooperation and Development. (2015b). *In it together: Why less inequality benefits all.* Retrieved August 11, 2016, from http://www.oecd.org/social/in-it-together-why-less-inequality-benefits-all-9789264235120-en.htm

Ostram, E. (1990). *Governing the commons: The evolution of institutions for collective action.* Cambridge: Cambridge University Press.

Ostry, J. D., Loungani, P. and Furceri, D. (2016). Neoliberalism oversold? International Monetary Fund. Retrieved August 11, 2016, from http://www.imf.org/external/pubs/ft/fandd/2016/06/ostry.htm

Piketty, T. (2014). *Capital in the twenty-first century.* Cambridge, MA: The Belknap Press.

Reich, R. (1991). *The work of nations.* New York: Knopf.

Rifkin, J. (2014). *The zero marginal cost society: The Internet of things, the collaborative commons, and the eclipse of capitalism.* Basingstoke: Palgrave/Macmillan.

Sandel, M. (2016, June 10–16). The energy of the Brexiteers and Trump is born of the failure of elites. *New Statesman.* Retrieved August 11, 2016, from http://www.newstatesman.com/politics/uk/2016/06/michael-sandel-energy-brexiteers-and-trump-born-failure-elites

Stiglitz, J. (2013). *The price of inequality.* London: Penguin.

Vercellonne, C. (2010). The crisis of the law of value and the becoming-rent of profit. In A. Fumagalli & S. Mezzadra (Eds.), *Crisis in the Global Economy:*

Financial Markets, Social Struggles, and New Political Scenarios (pp. 85–118). Los Angeles: Semiotext(e).

Willsher, K. (2016, June 16). French union leader vows to continue struggle against labour law. *The Guardian*. Retrieved August 15, 2016, from https://www.theguardian.com/world/2016/jun/16/french-union-leader-philippe-martinez-continue-struggle-labour-law

Winterson, J. (2016, June 25). Everything starts as a story. Every political movement begins as a challenge to an existing narrative. *The Guardian*, p. 3.

9

Alternatives: Exploring Possibilities

We have argued that capitalist modernity, particularly in its current unfettered neoliberal form, is failing large sections of humanity and the proportion is growing. Yet, governments, IGOs, many academics, corporations and much of the media have only one answer: yet more markets, competition, growth and technological change. Castoriadis's assessment of where we have reached under the current capitalist regime is chilling but perhaps apposite:

> We are witnessing a brutal, savage transitional phase on a much vaster scale, and over a much shorter lapse of time, than the other transitional phases that have occurred in the history of capitalism. … In such a situation, there is no point in discussing any 'rationality' of capitalism whatsoever. … Transnational firms, financial speculators, and even Mafias in the strict sense of the term are now roving the planet … guided solely by the short-term view of their profits. (2007: 121)

Previous chapters also pointed towards a series of overlapping crises we face in coming decades and the alternative futures to which they are likely to give rise. To different degrees all these are clearly signposted in the writings of some of the scholars and observers whose work we have discussed. There are several but three stand out as particularly ominous and potentially destructive in terms of their possible impact on the future of democracy, social order and economic security: widening inequality and the chasm opening up between the elites and everyone else; the prospect of a workless future for many; and the need to contain climate change and limit its impact fairly. In previous chapters we also considered whether capitalism as presently constituted can conjure solutions to these impending crises without massive supporting, directing and countervailing interventions by governments and, above all, citizens' political movements. The answer seemed to be a resounding 'no'. Placing this in a wider context it seems unlikely that humanity can resolve these issues and crises if we persist in trying to tackle them *solely* from within the paradigms that have dominated the thinking of moderns till now. Crucial is the presumption that the only valid and viable path to human 'progress' lies in the prioritization of material betterment over all other considerations and driven by the perpetual treadmill of competition for personal, company and national gain tied into economic growth.

Further alternatives are also disturbingly possible and may give rise to highly dystopic futures. These might include a slow (or rapid) disintegration of capitalism into a series of mini and localized crises that coalesce through globalization into a catastrophic financial collapse—with governments largely bereft of the fiscal and monetary resources they brought into play in 2008 and beyond. Then there are far more malign scenarios where the institutions of international governance are overwhelmed and some regions collapse into anarchy and violence or Frase's (2011) horrific prospect of 'exterminism' outlined at the end of Chap. 8.[1]

We now consider whether more democratic, equitable and ecologically sustainable futures are equally possible and ask where the resources needed for building such positive alternative might be found. Arguably, these would offer the prospect of remaining within the envelope of modernity as outlined by the original Enlightenment values: the exercise

---

[1] Scarred by intense long-standing sectarian and inter-state rivalries, both exacerbated by decades of Western intervention, parts of the Middle East and North Africa already demonstrate this possibility with its truncated and undemocratic modernization processes supported by vast oil wealth, the purchase of advanced military technology and underpinned, in some cases, by the availability of oppressed migrant rather than local workers.

of reason by free individuals living in societies which impose obligations in exchange for social protection but also the capacity to exercise self-realization. It would be foolish to deny, however, that reaching for such alternatives will mean overcoming some formidable constraints: gaining the support of citizens, many of whom are wedded to private aspirations for material betterment and in denial about globalization and climate change; the need to build cosmopolitan transnational alliances against the tides of nationalism and ethnic mistrust; the possible hostile reactions of the state and political elites who seem currently unable of imagining any future other than a neoliberal capitalist one; and the likely adverse responses of powerful capitalist interests—even when weakened by financial and other crises. There is also the question of resources. How would those seeking alternatives acquire skills and secure land, equipment and seed-corn finance from banks, economic elites and local–national stakeholders including communities, councils and so on? Here, we return to the importance of generating political movements and campaigns.

These constraints appear ominous. Yet, there are reasons for supposing that building alternative social economies may be more readily achievable than seems possible at first sight. Qualitatively different processes and institutions are already established and working both inside capitalist economies and as pre- or quasi-capitalist systems surviving on its periphery. These possess a logic running counter to capitalism. The latter has also failed to completely incorporate these into its own trajectory or entirely corrupt their values. Their survival provides models and levers around which to build alternatives. Second, more recent practises, growing directly out of the changing nature of capitalist modernity *per se,* are encouraging many to seek alternatives. The prospect of a workless future is likely to become one such powerful motivating factor. But there are also springboards for change which offer new opportunities for constructing viable and dynamic social alternatives. We now explore each of these prospects.

9.1 The Power of the Social Flourishing Within Capitalism

Gibson-Graham (2006: 53) contest what they call the 'discursive dominance' of capitalism: the presumption that capitalism has no possible 'outside' or 'any so-called alternatives' (2). They remind us that an inner core of non-capitalist orientations, aspirations and concrete practices have always flourished, and still do, despite the long era of capitalist dominance. Here, they are not referring to the cultural, familial and community institutions, we call 'society', which carries most of the burden of social reproduction, but to the social practices that buttress the 'innards' of economic life itself. Capitalism's perpetual clamour for attention—which as John Stuart Mill suggested in the nineteenth century—compels us to spend our time 'trampling, crushing, elbowing and treading on each other's heels' as the 'existing type of social life'[2]—distracts us from the power of this other side of economic life: namely, the social economy. Consequently we rarely reckon on its potential significance. Yet if we mentally turn capitalism inside we soon discover the dense and taken-for-granted web of ties and activities linked indirectly to economic processes which are social and ethical in intention. Looking to locations often far distant from the Western industrial heartlands we also discover social formations capitalism has failed to obliterate but which have co-existed alongside: indigenous peoples and peasant-farmers. Arguably both the social economy flourishing within the borders of capitalism and the worlds still existing outside point to perfectly viable practices we can transplant to alternative formations.

The Inside Social Core and Supporting Buttresses of Capitalism

In order to create a political space for their contrasting idea of 'the community economy', Gibson-Graham (2006: 79) set out two arguments. First, even when we concentrate on the economy *per se*, we discover that

---

[2] Cited by Albert (2006: 2) in his book *Realizing Hope: Life Beyond Capitalism*.

far from taking a single, dominant form capitalist economies actually consist of diverse practices. These include different types of transactions, varying kinds of market activities and a wide range of modes of labour engagement. Capitalism turns out to be no more than a 'small subset' (69) of actual economic life even in the advanced market economies.

Taking the case of paid workers in private companies, for example, we can think about this in terms of an iceberg where the fraction on view conceals a volume of supporting and largely unpaid social activities below. Among the many alternative ways in which work is produced, whether unpaid, paid in kind, through barter, self-payment, back-handers and so on, are the following: domestic chores and childcare within families; congregation members contributing to church events; parents helping in schools; slave labour which is increasing with rising migration; friends or retired people helping each other in home repairs or childcare commitments; informal baby-sitting arrangements; self-provisioning when individuals grow their own food in allotments, make and bottle jam, knit or sew clothes or manufacture other articles for their own or another's use; a wide range of self-employment supported by family employees; the members of cooperatives; those working in non-profit-making social enterprises; or illegal activities such as drug dealing, theft or moonlighting. Moreover, this list does not include the paid work in the public sector for health and so on. Nor does it take account of voluntary work conducted outside the household for charities, INGOs and so on, much of it unmeasured. Drawing on the research conducted by several IGOs, including the ILO and OECD, a Bank of England report in 2014 (presented by A.G. Haldane) suggested that in 2012 around 15 million people in the UK had acted as volunteers during the previous 12 months. In total, approximately 4.4 billion hours or an average of nearly 2 hours per week for each volunteer took place in Britain during that same year, equivalent to 10 per cent of all the hours worked by paid employees.[3] According to the OECD's figures, cited in this same report, Britain was ranked 12th out of 36 countries in respect to volunteering.

Secondly, Gibson-Graham (2006) discuss the vast array of ethically oriented activities taking place within modern economies. These mostly

---

[3] www.bankofengland.co.uk/publications/Document/speeches/2014/speech756.pdf.

relate to various concepts that prioritize 'care of the local community and its environment' (80) as opposed to making profits or pursuing materialistic goals. Additional features intrinsic to the community economy include: smallness of scale, diversification, cooperation, being autonomous, ownership and control by the community, attachment to particular places and concern with serving local markets, dedication to recycling any surplus back to the community and following principles of environmental sustainability (87). Underpinning the community economy is the principle of mutual interdependence and responsibility (95–96). The authors also allude to a series of ethically based actions frequently associated with running community economies: for example, joining fair-trade networks, participating in farmers' markets, joining anti-sweatshop or workers' buy-out or living-wage movements and engaging in green/ ethical consumption and investment practices (79–80). According to the 'Ethical consumer market report' published by the magazine *Ethical Consumer* (2013), for example, sales of ethical goods in the UK continued to grow between 2008 and 2013 despite the recession. For example, Fairtrade products expanded by 24 per cent (2010–2012), Rainforest Alliance goods grew by 47 per cent, spending on ecologically concerned travel products and transport rose by 157 per cent while the purchases of fish from sustainable stocks increased by 20 per cent. The same report also explained how the voluntary incomes accruing to Britain's top 500 charities rose by nearly a quarter (22 per cent) during the same period.

Gibson-Graham (2006: 213) alert us to the tendency for 'mainstream economic theory' to 'lump' together voluntary work, charities, INGOS, intra-community projects, cooperatives and so on, as 'third sector' activities—neither private nor public. But this term disparages and marginalizes the vibrancy and sheer volume of the social economy as well as people's desire to participate in it. Far from being merely 'variants of, or supports to, market exchange' involving—for economists and capital—irritatingly 'unenforceable' and even 'pathological practices' that undermine economic efficiency the social and community economy supports capitalism at no cost while compensating for the damage, neglect and lacuna in people's lives capitalism leaves in its wake. It also signposts the possibility of an alternative future even as it co-exists, as a pulsating, breathing force, at the heart of the market economy.

9.2 Social Economies Surviving on Capitalism's Periphery

In Chap. 8 we considered Ostram's (1990) work on small communities which have constructed social arrangements designed to ensure the survival of shared economic resources without state intervention or privatization. One of her examples involved alpine farmers and villagers who share around 80 per cent of the mountain pastures for summer cattle grazing entirely through self-managed social agreements. Not only have they done this for centuries but this continues today in one of the richest countries in Europe: Switzerland. There are, however, other examples of enduring situations worldwide where long-established economic systems are still partly grounded in socio-cultural relationships and values. Moreover, these have equipped those involved with resources that empower them to mount some resistance to competitive market capitalism. We refer here to indigenous peoples and the approximately two-and-a-half billion peasant-small family farms, most still flourishing in the Global South. Both bear scars from centuries of being battered by modernizing national and foreign governments along with global capitalism. Nevertheless they have adapted and retained much of their original alternative values and priorities.

Indigenous Peoples

There are around 5000 different indigenous peoples each with their own dialect or language. Their numbers are estimated at approximately 350–370 million, perhaps 5 per cent of the world's population (UN-DESA 2009: 21). Their cultures stretch across the Americas from the Inuit of Alaska and Canada down to the Maya and the many Indian peoples of Central and South America, including Mexico, Brazil, Ecuador and Bolivia. In the latter they constitute 60 per cent of the population. Across South America they number 40–55 million people (Martin and Wilmer 2008: 585). Indigenous peoples also exist across Northern Europe and Siberia, Africa, Australia, New Zealand and much of Asia. In India alone the 2001 census identified perhaps 600 distinctive groups and classified around 84 million people as belonging to indigenous societies and occupying 7 per cent of the territory (Starr and Adams 2003: 33). They also make up 15 per cent of the world's poorest people (UN-DESA 2009: 21). Pastoralists form a major subgroup. They are based on raising livestock often in savannah regions characterized by erratic rainfall, covering around one-quarter of the global land area. Included in this group are the Saami reindeer herders of Siberia and Northern Scandinavia, Mongol horse breeders and traders, the East African Massai whose economy revolves around cattle and the Saharan Tuareg camel breeders (UN-DESA 2009: 30).

The vast array of indigenous peoples, with their cultural diversity, wide range of livelihoods and occupation of a variety of often remote and climatically difficult terrains, almost defies clear definition. Nevertheless, they share unique features and common experiences singling them out not only as different from other surrounding social formations but also as possessing cultural and lifestyle attributes that highlight the limitations of capitalist modernity.

First, their core values contrast strikingly with those dominant in the West through Christianity, the Enlightenment and over two centuries of modernization. Their religious beliefs invariably revolve around ancestor worship not a single monotheistic god. Consequently burial sites are very significant to them and this has often brought them into conflict with modernizing states and incoming settlers. Indigenous peoples also possess a very different ontological understanding of nature since they regard animals, plants and other natural entities as possessing some kind of soul, rather like humans, and therefore are owed certain rights and obligations.[4] In general, the goal of protecting nature against the destructive aspects of relentless development brings the interests of indigenous peoples very much in line with those of environmental groups—though this does not always work out as footnote 4 suggests. Land is often

---

[4] One reason is the creation of around 6000 wildlife parks and many thousands of protected conservation areas—partly to attract tourists—since this often leads to the eviction of indigenous peoples (Vidal 2014: 240), as with the San people of the Kalahari in Botswana. The traditional grazing lands of the Saami reindeer herders of Northern Norway are also being threatened not only by mining interests and the government—for windfarms, tunnel and roads—but also by local conservation groups anxious to protect reindeer predators such as lynx, wolverine and eagles (Vidal 2016).

regarded as sacred and along with other resources is to be held and preserved for future generations. As such, their societies operate on the basis of communal rather than individual ownership which totally denies that *sine qua non* of capitalism—private property rights (Hall and Fenlon 2004: 156).

Second, for centuries, national and imperialist states and/or the surrounding majority ethnic societies have occupied their ancestral lands and forests or commandeered territory required for timber, mineral or other rights, often invoking violence or claiming legal precedence in the process (Hall and Fenlon 2008). Frequently, those societies affected by repeated attacks on their existence were compelled to migrate to safer regions. Often, too, their original presence in certain localities or their location following migration meant they straddled national borders so giving states further reasons to disrupt their habitations. In the face of such threats and the deepening thrust of modernizing and commercial values, many indigenous peoples have demonstrated an inventive capacity to adapt to the changing world. Indeed, this is partly what explains their capacity to survive at all (Schmidt 2007). Another reason for their resilience has been their conscious struggles to preserve as much of their traditional culture as possible. Hall and Fenlon (2004: 157) point to one recent example demonstrated by some Native American groups in the USA who have established tribal colleges offering courses in indigenous crafts, languages and customs. More generally indigenous peoples have responded to threats to their cultures by seeking allies such as the ILO and various UN agencies and by appealing to sympathetic world media interests. Helped by concerned anthropologists and human rights activists, they established their own organization in 1968, the International World Group for Indigenous Affairs (IWGIA). They have also participated in transnational social movements such as the Global Justice Movement: a vast alliance engaged in countering the spread of neoliberal capitalism from the late 1990s (see, Kiely 2005b; Munck 2007; Reitan 2007). They also participate in the World Social Forum (WSF).[5]

---

[5] An annual assembly of worldwide groups which has met most years since 2001. The latter's goal is summarized by the following statement: 'Another world is needed. Together, it is possible'.

In short, indigenous peoples present only a modest direct threat to capitalism and the project of modernity. But as Hall and Fenlon (2004: 173) suggest their continued presence and values constitute a challenge because they are 'organized according to a different logic'. They demonstrate that there is nothing about capitalism which suggests it is natural, inevitable or destined to last indefinitely and should it collapse alternative social systems with a proven viability are available.

Peasants–Small Farmers and Feeding the World

Like indigenous peoples small farmers have survived capitalist modernity and industrialization over more than two centuries. In doing so, at least some of their values, the family farm, membership of local communities and a relationship to the land and nature, still shape their lives though modified by commercial inducements and the promise of material comforts. Arguably, the continued viability of the small farm economy as a distinctive culture in its own right and its ability to co-exist with capitalism represents a further challenge to the latter's presumed hegemony. It also indicates that various additional and even new forms of social economy, less dominated by competition, individualism and the drive to accumulate, could emerge in the future and perhaps borrow elements of peasant values and practices.

There has been an upsurge of interest relating to small family farms by IGOs such as the UNEP and the Food and Agricultural Organization (FAO) but also by agronomists and development experts. For example, the UN declared 2014 as the 'International Year of Family Farming'. Estimates of their numbers vary a little but there is also wide agreement. The FAO has estimated that there are 500 million small farms and they constitute 90 per cent of all farms in the world (2014). In contrast the UNEP suggested that in total there are 525 million small farms involving 2.6 billion people (2011). What is clear, however, is that the vast majority cover under two hectares though what is defined as 'small' varies between countries. Nevertheless, in much of Asia and SSA 'small' actually means tiny and partly because of population growth the size of such farm plots is decreasing. Thus, The FAO's data (2014: 13) suggest that nearly three-quarters of those cultivating farm land held less than 1 hectare amounting to just 8 per cent of the world's agricultural land. In fact, 84 per cent of farmers worldwide cultivate food for their families and surrounding local inhabitants—plus some for urban markets—on less than two hectares of land. This amounts to only 12 per cent of all farm land worldwide.

Despite their small land areas there is wide agreement that by mostly using family and some additional local labour, they achieve commendable results with meagre resources. Two-thirds of small farmers deploy mixed methods—multiple crop cultivation alongside animals—and unlike large agri-businesses they use little or no artificial fertilizers or pesticides. They produce the bulk of the staple foods on which most people in their countries depend (UNEP 2011) and utilize a far wider range of crop varieties they have bred themselves than most industrial agricultural producers, thereby keeping a rich genetic stock in circulation. A high proportion of small family farms are headed by women, especially in SSA. Perhaps most impressive of all, although estimates vary, the UNEP (2011) study concluded that small family farmers produce 70 per cent of all the world's food (UNEP 2011). The FAO's (2014) corresponding estimate was higher at 80 per cent. What lies behind these impressive figures is that most small farmers produce higher average yields per hectare than the big industrial farms despite their comparatively scant resources (though their per capita production is far lower). Some of the reasons why agri-businesses often experience declining productivity, and the wider issues surrounding world food security, are examined in Chap. 8, Case Study 6.

Following from this, what are the unique characteristics of small farmers? First, scholars have usually distinguished between peasants and small farmers by regarding the former as oriented mainly towards family subsistence needs and the latter as more driven by the desire to expand through engagement with the market and a tendency to specialize. More recently, their common desire to preserve the farm as a family concern and to operate within a local community—and their joint exposure since the 1980s to pressures from agri-business and neoliberal globalization—has tended to override these differences. On the first point, the following comment by Nettie Wiebe in 2002, once the president of Canada's

National Farmers Union, highlights the underlying perspective shared by peasants and small farmers:

> If you actually ask what 'peasant' means, it means 'people of the land'. Are we Canadian farmers 'people of the land'? Well, yes, of course. ... We too are peasants and it's the land and our relationship to the land and food production that distinguishes us. We're not part of the industrial machine. We're much more closely linked to places where we grow food and how we grow food, and what the weather is there. (Cited in Edelman2003: 187)

Second, it is useful to recall that industrialization has always presented small farmers with difficulties. Chief among these was the demand for cheap food by urban workers and their employers, growing international farm competition and the tendency for crop prices to fluctuate or fall. Until the 1980s, many governments protected local agriculture from imports and from foreign companies wishing to buy land while subsidizing national produce on the grounds of preserving national food security and maximizing rural employment. The EU and North American governments still subsidize local farmers, impose trade restrictions on food imports from developing countries and even permit home producers to dump cheap produce onto the latter (Case Study 6).

However, recent economic policy and business changes have exposed small farmers everywhere to similar problems (Edelman 2003; Hendrickson and Heffernan 2002; Reitan 2007). From the 1980s neoliberal policies imposed by the IMF and WB in exchange for debt relief forced governments to reduce or eliminate their programmes of protection for small farmers such as low-interest loans, subsidized fertilizers and guaranteed prices. In Mexico, for example, previous legal protection for communal peasant land against commercialization was removed. During the 1990s the GATT, replaced by the WTO in 1995, persuaded governments to extend to agriculture and services the same free trade agreements previously introduced in manufacturing. One notable case was the North American Free Trade Association (NAFTA) between Canada, the USA, Mexico and the Central American Republics. Small farmers rightly perceived that large farmers would benefit and enlarge their farm holdings, but competition from cheap food imports would further undermine their own precarious livelihoods. The growth of international food corporations, helped by capital liberalization, presented another threat since their grip on some farmers often reduced the latter to contract-suppliers of specified produce in a global food system dominated by gigantic players including supermarkets such as Wal-Mart and Tesco. The latter's concentration of market share has often allowed them to impose lower prices on small famers plus regulations that work to their advantage while squeezing the livelihoods of farmers still further.

Third, confronted with these threats to their livelihoods, numerous small national farm organizations have joined in common cause despite the huge variation in respect to the average size of 'small' farms and national cultural differences. (This included Netti Wiebe whose words were quoted above.) They realized the main threat to their survival had shifted from the domestic to the global level. Transnational networking and collaboration was the only solution to countering this. In the 1990s, for example, Mexican, US and Canadian farmers' organizations combined in the attempt to resist the onset of NAFTA in 1994. The main vehicle for such transnational cooperation became *Via Campesina* (VC) (www.viacampesina.org) or 'the Peasants' Way' (see, Desmarais 2002). VC is an international movement supported by groups from 88 countries (in 2013) and was founded in Belgium in 1993. It claims to represent the interests of 200 million small- and middle-scale farmers as well as agricultural workers and indigenous communities. It has always emphasized its parallel commitment to the rights and full participation of rural women.[6] The introductory preamble on an earlier VC website, in 2010, summarized the organization's principle objective as follows: 'to develop solidarity and unity among small farm organizations in order to promote gender parity and social justice in fair economic relations: the preservation of land, water, seeds and other natural resources'.

The same website also emphasized the need to preserve food sovereignty and ecologically sustainable agriculture 'based on small and medium-sized food producers'. The idea of food sovereignty is crucial to the concerns of VC but also to many other international campaigns: for

---

[6] See especially: 'Declaration of Rights of Peasants – Women and Men', published in Seoul, March 2009.

example, *Global Justice*.[7] The idea goes to the heart of VC's interest in preserving their own survival but also in keeping the pressures of full-blown capitalist competition under restraint. Accordingly, VC defines food sovereignty in the following terms: agriculture should be free from trade agreements and rampant competition from agri-businesses, production should mostly be for local markets and at prices that allow workers and farmers to live in dignity and the food produced should reflect local cultural orientations, be healthy, affordable and based on environmentally sustainable methods.

As we saw in Chap. 7, the reality of climate change has placed a new agenda on the world's stage. Not just environmentalists but also agronomists, IGOS, governments and demographers, worried about future world food output, have taken a fresh look at farming methods. A major conclusion is that a holistic approach is now urgently needed. This recognizes the multi-functional nature of small farms both as key producers of local and global food but also their valuable contribution to ecologically sustainable agriculture for the following reasons: their minimum reliance on fossil-fuel and chemical-based farming practices, their use of multiple- and inter-cropping systems which reduces pests and conserves water, their dependence on animal and vegetable compost and so on. The contrast could hardly be greater between the relatively limited contribution to carbon emissions stemming from small farms, producing at least three-quarters of world food, and the high-tech, fossil-fuel-hungry global food industry emitting nearly half of all carbon emissions (see Case Study 6) but churning out a relatively small share of that overall total—most of it used disproportionately to feed cereal-guzzling pigs, cattle and poultry for meat production. Experts and IGOS, therefore, increasingly view small farmers as deserving of more concrete assistance. Indeed, there would seem every reason for optimism that if given financial and technical support and more sympathetic trade deals they will be able to increase their food productivity and output, thereby contributing to future world food security, while playing a major role in moving towards enhanced environmental sustainability. In a coming age of high technological unemployment it may also be worthwhile recalling that

---

[7] See: www.globaljustice/org.uk/what-is-food-sovereignty.

unlike big agri-businesses, and despite their smallness, these farms absorb a lot of family labour as well as local workers.

9.3 Replacing Capitalism from Within—The Collaborative Commons

As we saw in Chap. 8 a growing number of observers are excited by the prospect that the knowledge economy, or cognitive capitalism, is transforming certain capitalist businesses. In particular, the ability of ordinary citizens to repeatedly copy and transfer many kinds of information goods to others at zero- or near-zero marginal cost means that businesses are faced with the prospect of collapsing profits as they cannot easily charge customers for these same products. Indeed, some observers argue that the new knowledge economy—or what Mason (2015b) calls info-capitalism—may replace capitalism altogether. Building on the account developed in Chap. 8 we now focus specifically on the recent writings of Rifkin (2014) and Mason (2013, 2015b) in order to explore five main themes around this topic.

First, both stress the failure of neoliberal capitalism to move our economies beyond the post-2008 financial crisis or to resolve structural constraints that block further growth. Mason (2015b: 78) claims that this is linked to the defeat of organized labour, and so the absence of an effective opposition to neoliberalism, America's capacity as 'an unchallenged superpower' to 'create money out of nothing for a long time' thereby, perpetuating financial instability, but also the rise of the info-economy.

Second, both are adamant concerning the many positive gains for ordinary citizens, particularly the young, associated with ICT. These can be summarized as follows:

- We are seeing the rise of the networked individual, repeatedly connected to numerous others and enjoying vast realms of knowledge and information through the 'Internet of Things' and the social media;
- This partly frees participants from the influence of politicians and the techno-elites who dominant the mass media, leaving them less

conditioned by orthodox presumptions concerning what is possible and desirable and more open to the ideas and visions of fellow social media users;
- Instant communication via the Internet offers the prospect for participants to seek and express considerable personal autonomy. By the same token the technology also creates a space for forming and joining new and alternative communities where everything is negotiable;
- ICT also engenders fluidity in relationships and meanings—and therefore constant change and evolution—but also the ability to form loose coalitions or use swarming techniques in inter-personal relations and during political actions. These occur where multiple individuals in different locations use ICT to know where everyone is so they can engage in efficient and instantaneous cooperative acts even to the point where hierarchical organization is overcome or by-passed (Mason 2013: 82–83);
- Mason (2013: 80–83) further suggests that ICT and the social media empower participants to express individual freedom but within the simultaneous context of community collaboration and accountability.

The Position and Role of Youth

Thirdly, and as we have seen in earlier chapters, today's youth in Western countries face a problematical future of declining jobs, huge educational debts, the burden of supporting an ageing population, disappearing welfare support, a deepening environmental crisis and much else besides. Most realize that the 'whole offer of self-betterment has been withdrawn' (Mason 2013: 68). The possibility therefore of finding some kind of economic future in the collaborative commons is not only attractive in its own right but numerous young people will be driven to seek a living in that space through sheer necessity (Rifkin 2014: 132). In any case, their experience of growing up in the network economy, immersed in the social media, and their close familiarity with the skills and possibilities of the knowledge economy means that many young people are strongly disposed towards its orientations and seek flexibility and the opportunity for self-invention. According to Mason, therefore, their experience of ICT leaves many antipathetic to hierarchy, politicians, corporate power and conventional capitalist career structures. Instead, they seek work commensurate with the ability to exercise their own values and lifestyles within some kind of cooperative economic community. Mason (2013) argues that these same young people are also open to global culture, relatively indifferent to patriotic identities and hostile to patriarchal cultures. They also lean towards the life and culture found in global cities where the educated young mix on streets and in clubs and bars with their less-well-educated peers and the urban poor. Thus, their concerns are shared and pooled relatively easily across social borders (68–69). Rifkin (2014: 234–40) also suggests that the reality of free goods grounded in the collaborative commons predisposes many young people towards sharing far more than just the information goods they acquire on the Internet. Thus, bicycles, clothes, cars, bed space, music, books, study notes and so on are increasingly being swapped, exchanged and borrowed without cost. Adults, too, are learning to share children's toys, work skills and labour time and vegetables from urban allotments while utilizing the possibilities of farming out personal resources cheaply or on an exchange basis provided by various apps such as Airbnb.

Life Beyond Capitalism in the New Knowledge Economy

Fourthly, both these and other authors (e.g. Castells 1996) claim that for everyone the nature of economic life is undergoing a drastic transformation because of the knowledge economy. Rifkin is particularly upbeat concerning the long-term implications. Thus, he argues that although robotization will bring most factory jobs to an end within the next 20 or so years, and many other kinds of work, too, the advent of Big Data, algorithms, robotics and AI is also 'liberating hundreds of millions of people from work in the market economy' (2014: 121). As we have seen, in its place Rifkin envisages the emergence of the collaborative economy. This new world will no longer be characterized by the inherent scarcity which provided the starting point for theorizing the market economy by neo-classical economics. Rather, the economy we are heading towards will offer an abundance of time, goods, services and opportunities for self-expression through cooperation with others. This, in turn, is closely linked to three key changes which will hugely compensate for unemployment in the old economy. People will obviously benefit from the reality that ever more goods will be either available at zero- or near-zero cost or shared. Second, a great many new jobs will be created as people enjoy lower costs of living and many of these will cluster around the three areas affected most by the new technology: the switch to renewables as the primary source of energy, the sphere of logistics or transport and travel and, of course, the communication and knowledge industries, too. A third and crucial source of employment will come from the ability of citizens to use their free time in order to produce for themselves—probably through various forms of cooperative endeavour—some of the goods and services they once purchased on the market. They will become prosumers: people who both produce and consume—and share—their own goods in the not-for-profit and peer-to-peer-economy.

Rifkin's ideas resemble the claims of some notable earlier observers such as Gandhi and Schumacher and he makes explicit references to both (2014: 100 and 104–8). In the 1930s and 40s Gandhi contemplated India's possible future as it approached independence from Britain. Contrary to the vast industrializing ambitions of most of his elite compatriots, he saw the top-down mass production economies of the West as dangerously inappropriate to India given that it was primarily rural, extremely poor and where most people lived in tiny villages. True human fulfilment could only come from living in decentralized communities where respect for nature, collective life and the dignity of skilled craft labour in the pursuit of local and family self-sufficiency took central place over the pursuit of material betterment. Not mass production but production by the masses was needed. Schumacher's book (2011) *Small is Beautiful: A Study of Economics as if People Mattered,* and originally published in 1976, expressed similar ideas to Gandhi's and reached a wide audience. He argued that mass production technology is 'inherently violent, ecologically damaging … and stultifying for the human person'. In contrast, intermediate technology or 'self-help technology, or democratic or people's technology—technology to which everyone can gain admittance and which is not reserved for the rich and powerful' (127) is infinitely preferable because in addition to being far less environmentally destructive it depends on those resources that everyone possesses, 'their clever brains and skilful hands' (126–7).

Rifkin's rosy view of the collaborative commons is actually more pronounced that the previous outline suggests. He predicts that the open source software that is producing free or nearly zero cost information goods such as research data, film, design plans and so on will soon be extended to the production and distribution of an ever widening range of material objects. Indeed, this is already happening through the invention of smart three-dimensional printing machines (3-D printers). These can be instructed to direct 'molten plastic, molten metal, and other feedstocks inside a printer, to build a physical product layer by layer, creating a fully formed product, even with moveable parts' (2014: 89). Over time the cost of these printers will fall; they will become more efficient and linked up with cheap renewable energy sources. Moreover, the same principles of near-zero cost production will increasingly apply to a host of new small businesses using 3-D technology. These will provide jobs and cheap goods while individual citizens will increasingly produce some of their own physical goods using the same methods. This further mass democratization of economic life will also help in 'easing us out of the capitalist period and into the collaborationist era' (99).

Not everyone is equally convinced by Rifkin's extrapolation from what is possible in the knowledge economy to the world of industry, agriculture and construction. Evans and Tilly (2016: 665), for example, suggest that it may be possible 'to produce our own entertainment on YouTube and even various material gadgets via 3-D printers, but we will still depend on a range of products—from breakfast cereals to shoes—for which the marginal cost is not zero'. The same applies to the houses we need to live in. In any case, and despite the promise of peer production and the collaborative commons, we will need to work in order to earn the cash to pay for such goods. Mason (2015b: 140–1) is also sceptical. Observers like Rifkin talk as if the knowledge economy is already supplanting industrial capitalism but the latter continues to dominate across swathes of the Global South and North in factories, quarries, 'metal-bashing-shops' (140), agro-businesses, docks, airports and container yards. It is the access to cheap, exploited industrial and agricultural labour in the Global South made possible by an open, globalized economy, Mason argues, that largely underpins profitability and economic growth in the advanced economies.

Arriving at Post-Capitalism: When and How

Lastly, and in view of the above, what is the prognosis for old-style capitalism? In sharp contrast to what most past critics have insisted, particularly most Marxists, Mason (2015b: 243–4 and 253–4) argues that it is possible for a post-capitalist society to be built within and alongside the hulk of the existing system without the necessity for violent revolution though it will need to be designed and fostered with care. This will be even more likely if (a) state support is harnessed to the project and (b) this is coupled to the replacement of many types of market practice by a range of grassroots cooperative enterprises committed to social production rather than individual material aggrandizement (see also, Satgar 2014). While this transition will probably be slow and piecemeal, capitalism will undergo fundamental change under the weight of falling prices and profits as knowledge becomes the key productive but also shared resource.

Similarly, as robotization destroys many kinds of jobs and citizen spending power correspondingly declines along with business profitability, it is also likely that capital will try to commodify a range of previously non-commercial activities. In theory this will create new jobs and compensate for falling demand and profits. But Mason (2015b: 172–6) suggests that the only sphere of human activity still available for such investment relates to all those inter-personal micro-social services defined by intimacy, trust and reciprocity that until now have been given and exchanged between family and friends for free as intrinsic to sociality: looking after a neighbour's dog, visiting a sick elderly person or offering emotional support or sexual relief to those who are stressed or alone. If this occurs it will undermine the foundation of everyday social relationships and may also require governments to criminalize actions which defy the commands of money payment because people continue to offer their support for free. All this is likely to be resisted.

Mason (2015b: 144) is also quite clear that post-capitalism has not yet replaced capitalism. At present we are stuck with info-capitalism—in a hybrid economy—where a network logic and hierarchical private-corporate or public organizations operate side by side. Nevertheless, this unresolved conflict is an indication that the '240-year lifecycle of industrial capitalism may be nearing its end'.

9.4 Co-existing with Capitalism—Social Enterprise and Cooperatives

Social Enterprises

Social enterprises (SEs) are not new but they have grown in number and significance during the last 30 years. A SE is one that adopts 'a mission to create and sustain value' and this social mission is what distinguishes social entrepreneurs from their business counterparts. The mission concerns:

> social improvement that cannot be reduced to creating private benefits (financial returns or consumption benefits) for individuals. … Profit is not the gauge of value creation … social impact is the gauge. Social entrepreneurs look for … lasting improvements that can be sustained. (Dees 2001: 8)

A recent book by Martin and Osberg (2016: 7–8) pushes this argument further. Social entrepreneurs are neither advocates of social change designed to foster human improvement, such as Martin Luther King, nor are they social benefactors like Maria Theresa who worked to relieve the sufferings of destitute people in India. Rather, social entrepreneurs combine both these attributes but add further essential elements. They undertake direct actions in order to transform an existing society so that lasting improvement will become possible—not just temporary, humanitarian ameliorative measures. Similarly, while charities, food banks, churches, various social work services and so on operate as 'balms', helping to alleviate suffering, they do not achieve 'wholesale transformation' intended and designed to permanently alter society's equilibrium (37).

Martin and Osberg (2016) develop a more elaborate framework of steps they believe are crucial to effective social entrepreneurship. First, attain an understanding of how the world works in respect to a problematic area. Second, envision a possible and different future. Then construct a model showing how the vision could be put into practical effect before finally scaling up the solution so it has a real chance of transforming many lives. Like other observers on this subject the authors suggest that governments and private businesses have 'flourished together' in contributing to the 'advancement of humankind' (48). Governments provide public services for all and without trying to achieve profits. Capitalist entrepreneurs adopt innovations designed to provide new, better or cheaper goods and services that enhance their profits by attracting customers. Both public and private actions are transformative. But increasingly today's societies face challenges that are 'ill-suited to either of these modes' (48) of solving human problems such as cumulative disadvantages which leave people with no confidence to overcome difficulties. Social enterprise strives to fill the gap between public and private provision. This requires using 'business methods to tackle problems in society' (Ashton 2012) yet striving to maximize social advantage rather than economic gains.

Martin and Osberg (2016) discuss a number of notable instances of SEs including the Grameen Bank established in Bangladesh by Muhammad Yunus in 1976. His idea was to provide technical advice, communication links—later helped by the mobile phone—and microfinance for very poor people, with a central focus on women. This was grounded in a basic philosophy of self-help: helping the poor to address their own needs so that they could then reach their full potential. The project has since expanded into other countries such as India, has reached millions of people and has spawned sister organizations. The loan scheme mostly works on the basis of encouraging lenders to set up a weekly savings account which is then tied into a micro-loan repaid by a weekly instalment system at a rate of interest the individual can afford.[8] A system of solidarity lending has developed alongside where a small group of lenders

---

[8] This system is very similar to the 471 credit union schemes currently running across the UK.

in the same village monitor and support each other's loans and repayment arrangements while jointly accepting a set of social principles such as agreeing to send their children to school. Most loans are invested in buying livestock, seeds or agricultural equipment or on establishing small hand-driven wells. From the outset the Grameen system has worked with NGOS and government agencies, has drawn on donations from benefactors such as Bill Gates but has also increasingly turned to private businesses and banks for funding.

Turning to the British experience, the website www.socialenterprise.org.uk. reveals that the main principles guiding SEs consists of possessing a clear social/environmental mission, generating most income from trade or business and re-investing some profit into furthering the social mission. Among the examples of successful SEs are: Jamie Oliver's 'Fifteen' training project for disadvantaged youngsters, the 'Big Issue' newspaper the 'Eden Project' and 'Café Direct' selling fair-trade coffee. According to the *State of Social Enterprise Survey 2015*, the 2008 financial crisis, followed by years of government austerity, helped SEs to emerge and expand their turnover considerably faster than small- and medium-sized businesses, especially after 2011—the year when a 'start-up explosion' of SEs occurred (4). The report also explained how by 2015 there were approximately 70,000 SEs in the UK, employing nearly 1 million people and these added £24 billion to the economy. Two additional points stand out in the 2015 report. First, the emphasis is on earning money through trade and competing successfully in whatever market a particular SE operates. In this respect SEs are distinct from charities and other 'third sector' organizations and this difference needs to be clearly noted. Yet, 72 per cent of the business carried out by SEs in 2015 involved providing various services: for example, in education, business support and consultancy and employment training. In the case of trading with large organizations the public sector provided the bulk of business especially in the housing, social and health care (81 per cent) (8). Alongside this dependence on providing services and on the public sector SEs also rely on donations and grants from local authorities, charities and other third sector support agencies for some of their funding and this has diminished significantly because of government austerity measures.

The record of SEs is clearly impressive. It demonstrates once again the underlying viability and potential reach of the not-for-profit alternatives to capitalism. Yet, there are also limits to how far SEs—like other elements of the social economy—can hope to be effective in achieving their goals. As we have seen in the British case, most SEs depend on the public sector: only 17 per cent of trade was with firms in the private sector. Moreover, as Martin and Osberg (2016: 64–66) suggest, further growth in the number and size of SEs is almost certainly hampered by a lack of access to capital and will either depend on government support and/or philanthropy or an inflow of private investment from capitalist companies. In this respect they discuss the recent involvement of Ronald Cohen, a venture capital pioneer, who has tried to accelerate the growth of the social investment market by bringing in private equity and bank capital. To this end he established the 'Big Society Bank' in 2011 with approval from the Coalition Government. In total £600 million initial funding was set in place with some of the big banks committed to adding another £400 million in future—mostly coming from dormant accounts. The scheme will make grants and/or provide business training and skills to promising SEs.

There may be dangers lurking here, however. For example, according to Lee and David (2010) the take-up of microloans in India under the Grameen system rose by an average of 88 per cent each year between 2005 and 2010. It was spearheaded by a rapid increase in the number of middlemen scouting villages for custom. Originally they operated mainly as not-for-profit enterprises. But two things changed. Scenting the growing scope for making money as the project rapidly expanded, Indian private equity capital and private venture funds began to push capital into the scheme. Clearly the return they expected was often higher than the usual Grameen lending system. Second, and faced with pressure to take on more loans from thousands of hired lending agents, some borrowers began to use their loans not to improve their farms or tiny businesses but as a means to purchase cheap consumer goods. As with the subprime mortgage crisis in the USA, what followed was over-lending and an accumulation of unpayable debts by people whose livelihoods had little hope of growing fast enough to pay the interest and capital on their loans. This may well explain the spate of reported suicides among women in recent years, particularly in Andhra Pradesh.

Cooperatives

The public and scholarly interest in cooperatives has always been strong. There is a correspondingly vast literature relating to them (e.g. Zamagni and Zamagni 2010; Roelants and Sanchez Bajo 2011; Kelly 2012; Harrison 2013, to name just a few recent contributions) as well as innumerable websites. Cooperatives go back a long way but most observers regard the Rochdale Society of Equitable Pioneers, a consumer cooperative founded in 1844 by a small group of artisans to provide basic foodstuffs at affordable prices, as marking the onset of modern cooperatives. The principles established then provided a template for numerous later cooperatives: each member, including women, exercises one vote in the democratic and shared management of the enterprise; the stock and other resources is owned by all members; any financial gains are shared; and there is a commitment to return a portion of profits back into the community. Consumer cooperatives along these lines soon attracted many supporters and they spread across Britain and other countries. By WW1 co-ops in Britain controlled two-fifths of the national market for food distribution and owned a variety of other businesses including farms, factories, banks and shipping lines (Murray 2013). Moreover during the nineteenth century the same desire to prioritize a social rather than an economic mission and to remain autonomous from capitalism was borrowed by the agricultural cooperatives soon formed in Scandinavia, the credit unions that first evolved in Germany and the worker's cooperatives established in France (Zamagni and Zamagni 2010: 14–17).

Most farmers who participate in agricultural cooperatives combine in order to negotiate a better price from suppliers—tractors, fertilizers, seeds and so on—or as a strategy for demanding a fairer price for their produce. But in some poorer countries, farmers pool their resources in order to buy or lease inputs such as tools or machinery and/or they establish credit unions to assist each other with small loans. Worker's cooperatives vary a great deal but in addition to equal member/worker voting rights and influence over management through elected representatives, most shares are owned by the workforce and most of the latter own some shares. As with consumer cooperatives a portion of any yearly surplus is reserved both for re-investing in the enterprise and for social improvement.

The International Cooperative Alliance (ICA) (ica.coop), established in 1895, claims that by 2014 its affiliated members came from 95 countries encompassing nearly one billion individuals. In terms of full- or part-time employment, its affiliated organizations provided work in 2014 for 250 million people including approximately 100 million in worker's co-ops. Data from 2012 also revealed that the affiliated 300 largest co-ops achieved an average growth rate of 12 per cent and enjoyed a combined turnover value of $2.2 trillion for that year—equivalent to the size of Brazil's GDP.[9] The same site revealed that in 2007 36 per cent of Denmark's consumer retail market was managed by co-ops and in Japan 91 per cent of farmers belong to agricultural co-ops. In Canada two-fifths of the population are involved in some kind of co-op while the USA, with around 30,000 co-ops, includes over 250 million members and has the largest national membership.

The rapid development of technology for generating renewable energy combined with concern over climate change has created opportunities for local communities to own cooperatives using wind or solar power. Bioenergy has also become significant and is often managed by farming groups. However, some countries have been more willing to permit such not-for-profit small enterprises to take advantage of renewable energy schemes than others. In Germany the share of community ownership in renewable energy capacity was 34 per cent of the national total in 2012—reaching 50 per cent in the case of solar or photovoltaic energy. Denmark also has a long history of energy production by consumer co-ops, local communities and towns. Yet, recent restrictions on windmills mean that now only 20 per cent of projects are reserved for local ownership. Further, the big energy companies protested that the feed-in tariff system for households and small local groups investing in photovoltaic cells worked too strongly in the latter's favour. The government then imposed restrictions on how much solar capacity small groups were

---

[9] http://ica.coop/en/what-co-op/co-operative-facts-figures.

permitted to install each year and reduced the feed-in tariff rate for solar cells. Similar changes to government policies in regard to local/household versus corporate access to investment in renewables have also been introduced in Britain and the USA as we saw in Chap. 7. Legal obstacles and costs also make this process difficult. It seems likely that the question of who should own and manage renewables—corporations or local not-for-profit groups—will become an arena of future conflict.[10]

The Benefits of Cooperatives

Most writers view cooperatives as entirely positive. One crucial benefit is that they extend democracy from the sphere of politics and citizens' rights into economic life in marked contrast to capitalist companies. A second benefit is that those who form and join co-ops are expressing an 'irrepressible yearning for positive liberty' (Zamagni and Zamagni 2010: 28) through the possibility of exercising far greater autonomy than is possible in a capitalist enterprise. The reality that some individuals place the desire for liberty at the top of their 'scale of values' is what keeps co-ops alive (28). But equally it suggests that since for many people social benefits are at least as important as the prospect of pure material gain there is every reason to hope for the potential extension and deepening of a future social economy, particularly, perhaps, as educational levels rise. A third positive arising from co-ops is their capacity to offer inclusivity and a platform of participation to those who lack resources and who are rejected as either dis-functional or simply not needed by capitalism. Zamagni and Zamagni (2010: 2) even suggest that extending a space to the excluded may be 'the prime mission of the cooperative movement today', one that protects capitalism itself from the 'risk of a slow but steady degeneration'. This also demonstrates that the market economy is a hugely broad institution capable of accommodating a slew of agencies—everything from petty traders and peasants selling meagre household surpluses all the way to vast global corporations and including cooperatives: capitalist enterprises are 'merely one species within it' (2).

---

[10] See: 'About us': http://www.communitypower.eu/en/about-us.html.

It is worth noting that writers who would like to see capitalism's sway progressively dwindle are far from being opposed to markets. Instead they regard the operation of supply and demand as an expression of what people need and want, as a rational determinant of price in a competitive system. As such, markets are necessary and perfectly compatible with a democratic socialist society (e.g. Schweickart 2002: 22 and 47). Sklair (2002: 301) argues that not only markets but small private companies, too, may have a useful role to play during 'the transitional stage between capitalist and socialist globalization' (302). He is also quite clear that different types of producer-consumer cooperatives will provide the bedrock of economic activity during this transitional period and not just the primary form of an eventual socialist society. In the meantime cooperatives operate as 'tiny seeds of socialist globalization struggling to flower in capitalist societies' (303). As such they deserve strong support.

Mondragon and Other Industrial Cooperatives—And Issues Arising

Agricultural and retail cooperatives along with credit unions find it easier to endure in a predominantly capitalist environment than their industrial counterparts where the need for investment capital and access to a range of technical, design and advertising skills are prerequisites for competing successfully against large integrated private corporations. Despite these constraints, there are many cases of successful industrial co-ops. One example is Argentina, where, following the financial collapse and political crisis that struck the country in 2001, and the bankruptcy or abandonment of nearly 4000 factories, a number of workers decided to re-open some of these. Although the factories they have successfully established are mostly small, employing less than 50 workers, by 2012 they numbered over 200 firms spanning several industries—including textiles, shoes and transport. They also employed 9000 workers (Ellwood 2013: 32–33). The Emilia Romagna region of Italy provides a further example of an entire 'cooperative region' (Murray 2013: 23). Here, towns have built-up specialist skills in particular industries, public and cooperative banks support them through loans guaranteed by other artisan co-ops and a network of local professionals provide accountancy and other services. Some of these cooperatives in clothing and ceramics have become recognized industrial leaders across Europe. Mondragon, a federation of worker's cooperatives in the Basque region of Spain offers the most outstanding and frequently quoted case of a successful industrial cooperative.

Originally established in 1956 by a catholic priest and the engineering graduates and skilled workers trained by a local technical college, Mondragon had become the world's biggest worker cooperative with global sales of £13 billion by 2013 (Tremlett 2013). It was also one of Spain's ten largest businesses in 2010 (Wolff 2014). In 2010 it had 85,000 members, nearly half of them women. It actually consists of many smaller cooperatives ranging across four economic sectors: industry, including white goods, machinery, machine tools refrigeration equipment, bicycles and so on; retail; educational and business services; and finance—it has its own bank with deposits worth $25 billion in 2010 (Wolff 2014). Mondragon has established a university which enrolled more than 3000 students in the academic year 2009–2010 alone. It also endeavours to operate at the cutting edge of technological innovation by channelling a slice of its revenue each year into the research and development of new techniques and products. To this end the cooperative had a research team of more than 800 people in 2010 (Wolff 2014). Spain's exposure to the post-2008 global financial crisis hit Mondragon like many other national companies. But unlike the latter it has largely—not entirely—avoided adding huge number of workers to Spain's unemployment register. National unemployment reached 28 per cent in 2013. It has achieved this because it claims to be committed to a policy of preserving worker job security and through collaborative discussions employees agreed to accept a series of wage reductions rather than face job losses. This was rendered more acceptable because (a) the managers—usually appointed in consultation with the workforce—took the biggest cuts and (b) unlike private corporations the salaries of managerial staff are capped at eight times the wages level earned by the lowest paid workers (Tremlett 2013).

There are various criticisms of the Mondragon experiment and others like it and these hark back to much earlier debates within the socialist and cooperative movements. One nineteenth-century thinker who argued through speeches and writings for a more peaceful transition to an equitable society less ravaged by economic insecurity was the reformer Robert Owen. As an employer of the largest cotton factory in Britain, at New Lanark in Scotland, he reduced children's hours of work and established schools. Later he founded a cooperative, 'New Harmony' in Indiana, and another back in the UK, but disputes between their participants led to their failure. His idea of socialism lay in building a society consisting of inter-linked and mutually exchanging producer and consumer cooperatives, owned and managed collectively by the people who worked in them. Jossa (2005) argues that Marxists have held complex and changing views on cooperatives. This included Marx himself who for some time regarded producer cooperatives as important steps towards a socialist future, given that they were enterprises based on worker self-management of productive activity. But his interest seems to have waned following the failure of the Paris Commune in 1870. Some Marxists feared that cooperatives provided neither the organized political strength to confront the capitalist bourgeois state nor could they be relied on to fully develop the productive forces. Accordingly, the emphasis shifted progressively towards capturing the levers of state power as the only way of overcoming capitalism. Gurney (1996) shows how in Britain other transformations played into this wider socialist pattern of thinking. Thus, by the 1880s private retailers were increasingly swallowing up smaller private stores, forming syndicates where companies ran multiple outlets and using advertising to attract customers. The consumer cooperative movement of small local shops survived but found this competition difficult. For many socialists and trade unionists these trends seemed to point to a future of large organizations, including nationalized enterprises, and the necessity to concentrate on winning political power over the state as the way forward.

Returning to the debates surrounding Mondragon, various observers have criticized aspects of its recent policies. Gasper (2014), for example, outlines a list of practices at Mondragon that contradict its own stated principles. Increasingly, as the cooperative expanded, Mondragon came to more closely resemble private companies and became more integrated with the wider capitalist economy. Thus, from the 1990s, and in response to the EU's Single Market, salary differentials began to increase. In response to globalization and the import of cheap consumer goods,

Mondragon set up plants in low-wage economies such as Morocco, China and Egypt whose employees earn much lower wages than the Basque workers. It also entered joint ventures with some private capitalist companies in Spain. As the post-2008 recession hit the Spanish economy so around 20 per cent of Mondragon's workforce has become part-time employees or been forced to accept short-term contracts. When Fagor, one of its leading factories producing domestic appliances recently went bankrupt, some workers lost their jobs following failed attempts by the central Mondragon council to raise more capital instead. Mondragon explains these and other changes as unfortunate but inevitable responses to the unavoidable uncertainties of the capitalist market.

But Gasper argues it is exactly this need to compete in a capitalist system that constitutes the fundamental problem. Cooperatives competing against a host of rival private companies have no choice but to adopt some, at least, of the latter's tactics such as wage-cutting, creating a buffer against market fluctuations with a part-casualized labour force, engaging in price-fixing with competitors and so on. A failure to do so risks losing market share and earning sufficient 'profits' to finance innovation and investment. Many co-ops face additional problems (Gaus 2003). To grow they need capital and banks are often uneasy about lending. As a result workers often put in their own savings and this probably deters many from becoming engaged in the movement. Others, being small, rely on voluntary labour. For these and other reasons co-ops often struggle to survive even in towns and cities with a history of trade unions and quasi-Left traditions. In short, as with social enterprises, situations arise where the social economy in general is forced to compete with private capital and play by the latter's rules (Gaus 2003; Satgar 2014; Williams 2014) thereby placing the exercise in jeopardy.

9.5 Breaking Away—The Solidarity Economy

For nearly 200 years people have been trying to create a fairer society and to defend their collective interests against the penetration of capitalism and the insecurities it brings in its wake by building a social economy. Indeed, as Williams suggests (2014: 43–44), today, with the retreat of state protection and welfare under the onslaught of neoliberal globalization, citizens and workers are being thrown back onto re-building the social economy once again. Since the 2008 financial crisis, too, a growing number of IGOs such as the ILO, OECD and WB in addition to the G20 group, the WEF, individual governments and private corporations have all spoken in favour of the social economy. According to Satgar (2014) and Williams (2014) there are several explanations. By generating jobs and an element of socio-economic inclusion, the expansion of credit unions, charities, co-ops, social enterprises, NGOs and so on help to ease the effects of austerity measures, compensate for shrinking welfare protection, preclude the necessity to raise taxes on the wealthy and lock economies, including those in the Global South, into neoliberal globalization policies.

But this attempt to alleviate social problems through such 'targeted interventions' (46) keeps everyone within the umbrella of capitalism and merely offsets the latter's negative effects. Moreover, encouraging a more 'humane capitalism' (Williams 2014: 49) mainly serves to ameliorate (43) its impact by 'offsetting' (45) its negative effects, and binds citizens more tightly to the neoliberal discourse. Williams further suggests that the limits on what the social economy can achieve are also revealed by two further realities. One is that under globalized capitalism the nation-state now functions as little more than an organization for imposing discipline on citizens since its affiliation is to the market not to society (40). Second, social enterprises of different kinds demonstrate little or no capacity or even intention to alter the underlying labour/capital and community power relations that created the poverty and exclusion they are attempting to alleviate in the first place (49–50). A much more genuinely transformative social economy would need to build deep roots within the underlying productive, and not just the services and retail, economy thereby integrating economic and social actions.

Yet, as we have seen, despite such limitations the social economy is a force for positive change. In the case of co-ops, Satgar (2014: 13) reminds us that nineteenth-century thinkers and activists who supported them tended either to be social reformers, dedicated to helping ordinary people to better survive the harshness of the market through institutions dedicated to democratic self- and community support, or they held utopian ideals of transforming society by shifting economic power to the grassroots. Robert Owen and Marx, too, for a time, belonged to the second group (Satgar 2014: 13). One answer to the problem of competing with private businesses might be to move all the way towards establishing a socialist alternative. Even if this was currently possible there seems little enthusiasm for it on the part of most groups on the Left. Replacing market with plan and private with state ownership seem far less attractive as a solution to social injustice, and the lack of democracy than it did for many in the twentieth century. Nor was the environmental record of socialist regimes such as the USSR's any better than that of capitalism given its absolute commitment to rapidly developing the productive forces above all other goals. Satgar (2014: 13) certainly argues that he has no wish to offer a 'socialist blueprint' for the twenty-first century thereby replacing the dogma of neoliberal global capitalism with another. Instead, he and his colleagues call for the solidarity economy which must be clearly distinguished in theory and practice from the idea of a social economy. Thus, solidarity economies are transformative rather than ameliorative. They are based on bottom-up struggles to completely re-define and re-build economic and social life and they are fundamentally committed to, and constructed around, the values of cooperation, solidarity, reciprocity, pluralism, equity and environmental sustainability. Instead of society operating at the service of the economy, as at present, the latter would serve the needs of the former.

Above all solidarity economies look beyond the market and engage in 'strengthening community ties and transforming economic culture in a way that delinks production from capital' (Esteves 2014: 131). The dilemma posed by endlessly needing to compete with capitalism, with all the insecurity, inequity, exclusion and hollow autonomy it brings, can then be resolved. Solidarity communities also reach out to the excluded, build extensive local and transnational networks with participants in other economies and establish backward and forward enterprise linkages in order to broaden the base and the autonomy of the emerging solidarity sector as a whole. Since the mid-1990s, in countries such as the USA, South Africa and Brazil, they have often overlapped with the social economy and this provided a basis for penetrating the latter and perhaps bringing some activities into the solidarity economy. They have also experimented with new forms rather than offering a blueprint for a future socialist or post-capitalist world—though this might emerge at some future time. Their work in progress requires them to separate from capitalism but not from society (Williams 2014: 50; Esteves 2014: 131–2).

A number of resources are available to those establishing solidarity economies and others may appear in time. One such resource consists in the sheer scale and escalating economic marginalization that forms the background experience of many young people, the urban unemployed, those living in shanty towns, members of the precariat, workers whose former skills have been superseded by technology and many others. In a globalized world of searing visual images, instant communication and the sharing and connecting possibilities of the Internet, the accumulating failures of capitalism constitute a driving force propelling many to search for alternatives. Capitalism becomes a potential and gigantic recruiting agency for the solidarity economy.

Wainwright (2014) points to a second potential resource. Intriguingly, she suggests that it is capitalism that is in crisis not the labouring people of the world. Businesses go bankrupt, machines become obsolete, property values can plummet and financial values collapse. Although such events obviously hurt all kinds of workers the skills, knowledge, social relationships and connections they have previously accumulated and the ever-present possibility that they can learn new skills, form additional relationships and so on insulate them from the prospect of total collapse. Capital goes into crisis but human capacity in all its forms endures and is potentially always poised ready to follow different paths if and when the need or opportunity arises. Accordingly, Wainwright suggests we need to re-think what we mean by 'labour' because until now academic and social democratic thought has primarily regarded the human worker as a voter, a factor of production or a consumer. But a far more useful notion of 'labour' would focus on human learning and creativity—both potential and actual. This allows us to view individual and collective social action as a form of common property which when assembled, shared and articulated anew opens the door not just to a new kind of political economy but perhaps, also, to a very different and transformative society built on community, solidarity and emancipation from the need to create value for capital. Wainwright's argument is very similar to that of Hardt and Negri (2004) when they observe that economic activity has always depended on immanent labour (see Chaps. 5 and 8): the human social capacity to forge understandings and cooperation and to share meanings and affections. Since immanent labour is generated by individuals as autonomous human beings in social situations we can readily project it into new social arrangements beyond the reach of capital if we choose to do so.

Taking just one case study, and turning to Mance's (2014) work on Brazil, we find that government support under the presidency of Lula da Silva and the election of his worker's party in 2002 proved to be another key resource which helped to promote a flowering of solidarity economies. In Brazil's case additional factors were also important. For one thing it has a history of runaway slave communities and trade union struggles. More recently many additional grassroots initiatives have bubbled up: the landless worker's movement, operating in most Brazilian states and with an estimated 1.5 members, urban community-based farms, consumer co-ops, workers taking over bankrupt factories, community banks and bartering systems. Much of this was supported by the Catholic and evangelist churches, NGOS, some universities and others. The foundation of the World Social Forum (WSF) in Porto Alegre in 2001, and then the second and third forums in the following two years, based in the same location, led to follow-up workshops and created a momentum for change around the theme of resistance to neoliberal global capitalism and so helped to reinforce radical political expectations. Ultimately all this converged around the da Silva government and in 2003 the Brazilian Forum of the Solidarity Economy was established with its support (Mance 2014: 154). This was followed by a government-sponsored survey of the burgeoning collective initiatives taking place at that time and based on self-management and solidarity. In 2007 it revealed the existence of more than 22,000 initiatives, half of them generated between 2001 and 2007, and employing in total 1.7 million workers with half of these being new jobs created during the previous few years. Nearly three-quarters of these initiatives were financed from the members' own resources and more than four-fifths of the output produced is funnelled into local consumption (172). Mance (2014: 155–6) stresses that the participants in these mainly solidarity economies possess very diverse priorities and expectations. What unites them is their joint view that their various experiments constitute 'alternatives to capitalism'.

9.6 Summary and Conclusions

Against the tide of current economic priorities, orthodoxies and elite interests, we can try to imagine that the world moves speedily towards heeding Stephen Hawking's recent compassionate words:

> Our planet and the human race face multiple challenges. … Such pressing issues will require us to collaborate, all of us, with a shared vision and cooperative endeavour to ensure that humanity can survive. We will need to adapt, rethink, refocus and change some of our fundamental assumptions about what we mean by wealth, by possessions, by mine and yours. Just like children, we will have to learn to share. (Stephen Hawking 2016)[11]

We do not know exactly what changes Hawking had in mind when he wrote those words but we are entitled to fill in the gaps with our own follow-up questions and concerns. Chief among these is the urgent necessity to re-design the project of capitalist modernity through intergovernmental collaboration. This, in turn, surely entails bringing capitalism back under substantial control so that the core economic engines and elite plutocrats currently driving it cease to be largely disengaged from the needs of everyone else and the planet. As a minimum this requires: the re-regulation of finance and a radical attack on tax evasion; drastic policies of income and wealth re-distribution; a rapid and fundamental shift into renewable energy; and dismantling much of the current industrial food system. A balance is also sought between preserving the gains from a relatively open global economy while providing scope for governments to protect their populations and environments from total exposure to global competitive pressures.

---

[11] *The Guardian*, July 29, p. 30.

Whether such reforms take place or not and irrespective of their likely success or failure we can point to various benevolent and non-dystopic alternatives discussed in this final chapter that are equally possible. In doing so it may prove advantageous to learn from and draw on the repertoire of socio-economic and cultural practices that survived during the long preceding 'traditional' and early modern eras. None can be transplanted directly into our present situation but perhaps a version of these can be filtered out and imitated if that seems desirable. The long history and culture of family farming may be one obvious example particularly as there is a growing awareness that the current global food system is a major cause of climate change and is unsustainable. Moreover, the world's small farmers are far more inclined and able to work with rather than against nature and are driven not by competitive pressures but by the desire to preserve their family, local and community life above all else. The same is equally true in the case of the many kinds of worker, credit, farmer, industrial and consumer cooperatives that sometimes thrive in the face of far more powerful competitive businesses and financial pressures.

In both cases what has made them resilient is not just economic necessity and the dearth of opportunities provided by capitalism but the kinds of qualities expounded by Wainwright (2014): the ability to draw on the resources all humans share of creativity, the capacity to learn, to express affectivity and the need and desire to seek social as well as material rewards and identities. It seems possible and indeed likely that the impending large-scale technological unemployment soon to hit many who are locked inside the capitalist economy and the environmental benefits of moving to more localized, small-scale economies will encourage many future humans—rendered superfluous to, and by, capital—to join with others not just in falling back on the social economy but in constructing the kinds of solidarity economies, largely outside and separate from capitalism, outlined above. Perhaps, too, and against most current trends, even some politicians and governments will follow in da Silva's Brazilian footsteps and become converted to the idea of taking practical measures to foster parallel social and solidarity systems by making material resources available and instituting—at the very least—a citizen's income. Certainly, we have to hope for this.

Turning to capitalism, two processes may shape and hasten its future prospects. One is that a growing spectrum of alternative economies operating outside its sphere of operation and refusing to compete with it, will become ever more autonomous strengthened by forging local and transnational linkages with multiple others. But this may progressively diminish the market demand for capitalism's products pushing it into severe crisis even to the point where it collapses altogether. The bifurcation of capitalism discussed in Chap. 8 may leave the plutonomous elites unharmed since they have outgrown any former reliance on the market, savings and labour of the majority 'plebian' economy. Yet, this possibility only reinforces the likelihood that ordinary people may be driven to join and construct entirely separate solidarity economies. Then, there is the promise of the collaborative commons and the expansion of the embryonic not-for-profit economy, promised by observers such as Rifkin (2014) and currently ticking away inside capitalism. If his analysis and that of others are accurate then we are witnessing the birth of a society whose citizens produce, share and exchange a plethora of their own and other's products and services outside the market. Perhaps, too, some of the same people will be persuaded to join the solidarity economy. Add to this the reality that dealing with the crises caused by growing inequality, and the resulting fracturing of societies along the lines of class, age, gender, ethnicity and education, in addition to those engendered by climate change and mass technological unemployment, and it becomes difficult to believe that neoliberal or perhaps any known version of capitalism can remain the sole and overwhelmingly dominant form of future economic life.

Like capitalism our future looks increasingly uncertain. Yet it also offers interesting possibilities that are simultaneously worrying and inviting, dangerous and exciting. The only certainty is that no one will avoid becoming entangled in these various future possibilities and everyone has an equal right to declare their own interest in whatever may or may not be on offer.

Bibliography

Albert, M. (2006). *Realizing hope: Life beyond capitalism*. London: Zed Books.
Ashton, C. (2012, February 21). Why are social enterprises thriving in the UK? *BBC Radio*, p. 4. Retrieved May 5, 2016, from http://www.bbc.co.uk/news/uk-17104953
Castells, M. (1996). *The rise of the network society*. Oxford: Blackwell.
Castoriadis, C. (2005). [electronic publication date] *Figures of the unthinkable*. [Anonymous translation.] Retrieved August 9, 2016, from http://www.notbored.org/FTPK.pdf
Ethical Consumer. (2013). Ethical consumer markets report 2013. https://www.ethicalconsumer.org/portals/O/downloads/ethical_consumer_markets_report_2013.pdf
Dees, J. D. (2001). The meaning of entrepreneurship. Retrieved May 19, 2016, from http://entrepreneurship.duke.edu/news-item-category/spotlight
Desmarais, A. (2002). The via Campesina: Consolidating and international peasant and farm movement. *Journal of Peasant Studies, 29*(2), 91–124.
Edelman, M. (2003). Transnational peasant and farmer movements and networks. In H. Anheier, M. Glasius, & M. Kaldor (Eds.), *Global civil society 2003* (pp. 185–218). Oxford: Oxford University Press.
Ellwood, W. (2013). Can co-ops crowd out capitalism? In R. Harrison (Ed.), *People over capital: The co-operative alternative to capitalism* (pp. 31–39). Oxford: New Internationalist Publications.
Esteves, A. M. (2014). The emergence of the United States solidarity economy network. In V. Satgar (Ed.), *The solidarity economy alternative: Emerging theory and practice* (pp. 129–149). Scottsville: University of KwaZulu-Natal Press.
Evans, P., & Tilly, C. (2016). The future of work: Escaping the current dystopian trajectory and building better alternatives. In S. Edgell, G. H., & E. Granter (Eds.), *The sociology of work and employment* (pp. 651–671) . London: Sage.Public policies for private corporations: The British corporate welfare state
Food and Agricultural Organization (FAO). (2014). The state of food and agriculture: Innovation in family farming. Rome. Retrieved July 28, 2016, from www.fao.irg/3/a-i1404e.pdf
Frase, P. (2011, December). Four futures: Life after capitalism. *Jacobin*. Retrieved August 10, 2016, from https://www.jacobinmag.com/2011/12/four-futures/

Gasper, P. (2014). Are worker's cooperatives the alternative to capitalism? *International Socialist Review*, Issue #93. Retrieved August 3, 2016, from http://isreview.org/issue/93/are-workers-cooperatives-alternatives–capitalism

Gaus, M. (2003, August 1–7). Workers Coops. *Z Magazine*. Retrieved August 22, 2016, from https://zcomm.org/magazine/worker-co-ops-by-mischa-gaus

Gibson-Graham, J. K. (2006). *A postcapitalist politics*. Minneapolis: University of Minnesota Press.

Gurney, P. (1996). *Co-operative culture and politics of consumption in England, 1870–1930*. Manchester: Manchester University Press.

Hall, T. H., & Fenlon, J. V. (2004). The future of indigenous peoples: 9–11 and the trajectory of indigenous survival and resistance. *Journal of World Systems Research, 10*(1), 153–197.

Hall, T. H., & Fenlon, J. V. (2008). Indigenous movements and globalization: What is different? What is the same? *Globalizations, 5*(1), 1–12.

Hardt, M., & Negri, A. (2004). *Multitude: War and democracy in the age of empire*. New York: Penguin Press.

Harrison, R. (Ed.). (2013). *People over capital: The co-operative alternative to capitalism*. Oxford: New Internationalist Publications.

Hawking, S. (2016, July 29). A new approach to wealth could save us in perilous times. *The Guardian*, p. 30.

Hendrickson, M. K., & Heffernan, W. D. (2002). Opening spaces through relocalization: Locating potential resistance in the weakness of the global food system. *Sociologia Ruralis, 42*(4), 347–369.

Jossa, B. (2005). Marx, Marxism and the cooperative movement. *Cambridge Journal of Economics, 29*(1), 3–18. Retrieved August 16, 2016, from http://www.researchgate.net/publications/5208466_Marx_Marxism_and_the_cooperative-movement

Kelly, M. (2012). *Owning our own future: The Emerging ownership revolution*. Oakland, CA: Berrett-Koeler Publishers.

Kiely, R. (2005b). *The clash of globalizations: Neo-liberalism, the third way and anti-globalisation*. Leiden: Brill.

Lee, Y. and David, R. (2010). Suicided in India revealing how men made a mess of microcredit. Bloomberg Markets. Retrieved August 18, 2016, from www.bloomberg.com/news/articles/2012-12-28/suicides-among-borrowers-in-india-show-how-men-made-a-mess-of-microcredit

Mance, E. (2014). The solidarity economy in Brazil. In V. Satgar (Ed.), *The solidarity economy alternative: Emerging theory and practice* (pp. 150–176). Scottsville: University of KwaZulu-Natal Press.

Martin, R. L., & Osberg, S. R. (2016). *Getting beyond better: How social enterprise works*. Boston: Harvard University Press.

Martin, P., & Wilmer, F. (2008). Transnational normative struggles and globalization: The case of indigenous peoples in Bolivia and Ecuador. *Globalizations, 5*(4), 583–598.

Mason, P. (2013). *Why it's still kicking off everywhere: The new global revolutions*. London: Verso.

Mason, P. (2015a, November 2). Apocalypse now: Has the next giant financial crash already begun? *The Guardian*. Retrieved August 10, 2016, from https://www.theguardian.com/commentisfree/2015/nov/01/financial-armageddon-crash-warning-signs

Munck, R. (2007). *Globalization and contestation*. Oxford: Routledge.

Murray, R. (2013). The potential for an alternative economy. In R. Harrison (Ed.), *People over capital: The co-operative alternative to capitalism* (pp. 20–30). Oxford: New Internationalist Publications.

Ostram, E. (1990). *Governing the commons: The evolution of institutions for collective action*. Cambridge: Cambridge University Press.

Reitan, R. (2007). *Global activism*. London: Routledge.

Rifkin, J. (2014). *The zero marginal cost society: The Internet of things, the collaborative commons, and the eclipse of capitalism*. Basingstoke: Palgrave/Macmillan.

Roelants, B., & Sanchez Bajo, C. (2011). *Capital and the debt trap: Learning from cooperatives*. Basingstoke: Palgrave.

Satgar, V. (2014). The crisis of global capitalism and the solidarity economy alternative. In V. Satgar (Ed.), *The solidarity economy alternative: Emerging theory and practice* (pp. 1–34). Scottsville: University of KwaZulu-Natal Press.

Schmidt, E. (2007). 'Whose "culture"; Globalism, localism and the expansion or tradition: The case of the Hñähñu of Hidalgo, Mexico and Clearwater, Florida. *Globalizations, 4*(1), 101–114.

Schumacher, E. F. (2011). *Small is beautiful; A study of economics as if people mattered*. London: Vintage Books.

Schweickart, D. (2002). *After capitalism*. Oxford: Rowan and Littlefield.

Sklair, L. (2002). *Globalization, capitalism and its alternatives* (3rd ed.). Oxford: Oxford University Press.

Starr, A., & Adams, J. (2003). Anti-globalization: The global fight for local autonomy. *New Political Science, 25*(1), 20–42.

Tremlett, G. (2013, March 7). Mondragon: Spain's giant co-operative where times are hard but few go bust', *The Guardian*. Retrieved May 10, 2016, from http://www.theguardain.com/world/2013/mar/07/mondragon-spains-giant-cooperative

UN. Department of Economic and Social Affairs (DESA). (2009). The state of the world's indigenous peoples. New York. Retrieved August 8, 2016, from www.un.org/esa/socdev/unpfii/documents/SOWIP/en/SOWIP_web.pdf

United Nations Environment Programme (UNEP). (2011). Towards a green economy: Pathways to sustainable development and poverty eradication. Retrieved August 1, 2016, from http://web.unep.org/greeneconomy/resources/green-economy-report

Vidal, J. (2014, November 16). The hunters hunted—How tribespeople are being evicted to make way for "wilderness". *The Guardian*, p. 24.

Vidal, J. (2016, February 21). Sami reindeer herders battle conservationists and miner to cling on to Arctic culture. *The Guardian*. http://www.theguardian.com/global-development/2016/feb/21/sami-people-reindeer-herders-arctic-culture

Wainwright, H. (2014). Notes for a political economy of creativity and solidarity. In V. Satgar (Ed.), *The solidarity economy alternative: Emerging theory and practice* (pp. 64–100). Scottsville: University of KwaZulu-Natal Press.

Williams, M. (2014). The solidarity economy and social transformation. In V. Satgar (Ed.), *The solidarity economy alternative: Emerging theory and practice* (pp. 37–63). Scottsville: University of KwaZulu-Natal Press.

Wolff, R. (2014, June 24). Yes, there is an alternative to capitalism: Mondragon shows the way. *The Guardian*. Retrieved June 7, 2016, from http://www.theguardian.com.commentisfree/2012/jun/24/alternative-capitalismmondragon.

Zamagni, S., & Zemagni, V. (2010). *Cooperative enterprise: Facing the challenge of globalization*. Cheltenham: Edward Elgar.

Bibliography

Acemoglu, D. and Autor, D. (2011). Skills, tasks and technologies: Implications for employment and earnings. *Handbook of Labour Technologies*. National Bureau of Economic Research. Retrieved August 9, 2016, from http://www.nber.org/papers/w16082

Adams, P. (2015a). *The truth about China: Why Beijing will resist demands for abatement.* Global Warming Policy Foundation. Retrieved August 9, 2016, from http://www.thegwpf.org/content/uploads/2015/12/Truth-about-China.pdf

Adams, T. (2015b, November 29). The future of work. *The Observer.*

Ahmed, M. (2012). *Youth unemployment in the MENA Region: Determinants and challenges.* International Monetary Fund. Retrieved August 8, 2016, from https://www.imf.org/en/News/Articles/2015/09/28/04/54/vc061312

Albert, M. (2006). *Realizing hope: Life beyond capitalism.* London: Zed Books.

Amin, A. (1994). *Post-fordism: A reader.* Oxford: Wiley-Blackwell.

Amsden, A. (1989). *Asia's next giant: South Korea and late industrialization.* New York: Oxford University Press.

Anderson, B. (1983). *Imagined communities: Reflections on the origins and spread of nationalism.* London: Verso.

Anderson, K. (2015) *The hidden agenda: How veiled techno-utopias shore up the Paris Agreement.* Retrieved August 9, 2016, from http://kevinanderson.info/

blog/the-hidden-agenda-how-veiled-techno-utopias-shore-up-the-paris-agreement/
Ashton, C. (2012, February 21). Why are social enterprises thriving in the UK? *BBC Radio*, p. 4. Retrieved May 5, 2016, from http://www.bbc.co.uk/news/uk-17104953
Autor, D. (2011). The polarization of job opportunities in the US labor market: Implications for employment and earnings. *Community Investment, 43*(2), 11–18.
Autor, D. H., Katz, L. F., & Krueger, A. B. (1998). Computing inequality: Have computers changed the labor market. *The Quarterly Journal of Economics, 113*(4), 1169–1213.
Axford, B. (2013). *Theories of globalization*. Cambridge: Polity.
Bartlett, J., Birdwell, J., & Littler, M. (2011). *The new face of digital populism*. London: Demos.
Batt, R. L. and Appelbaum, E. (2013). *The impact of financialization on management and employment outcomes*. W. E. Upjohn Institute for Employment Research. Retrieved August 9, 2016, from http://research.upjohn.org/cgi/viewcontent.cgi?article=1208&context=up_workingpapers
Baudrillard, J. (1988). *Selected writings* (ed. M. Poster). Cambridge: Polity.
Bauman, Z. (1998). *Globalization: The human consequences*. Cambridge: Polity.
Bauman, Z. (2000). *Liquid modernity*. Cambridge: Polity.
Bauman, Z. (2002). *Society under siege*. Cambridge: Polity.
Beck, U. (1992). *The risk society: Towards a new modernity*. London: Sage.
Beck, U. (2000). *The Brave new world of work*. Cambridge: Polity.
Beck, U. (2009). *World at risk*. Cambridge: Polity.
Beck, U., & Beck-Gernsheim, E. (2002). *Individualization*. London: Sage.
Benkler, Y. (2006). *The wealth of networks: How social production transforms markets and freedom*. New Haven, CT: Yale University Press.
Berking, H. (2000). Solidary individualism. In S. Lash, B. Szersynski, & B. Wynne (Eds.), *Risk, environment and modernity: Towards a new ecology* (pp. 185–201). London: Sage.
Berman, M. (1982). *All that is solid melts into air*. New York: Simon and Schuster.
Beynon, H. (1973). *Working for ford*. Harmondsworth: Allen Lane.
Boren, Z. D. (2015) *China's coal bubble: 155 coal-fired power plants in the pipeline despite overcapacity*. Retrieved August 9, 2016, from http://energydesk.greenpeace.org/2015/11/11/chinas-coal-bubble-155-new-overcapacity/
Bourdieu, P. (1984). *Distinction: A social critique of the judgement of taste*. Cambridge, MA: Harvard University Press.

Bowman, A., Froud, J., Johal, S., Law, J., Leaver, A., Moran, M., & Williams, K. (2014). *The end of the experiment: From competition to the foundational economy.* Manchester: Manchester University Press.

Boyle, J. (2003). The second enclosure movement and the construction of the public domain. *Law and Contemporary Problems, 66*(1/2), 33–74.

Brower, K. (2010). The danger of cosmic genius. *The Atlantic.* Retrieved August 9, 2016, from http://www.theatlantic.com/magazine/archive/2010/12/the-danger-of-cosmic-genius/308306/

Brubaker, R. (1984). *The limits of rationality: An essay on the social and moral thought of Max Weber.* London: Allen and Unwin.

Brynjolfsson, E. and McAfee, A. (2014) *The second machine age: Work, progress and prosperity in a time of brilliant technologies.* New York: W.W. Norton and Company.

Cann, O. (2016). *What are the top global risks for 2016?* World Economic Forum. Retrieved August 9, 2016, from https://www.weforum.org/agenda/2016/01/what-are-the-top-global-risks-for-2016/

Carbon Dioxide Information Analysis Centre. (2012). *800,000-year ice-core records of atmospheric carbon dioxide (CO_2).* Retrieved August 9, 2016, from http://cdiac.ornl.gov/trends/co2/ice_core_co2.html

Carbon Tracker. (2013). *Unburnable carbon: Wasted capital and stranded assets.* Retrieved August 9, 2016, from http://carbontracker.live.kiln.digital/Unburnable-Carbon-2-Web-Version.pdf

Carr, N. (2014). *The glass cage: Automation and US.* New York: W. W. Norton and Company.

Carrington, D. (2016, March 18). Hinkley Point C nuclear deal contains £22bn 'poison pill' for taxpayer. *The Guardian.* Retrieved August 9, 2016, from https://www.theguardian.com/uk-news/2016/mar/18/hinkley-point-c-nuclear-deal-22bn-poison-pill-taxpayer

Carrington, D. and Slezak, M. (2016, March 15). February broke global temperature records by 'shocking' amount. *The Guardian.* Retrieved August 9, 2016, from https://www.theguardian.com/science/2016/mar/14/february-breaks-global-temperature-records-by-shocking-amount

Carroll, W. K., & Carson, C. (2003). The network of global corporations and elite policy groups: A structure for transnational capitalist class formation. *Global Networks: A Journal of Transnational Affairs, 3*(1), 29–59.

Castells, M. (1996). *The rise of the network society.* Oxford: Blackwell.

Castoriadis, C. (2007). [electronic publication date] *Figures of the unthinkable*. [Anonymous translation.] Retrieved August 9, 2016, from http://www.notbored.org/FTPK.pdf

Chakrabortty, A. (2008, July 3). Secret report: Biofuel caused food crisis. *The Guardian*. Retrieved August 9, 2016, from https://www.theguardian.com/environment/2008/jul/03/biofuels.renewableenergy

Chen, T. (2015) *American household credit card debt statistics: 2015*. Retrieved August 9, 2016, from https://www.nerdwallet.com/blog/credit-card-data/average-credit-card-debt-household/

Chen, S. and Ravallion, M. (2008). *The developing world is poorer than we thought, but no less successful in the fight against poverty.* World Bank. Retrieved August 9, 2016, from http://elibrary.worldbank.org/doi/abs/10.1596/1813-9450-4703

CIA World Factbook. (2011). Washington, DC: Central Intelligence Agency.

Cohen, R., & Kennedy, P. (2007). *Global sociology* (2nd ed.) and (3rd ed.) 2013. New York: New York University Press.

Community Power. (2016). About us. Retrieved August 10, 2016, from http://www.communitypower.eu/en/about-us.html

Ethical Consumer. (2013). Ethical consumer markets report 2013. https://www.ethicalconsumer.org/portals/0/downloads/ethical_consumer_markets_report_2013.pdf

Crouch, C. (2013). *Making capitalism fit for society*. Cambridge: Polity.

Cummings, B. (1987). Northeast Asian political economy. In F. C. Deyo (Ed.), *Political economy of the New Asian industrialization* (pp. 44–83). Ithaca, NY: Cornell University Press.

Da Costa, P. N. (2015, February 4). China's total debt load equal 282 per cent of GDP, raises economic risks. *Wall Street Journal*. Retrieved August 9, 2016, from http://blogs.wsj.com/economics/2015/02/04/chinas-total-debt-load-equals-282-of-gdp-raising-its-economic-risks/

Dabla-Norris, E., Kochhar, K., Suphaphiphat, N., Ricka, F. and Evridiki, T. (2015). *Causes and consequences of income inequality: A global perspective*. International Monetary Fund. Retrieved August 12, 2016, from https://www.imf.org/external/pubs/ft/sdn/2015/sdn1513.pdf

Darby, M. (2015) *Investors pressure mining giants to phase out coal*. Climate Home. Retrieved August 9, 2016, from http://www.climatechangenews.com/2015/12/17/investors-pressure-mining-giants-to-phase-out-coal/

Darby, M. (2016) *Shareholder activists target ExxonMobil on 2C climate risk.* Climate Home. Retrieved August 9, 2016, from http://www.climatechangenews.com/2016/01/19/28330/

Dardot, P. and Laval, C. (2013). *The new way of the World: On neo-liberal society* (trans: Elliot, G.). London: Verso.

Dasgupta, R. (2014). *Capital: A portrait of twenty first century Delhi.* Edinburgh: Canongate Books.

Davis, M. (2006). *Planet of slums.* London: Verso.

Davis, M. (2010). Who will build the ark? *New Left Review, 61* (January–February edition).

De Rivero, O. (2001). *The myth of development.* London: Zed.

Dean, J. (2009). *Democracy and other neoliberal fantasies: Communicative capitalism and left politics.* Durham: Duke University Press.

Debord, G. (1983). *Society of the spectacle.* Detroit: Black and Red.

Dees, J. D. (2001). The meaning of entrepreneurship. Retrieved May 19, 2016, from http://entrepreneurship.duke.edu/news-item-category/spotlight

DeLong, J. B. and Summers, L. H. (2001). *The 'new economy': Background, historical perspective, questions, and speculations.* Federal Reserve Bank of Kansas City. Retrieved August 9, 2016, from https://www.kansascityfed.org/publicat/econrev/Pdf/4q01delo.pdf

Derrida, J. (1978). *Writing and difference.* London: Routledge and Kegan Paul.

Desmarais, A. (2002). The via Campesina: Consolidating and international peasant and farm movement. *Journal of Peasant Studies, 29*(2), 91–124.

Dew-Becker, I. and Gordon, R. J. (2005). *Where did the productivity growth go? Inflation dynamics and the distribution of income.* National Bureau of Economic Research. Retrieved August 9, 2016, from http://www.nber.org/papers/w11842

Dicken, P. (2003). *Global shift: Reshaping the global economic map in the 21st century.* London: Sage.

Dohse, K., Jurgens, V., & Malsch, T. (1985). From fordism to toyotism. *Politics and Society, 14*(2), 115–146.

Domhoff, G. W. (2016) *Wealth, income, and power.* Who Rules America? Retrieved August 10, 2016, from http://www2.ucsc.edu/whorulesamerica/power/wealth.html

Donoso, D. and Merkl, A. (2016, September 9). By 2025, our seas may be filled with one ton of plastic for every three tons of fish. *The Guardian.* Retrieved August 10, 2016, from https://www.theguardian.com/sustainable-business/2015/sep/30/dow-chemical-the-ocean-conservancy-ocean-plastics-pollution

Drucker, P. (1993). *Post-capitalist society*. Oxford: Butterworth Heinemann.

Durden, T. (2012) *Manipulation and abuse confirmed in $359 trillion market*. Retrieved August 10, 2016, from http://www.zerohedge.com/news/manipulation-and-abuse-confirmed-350-trillion-market

Eckersley, R. (2012). Understanding the interplay between the climate and trade regimes. In *Climate and trade in a post-2012 world* (pp. 11–18). Geneva: United Nations Environmental Program.

Edelman, M. (2003). Transnational peasant and farmer movements and networks. In H. Anheier, M. Glasius, & M. Kaldor (Eds.), *Global civil society 2003* (pp. 185–218). Oxford: Oxford University Press.

Edgell, A. (2012). *The sociology of work: Continuity and change in paid and unpaid work*. London: Sage.

Edgell, S., & Duke, V. (1991). *A measure of Thatcherism: A sociology of Britain*. London: Harper-Collins.

Elliott, L. (2016a, January 1). Richest 62 people as wealthy as half the world's population, says Oxfam. *The Guardian*. Retrieved August 9, 2016, from https://www.theguardian.com/business/2016/jan/18/richest-62-billionaires-wealthy-half-world-population-combined

Elliott L. (2016b). Brexit could spread shockwaves through global economy, says OECD. Retrieved August 9, 2016, from https://www.theguardian.com/business/2016/jun/01/brexit-could-spread-shockwaves-trough-global-economy-says-oecd

Elliott, L., & Atkinson, D. (2008). *The gods that failed: How blind faith in markets has cost us our futures*. London: Bodley Head.

Ellwood, W. (2013). Can co-ops crowd out capitalism? In R. Harrison (Ed.), *People over capital: The co-operative alternative to capitalism* (pp. 31–39). Oxford: New Internationalist Publications.

Esteves, A. M. (2014). The emergence of the United States solidarity economy network. In V. Satgar (Ed.), *The solidarity economy alternative: Emerging theory and practice* (pp. 129–149). Scottsville: University of KwaZulu-Natal Press.

European Commission. (2008). *The EU emissions trading system (EU ETS)*. Retrieved August 10, 2016, from http://ec.europa.eu/clima/policies/ets/faq_en.htm

Evans, P., & Tilly, C. (2016). The future of work: Escaping the current dystopian trajectory and building better alternatives. In S. Edgell, G. H., &

E. Granter (Eds.), *The sociology of work and employment* (pp. 651–671). London: Sage.Public policies for private corporations: The British corporate welfare state

Farnsworth, K. (2013). Public policies for private corporations: The British corporate welfare state. *Renewal, 21*(4), 51–65.

Featherstone, M. (1992). *Consumer culture and postmodernism*. London: Sage.

Fieschi, C., Morris M. and Caballero, L. (2012). *Recapturing the reluctant radical: How to win back Europe's populist vote*. Online: Counterpoint. Retrieved August 10, 2016, from http://counterpoint.uk.com/wp-content/uploads/2013/02/E-version-Recapturing-the-Reluctant-Radical-September-2012.pdf

Fisher, M. (2009). *Capitalist realism: Is there no alternative?* Winchester: Zero Books.

Fleming, N. (2016, June 2). Farming innovators nurture seed capital. *The Guardian*.

Food and Agricultural Organization (FAO). (2014). The state of food and agriculture: Innovation in family farming. Rome. Retrieved July 28, 2016, from www.fao.irg/3/a-i1404e.pdf

Forbes. (2016). *The world's billionaires*. Retrieved August 10, 2016, from www.forbes.com/billionaires/.

Ford, J. and Larsen, P. T. (2009, November 18). How to shrink the banks. *Prospect*. Retrieved August 9, 2016, from http://www.prospectmagazine.co.uk/features/how-to-shrink-the-banks

Foucault, M. (1977). *Discipline and punish: The birth of the prison*. London: Allen Lane.

Foucault, M. (1980). *Power/knowledge: Selected interviews and other writings, 1972–77* (ed.: Gordon, C.). New York: Pantheon Books.

Foucault, M. (2008) *The birth of biopolitics: Lectures at the College de France, 1978–79* (ed.: Arnold, I.). Basingstoke: Palgrave Macmillan.

Frase, P. (2011, December). Four futures: Life after capitalism. *Jacobin*. Retrieved August 10, 2016, from https://www.jacobinmag.com/2011/12/four-futures/

Frayne, D. (2016). Critiques of work. In S. Edgell, H. Gottfried, & E. Granter (Eds.), *The sociology of work and employment* (pp. 616–633). London: Sage.

Freeland, C. (2012). *Plutocrats: The rise of the new global super-rich and the fall of everyone else*. New York: Penguin.

Freeman, R. B. (2007). The challenge of the growing globalization of labour markets to economic and social policy. In E. Paus (Ed.), *Global capitalism unbound: Winners and losers in offshore outsourcing* (pp. 23–40). Basingstoke: Palgrave.

Frey, C. B. and Osborne, M. A. (2013). *The future of employment: How susceptible are jobs to computerisation?* Oxford University Engineering Sciences Department. Retrieved August 9, 2016, from http://www.oxfordmartin.ox.ac.uk/downloads/academic/The_Future_of_Employment.pdf

Fuhr, L. and Hällström, N. (2016) *The myth of net- zero emissions.* Retrieved August 10, 2016, from https://www.project-syndicate.org/commentary/net-zero-emissions-not-enough-by-lili-fuhr-and-niclas-h-llstr-m-2014-12

Funnell, B. (2009, July 30). Debt is capitalism's dirty little secret. *Financial Times.* Retrieved August 10, 2016, from http://www.ft.com/cms/s/0/e23c6d04-659d-11de-8e34-00144feabdc0.html#axzz4GvQlbNjv

Gamble, A. (2014). *Crisis without end? The unravelling of western prosperity.* Basingstoke: Palgrave.

Garside, J. (2014, April 20). The age of artificial intelligence may be getting closer." *The Guardian,* p. 30.

Gasper, P. (2014). Are worker's cooperatives the alternative to capitalism? *International Socialist Review,* Issue #93. Retrieved August 3, 2016, from http://isreview.org/issue/93/are-workers-cooperatives-alternatives–capitalism

Gaus, M. (2003, August 1–7). Workers Coops. *Z Magazine.* Retrieved August 22, 2016, from https://zcomm.org/magazine/worker-co-ops-by-mischa-gaus

Gershenkron, A. (1966). *Economic backwardness in historical perspective.* Cambridge, MA: Harvard University Press.

Ghosh, J. (2015, August 23). Is the game up for China's much emulated growth model? *The Guardian.* Retrieved August 10, 2016, from https://www.theguardian.com/commentisfree/2015/aug/23/china-growth-model-brics

Gibson-Graham, J. K. (2006). *A postcapitalist politics.* Minneapolis: University of Minnesota Press.

Giddens, A. (1985). *The nation state and violence.* Cambridge: Polity.

Giddens, A. (1990). *The consequences of modernity.* Cambridge: Polity.

Giddens, A. (1991). *Modernity and self-identity: Self and society in the late modern age.* Cambridge: Polity.

Giddens, A. (1992). *The transformation of intimacy.* Cambridge: Polity.

Giddens, A. (1994). Living in a post-traditional society in Beck, U., Giddens, A. and Lash, S. [Eds.] *Reflexive modernity: Politics, tradition and aesthetics in the modern social order.* Cambridge: Polity, pp. 56-108.

Giddens, A. (2009). *The politics of climate change.* Cambridge: Polity.

Giugliano, F. (2015, July 25). BoE's Haldane says corporations putting shareholders before economy. *Financial Times*. Retrieved August 9, 2016, from http://www.ft.com/cms/s/0/7d347016-32f4-11e5-b05b-b01debd57852.html#axzz4GvQlbNjv

Global CCS Institute. (2015). *The global status of CCS: 2015, summary report*. Retrieved August 10, 2016, from https://www.globalccsinstitute.com/publications/global-status-ccs-2015-summary-report

Global Financial Integrity. (2015). *Illicit financial flows from developing countries, 2004–2013*. Retrieved August 10, 2016, from http://www.gfintegrity.org/report/illicit-financial-flows-from-developing-countries-2004-2013/

Global Justice. Retrieved July 9, 2016, from www.globaljustice.org.uk/what-is-food-sovereignty

Goldberg, S. (2016, January 27). UN urges business leaders to double investment in green energy by 2020. *The Guardian*. https://www.theguardian.com/environment/2016/jan/27/un-urges-business-leaders-to-double-investment-in-green-energy-by-2020

Goos, M. and Manning, A. (2003). *Lousy jobs and lovely jobs: The rising polarization of work in Britain*. Centre for Economic Performance. Retrieved August 10, 2016, from http://eprints.lse.ac.uk/20002/1/Lousy_and_Lovely_Jobs_the_Rising_Polarization_of_Work_in_Britain.pdf

Gordon, R. J. (2012). *Is U.S. economic growth over? Faltering innovation confronts the six headwinds*. National Bureau of Economic Research. Retrieved August 10, 2016, from http://www.nber.org/papers/w18315

Gorz, A. (1989). *Critique of economic reason*. London: Verso.

Gottfried, H. (2013). *Gender, work, and economy: Unpacking the global economy*. Cambridge: Polity.

Gowan, P. (2009). Crisis in the heartlands: Consequences of the new Wall Street system. *New Left Review, 55*, 5–28.

GRAIN. (2015). *The land-grabbers of the Nacala Corridor*. Retrieved August 10, 2016, from https://www.grain.org/article/entries/5137-the-land-grabbers-of-|the-nacala-corridor

GRAIN. (2016). *Is industrial farming a tech-fix or a dead end for tackling climate change?* Retrieved August 9, 2016, from https://www.grain.org/es/article/entries/5373-is-industrial-farming-a-tech-fix-or-dead-end-for-tackling-climate-change

Gray, J. (1995). *Enlightenment's wake*. London: Routledge.

Gray, J. (1998). *False dawn: The delusions of global capital*. London: Granta Publications.

Greenfacts. (2016). *The living planet index, 1970–2000.* Retrieved August 9, 2016, from http://www.greenfacts.org/en/biodiversity/figtableboxes/1037-living-planet.htm

Gurney, P. (1996). *Co-operative culture and politics of consumption in England, 1870–1930.* Manchester: Manchester University Press.

Haldane, A. G. (2014). In giving, how much do we receive: The social value of volunteering. Speech given to the Bank of England. Retrieved September 9, 2014, from www.bankofengland.co.uk/publications/speeches/2014/speeches.756.pdf

Hall, T. H., & Fenlon, J. V. (2004). The future of indigenous peoples: 9–11 and the trajectory of indigenous survival and resistance. *Journal of World Systems Research, 10*(1), 153–197.

Hall, T. H., & Fenlon, J. V. (2008). Indigenous movements and globalization: What is different? What is the same? *Globalizations, 5*(1), 1–12.

Harari, Y. N. (2016). *Homo Deus.* London: Secker.

Hardin, G. (1968). The tragedy of the commons. *Science, 162*(3859), 1243–1248.

Hardt, M., & Negri, A. (2004). *Multitude: War and democracy in the age of empire.* New York: Penguin Press.

Hardt, M., & Negri, A. (2009). *Commonwealth.* New Haven, CT: Harvard University Press.

Harris, J. (2015). Transnational capital and the technology of domination and desire. *Race and Class, 57*(1), 3–19.

Harris, J. (2016a). Green capitalism and social justice. *Global Capitalism and the Crisis of Democracy, 4*, 103–142 Atlanta, Georgia: Clarity Press, chapter 4.

Harris, J. (2016b, June 17). Britain is in the midst of a working-class revolt. *The Guardian.* Retrieved August 9, 2016, from https://www.theguardian.com/commentisfree/2016/jun/17/britain-working-class-revolt-eu-referendum

Harrison, R. (Ed.). (2013). *People over capital: The co-operative alternative to capitalism.* Oxford: New Internationalist Publications.

Harvey, D. (2005). *A brief history of neoliberalism.* Oxford: Oxford University Press.

Harvey, D. (2011). *The enigma of capital.* London: Profile Books.

Hawking, S. (2016, July 29). A new approach to wealth could save us in perilous times. *The Guardian*, p. 30.

Hayek, F. A. (1944). *The road to Serfdom.* London: Routledge.

Hebdige, D. (1998). Postmodernism and 'The Other Side'. In J. Storey (Ed.), *Cultural theory and popular culture: A reader*. Dorchester: Pearson/Prentice Hall.

Held, D., Goldblatt, A., & Perraton, J. (1999). *Global Transformations*. Cambridge: Polity.

Hendrickson, M. K., & Heffernan, W. D. (2002). Opening spaces through relocalization: Locating potential resistance in the weakness of the global food system. *Sociologia Ruralis, 42*(4), 347–369.

Henry, J. S. (2012). *The price of offshore revisited*. Tax Justice Network. Retrieved August 10, 2016, from http://www.taxjustice.net/cms/upload/pdf/Price_of_Offshore_Revisited_120722.pdf

Hoare, P. (2016, March 30). Whales are starving—Their stomachs full of plastic waste. *The Guardian*. Retrieved August 10, 2016, from https://www.theguardian.com/commentisfree/2016/mar/30/plastic-debris-killing-sperm-whales

Hobsbawm, E. (1994). *Age of extremes: The short twentieth century, 1914–1991*. London: Michael Joseph.

Hochschild, A. R. (2003). *The managed heart: Commercialization of human feeling*. Berkley: University of California Press.

Hoogvelt, A. M. (1997). *Globalization and the post-colonial world: The new political economy of development*. Basingstoke: Macmillan.

Hubert Reeves, H., & Jouzel, J. (2010). *Climate refugees*. Massachusetts: Massachusetts Institute of Technology.

Humphrey, K. (2010). *Excess: Anti-consumption in the West*. Cambridge: Polity.

Hutton, W. (2007). *The writing on the wall: China and the West in the 21st century*. London: Abacus.

Hutton, W. (2015, October 11). The world economic order is collapsing and this time there seems no way out. *The Guardian*. Retrieved August 10, 2016, from https://www.theguardian.com/commentisfree/2015/oct/11/world-order-collapse-refugees-emerging-economies-china-slowdown-recession

Hutton, W. (2016, January 17). Why are we looking on helplessly as markets crash all over the world? *The Guardian*. Retrieved August 10, 2016, from https://www.theguardian.com/commentisfree/2016/jan/17/china-economic-crisis-world-economy-global-capitalism

Hwang, T. and Elish, M. C. (2015) *The mirage of the marketplace: The disingenuous ways Uber hides behind its algorithm*. Slate. Retrieved August 10, 2016, from http://www.slate.com/articles/technology/future_tense/2015/07/uber_s_algorithm_and_the_mirage_of_the_marketplace.html

Inman, P. (2015, October 7). Risk of global financial crash has increased, warns IMF. *The Guardian*. Retrieved August 10, 2016, from https://www.theguardian.com/business/2015/oct/07/risk-global-financial-crash-increased-imf-emerging-economies-eurozone-stability-report

Intergovernmental Panel on Climate Change. (2013). *Climate change 2013: The physical science basis, summary for policy makers*. Cambridge: Cambridge University Press.

Intergovernmental Panel on Climate Change. (2014). *Climate change 2014: Mitigation of climate change: Summary for policymakers and technical summary*. Cambridge: Cambridge University Press.

International Assessment of Agricultural Knowledge, Science and Technology for Development (IAASTD). (2009). *Agriculture at the crossroads: Synthesis report*. Retrieved August 12, 2016, from http://www.unep.org/dewa/agassessment/reports/IAASTD/EN/Agriculture%20at%20a%20Crossroads_Synthesis%20Report%20(English).pdf

International Co-operative Alliance (ICA). Retrieved August 10, 2016, from http://ica.coop/en/facts-and-figures

International Labour Organization. (2008). *World of Work Report 2008—Income inequalities in the age of financial globalization*. Retrieved August 10, 2016, from http://www.ilo.org/global/publications/ilo-bookstore/order-online/books/WCMS_100354/lang--en/index.htm

International Labour Organization. (2015). *World employment and social outlook—Trends 2015*. Retrieved August 10, 2016, from http://www.ilo.org/global/research/global-reports/weso/2015/lang--en/index.htm

International Labour Organization. (2016). *World employment and social outlook: Trends 2016*. Retrieved August 10, 2016, from http://www.ilo.org/global/research/global-reports/weso/2016/WCMS_443480/lang--en/index.htm

International Monetary Fund. (2015) *Counting the cost of energy subsidies*. Retrieved August 10, 2016, from http://www.imf.org/external/pubs/ft/survey/so/2015/new070215a.htm

International Work Group for Indigenous Affairs (IWGIA). www.iwgia.org

James, P. (2005). Arguing globalizations: Proposition towards an investigation of global formations. *Globalizations, 2*(2), 193–209.

Jameson, F. (1992). *Postmodernism or the cultural logic of late capitalism*. London: Verso.

Jameson, F. (2011). *Representing capital: A reading of volume one*. London: Verso.

Jennings, W. (2016, July 5). North v south, young v old—The new political faultlines. *The Guardian*. Retrieved August 10, 2016, from http://www.theguardian.com/politics/2016/jun/04/eu-referendum-campaign-polls-fault-lines-politics

Johnson, C. (1982). *MITI and the Japanese miracle*. Stanford, CA: Stanford University Press.

Jones, O. (2014, August 9). "It's socialism for the rich and capitalism for the rest of us in Britain." *The Guardian*. Retrieved August 10, 2016, from https://www.theguardian.com/books/2014/aug/29/socialism-for-the-rich

Jossa, B. (2005). Marx, Marxism and the cooperative movement. *Cambridge Journal of Economics, 29*(1), 3–18. Retrieved August 16, 2016, from http://www.researchgate.net/publications/5208466_Marx_Marxism_and_the_cooperative-movement

Justice, F. (2010). *The report of the food and fairness inquiry*. Brighton: Food Ethics Council.

Kapur, A., Macleod, N., & Singh, N. (2006). *Revisiting plutonomy: The rich getting richer*. London: Citigroup Global Markets.

Kelly, M. (2012). *Owning our own future: The Emerging ownership revolution*. Oakland, CA: Berrett-Koeler Publishers.

Kennedy, P. (2010). *Local lives and global transformations: Towards world society*. Basingstoke: Palgrave-Macmillan.

Kenway, J., Kraack, A., & Hickey-Moody, A. (2006). *Masculinity beyond the metropolis*. Basingstoke: Palgrave-Macmillan.

Kiely, R. (2005a). *Empire in the age of globalisation*. London: Pluto.

Kiely, R. (2005b). *The clash of globalizations: Neo-liberalism, the third way and anti-globalisation*. Leiden: Brill.

Kiely, R. (2007). *The new political economy of development: Globalization, imperialism, hegemony*. Basingstoke: Palgrave.

Kiely, R. (2015). *The BRICs, US 'Decline' and global transformations*. Basingstoke: Palgrave.

Klein, N. (2000). *No logo: No space, no choice, no jobs*. London: Flamingo.

Klein, N. (2007). *The shock doctrine: The rise of disaster capitalism*. New York: Metropolitan Books.

Klein, N. (2014). *This changes everything: Capitalism vs the climate*. London: Allen Lane.

Kliman, A. (2012). *The failure of capitalist production; Underlying causes of the great recession*. London: Pluto Press.

La Via Campesina. (2013). *Declaration of the rights of peasants—Women and men*. Retrieved July 6, 2016, from www.viacampesian.org

Lansley, S. (2011). *The cost of inequality: Why economic equality is essential for recovery*. London: Gibson Square.

Lapavitsas, C. (2013). *Profits without producing: How finance exploits us all*. London: Verso.

Lash, S., & Urry, J. (1994). *Economies of signs and spaces*. London: Sage.

Lee, Y. and David, R. (2010). Suicided in India revealing how men made a mess of microcredit. Bloomberg Markets. Retrieved August 18, 2016, from www.bloomberg.com/news/articles/2012-12-28/suicides-among-borrowers-in-india-show-how-men-made-a-mess-of-microcredit

Lelieveld, J., Evans, J. S., Fnais, M., Giannadaki, D., & Pozzer, A. (2015). The contribution of outdoor air pollution sources to premature mortality on a global scale. *Nature, 525*, 367–371.

Liang, C. S. (2007). Europe for the 'Europeans': The foreign and security policy of the populist radical right. In C. S. Liang (Ed.), *Europe for the Europeans: The foreign and security policy of the populist radical right* (pp. 1–32). Aldershot: Ashgate.

Lyotard, J.-F. (1986). *The postmodern condition: A report on knowledge*. Manchester: Manchester University Press.

Macalister, T. (2016, April 17). Clouds gather over the solar power sector after golden years of success. *The Guardian*. Retrieved August 10, 2016, from https://www.theguardian.com/environment/2016/apr/16/solar-power-clouds-gather-six-years-success-uk

Maddison, A. (2001). *The world economy: A millennial perspective*. OECD. Retrieved August 10, 2016, from http://theunbrokenwindow.com/Development/MADDISON%20The%20World%20Economy--A%20Millennial.pdf

Maguire, J. (1999). *Global sport identities, societies, civilizations*. Cambridge: Polity.

Mance, E. (2014). The solidarity economy in Brazil. In V. Satgar (Ed.), *The solidarity economy alternative: Emerging theory and practice* (pp. 150–176). Scottsville: University of KwaZulu-Natal Press.

Mann, M. (1986). *The sources of social power: A history of power from the beginning to AD 1760*. Cambridge: Cambridge University Press.

Manning, A. (2004) *We can work it out: The impact of technological change on the demand for low-skilled workers*. Centre for Economic Performance; Discussion Paper No. 640. London School of Economics.

Martin, R. L., & Osberg, S. R. (2016). *Getting beyond better: How social enterprise works*. Boston: Harvard University Press.

Martin, H.-P., & Schumann, H. (1997). *Global trap: Globalization and the assault on prosperity and democracy*. London: Zed Books.

Martin, P., & Wilmer, F. (2008). Transnational normative struggles and globalization: The case of indigenous peoples in Bolivia and Ecuador. *Globalizations, 5*(4), 583–598.

Marx, K. (1967). *Capital volume one: A critique of political economy*. New York: International Publishers.

Marx, K., & Engels, F. (1967). *The communist manifesto*. Harmondsworth: Penguin.

Mason, P. (2013). *Why it's still kicking off everywhere: The new global revolutions*. London: Verso.

Mason, P. (2015a, November 2). Apocalypse now: Has the next giant financial crash already begun? *The Guardian*. Retrieved August 10, 2016, from https://www.theguardian.com/commentisfree/2015/nov/01/financial-armageddon-crash-warning-signs

Mason, P. (2015b). *Postcapitalism: A guide to our future*. Milton Keynes: Allen Lane.

Mathieson, K. (2015, July 22) "How will the government subsidy cuts impact on the UK's solar industry?" *The Guardian*. Retrieved August 10, 2016, from https://www.theguardian.com/environment/2015/jul/22/how-will-government-subsidy-cuts-impact-the-uks-solar-industry

Mattei, U. (2012). Providing direct access to social justice by renewing common sense: The state, the market and some preliminary questions about the commons" in *Redefining and combating poverty. Human Rights, Democracy and Common Goods in Today's Europe* (pp. 307–324). Council of Europe.

Mazzucato, M. (2011). The entrepreneurial state. *Renewal: A Journal of Social Democracy, 19*(3/4), 1–11. http://www.renewal.org.uk/articles/the-entrepreneurial-state/

McAfee, K. (1999). Selling nature to save it? Biodiversity and green developmentalism. *Environment and Planning D: Society and Space, 17*(2), 133–154.

McAfee, K. (2012). The contradictory logic of global ecosystem services markets. *Development and Change, 43*(1), 105–131.

McKibben, B. (2012, July 7). Global warming's terrifying new math. *Rolling Stone*. Retrieved August 10, 2016, from http://www.rollingstone.com/politics/news/global-warmings-terrifying-new-math-20120719

McMicheal, P. (2000). *Development and social change: A global perspective.* Thousand Oaks, Ca.: Pine Forge.

Meltzer, T. (2014, July 16). Computer says go. *The Guardian, G2*, pp. 9–11.

Mengin, G., Johanna, F., and Damassa, T. (2014). *6 Graphs explain the world's top 10 emitters.* World Resources Institute (2014). Retrieved August 11, 2016, from http://www.wri.org/blog/2014/11/6-graphs-explain-world%E2%80%99s-top-10-emitters

Milanovic, B. (2012). *The real winners and losers of globalization.* The Globalist. Retrieved August 11, 2016, from http://www.theglobalist.com/the-real-winners-and-losers-of-globalization/

Miller, T., Lawrence, G., McKay, J., & Rowe, D. (2001). *Globalization and sport: Playing the World.* London: Sage.

Milman, O. (2014, December 10). Full scale of plastic in the world's oceans revealed for the first time. *The Guardian.* Retrieved August 11, 2016, from https://www.theguardian.com/environment/2014/dec/10/full-scale-plastic-worlds-oceans-revealed-first-time-pollution

Milne, S. (2013, January 8). There is a problem with welfare, but it's not the 'shirkers'. *The Guardian.* Retrieved August 11, 2016, from https://www.theguardian.com/commentisfree/2013/jan/08/welfare-problem-real-scroungers-greedy

Mirowski, P. (2013). *Never let a serious issue go to waste: How neoliberalism survived the financial crisis.* London: Verso.

Mitchell, S. (2014). *How the Walton family is threatening our clean energy future.* Institute For Local Self-Reliance. Retrieved August 11, 2016, from http://ilsr.org/wp-content/uploads/2014/10/ILSR-WaltonSolar-Report-Final.pdf

Montgomery, D. (1987). *The fall of the house of labour: The workplace, the state, and american labour activism, 1865–1925.* Cambridge: Cambridge University Press.

Morozov, E. (2011). *The net delusion: How not to liberate the world.* London: Allen Lane.

Morozov, E. (2015, June 7). Where Uber and Amazon rule: Welcome to the world of the platform. *The Guardian.* Retrieved August 11, 2016, from https://www.theguardian.com/technology/2015/jun/07/facebook-uber-amazon-platform-economy

Mouzelis, N. (1999). Modernity: A non-European conceptualization. *British Journal of Sociology, 50*(1), 141–159.

Mudde, C. (2007). *Populist radical right parties in Europe.* Cambridge: Cambridge University Press.

Munck, R. (2007). *Globalization and contestation*. Oxford: Routledge.
Murray, R. (2013). The potential for an alternative economy. In R. Harrison (Ed.), *People over capital: The co-operative alternative to capitalism* (pp. 20–30). Oxford: New Internationalist Publications.
Mythen, G. (2005). Employment, individualization and insecurity: Rethinking the risk society perspective. *The Sociological Review, 53*(1), 129–149.
Nolan, P. (2004). *China at the crossroads*. Cambridge: Polity.
O'Connor, J. (2015, October 8). The human cloud: A new world of work. *Financial Times*. Retrieved August 11, 2016, from http://www.ft.com/cms/s/2/a4b6e13e-675e-11e5-97d0-1456a776a4f5.html#axzz4H1SfS8MS
Offe, C. (1985). *Disorganized capitalism*. Cambridge: Polity.
Organization for Economic Cooperation and Development. (2014). *Focus on inequality and growth*. Directorate for Employment, Labour and Social Affairs. Retrieved August 9, 2016, from https://www.oecd.org/social/Focus-Inequality-and-Growth-2014.pdf
Organization for Economic Cooperation and Development. (2015a). *Improving job quality and reducing gender gaps are essential to tackling poverty*. Retrieved August 9, 2016, from http://www.oecd.org/social/reducing-gender-gaps-and-poor-job-quality-essential-to-tackle-growing-inequality.htm
Organization for Economic Cooperation and Development. (2015b). *In it together: Why less inequality benefits all*. Retrieved August 11, 2016, from http://www.oecd.org/social/in-it-together-why-less-inequality-benefits-all-9789264235120-en.htm
Ostram, E. (1990). *Governing the commons: The evolution of institutions for collective action*. Cambridge: Cambridge University Press.
Ostry, J. D., Loungani, P. and Furceri, D. (2016). Neoliberalism oversold? International Monetary Fund. Retrieved August 11, 2016, from http://www.imf.org/external/pubs/ft/fandd/2016/06/ostry.htm
Panitch, L., & Gindin, S. (2004). Global capitalism and American Empire. In L. Panitch & C. Leys (Eds.), *The socialist register* (pp. 1–42). London: Merlin.
Patel, A. (2015, Febuary 4). India has the world's third largest number of billionaires. *Wall Street Journal*. Retrieved August 11, 2016, from http://blogs.wsj.com/indiarealtime/2015/02/04/india-has-worlds-third-largest-number-of-billionaires/
Paus, E. (2007). Winners and losers from offshore outsourcing: What is to be done? In E. Paus (Ed.), *Global capitalism unbound: Winners and losers in offshore outsourcing* (pp. 3–20). Basingstoke: Palgrave.

Perez, C. (2009). *Technological revolutions and techno-economic paradigms.* Tallinn University of Technology. Retrieved August 11, 2016, from http://technologygovernance.eu/files/main/2009070708552121.pdf

Pew Research Center. (2014). *For most workers real wages have barely budged for decades.* Retrieved August 11, 2016, from http://www.pewresearch.org/fact-tank/2014/10/09/for-most-workers-real-wages-have-barely-budged-for-decades/

Piketty, T. (2014). *Capital in the twenty-first century.* Cambridge, MA: The Belknap Press.

Polanyi, K. (1944). *Origins of our time: The great transformation.* London: Victor Gollanz.

Population Reference Bureau. (2011). Retrieved August 8, 2016, from http://www.prb.org/Publications/Articles/2011/agingpopulationclocks.aspx

Quiggin, J. (2010). *Zombie economics: How dead ideas still walk among us.* Princeton, NJ: Princeton University Press.

Reeves, H., & Jouzel, J. (2010). *Climate refugees.* Paris: Massachusetts Institute of Technology.

Reich, R. (1991). *The work of nations.* New York: Knopf.

Reinert, E. S. (2007). *How rich countries got rich… and poor countries stay poor.* London: Constable.

Reitan, R. (2007). *Global activism.* London: Routledge.

Rifkin, J. (1995). *The end of work: The decline of the global labour force and the dawn of the post-market era.* New York: Putnam Publishing.

Rifkin, J. (2014). *The zero marginal cost society: The Internet of things, the collaborative commons, and the eclipse of capitalism.* Basingstoke: Palgrave/Macmillan.

Ritzer, G. (2004). *The globalization of nothing.* London: Pine Forge.

Roberts, K. (2016). Unemployment. In S. Edgell, H. Gottfried, & E. Granter (Eds.), *The sociology of work and employment* (pp. 469–484). London: Sage.

Robertson, R. (1992). *Globalization: Social theory and social culture.* London: Sage.

Robinson, W. I. (2002). Capitalist globalization and the transnationalization of the state. In M. Rupert & H. Smith (Eds.), *Historical materialism and globalization* (pp. 210–229). London: Routledge.

Robinson, W. I., & Harris, J. (2000). Towards a global ruling class? Globalization and the transnational capitalist class. *Science and Society, 64*(1), 11–54.

Rodrik, D. (1998). 'Who needs capital-account convertibility?' Harvard University. Retrieved August 11, 2016, from http://www.uvm.edu/~wgibson/PDF/Rodrik%20convertibility.pdf

Roelants, B., & Sanchez Bajo, C. (2011). *Capital and the debt trap: Learning from cooperatives.* Basingstoke: Palgrave.

Rosenberg, J. (2005). Globalization theory: A post-mortem. *International Politics, 42*(1), 2–74.

Rustin, M. (1994). Incomplete modernity: Ulrich Beck's risk society. *Radical Philosophy, 67*, 3–11.

Ryan, F. (2015, August 18). China's flight of capital causes global ripples. *The Guardian.* Retrieved August 11, 2016, from https://www.theguardian.com/world/2015/aug/19/chinas-flight-of-capital-causes-global-ripples

Sandel, M. (2016, June 10–16). The energy of the Brexiteers and Trump is born of the failure of elites. *New Statesman.* Retrieved August 11, 2016, from http://www.newstatesman.com/politics/uk/2016/06/michael-sandel-energy-brexiteers-and-trump-born-failure-elites

Sapinski, J. P. (2016). Constructing climate capitalism: Corporate power and the global climate policy-planning network. *Global Networks, 16*(1), 89–111.

Sassen, S. (2000). *Cities in a world economy.* Thousand Oaks, CA: Pine Forge.

Sassen, S. (2002). Introduction: Locating cities in global circuits. In S. Sassen (Ed.), *Global networks: Linked cities* (pp. 1–37). New York: Routledge.

Satgar, V. (2014). The crisis of global capitalism and the solidarity economy alternative. In V. Satgar (Ed.), *The solidarity economy alternative: Emerging theory and practice* (pp. 1–34). Scottsville: University of KwaZulu-Natal Press.

Schmidt, E. (2007). 'Whose "culture"; Globalism, localism and the expansion or tradition: The case of the Hñähñu of Hidalgo, Mexico and Clearwater, Florida. *Globalizations, 4*(1), 101–114.

Schumacher, E. F. (2011). *Small is beautiful; A study of economics as if people mattered.* London: Vintage Books.

Schumpeter, J. A. (1934). *The theory of economic development.* Cambridge, MA: Harvard University Press.

Schweickart, D. (2002). *After capitalism.* Oxford: Rowan and Littlefield.

Seidman, S. (1998). *Contested knowledge: Social theory in the postmodern era.* Oxford: Blackwell.

Sennett, R. (1998). *The corrosion of character: The personal consequences of work in the new capitalism.* New York: W. W. Norton and Company.

Sennett, R. (2006). *The culture of the new capitalism*. London: Yale University Press.
Shaxson, N. (2011). *Treasure islands and the men who stole the world*. London: Vintage.
Simms, A. (2016) *Toxic time capsule: Why nuclear energy is an intergenerational issue*. The Intergenerational Foundation. Retrieved August 11, 2016, from http://www.if.org.uk/wp-content/uploads/2016/04/Toxic-Time-Capsule_Final_28-Mar.pdf
Skidelski, R., & Skidelski, E. (2012). *How much is enough? Money and the good life*. London: Penguin.
Sklair, L. (2001). *The transnationalist capitalist class*. London: Blackwell.
Sklair, L. (2002). *Globalization, capitalism and its alternatives* (3rd ed.). Oxford: Oxford University Press.
Skocpol, T. (1979). *States and revolutions: A comparative analysis of France, Russia and China*. Cambridge: Cambridge University Press.
Slater, D. (1997). *Consumer culture and modernity*. Cambridge: Polity.
Sloterdijk, P. (2014). *In the world interior of capital*. Cambridge: Polity.
Social Enterprise UK. (2015). State of social enterprises survey 2015). Retrieved August 11, 2016, from http://socialenterprise.org.uk/public/uploads/editor/SEUK_StateofSocialEnterprise_FINAL_WEB.pdf
Social Enterprise UK. Retrieved August 3, 2016, from www.socialenterprise.org.uk/about/about-social-enterprise
Standing, G. (2009). *Work after globalization: Building occupational citizenship*. Cheltenham: Edward Elgar.
Standing, G. (2011). *The precariat: The new dangerous class*. London: Bloomsbury Academic.
Starr, A., & Adams, J. (2003). Anti-globalization: The global fight for local autonomy. *New Political Science, 25*(1), 20–42.
Starrs, S. (2013). American economic power hasn't declined—It globalized. Summarizing the data and taking globalization seriously. *International Studies Quarterly, 57*(4), 817–830.
Stern, N. (2007). *The economics of climate change: The stern review*. Cambridge: Cambridge University Press.
Stigler, C. J. (1971). The theory of economic regulation. *The Bell Journal of Economics and Management Science, 2*(1), 30–21.
Stiglitz, J. (2013). *The price of inequality*. London: Penguin.
Streek, W. (2012). Citizens as consumers: Consideration on the new politics of consumption. *New Left Review. 76* (July–August edition), pp. 27-48.

Streek, W. (2014). *Buying time: The delayed crisis of democratic capitalism.* London: Verso.

Taibbi, M. (2010, April 5). The great American bubble machine. Rolling Stones, 5/4/2010. Retrieved August 15, 2016, from www.rollingstones.com/politics/news/the-great-american-bubble-machine-20100405

Taylor, P. L. (2004). *World city network: A global urban analysis.* London: Routledge.

The Economist. (2007, April 7). Has globalization hurt workers in rich countries? The IMF wades in, p. 84.

The Economist. (2012, October 10). *For richer, for poorer.* Retrieved August 11, 2016, from http://www.economist.com/node/21564414

The Economist. (2014, March 15). *Planet plutocrat: Our crony-capitalist index.* Retrieved August 11, 2016, from http://www.economist.com/news/international/21599041-countries-where-politically-connected-businessmen-are-most-likely-prosper-planet

The Economist. (2015). *The global debt clock.* Retrieved August 11, 2016, from http://www.economist.com/content/global_debt_clock

The Observer. (2016, June 5). *Editorial: An economic fight that goes to the heart of French existence.*

Therborn, G. (2013). *The killing fields of inequality.* Cambridge: Polity.

Thompson, E. P. (1963). *The making of the english working class.* London: Victor Gollanz.

Tomlinson, J. (1999). *Globalization and culture.* Cambridge: Polity.

Touraine, A. (1995). *Critique of modernity.* Oxford: Blackwell.

Treanor, J. (2012, October 21). Twenty-two more face investigation over potential Libor rigging. *The Guardian.* Retrieved August 11, 2016, from https://www.theguardian.com/business/2013/oct/21/sfo-investigation-libor-22

Treanor, J. (2016, January 20). Automation will hit poor nations and the unskilled. *The Guardian.*

Tremlett, G. (2013, March 7). Mondragon: Spain's giant co-operative where times are hard but few go bust', *The Guardian.* Retrieved May 10, 2016, from http://www.theguardain.com/world/2013/mar/07/mondragon-spains-giant-cooperative

Turner, R. S. (2008). *Neo-liberal ideology: History, concepts and policies.* Edinburgh: Edinburgh University Press.

UN. Department of Economic and Social Affairs (DESA). (2009). The state of the world's indigenous peoples. New York. Retrieved August 8, 2016, from www.un.org/esa/socdev/unpfii/documents/SOWIP/en/SOWIP_web.pdf

UN-HABITAT. (2003). *The challenge of slums: Global report on human settlement*. London: Earthscan.

UNICEF. (2012). *Measuring child poverty*. Retrieved August 11, 2016, from https://www.unicef-irc.org/publications/pdf/rc10_eng.pdf

United Nations Conference on Trade and Development. (2013). *Trade and environment review: Wake up before it is too late*. Retrieved August 11, 2016, from http://unctad.org/en/PublicationsLibrary/ditcted2012d3_en.pdf

United Nations Department of Economic and Social Affairs. (2009). *State of the world's indigenous peoples*. www.un.org/esa/socdev/impfii/documents/SOWIP/en/SOWIP_web.pdf

United Nations Development Program. (2007). *UN Human Development Report 2007/8: Fighting Climate Change, Human Solidarity in a Divided World*. Basingstoke: Palgrave.

United Nations Environment Programme (UNEP). (2011). Towards a green economy: Pathways to sustainable development and poverty eradication. Retrieved August 1, 2016, from http://web.unep.org/greeneconomy/resources/green-economy-report

Urry, J. (2011). *Climate change and society*. Cambridge: Polity.

Vercellonne, C. (2010). The crisis of the law of value and the becoming-rent of profit. In A. Fumagalli & S. Mezzadra (Eds.), *Crisis in the Global Economy: Financial Markets, Social Struggles, and New Political Scenarios* (pp. 85–118). Los Angeles: Semiotext(e).

Vidal, J. (2014, November 16). The hunters hunted—How tribespeople are being evicted to make way for "wilderness". *The Guardian*, p. 24.

Vidal, J. (2016, February 21). Sami reindeer herders battle conservationists and miner to cling on to Arctic culture. *The Guardian*. http://www.theguardian.com/global-development/2016/feb/21/sami-people-reindeer-herders-arctic-culture

Wade, R. (1990). *Governing the market: Economic theory and the role of government in East Asian industrialization*. Princeton, NJ: Princeton University Press.

Wagner, P. (1994). *A sociology of modernity: Liberty and discipline*. New York: Routledge.

Wagner, P. (2001). *Theorizing modernity: Inescapability and attainability in social theory*. London: Sage.

Wainwright, H. (2014). Notes for a political economy of creativity and solidarity. In V. Satgar (Ed.), *The solidarity economy alternative: Emerging theory and practice* (pp. 64–100). Scottsville: University of KwaZulu-Natal Press.

Weber, M. (1968). *Economy and society, Volume 1*. New York: Bedminster Press.
Weber, M. (1992). *The protestant ethic and the spirit of capitalism*. London: Routledge.
Webster, F. (2002). *Theories of the information society*. London: Routledge.
White, G. (1988). *Developmental states in East Asia*. Basingstoke: Macmillan.
Williams, M. (2014). The solidarity economy and social transformation. In V. Satgar (Ed.), *The solidarity economy alternative: Emerging theory and practice* (pp. 37–63). Scottsville: University of KwaZulu-Natal Press.
Willsher, K. (2016, June 16). French union leader vows to continue struggle against labour law. *The Guardian*. Retrieved August 15, 2016, from https://www.theguardian.com/world/2016/jun/16/french-union-leader-philippe-martinez-continue-struggle-labour-law
Winterson, J. (2016, June 25). Everything starts as a story. Every political movement begins as a challenge to an existing narrative. *The Guardian*, p. 3.
Wolff, R. (2014, June 24). Yes, there is an alternative to capitalism: Mondragon shows the way. *The Guardian*. Retrieved June 7, 2016, from http://www.theguardian.commentisfree/2012/jun/24/alternative-capitalism-mondragon
World Bank. (2015). *Gross domestic product 2015*. Retrieved August 11, 2016, from http://data.worldbank.org/data-catalog/GDP-ranking-table
World Bank. (2016) *Shock waves: Managing the impact of climate change on poverty*. Retrieved August 11, 2016, from https://openknowledge.worldbank.org/bitstream/handle/10986/22787/9781464806735.pdf
World Meteorological Organization. (2015). *WMO statement on the status of the global climate 2015*. Retrieved August 11, 2016, from http://public.wmo.int/en/resources/library/wmo-statement-status-of-global-climate-2015
World Wealth Report. (2015). *Global HNWI population and wealth expanded, but at a slower pace*. Retrieved August 11, 2016, from https://www.worldwealthreport.com/Global-HNWI-Population-and-Wealth-Expanded
World Wildlife Fund. (2016). *How many species are we losing?* Retrieved August 9, 2016, from http://wwf.panda.org/about_our_earth/biodiversity/biodiversity/
Worldwatch Institute. (2016). *Fossil fuels dominate primary energy*. Retrieved August 11, 2016, from http://www.worldwatch.org/fossil-fuels-dominate-primary-energy-consumption-0
YouGov/The Times Survey Results. (2016). https://d25q2506sfb094s.cloudfront.net/cumulus_uploads/documents/0ofltfa592/Times_Results

Zamagni, S., & Zemagni, V. (2010). *Cooperative enterprise: Facing the challenge of globalization*. Cheltenham: Edward Elgar.

Žižek, S. (2011). *Living in the end times*. London: Verso.

Žižek, S. (2014). *Trouble in paradise: From the end of history to the end of capitalism*. London: Allen Lane.

Zucman, G. (2015, October 11). Inequality is the great concern of our age: So why do we tolerate rapacious, unjust tax havens?" *The Guardian*. Retrieved August 11, 2016, from https://www.theguardian.com/commentisfree/2015/oct/11/inequality-will-continue-until-corporations-stop-avoiding-tax

Index

A

account–mid-twentieth-century events, 62–4
Adams, P., 219
Adams, T., 139, 145
agricultural supplies, 89
AI. *See* artificial intelligence
Alliance of Small Island States (AOSIS), 123n12
All That Is Solid Melts Into Air (1982), 10
Al-Qaeda, 2
Anderson, K., 222
Anglo-American, 224
Anglo-Saxon countries, 246
Anthropocene Age, of climate change, 204–10
anti-capitalist movements, 62
AOSIS. *See* Alliance of Small Island States
aphorism, 162
Appelbaum, E., 79
Arab Spring to the Occupy Movement, 110
Arctic sea ice, summer, 208
Argentina, 300
artificial intelligence (AI), 7, 14, 23, 101, 132, 142, 144, 147, 162, 264–7, 289
Asian 'Tiger' economies, 91
asset prices, 36
atmospheric levels, of CO_2 and GHGs, 206
austerity policies, 116
automation, 246
automation complacency, 159
autopsies, in Germany, 214
Autor, D.H., 139

Note: Page numbers followed by 'n' refer to foot notes.

B

baby boomer, 110
bad fairy curse, at modernity christening, 211–14
Bangladesh, coastline of, 208
Ban Ki-moon, UN Secretary General, 227
Bank of England, 277
Batt, R.L., 79
Baudrillard, J., 180
Bauman, Z., 88, 159, 171, 172, 181–3, 194–8
Beck-Gernsheim, 171, 175, 177, 194
Beck, U., 137, 148–51, 153, 154n5, 163, 171, 175, 177, 194, 265
　analysis, 154
　argument of, 149
　theory, 152
Benkler, Y., 252, 255, 259, 269
Berking, H., 177
Berman, M., 10
Berners-Lee, Tim, 155, 255
Big Society Bank, 296
biodiversity, 213–14
bioenergy resources, 210
biopolitical labour, 252
bio-power concept, 75
biosphere, 203–35
　absorbing capacity of, 205
　adverse effect on, 204
Blair, Tony, 51
blogosphere, 252
Bloomberg, Michael, 227
Bolshevik communist revolution, 62
Boyle, J., 252–5, 259
Branson, Richard, 157
The Brave New World of Work, 265

Brazil, 134
Brazilian Forum, of Solidarity Economy, 307
Bretton Woods conference, 80
Bretton Woods system, 81
Brexit, 3
BRIC countries, 43
brilliant technologies, 157
Britain's case, 33
Britain's Conservative Government, 116
Britain's industrial revolution, 211
Brower, K., 164
Brynjolfsson, E., 144, 147, 157, 158
Bush, G.B., 44, 54
business armies, 56
business-only model, 115
business schemes, 33

C

cacophony, 105
California, drought in, 208
capitalism, 133, 216, 233–4, 239–69
　account–mid-twentieth-century events, 62–4
　climate, 227–8
　as climate change, 223–8
　co-existing with, 293–303
　cognitive, 137
　community economy, 278
　crony, 50, 51
　discursive dominance of, 276
　disintegration of, 274
　end game for, 248–61
　global, 203–35
　green/climate, 227–8
　humane, 304

and knowledge economy, 252–8
market, 115
and modernity, partnership of, 8–12
from networked economy, threat to, 260–1
in new knowledge economy, 289–92
partnership of, 8–12
post-capitalism, 292–3
privatization, 115–19
problems, 262–4
prospects for economic growth, 241–3
reform, 65
replace, 287–93
social core and supporting buttresses of, 276–8
social economies surviving on, 279–87
social flourishing power within, 276–8
capitalist-market-public sector, 265
capitalist modernity, 1–26
connection between fossil fuels and, 211–16
end game for, 21
market, 31
miracle of, 12–20
partnership of capitalism and modernity, 8–12
solutions, obstacles to, 228–33
carbon, 211–14, 219
bad fairy's curse at modernity christening, 211–14
budget, fossil-fuel reserves *vs.*, 217–19
economy, 214–15
emissions, 225
markets, 263
sinks, 221
trading, 226
and twentieth-century consumer binge, 214–16
carbon capture and storage (CCS) systems, 219–20
carbon dioxide (CO_2), 204–7
annual emission of, 216
negative emissions, 222
carbon-reducing techniques, 212
Carbon Tracker, 217–20
Carnegie, Andrew, 42
Carr, N., 159, 160, 163–4
Carroll, W.K., 51
Carson, C., 51
Castells, M., 137
Castoriadis, C., 115
Cayman Islands, 48
CCS. *See* carbon capture and storage
cement production, 204–5
CEO. *See* Chief Executive Officer
CEPGS. *See* corporate-funded climate and environmental policy groups
CERES Sustainable Business Network, 227
Chernobyl plant, 220–1
Chief Executive Officer (CEO), 34, 35, 39, 41, 51, 53, 246
China
economy, 87, 109
system, 219
CIA World Factbook 2011, 89
cinema, 14
Citibank, in USA, 86
Citigroup Research report, 243–6

citizen-consumer process, 196
citizens, 196
  dangers of war, 63
citizenship, 197
climate change
  Anthropocene Age of, 204–10
  capitalism as, 223–8
  explanations of, 203
  impact of, 203, 207–10
  manage, 223–6
  and market economy, 262–4
  through technology, 216–23
Climate Change and Society, 214
climate-denial movement, 213
climatically benign economy, 228
Clinton, 44, 45, 54
CO_2. *See* carbon dioxide
cognitive capitalism, 137, 250–2
cognitive economy, vampirism hijacks, 258–60
cognitive labour, 251
Cohen, Ronald, 296
collateral debt obligations (CDO), 54
collective solidarity, 198–9
collectivism, 65
commercial advertising campaigns, 196–7
Communist Manifesto, 6
Communist Party, 56
community economy, 276–8
compensatory employment, 41
Conference of Paris (COP), 123n12
consumer cooperative movement, 302
consumer culture, and decline of work identity, 184–93
consumerism, to rescue, 190–3

continued growth, climate change, 223–6
control techniques, 189–90
cooperatives, 297–9
  benefits of, 299–300
  mondragon and, industrial, 300–3
  social enterprise and, 293–7
COP. *See* Conference of Paris
Corn Laws in 1846, 70
corporate-funded climate and environmental policy groups (CEPGS), 228
corporate–industrial–agriculture, issues in, 247–8
corruption, 55, 56
  of politics, 196–9
counter-arguments, 8, 12–20
credit card, 40, 54, 216
  debt, 110
cropland management, 222
Crystal Palace, 88
cultural identity crises, 114
The Culture of the New Capitalism, 188
cybernetic revolution, 155
Cyclone Patricia, 208

D

Dardot, P., 68, 84, 85, 100
David, R., 296
Davis, M., 161, 162, 210
Dean, J., 192–4, 196–8
debt card, way of life, 108–11
'the debt state', 106
'debt surge', 106
decision-making process, 33

Deleuze, 189
DeLong, J.B., 250, 260–1, 261, 269
demographic time bombs, 123
Denmark, 298
deregulation, 85
De Rivero, O., 162
Derrida, J., 179
Detroit, 66
Deutsche Telekom, 257–8
Dew-Becker, I., 39
Dhaka, 209
digitalization, and jobless future, 141–8
downward spiral, 100–14
Drucker, P., 137

E

EA. *See* East Asia
earth geology, adverse effect on, 204
East Asia (EA), 247
Eckersley, R., 212
economic growth, 212
   perpetual competition and, 119–24
   prospects for, 241–3
economic migrants, 134
economic rationality, 121
economic retrenchment, 226
The Economics of Climate Change, 210
economic system, 218
economy
   capitalism in new knowledge, 289–92
   on capitalism periphery, social, 279–87
   climatically benign, 228
   community, 276–8
   gig, 137, 145–6
   knowledge, 252–8
   Smithian, 260
   solidarity, 303–8
   Spanish, 303
ecosystem services, 224, 225
Edgell, S., 57n10
Egypt, 134
elasticity consumption, 245
electronic point of sale systems (EPOS), 186
Emilia Romagna region, of Italy, 300–1
emissions
   carbon, 225
   CO_2, 206–7
   GHGs, 212, 213, 215, 219, 221, 222, 226, 227, 229, 247, 262, 263, 268
emotional labour, 144
employment
   technology and future of, 132–41, 146–8
   until 1970s, 133–7
   vulnerable, 160
empowered investors, 34
energy sources, 211
Engels, F., 172
entrepreneurial society, 73
EPOS. *See* electronic point of sale systems
EPZs. *See* Export Processing Zones
Ethical Consumer (2013), 278
EU. *See* European Union
EUETS. *See* European Union Emissions Trading System
Eurodollar market, 82

European science, 9
European Union (EU), 2, 3, 64, 86, 89, 134
  Britain votes to leave, economic discontent, 113–14
  Climate Action report, 226
  government, 284
European Union Emissions Trading System (EUETS), 226
Evans, P., 291
Export Processing Zone, (EPZ), 91
extractivism, 156
Exxon Mobile, 224

F

Facebook, 258
factory production, 13–14
fall-back strategy, 222
FAO. *See* Food and Agricultural Organization
Farnsworth, K., 46, 47
Far-right populist parties, 3
Federal Government revenue, 45
Federal Reserve's policy, 71, 84
female employment, 134
Fenlon, J.V., 281, 282
finance, failure to re-regulate, 111–13
financial capitalism, 79
financial crash, 234
financial crisis, 304
  2007–2008, 112
  2008–2009, 85–7
financialization, 79–87
financial liberalization, politics of, 82–5
financial services industry, 48

Financial Times, 43
fiscal crisis, 106
Fisher, M., 108, 189
550ppm figure, 217
flexible specialization, impact of work culture, 188–90
Food and Agricultural Organization (FAO), 282–3
food sovereignty, 285–6
Ford, Henry, 66
Fordism, 33
Fordist manufacturing techniques, 135–6
Fordist model, 14
Fordist system, 66, 67, 101, 135–6
Forest Carbon Partnership Facility, 222
formal rationality, 99
fossil-fuel combustion, 204–5
fossil-fuel reserves, *vs.* carbon budget, 217–19
fossil fuels
  and capitalist modernity, connection between, 211–16
  phasing out, 229–30
fossil stores, 211
Foucault, M., 74, 75
Foxconn, 143
France, 63
Frase, P., 267, 274
Freedland, 43, 104
Freeland, 42, 43, 56, 243, 245
Freeman, R.B., 92
free markets economy, 65
'free' private capitalism, 115
Frey, C.B., 138–9, 141–3, 145
Fuhr, L., 222

Furceri, D., 242
future techno-utopias, 222

G
Gamble, A., 111
gases, volumes of, 205–6
Gasper, P., 302, 303
Gates, Bill, 157
GATT. *See General Agreement on Trade and Tariffs*
GDP. *See* gross domestic product
General Agreement on Trade and Tariffs (GATT), 212
general purpose technologies (GPTs), 118
geoengineering projects, 156
geo-politics, 2, 4
German Government's Animal Welfare Report, 211n6
Germany, 222, 298
  autopsies in, 214
GHGs. *See* greenhouse gases
Ghosh, J., 111, 112
Gibson-Graham, J.K., 276–8
Giddens, A., 10, 171, 175–6, 194, 199, 220, 230
gig economy, 137, 145–6
Gilded Age, 42
Gindin, S., 80, 81, 84, 93
Glass-Steagall Act of 1933, 85
Glencoec, 224
Global CCS Institute, 219
'Global Debt Clock', 109
Global Financial Integrity, 49
global financial system, 188
globalization, 87–92
globalizing process (1960s), 88–92

Global Justice Movement, 281
global liberalization, 46
global neoliberal capitalism, 203
Global North, 209–10, 225
global plutocrats, 104
Global South, 7, 13, 19, 23, 25, 37, 38, 42, 43, 43n5, 55–7, 61, 83, 87–9, 91, 93, 101, 105, 111n6, 112, 120, 123–5, 134, 137, 158, 161–3, 163, 210, 215, 225, 279, 291, 292, 304
global supply chains, 89
global warming, 205–6, 209
Google, 258
Goos, M., 140
Gordon, R.J., 39
Gowan, P., 84
GPTs. *See* general purpose technologies
Grameen system, 295, 296
Gray, J., 148–9
grazing land management, 222
Great Depression, 63, 65, 80, 100
green capitalism, 227–8
green developmentalism, 224
greener technologies, 225
greenhouse gases (GHGs), 204–7
  emissions, 212, 213, 215, 219, 221, 222, 226, 227, 229, 247, 262, 263, 268
Green New Deal, 227
Greenspan, Alan, 243
gross domestic product (GDP), 19, 40, 41, 54, 67, 79, 105, 109, 116, 119, 218–19
growth cycle, 120
Gurney, P., 302

H

Haldane, A.G., 35–6
Hällström, N., 222
Hall, T.H., 281, 282
Hardin, G., 253
Hardt, M., 43, 155, 163, 250, 250n6, 256, 259
Harris, J., 218, 227, 232
Harvey, D., 4, 71
Hawking, S., 308
Hayek, F. A., 6, 18, 64, 65, 73
heatwaves, 208
Held, D., 87
Henry, J.S., 50
  2012 report, 49
High Net Worth Individuals (HNWIs), 41, 50
Hispanic peoples, 134
HNWIs. *See* High Net Worth Individuals
Hobsbawm, E., 62
Hochschild, A.R., 144
Holocene, 204
Human Development Index, 119
humane capitalism, 304
human influence, 204
human life, history of, 205
human-machine co-operations, 211
Hutton, W., 3, 5, 37, 57, 112
hydraulic fracking, development of, 156
hyperreal space, floating in, 178–81

I

IAASTD. *See* International Assessment of Agricultural Knowledge, Science and Technology for Development
ICA. *See* International Cooperative Alliance
ICT. *See* Information and Communication Technology
identities, lost and incomplete, 183–4
IF. *See* Intergenerational Foundation
IGOs. *See* intergovernmental organizations
ILO. *See* International Labour Organization
IMF. *See* International Monetary Fund
immaterial labour, 251
India, census in, 279–80
indigenous peoples, 279–82
individual
  free, 181–3
  neoliberal, 177–8
  reflexive, 175–7
individualism, 198
individualization, 170–5
  and deficits, 193–9
industrial capitalism, 9, 11, 13, 19
industrialization, 205, 206, 233–4
industry, 161
inequality, dangers of growing, 102–5
Information and Communication Technology (ICT), 145–6
  corporations, 259
  revolution, 248–61, 264
information technology (IT), 92
instrumental rationality, 9, 99
integrated production system, 135
integrated steel corporation company, 138
Intergenerational Foundation (IF), 220

inter-governmental competition, 46
intergovernmental organizations
    (IGOs), 38, 48, 51, 209, 240,
    241, 243
  ecosystem services, 225
  marketing nature, 225
Intergovernmental Panel on Climate
    Change (IPCC), 156, 205–7,
    205n4, 216, 221–2
  2014 report of, 209–10
International Assessment of
    Agricultural Knowledge,
    Science and Technology for
    Development (IAASTD), 270,
    326
International Cooperative Alliance
    (ICA), 298
International Energy Agency's, 205
international food corporations,
    growth of, 285
international Internet governance,
    257
International Labour Organization
    (ILO), 38
  report, 242
  unemployment definition of, 161
  *World Employment and Social
    Outlook-Trends 2015*, 160
International Monetary Fund (IMF),
    51, 80, 82, 83, 92, 105, 112,
    123, 125, 242, 243
international trade, expansion of,
    212
International World Group for
    Indigenous Affairs (IWGIA),
    281
International Year of Family
    Farming, 282
Internet, 252

inter-state collaboration, 12
IPCC. *See* Intergovernmental Panel
    on Climate Change
iron cage, 99, 100
IT. *See* information technology
Italy, Emilia Romagna region of,
    300–1
IWGIA. *See* International World
    Group for Indigenous Affairs

J

Jameson, F., 162, 181
Japanization of Western industry, 90
Jobseeker's Allowance, 47
jobs, under threat, 138–41
Johnson, C., 67
Jones, O., 116
Jossa, B., 302

K

Katz, L.F., 139
Kenway, J., 191
Keynesian demand-management
    economic policies, 62, 66, 67
Kiely, R., 198n5
Klein, N., 84, 213, 223
Kliman, A., 4, 5
knowledge economy, 250–2, 252–8
  capitalism and, 252–8
Krueger, A.B., 139

L

labour costs, 117
laissez faire economy, 68–70
Lake Blarigui, 209
Lansley, S., 40, 103

Index

Lapavitsas, C., 40, 79
Latin America, 225
Laval, C., 68, 84, 85, 100
lead investor, technological developments, 118
lean production system, 90
Lee, Y., 296
Lehman Brothers, 85
Lelieveld, J., 214
Liquid Modernity, 172
The Living Planet Index, 213
London Interbank Offer Rate (LIBOR), 54, 55
long-term capital investment, 242
long-term growth, 33
Loungani, P., 242
low-carbon economy, 229
low-grade service work, 101
Lyotard, J.-F., 179

M

mainstream economic theory, 278
Mance, E., 307
Manhattan Project, 151
Mann, Catherine, 241
Manning, A., 139–41, 147–8
Mann, M., 10
marine life, 205, 213–14
market
    approaches, 263
    capitalism, 115
    capitalist, 31
    competition, 223–6
    issues relating to, 229–30
    mechanisms, 228
market-based approach, 226
'marketing nature', 225

market justice, 115
market-oriented policies, 34
Marrakesh, 208
Marshall Aid to Europe, 80
Martin, H.-P., 137
Martin, R.L., 293–6
Marxists, 292, 302
Marx, K., 4, 6, 17, 22n4, 70, 74, 108, 135, 172
Mason, P., 110, 252, 255, 259, 269, 287–9, 292, 293
Massachusetts Institute of Technology (MIT), 157
Mattel, 124
Mazzucato, M., 117, 118
McAfee, A., 144, 147, 157, 158
McAfee, K., 222, 225, 262
'McJobs', 101
McKibben, B., 217–18
mechanical substitutes, 211
Meiji Restoration, 11
MENA. *See* Middle East and North Africa
methane, 204–5
Mexico, 284
    maquiladoras, 91
Microsoft, 258
Middle East and North Africa (MENA), 123
Mill, John Stuart, 276
Mirowski, P., 65, 68, 70–6, 85
MIT. *See* Massachusetts Institute of Technology
modernity, 131, 233–4
    christening, bad fairy curse at, 211–14
    partnership of capitalism and, 8–12

principles of, 132
reflexive, 176
rise of risk society, 149–51
solid, 173
Mondragon experiment, and industrial cooperatives, 301–3
Morocco, 208
Morozov, E., 159n6
Mouzelis, N., 9
Multitude, 43

N

NAFTA. *See* North American Free Trade Association
narcissistic individualism, 174
NASA. *See* National Aeronautics Space Administration
National Aeronautics Space Administration (NASA), 207–8
National Farmers Union, 284
National Health Service (NHS), 117
National People's Congress, 56
national security, 257
national unemployment, 301
natural processes, 205
Nazi
 government intentions, 65
 war-machine, 62
negative emission technologies, 221–3
Negri, A., 43, 155, 163, 250, 250n6, 256, 259, 307
neo-classical economic theory, 52
neoliberal
 argument, 68–72
 economics, 100–14

environmentalism, 212, 224, 262–3
ideology, critical reflections on, 76–9
individualism, 177–8
market-based approach, 224
market policy, 231
moment, 1970s crises of, 64–8
policies, 284
presumptions, trio of core, 72–6
reform, 120
shrinking state, 115–19
neoliberalism, 5, 16, 61, 64–79, 108, 115, 124, 125, 174, 175, 178, 197, 213, 215–16, 242, 253, 266, 269, 287
Neoliberal Thought Collective (NLT), 65
networked economy, threat to capitalism from, 260–2
New Deal policies, 71, 81
New Labour, 103
Newly Industrializing Countries (NIC), 89–90
New York's banks, 48
NGO. *See* non-governmental organization
NHS. *See* National Health Service
NIC. *See* Newly Industrializing Countries
nitrous oxide, 204–5
Nixon, Richard M. (President), 82
NLT. *See* Neoliberal Thought Collective
non-financial firms (1980s), 79
non-governmental organization (NGO), 213

non-stop economic growth, treadmill of, 124
North American Free Trade Association (NAFTA), 284, 285
North American government, 284
North Atlantic Treaty Organization (NATO), 2
nuclear energy, 220–1

O

occluded society, 115–19
Ocean Conservancy, 213–14
oceans, plastics in, 213–14
offshore banking system, 82–5
offshoring actions, 37
Oil Sheiks, 34
Oliver, Jamie, 295
one-dimensional
　capitalism, 31, 99, 100, 115
　rationality, 9
OPEC. *See* Organization of Petroleum Exporting Countries
Organization for Economic Cooperation and Development (OECD), 15, 49, 122, 125, 241, 242
Organization of Petroleum Exporting Countries (OPEC), 82
organized labour, 67
Osberg, S.R., 293–6
Osborne, M.A., 138–9, 141–3, 145
Ostram, E., 253–4, 279
Ostry, J.D., 242
over-borrowing abuse, 54
over-lending abuse, 54
Oxfam, 103

P

paid workers, 148, 158, 277, 301
panic set, 86
Panitch, L., 80, 81, 84, 93
Paris Agreement, 204, 222–4, 234
Paris emergency, 48
Paris environmental conference, 120
Parts Per Million (PPM), 206
Paulson, Hank, 227
Payment for Ecosystem Services (PES), 224–5
Peabody coal company, 224
peasants–small farmers, 282–7
Pelerin, Mont, 64–5
Perez, C., 137
perpetual competition, and economic growth, 119–24
PES. *See* Payment for Ecosystem Services
PES projects, 225
Pew Research Center, 101
Piketty, T., 40n3, 41, 62, 67, 102–4, 104n1, 105, 121, 246, 266
pirate banking services, 48
plastics, in oceans, 213–14
plutonomies, 244–6
Polanyi, K., 69
politics, corruption of, 196–9
Poor Law Act of 1834, 70, 74
populist-cultural protest, 113–14
post-capitalism, 292–3
postmodern fragmented self, 178–81
postmodern theory, 181n2
potential shareholders, 33
PPM. *See* Parts Per Million
private businesses, 30
Private Equity Companies (PECs), 37

private military contractors, 267
private property, 253
privatization, capitalism, 115–19
productivist society, 192
profit-making, 32
profit maximization strategies, 32
profit, rent *vs.*, 258–60
public expenditure, 46

Q

quasi-feudal system, 11
Queen Elizabeth, 132

R

rainfall, extreme, 208
Rainforest Alliance, 278
rationality
  dangerous extremes of, 154–60
  one-dimensional, 9
rationalization process, 99
Reagan
  administration, 44
  government, 83
  political agenda, 115
referendum campaign, 113–14
reflexive
  individual, 152, 154, 175–7, 182, 194, 195
  modernity, 149, 152, 176, 230
reform capitalism, 65
Reich, R., 137
renewable energy sources, issues relating to, 230–3
renminbi, 112
rent, *vs.* profit, 258–60
Republican Party, 113

re-regulate finance, failure to, 111–13
research, IPCC, 206
resource-based approach, 216
revenue tax, forbidden path to raising, 105–8
Rifkin, J., 136–8, 145, 249, 252, 257–9, 259, 269, 287, 289–91
Rio Tinto, 224
The Rise of the Network Society: The Information Age: Economy, Society and Culture (1996), 137
risk society, modernity and rise of, 149–51
'Risky Business Project', 227
Ritzer, G., 191
robotization, 246, 264–7
Rochdale Society of Equitable Pioneers, 297
rooftop energy systems, 233
Roosevelt, 65, 85
  New Deal government, 85
Royal Mail, 116
Russian Oligarchs, 34
Rustin, M., 154–5

S

SA. *See* South Asia
Sapinski, J.P., 227–9
SAPs. *See* structural adjustment policies
Sassen, S., 81
satellite data, 216
Satgar, V., 304–5
Schumacher, E.F., 290
Schumann, H., 137
Schumpeterian-type innovations, 118

science-technology, 148–60
scientific ability, 206
scientific evidence, 203–7
Scott, 137
Seidman, S., 9, 10
self-actualization, 171
self-employment economy, 137
self-realization, 171
Sennett, R., 180, 183–4, 186, 188, 190, 191, 198
sensory technological advancement, 142–6
SEs. *See* social enterprises
shale gas, 156
Shanghai stock market, 112
share prices, 33, 34, 36, 37
Shaxson, N., 48
The Shock Doctrine (2007), 84
Shock Waves: Managing the Impacts of Climate Change on Poverty, 210, 224
short-term capital investment, 242
Siberian semi-frozen tundra, 206
Silicon Valley, 118
skewed distribution, 102
Sklair, L., 300
Slaughterhouse Five, 195
Sloterdijk, P., 88, 211–12, 211n6
Small is Beautiful: A Study of Economics as if People Mattered, 290
smart robots, 246
Smith, Adam, 30
Smithian economy, 260
social deficits, 190
social economy, 296
social enterprises (SEs), 293–7
socialist blueprint, 305

social justice, 115
social media giants, 258
Society Under Siege (2002), 182
solidarity
  economy, 303–8
  weak social, 196–9
solid modernity, 173
South Asia (SA), 102, 161
Soviet Union, 62, 65, 66, 92
space exploration, 216
Spanish economy, 303
spatial optimization strategies, 101
'special economic zones', 91
sport consumption, changing character of, 187
SSA. *See* Sub-Saharan Africa
stagflation, 67
stakeholders, 33
State of Social Enterprise Survey 2015, 295
state systems, 132
Status of the Global Climate, 208
Stern, N., 210, 213
Stiglitz, J., 44, 45, 53, 55, 84, 85, 258–9
Stonehenge, 132
Streek, W., 46, 105–7, 109, 115, 197, 197n4
structural adjustment policies (SAPs), 84, 89
subprime US mortgage crisis, 86
Sub-Saharan Africa (SSA), 102, 123
subsidy, bulk of, 231
substantive rationality, 99
Summary Report, 219
Summers, L.H., 250, 260–1, 261, 269
surplus

GHGs, 205
  to requirements, 160–3
sustainable management, of forests, 221–2
Sweden, 222
Swiss Bank USB, 162

T
tautological theory, 88
tax avoidance, 44
tax-avoidance, 44
  services, 48
  strategies, 32
tax evasion, 44
Tax Justice Network (TJN), 47, 49, 50
tax revenues, 105–8
Taylor, P.L., 81
technical knowledge, 74
technological plateau, 144
technological rationality, 121
technological unemployment, 138–41
techno-scientific rationality, 154
temperature
  global, 208, 217
  rise of, 206
  risk of, 204
terrorist groups, 49
Thatcher, Margaret, 63, 68
The Economist, 41, 51, 92, 109
The Enigma of Capital and the Crises of Capitalism (2011), 4
The Entrepreneurial State (2011), 117
The Price of Offshore Revisited, 49
thermal oceanic expansion, 208
The World Wealth Report of 2015, 41

Third World Debt Crisis of the 1980s, 83
threat, jobs under, 138–41
3-D technology, 291
'tiger' economies, 89, 90
Tilly, C., 291
TNC. *See* transnational corporations
Touraine, A., 172, 174, 192, 199–200
Toxic Time Capsule, 220–1
trade unions, 62
Tragedy of the Commons, 253
Transatlantic Trade and Investment Partnership deal (TTIP), 6n2
transnational corporation (TNC), 50, 81, 82, 84, 89, 92, 262
Trump, Donald, 113
trumpism, economic discontent, 113
Turner, R.S., 68
Tuvalu, 209
twentieth-century consumer binge, 214–16
twenty-first-century
  capitalism, 99–126
  neoliberal economics, 100–14
  privatization, shrinking state and occluded society, 115–19
  twin treadmills, 119–24
  two capitalist universes of, 243–6
  world risk society, 152–4
Twitter, 258

U
UK
  government, 232
  taxpayers, 221

UK Independence Party (UKIP), 114
UKIP. *See* UK Independence Party
UK Prime Minister Margaret Thatcher, 170–1
UN. *See* United Nations
unaccountable capitalism, era of, 64–79
'unburnable carbon', 218
Understanding Slums: Case Studies for the Global Report on Human Settlements (UN-HABITAT), 161
UNDP. *See* United Nation Development Programme
UNEP. *See* United Nations Environment Programme
United Nation Development Programme (UNDP), 119
United Nations Environment Programme (UNEP), 282, 283
United Nations (UN), *Human Development Report 2007/8*, 210
UN-sponsored international forums
urban
  air pollution, 214
  air quality, 213–14
  population, 161
Urry, J., 137, 214–15, 215n7, 223, 231
USA
  employment, 134
  financial organization, 218
  Republican Party, 229
US Bureau of Labour Statistics, 140
'U' shaped curve, 141
US legal system, 53

V
vampire capitalism, roots of, 61–93
  account—mid-twentieth-century events, 62–4
  financialization, 79–87
  globalization, 87–92
  neoliberalism and era of unaccountable, 64–79
VC. *See* Via Campesina
Vercellone, 259
Via Campesina (VC), 285–6
Vietnam War, 67
von Mises, Ludwig, 64, 65
voters, 196
vulnerable employment, 102, 160

W
wage stagnation, 100–2
Wagner, P., 10
Wainwright, H., 306–8
Wall Street, 63, 84
Wall Street Journal, 109
Walmart company, 233
Washington Consensus, 56, 83–4, 92
WB. *See* World Bank
Weber, M., 5, 31, 99, 100, 115, 149
WHO. *See* World Health Organization
Wiebe, Nettie, 283–4
Wikipedia, 255
Williams, M., 303–4
WMO. *See* World Meteorological Office
word risk society, twenty-first-century, 148–60
work identity

rise of consumer culture and decline of, 184–93
work security
  consumer as co-conspirator in decline of, 185–7
World at Risk (2009), 152
World Bank (WB), 80, 82–4
  approach, 224
  ecosystem services, 225
  Forest Carbon Partnership Facility, 222
  marketing nature, 225
World Bank publication, 210
World Economic Forum, 120, 223–4
World Economic Forum (WEF), 51
World Employment Social Outlook, Trends 2016, 242
world food security, issues in, 247–8
World Health Organization (WHO), 214
World Meteorological Office (WMO), 208
World of Work, 38
world population growth, 207
world poverty, 234
World Resources Institute, 209
world risk society
  science-technology and, 148–60
  twenty-first-century, 152–4

world-shattering events, 64
World's Largest Economies (G20), 48, 304
World Social Forum (WSF), 281
World's working population, 162
World Trade Organization (WTO), 2
Worldwatch Institute, 205
World Wide Web Consortium, 257
WSF. *See* World Social Forum
WTO. *See* World Trade Organization
World War One (WW1), 62–3, 66
World War Two (WW2), 62–5, 67, 80, 90, 93
WW1. *See* World War One
WW2. *See* World War Two

Y

young people, 110, 160, 288, 289, 306
youth, position and role of, 288–9
YouTube, 252

Z

Zamagni, S., 298
'zero-carbon energy', 222
Žižek, S., 56, 64, 108, 113
Zucman, G., 50

The manufacturer's authorised representative in the EU is Springer Nature Customer Service Centre GmbH, Europaplatz 3, 69115 Heidelberg, Germany. If you have any concerns regarding our products, please contact ProductSafety@springernature.com

Printed and bound by CPI Group (UK) Ltd, Croydon, CR0 4YY

23/03/2026

02076662-0013